The Dead Sea Scrolls

Gary A. Rendsburg, Ph.D.

THE
GREAT
COURSES®

PUBLISHED BY:

THE GREAT COURSES
Corporate Headquarters
4840 Westfields Boulevard, Suite 500
Chantilly, Virginia 20151-2299
Phone: 1-800-832-2412
Fax: 703-378-3819
www.thegreatcourses.com

Copyright © The Teaching Company, 2010

Printed in the United States of America

This book is in copyright. All rights reserved.

Without limiting the rights under copyright reserved above,
no part of this publication may be reproduced, stored in
or introduced into a retrieval system, or transmitted,
in any form, or by any means
(electronic, mechanical, photocopying, recording, or otherwise),
without the prior written permission of
The Teaching Company.

Gary A. Rendsburg, Ph.D.
Blanche and Irving Laurie Chair
in Jewish History
Rutgers University

Professor Gary A. Rendsburg holds the Blanche and Irving Laurie Chair in Jewish History in the Department of Jewish Studies at Rutgers University. He also serves as Chair of the Department of Jewish Studies and holds an appointment in the History Department. He previously taught at Canisius College from 1980 to 1986 and at Cornell University from 1986 to 2004.

Professor Rendsburg majored in English and Journalism at the University of North Carolina at Chapel Hill and received his B.A. in 1975. He then pursued graduate work in Hebrew Studies at New York University and received his Ph.D. in 1980.

Professor Rendsburg's areas of special interest include literary approaches to the Bible, the history of the Hebrew language, the history of ancient Israel, and the development of Judaism in the postbiblical period. It is this last field that the subject of the Dead Sea Scrolls fits most prominently.

Professor Rendsburg held a National Endowment for the Humanities fellowship and taught as a visiting professor at the University of Pennsylvania, Colgate University, the State University of New York at Binghamton, and the University of Sydney. He is a frequent guest of the Hebrew University of Jerusalem, where he has twice served as Visiting Research Professor and has twice held the position of Visiting Fellow at the university's Institute for Advanced Studies.

Professor Rendsburg is the author of 6 books and more than 120 scholarly articles. His most popular book is a general survey of the biblical world entitled *The Bible and the Ancient Near East* (1997), coauthored with the late Cyrus H. Gordon. His most recent book is *Solomon's Vineyard: Literary and Linguistic Studies in the Song of Songs* (2009), coauthored with Scott B. Noegel.

Professor Rendsburg has visited all the major archaeological sites in Israel, Egypt, and Jordan and has participated in excavations at Tel Dor and Caesarea. Most pertinent to this course, he has visited Qumran, the site of the discovery of the Dead Sea Scrolls, repeatedly over the span of several decades.

For more about Professor Rendsburg, visit http://jewishstudies.rutgers.edu/link/grendsburg. ∎

Table of Contents

INTRODUCTION

Professor Biography i
Course Scope 1

LECTURE GUIDES

LECTURE 1
The Discoveries and Their Significance 4

LECTURE 2
The First Seven Scrolls 18

LECTURE 3
Opening and Reading the First Scroll 31

LECTURE 4
The Historical Backdrop of Ancient Judaism 45

LECTURE 5
The Rise of the Jewish Sects 61

LECTURE 6
The Dead Sea Site of the Qumran Sect 76

LECTURE 7
The Emergence of the Rabbinic System 92

LECTURE 8
A Dead Sea Scroll from Medieval Cairo 106

LECTURE 9
Pesher Interpretation—Prophecy Read Anew 120

LECTURE 10
The War Scroll and Other Apocalyptic Texts 134

Table of Contents

LECTURE 11
Biblical Manuscripts at Qumran 147

LECTURE 12
Alternative Views of Qumran and the Scrolls 162

LECTURE 13
Stops and Starts En Route to Publication 176

LECTURE 14
The Qumran Vision for a New Temple 190

LECTURE 15
Daily Life at Qumran 205

LECTURE 16
The Halakhic Letter—Rituals Define the Sect 219

LECTURE 17
The Qumran Biblical Canon 234

LECTURE 18
The Qumran Calendar 248

LECTURE 19
Jewish Scholars and Qumran Ritual Practices 263

LECTURE 20
Prayers, Hymns, and the Synagogue 278

LECTURE 21
Qumran Hebrew as an Anti-Language 292

LECTURE 22
The Enigma of the Copper Scroll 305

LECTURE 23
Connections to Christianity 321

Table of Contents

LECTURE 24
Scroll Fragments and a New View of Judaism 338

SUPPLEMENTAL MATERIAL

Timeline 354
Glossary 361
Biographical Notes 371
Bibliography 382
Credits 387

The Dead Sea Scrolls

Scope:

In 1947, the discovery of ancient documents in caves near the Dead Sea shook the world of biblical studies. The Dead Sea Scrolls contain not only our oldest copies of the Bible but Jewish texts from the 3rd century B.C.E. through 68 C.E. that provide an unprecedented view of Jewish history, culture, and religion from before and during the time of Jesus.

All told, 930 individual documents emerged from the caves of Qumran, located on the northwestern shore of the Dead Sea; 230 of these are biblical manuscripts, representing every book of the Jewish Bible save Esther, with Isaiah, Psalms, and Deuteronomy the best represented. These texts greatly enhance our knowledge of how the Bible was transmitted in that age, representing an intermediate phase between the period of their authorship in ancient Israel and the appearance of the great medieval codices.

The remaining 700 documents provide extraordinary evidence about Jewish life during the late Second Temple epoch. Some 100 of the texts are too fragmentary to permit firm identification or classification. Another 250 of the texts are the common legacy of all Jewish groups during this period. Of greatest importance, however, are the approximately 350 texts that reflect the theological stance and ritual observance of a group known as the *Yahad*, a Jewish sect most likely related to the Essenes.

Since the *Yahad* was in constant contact and conflict with other Jewish groups of the period, we can also learn much about the Sadducees and the Pharisees from the Dead Sea Scrolls. From these documents, we learn that the Qumran sect considered the Temple to be totally impure and polluted, and thus they withdrew from the main focus of Jewish religious life and did not participate in the Temple cult in Jerusalem. Instead, they considered their body politic holy unto itself, a surrogate for the holiness inherent in the Temple.

The *Yahad* led a communal lifestyle, keeping no personal possessions and eating their meals communally. To enter the *Yahad*, one had to pass through certain initiation rites. The group applied the strictest interpretation to Jewish law, or Halakah, going so far as to refrain from toileting on the Sabbath. The group held that man had no free will but rather that all was predetermined or predestined by God. These positions conform to Josephus's description of the Essenes, leading scholars to make the connection between the Qumran sect and the Essenes.

We further learn that the Qumran group held to apocalyptic beliefs, anticipating a cosmic conflict in which the "sons of light" would defeat the "sons of darkness." Many of these beliefs resonate with the Christian movement, which began as a Jewish sect of the 1st century C.E. and which also was characterized by a communal lifestyle, distanced itself from the sacrificial system, and held apocalyptic beliefs. There are further points of similarity between the Dead Sea Scrolls community and the Jesus movement: Both groups believed in an ongoing revelation, both placed an emphasis on ritual immersion (baptism) not only for purification but for initiation, and both believed that the prophetic texts of old spoke to the present with new meaning and interpretation. This is not to say that Christianity and the Qumran community should be seen as one and the same—far from it, for as we stress in the course, the former relaxed Jewish law as much as possible, while the latter held to the most stringent interpretation of Halakah.

All of this information is forthcoming from the major documents, and we will read these compositions—namely, the Community Rule, the Damascus Document, Pesher Habakkuk, the War Scroll, the Temple Scroll, the Halakhic Letter, and the Thanksgiving Hymns. We progress both chronologically and thematically, beginning with the first scrolls to emerge from Cave 1, through which scholars determined the basic theological positions of the *Yahad*, and then proceeding to the legal texts, which were discovered and published only later, through which researchers learned about the strictures of the sect, especially in comparison to other, more moderate approaches attested in ancient Judaism. At times, we also will read more fragmentary texts, for even a few lines of a Qumran manuscript often reveal much about the sect's unique theological stance.

The course also tells the remarkable story of the scrolls' discovery, research, and publication. The first scrolls were found by accident by a Bedouin shepherd lad who was chasing a stray goat that had wandered into one of the Qumran caves. Scholars systematically explored other caves in the region until eventually 11 individual caves yielded texts. An international team was established to publish the manuscripts, although years, even decades, passed without sufficient progress. Finally, in 1991, developments both in the United States and Israel led to a new generation of researchers gaining access to the scrolls, until eventually all of the documents were made available to both scholars and the public. Throughout this period, archaeologists excavated the nearby site of Qumran, and we will review these finds as well.

In short, history, religion, archaeology, textual study, Bible transmission, and more all play a role in this course. These disparate approaches—all necessary given the great diversity of rich material from Qumran—combine to bring the Dead Sea Scrolls to light for a 21st-century audience. ■

The Discoveries and Their Significance
Lecture 1

Virtually all scholarship about the crucial historical period approximately 2,000 years ago has been affected by Dead Sea Scrolls research.

The Dead Sea Scrolls are a group of 930 documents found at Qumran, on the northwest shore of the Dead Sea, between 1947 and 1954. The texts date to 250 B.C.E.–50 C.E., although the heyday of Qumran was 150–50 B.C.E. The texts are divided into three groups. First, 230 (25 percent) of them are copies of the books of the Jewish Bible—our oldest biblical manuscripts. Then 250 (27 percent) are compositions that were read and used by various Jewish groups of the period. Finally, 350 (38 percent) are the sectarian works, which provide a window into the theology, beliefs, and practices of a unique Jewish sect. Outside of these three categories are another 100 texts (11 percent) too fragmentary to be identified as either sectarian or nonsectarian.

It is not always easy to distinguish between sectarian and nonsectarian text. As one scholar stated, one of the goals in Dead Sea Scrolls scholarship is to identify "sectually explicit" literature. Most importantly, the scrolls shed unprecedented light on both the transition from biblical to postbiblical Judaism during the last two centuries B.C.E. and the development of Christianity as an offshoot of Judaism during the 1st century C.E.

The discovery of the Dead Sea Scrolls created great excitement among scholars.

The discovery of the Dead Sea Scrolls created great excitement among scholars during the late 1940s and early 1950s that exists to the present day. We will attempt to do a number of things at once during this course as we move back and forth among a variety of subjects. First and foremost, we will spend a lot of time reading the actual scrolls (always in English translation, of course), with an eye to uncovering the religious practices and theological ideas expressed. Second, we will return to the narrative of the discovery, publication, and dissemination of the material, which at times will read like a spy novel or thriller. Third, we will study some background information as we situate the Dead Sea Scrolls and the Qumran community in the greater world of early Judaism—the epoch of the Maccabees and the Roman Empire. Fourth, we will note points of contact between the Dead Sea Scrolls and the development of both rabbinic Judaism and early Christianity.

Let us review some highlights of the scrolls' discovery process. In 1947, seven scrolls in earthenware jars were accidentally discovered in a cave by a Bedouin shepherd. In 1948, the scrolls reached scholars in Jerusalem and were quickly published. Between 1948 and 1954, the nearby caves were systematically combed, and 11 yielded scrolls. The mother lode was found in Cave 4: more than 500 documents, though most were fragmentary. Pottery, textiles, and remains of foodstuffs were found as well. From the 1950s to the 1970s, the scrolls were in the hands of an international team of scholars. Some scrolls were published quickly; for others the road to publication was long and arduous. In 1967, the largest scroll, called the Temple Scroll (11QT), finally came into the hands of scholars; it would be published 10 years later. The existence of one of the most important documents, the Halakhic Letter (4QMMT), was not announced until 1984, 30 years after it was discovered! It took yet another 10 years from announcement to publication. Finally, in 2002, scholars could truthfully state that they had published all of the Dead Sea Scrolls, 55 years after their initial discovery.

The vast majority of the texts are in Hebrew, with a few in Aramaic and Greek. The amount of material in Hebrew is probably about 90 percent. The vast majority of the documents are written on parchment. A small number of documents are written on papyrus. One unique text is written on copper! Almost none of the scrolls were found intact. Nevertheless, about a dozen of the scrolls are lengthy enough and sufficiently well preserved to allow scholars a continuous read.

There are many different translations of the Dead Sea Scrolls, though generally these do not differ in any substantive manner. In our course, I will typically present my own translations of the original texts. The standard

English translation, Geza Vermes's *The Complete Dead Sea Scrolls in English*, comprises about 500 pages, a bit less than half the length of the Jewish Bible.

What did scholars know about early Judaism and nascent Christianity before the discovery of the scrolls? The original Hebrew or Aramaic versions of the books of Enoch, Jubilees, and Maccabees, which were not canonized by Judaism, were lost; we only had later translations. We had the New Testament, although in the main scholars did not use these books to reconstruct ancient Judaism. The writings of Philo (c. 20 B.C.E.–c. 50 C.E.), a great Hellenistic Jewish philosopher who lived in Egypt, informed us about Jewish life in the Greek-speaking diaspora. The works of Josephus (c. 37–c. 100 C.E.), a great Jewish historian, have been invaluable in reconstructing not only the history but also the belief system of the times. We had the later rabbinic corpus, including the Mishna and the Talmud, but these works date from the 3rd century C.E. onward. Thus before the discovery of the Dead Sea Scrolls, scholars typically viewed Judaism through a single lens—namely, the rabbinic one. The Qumran documents reminded us how variegated Jewish life was during the last few centuries B.C.E. and the 1st century C.E.

Josephus, as well as other sources, we know of three main sects within Judaism: Pharisees, Sadducees, and Essenes. Only Josephus refers to all three groups; he also provides detailed descriptions of them. Rabbinic texts strongly suggest that the rabbis are the heirs to the Pharisees. In addition, on occasion, the rabbinic sources mention the Sadducees. Philo mentions the Essenes as an unusual sect of Jews, plus he refers to a group called the Therapeutae in Egypt, somehow related to the Essenes. The New Testament books refer to the Sadducees and the Pharisees. The Roman polymath Pliny the Elder (23–79 C.E.) refers to the Essenes. Pliny, Philo, and Josephus all refer to some among the Essenes as practicing celibacy. But of all these groups, the only one that has a true voice is the Pharisees, via the later rabbis—which is to say, none of these groups speaks for itself in the period while the three are competing on theological and other grounds. The Dead Sea Scrolls changed all of that! Finally, we have the voice of a specific Jewish sect from the 1st century B.C.E., and with these texts we finally realize how little we knew about the period. Of all the Jewish groups of the period, which is responsible for these documents? Most scholars, as we shall see, accede to the Essene hypothesis, though we will examine alternative views as well. ■

Essential Reading

Vermes, *The Complete Dead Sea Scrolls in English*, 1–25.

VanderKam, *The Dead Sea Scrolls Today*, 1–12.

VanderKam and Flint, *The Meaning of the Dead Sea Scrolls*, 3–17.

Schiffman, *Reclaiming the Dead Sea Scrolls*, 3–19.

Supplementary Reading

Cohen, *Josephus in Galilee and Rome.*

Feldman, "Flavius Josephus Revisited."

Questions to Consider

1. Imagine yourself a scholar of ancient Judaism and early Christianity. What kind of expertise would you need to master your field of inquiry? What languages would you need to know?

2. What kind of manuscript discovery, real or imagined, would be able to compete with Albright's description of the Dead Sea Scrolls as "the greatest manuscript discovery of modern times"?

The Discoveries and Their Significance
Lecture 1—Transcript

Welcome to our course on the Dead Sea Scrolls. Hello, I am Professor Gary Rendsburg, and I hold the Blanche and Irving Laurie Chair in Jewish History at Rutgers, the State University of New Jersey, located in New Brunswick, with appointments in both the Department of Jewish Studies and the Department of History. I invite you to join me in this course, as we will study together, read together, and marvel at together the fascinating collection of ancient texts known as the Dead Sea Scrolls.

In this introductory lecture, I want to provide some basic information about the scrolls, including the story of their initial discovery during the years 1947–1954, subsequent developments during the rest of the decade of the 1950s and into the 1960s, and, indeed, into the 21st century; the path of scholarship on the scrolls; and, of course, the most important aspects of the contents of these ancient documents. In order to fully comprehend the significance of this major archaeological discovery, we will present the state of scholarship concerning ancient Judaism and early Christianity in the mid-20th century, before the discovery of the Dead Sea Scrolls, and show how relatively little scholars really knew. Only by understanding the state of research before these texts came to light can we fully appreciate how radically the discovery of the Dead Sea Scrolls has changed that picture. Most importantly, we will note how virtually every aspect of the crucial historical period approximately 2000 years ago has been affected by Dead Sea Scrolls research, including our understanding of such Jewish groups as the Pharisees, Sadducees, and Essenes, along with the nascent Jesus movement that spawned Christianity.

We begin by asking the question: What are the Dead Sea Scrolls? The scrolls comprise a group of 930 documents found at a site called Qumran on the northwestern shore of the Dead Sea. The scrolls were found during the years 1947–1954. These texts date to the years 250 B.C.E.–50 C.E.—a 300-year period—though the heyday of Qumran was the period of 150–50 B.C.E, a 100-year slot within that longer 300-year period.

The texts are divided into three groups; and I'll present for you now the number of texts as well in each of these groups, although they are rough estimates, except for the first figure I will give you: 230. 230, or 25 percent, of the Dead Sea Scrolls are copies of the books of the Jewish Bible; every book in the Jewish canon except for the Book of Ester is represented among these 230 documents. As a whole, this group of texts represents our oldest biblical manuscripts. Prior to the discovery of the Dead Sea Scrolls, our oldest biblical manuscripts were from the early Middle Ages; that is, about 1,000 years later than our Dead Sea Scroll documents. The second group of texts: About 250 of them, or 27 percent of the corpus, are compositions that were part of common Judaism at the time; that is, they were read and used by various different Jewish groups during the period under consideration. Our third group of texts numbers about 350, or 38 percent of the 930 total documents found at Qumran. These are the sectarian works that comprise the most important aspect of the Dead Sea Scrolls, since these texts provide a window into the theology, beliefs, and practices of a unique Jewish sect in the century or two before the time of Jesus, the Roman destruction of Jerusalem and its Temple, and the bifurcation of Judaism and Christianity, leading to the establishment of two separate monotheistic traditions. Our fourth group consists of about 100 texts, or 11 percent of the Dead Sea Scroll corpus. These are too fragmentary to be identified as either sectarian or non-sectarian; that is, belonging to the Qumran sect or whether they were part of common Judaism. We can be certain that they don't belong to our first group of texts, they clearly are not biblical scrolls; even just a few words, sometimes even a few letters, of Hebrew would be sufficient to allow us to determine that we're dealing with a copy of the Bible. So 100 texts are too fragmentary to be classified other than the fact that we can state that they are not biblical manuscripts; and those groups together add up to the 930 Dead Sea Scroll documents.

It is not always easy to distinguish between the second and third categories that I've outlined for you. Certain works may have been read by all Jews and therefore would fall into our second category—that is to say, common Jewish texts—but may have had greater currency among the people responsible for the Dead Sea Scrolls, in which case, perhaps they belong in category number three; they are sectarian texts. As one scholar stated, one of the goals in Dead Sea Scrolls scholarship is to identify "sectually explicit" literature. I hope you've caught that: "sectually explicit" literature, what a lovely pun; that is to say, texts from among the Dead Sea Scrolls that we can use to build our knowledge of the Qumran sect that has left us these documents.

These data give you a sense of what the Dead Sea Scrolls are, but I need to say more here at the onset of our course to convey to you the true significance of these precious ancient documents. Most importantly, the Dead Sea Scrolls shed unprecedented light on both the transition from biblical to postbiblical Judaism during the last two centuries B.C.E. and the development of Christianity as an offshoot of Judaism during the 1st century C.E. Which is to say, nothing short of the very origins of both Judaism and Christianity, at a crucial turning point in religious history, at a true defining moment; the Dead Sea Scrolls shed light on this and on much more.

As you can imagine, the discovery of these documents created great excitement among scholars during the late 1940s and early 1950s, and we continue to share in that excitement to the present day. To put this differently, if you had told scholars in 1930 or 1940, or even 1945, that in just a few years more than 200 copies of the biblical books from the time of Jesus would be discovered, they never would have believed you. It is against this background that one can understand the famous declaration of William F. Albright of Johns Hopkins University, the doyen of biblical archaeologists in the 20th century, that the scrolls represent "the greatest manuscript discovery of modern times." As we shall see in Lecture Eight, depending on how one understands the phrase "modern times," Albright may have overstated the case, but this does not detract from the sensational nature of this singular archaeological discovery.

Let me say a word about the organization of our course. We will attempt to do a number of things at once during this course as we move back and forth between and among a variety of subjects. First and foremost, we will spend a lot of time reading the actual scrolls—always in English translation, of course—with an eye to uncovering the salient religious practices and theological ideas expressed in these ancient documents. Second, in no other field of scholarship is the actual subject matter so intertwined with the story of the discovery, publication, and dissemination of the material. Accordingly, we will constantly return to this narrative, which at times will read like a spy novel or a thriller: how the texts were found, how they came into the hands of the scholars, how they were published, and so on. Third, we will need background information throughout as we situate the Dead Sea Scrolls and the Qumran community in the greater world of early Judaism, the period of the Maccabees and the Roman Empire. Fourth, it was at this very time that the two streams of rabbinic Judaism and early Christianity emerged, and thus we repeatedly will note points of contact between the Dead Sea Scrolls and these two more famous religious developments.

Let me now tell you something about how the scrolls were discovered; a few highlights of the entire discovery process throughout the decades. The story begins in 1947 with the accidental discovery by Bedouin shepherds in the Judean desert near the shore of the Dead Sea of seven ancient scrolls—parchment scrolls—kept in earthenware jars found in a cave in that region. Later in 1947, and into the year 1948, the scrolls reach scholars in Jerusalem, and they quickly are published. If you find ancient documents in a cave on the shore of the Dead Sea near the site of Qumran, perhaps there are more scrolls awaiting discovery in different caves. This was the thought process of those scholars in the early years of Qumran research; and so they set about to systematically comb the caves in the area with the help of the Bedouin, because the Bedouin, after all, know this terrain better than anyone else (certainly better than scholars who spend their lives in libraries and university campuses in Jerusalem, for example). This led to success: 10 other caves yielded scrolls, giving us eventually 11 caves of Qumran—the original Cave 1 and the other 10 caves now known as Caves 1–11—these caves gave us ancient documents. As I mentioned, 930 altogether, with the mother lode coming from Cave 4 which yielded more than 500 documents—more than half of the Dead Sea Scrolls from Cave 4—though most of these texts are in a very fragmentary state. Not just written remains, by the way, were found in the caves, but also artifacts including pottery, textiles, and even the remains of foodstuffs such as charred date pits and the like.

Not far from these caves is an archaeological site known as Khirbet Qumran—*khirbet* is the Arabic word for "archeological ruin"; Qumran is the name of this region—and scholars assumed because of the close proximity of the caves to this archaeological site that there was most likely a connection between the two; and therefore, during the subsequent years 1951–1956 archaeologists excavated the site of Qumran. We will, of course, deal with these excavations as well in a future lecture.

Throughout the 1950s, 1960s, and into the 1970s, the scrolls were placed into the hands of an international team of scholars to publish. Some of these scholars published their texts very quickly; for others, the road to publication was a long and arduous one. We'll revisit that in a future lecture as well. In 1967, the largest scroll—the Temple Scroll—was still in private hands, until it, too, finally came into the hands of scholars; 20 years after the original discovery in 1967, the largest of all these scrolls, the Temple Scroll, found its way into the hands of scholars and it then took an additional 10 years to publish this scroll. We'll read the Temple Scroll; we'll study its contents in Lecture Fourteen. The existence of one of the most important documents from Qumran, a text known as the Halakhic Letter, was not announced until 1984; that's right: the existence of a crucial text was not made public until 1984, 30 years after it was discovered in Cave 4 in 1954. Then, again, it took another 10 years until this text was published in 1994. We'll study this text, the Halakhic Letter, dealing with aspects of Jewish law, in Lecture Sixteen. Finally, in 2002, scholars could state that they had completed the task of publishing all the Dead Sea Scrolls, 55 years after the initial discovery, from 1947–2002. We'll describe that process when we reach Lecture Nineteen.

Perhaps this would be a good place to dispel any misconceptions about the Dead Sea Scrolls, especially since these texts have received so much public attention over the years. First, while there were major delays in the publishing of the texts—as I indicated, more than half a century would pass before all the scrolls were published and were made available to the scholarly community and to the public at large—not withstanding those delays, there never was and there is no conspiracy of silence, as if the Church or any subgroup of Christians or even Jews suppressed the material for fear that major dogmas and teachings would be upset by the revelations forthcoming from the scrolls. Sheer utter nonsense; no truth to these rumors whatsoever. Second misconception: that an esoteric reading of the Dead Sea Scrolls could reveal the "true" meaning of Judaism and the "true" meaning of Christianity, which would completely overturn all earlier understandings of the two great religious traditions. Again, utter nonsense. We leave such musings for the world of fiction, from the pen of Dan Brown and other such authors.

Let me provide for you here some additional information about the Dead Sea Scrolls corpus as a whole. The vast majority of the texts are written in the Hebrew language. Of the 700 non-biblical scrolls—I should state here: 230 biblical scrolls, almost all in Hebrew because the Bible is almost all in Hebrew except for a few chapters in Aramaic—560, or 80 percent, are written in Hebrew; 120, or 17 percent, are written in Aramaic; and a small number, 20 out of the 700 non-biblical scrolls, representing about 3 percent, are written in Greek. We also need to note that the longest scrolls, with one exception perhaps, are in Hebrew; so that while 80 percent of our texts are in Hebrew, the amount of material in Hebrew is probably about 90 percent. The vast majority of the documents are written on parchment, which was the main mode of writing during this period. A small number of documents are written on papyrus; and as we shall see in Lecture Twenty-Two, one unique text is written on copper. Almost never are any of these scrolls found intact. Nevertheless, about a dozen of the scrolls are lengthy enough and sufficiently well-preserved to allow scholars a "continuous read"; that is, that one can begin in the beginning and read to the end and get a coherent message being transmitted from these ancient texts. The vast majority of the texts, however, are extremely fragmentary, but a scholar with a broad knowledge of the material usually can determine the context of even the most fragmentary document.

Throughout our course I will refer to a text by a name or by its scholarly numeric designation; and then, when citing a particular passage, I'll give you the column number and the line number. Let me add a word about this: Each scroll is comprised of columns—vertical columns—and in each column there are about 20 lines of text per column, more or less; sometimes a little bit more than 20, sometimes less than 20. Remember that we're dealing here mainly with Hebrew and Aramaic texts, which means that the direction is from right to left. A small scroll would have just a few columns perhaps, while the longest of them—which I mentioned, the Temple Scroll—consists of 67 columns, it takes up nine meters. Normally there were several columns written on a single sheet of parchment, and then the parchment sheets were sewn together to create the single scroll. This technique, incidentally, remains in practice down to the present day in Judaism in the writing of scrolls of Torah for liturgical use in the synagogue: ink on parchment, several columns to a sheet, with the sheets sewn together to create a single scroll.

There are many different translations of the Dead Sea Scrolls, though generally these do not differ in any substantive manner. In our course, however, I will present my own translations of the original texts. To give you a sense of how much material we have, the standard English translation, by Geza Vermes of Oxford University entitled *The Complete Dead Sea Scrolls in English*, comprises about 500 pages. This amounts to, say, a bit less than half the size of the Jewish Bible, or perhaps one-third the size of the Christian Bible that includes the New Testament, just to give you a very loose approximation of the amount of material that we have here.

What did scholars know about Early Judaism and nascent Christianity before the discovery of the scrolls? Our sources include the following texts, genres, and authors: We have compositions such as Enoch, Jubilees, and Maccabees, that were not canonized by Judaism, and thus the original Hebrew or Aramaic versions of these books were lost, but these texts were preserved in various translations into Greek and Ethiopic by various Christian communities; though since these compositions were not included in both the Jewish and Protestant Bibles, in truth they were very little studied before the discovery of the Dead Sea Scrolls. The New Testament: This was an important source for the 1st century, though in the main scholars did not use these books to reconstruct ancient Judaism, since the 1,900-plus years of Jewish-Christian theological tension had moved these works squarely into the Christian sphere, even though Jewish themes dominate these books at every turn. Then we have Philo; Philo's dates are circa 20 B.C.E.–circa 50 C.E. He was the great Hellenistic Jewish philosopher. He lived in Alexandria, Egypt, which means that most of his writings inform us much more about Jewish life in the Greek-speaking Diaspora; that is to say, outside the land of Israel. But we will return to Philo again and again in this course.

Then there's Josephus; Josephus's dates: 37 C.E., dies approximately 100 C.E.; that is to say, he is active in the second half of the 1st century C.E. Josephus is the great Jewish historian whose works have always been invaluable in reconstructing not only the history of the times but also the belief system of the times. Then we have the later rabbinic corpus: this includes texts such as the Mishna and the Talmud; but these works date from the 3rd century C.E. onward, and thus one needs to wonder how useful they can be for the period several centuries earlier, a topic to which we will return in our course.

Before the discovery of the Dead Sea Scrolls, scholars typically viewed Judaism through a single lens; namely, the rabbinic one, since the rabbis would emerge as the dominant stream within Judaism after the destruction of the Temple in 70 C.E. at the hands of the Romans. The Qumran documents, however, now remind us how variegated Jewish life was during the last few centuries B.C.E. and the 1st century C.E. The result of this is a dramatic turn to reading the New Testament books as sources for Judaism in late antiquity. Similarly, books that were not canonized by Judaism—such as Enoch and Jubilees, to which I referred a few moments ago—aroused new scholarly interest, especially since Aramaic and Hebrew originals of Enoch and Jubilees were discovered among the Qumran manuscripts.

You'll note up until now that I have used the abbreviations B.C.E. and C.E.; let me explain those terms if you're not familiar with them. B.C.E. stands for "Before the Common Era" and C.E. stands for "the Common Era"; and we use these terms in contrast to the more generally used B.C., "Before Christ," and A.D., "Anno Domini," Latin for "In the Year of Our Lord" with reference to Jesus. We use the B.C.E. and C.E. terminology as opposed to the B.C./A.D. terminology because scholars of religion realized that the latter terms reflect a Christian view of the world: that everything changes with the arrival of Jesus onto the scene of history. While that remains a historical truism, we refrain from using these theologically charged terms "Before Christ" and "Anno Domini," and instead use theologically neutral terms B.C.E., "Before the Common Era," and C.E., "the Common Era."

From Josephus especially, and from our other sources, we learn of three main sects within Judaism at this time: Pharisees, Sadducees, and Essenes. Only Josephus refers to all three groups, plus he provides detailed descriptions of them. Rabbinic texts such as the Mishna suggest strongly that the rabbis are the heirs to the Pharisees. In addition, on occasion, the rabbinic sources mention the Sadducees. Philo, the philosopher, mentions the Essenes as an unusual sect of Jews, plus he refers to a group called the Therapeutae in Egypt, somehow related to the Essenes. The New Testament books refer to the Sadducees and the Pharisees; and the Roman polymath Pliny the Elder refers to the Essenes as well. Pliny, one of the most remarkable humans who ever walked this planet; Pliny was a scientist, a naturalist, a geographer, an admiral in the Roman navy. He did all of these things, and he traveled the world—the known world; the Mediterranean basin of the Roman Empire—exploring and explaining natural phenomena that he saw; and he eventually wrote a large work called the *Natural History*. He had to visit the Dead Sea, of course, because he'd heard about the geological wonder of the Dead Sea—saltiest water on Earth; lowest spot on Earth—and while in the Dead Sea region during his travels, he encountered Essenes, so naturally he includes reference to the Essenes when he writes up his *Natural History*. Pliny describes the Essenes as *sine ulla femina, omni venere abdicata, sine pecunia, socia palmarum* ("with no women among them, renouncing desire entirely, without money, with [only] palm trees for company," *Natural History*, Book 5). In line with Pliny's statement, Philo and Josephus also refer to some among the Essenes as practicing celibacy.

But of all these groups, the only one that has a true voice are the Pharisees, that is, via the later rabbis; which is to say, none of these groups speaks for itself in the period while the three are competing on theological and other grounds. The Dead Sea Scrolls change all of that. Finally, we have the voice of a specific Jewish sect from the 1st century B.C.E.—from a half-century before the life of Jesus; from a century before the destruction of Jerusalem and the Temple—and with these texts, we finally realize how little we knew about the period, notwithstanding all of the above sources, the Dead Sea Scrolls have provided information in every area including theological beliefs, the calendar, religious practices, daily life, and much more. Naturally, the discovery of the scrolls leads to the question: Of all the Jewish groups of the period, which is responsible for these documents? Most scholars, as we shall see, will accede to the Essene hypothesis, and that is the approach that we will follow in this course; though naturally, I will present alternative views as well, since there is far from a scholarly consensus on this important matter.

I add here a word about my own personal involvement with Dead Sea Scrolls scholarship. I came to the subject as someone concerned mainly with the literature of the Hebrew Bible, the history of ancient Israel, and the history of the Hebrew language. I suppose that it was my interest in the last of these three subjects—the history of the Hebrew language—that brought me to Dead Sea Scrolls research in the first place; for as we shall see in Lecture Twenty-One, the Hebrew of the Dead Sea Scrolls exhibits some very peculiar grammatical features. But the more and more I read these scrolls, the more and more I became interested not just in their linguistic profile, but in their contents as well; and it was very easy to get hooked, for their contents are simply fascinating. In fact, for about three decades now, I have read the scrolls, taught the scrolls, and like everyone else, have been fascinated by the scrolls.

I am very excited about sharing my own fascination with the scrolls with you in this course. We will learn much together, and we will constantly be surprised with the findings forthcoming from these unparalleled documents from late antiquity. In our next lecture, we will narrate the story of the discovery of the Dead Sea Scrolls in greater detail. In so doing, we will present our first surprise: the fact that the Dead Sea Scrolls, the greatest discovery of ancient documents in the 20th century, first came to light purely by accident.

The First Seven Scrolls
Lecture 2

Two of the seven scrolls are copies of Isaiah that are approximately 1,000 years older than our hitherto oldest copies. Most striking is that one Isaiah manuscript adheres closely to our medieval copies but the other differs radically.

The Bedouin who accidentally discovered the scrolls in spring 1947 took them to Kando, an antiquities dealer in Bethlehem. Kando quickly sold four of the scrolls to Mar Samuel, the Metropolitan of the Syrian Orthodox Church in Jerusalem and the other three to Professor Eliezer Sukenik of the Hebrew University of Jerusalem. Mar Samuel turned to American and British scholars associated with the American Schools of Oriental Research in East Jerusalem, and granted them permission to publish the remaining four documents—but he did not actually sell them to the school. All seven scrolls were published as quickly as possible, with excellent photographs and transcriptions into modern Hebrew typeface, so that by 1951 scholars around the world could marvel at these unique documents.

At a very early stage, scholars began to see correspondences between the Dead Sea Scrolls and the Essenes. In fact, Sukenik himself suggested such connections, though he did not fully develop the thesis. The full Essene hypothesis was developed by a French scholar, André Dupont-Sommer, in his monograph *Aperçus préliminaires sur les manuscrits de la Mer Morte* (*The Jewish Sect of Qumran and the Essenes*). The Essene hypothesis would become the dominant view of scholars.

The three scrolls obtained by Sukenik were as follows.(1) An incomplete manuscript of the book of Isaiah, resembling very closely the medieval copies on which our modern printed editions are based. (2) The Thanksgiving Hymns, a collection of hymns in praise of God, somewhat like the book of Psalms. (3) And the War Scroll, describing the conflict between the sons of light and the sons of darkness, using explicit and specific military terms to detail the expected cataclysmic battle that would usher in the messianic age.

The American Schools of Oriental Research published four scrolls: (1) A complete manuscript of the book of Isaiah, only this one differs remarkably from the medieval copies; (2) the Community Rule, which lays out the basic theological underpinnings of the community (eventually to be called "the Qumran sect" by scholars), along with the rules that govern day-to-day life; (3) Pesher Habakkuk, a commentary on the biblical book of Habakkuk; and (4) a scroll too brittle to open and read, though later efforts revealed it to be the Genesis Apocryphon, which provides expansive retellings of portions of the book of Genesis.

How did these texts wind up in a cave above Qumran?

How did these texts wind up in a cave above Qumran? The general consensus is that a community of Jews lived nearby, in the archaeological ruin easily visible from this cave known as Khirbet Qumranand that this group stored their most valued possessions, namely, their sacred writings, in the cave shortly before the Roman army advanced towards the Dead Sea region. No doubt these Jews hoped to return to the area and reclaim these scrolls, though history had something else in store. Thus the scrolls remained in the cave until a goat strayed from the herd some time in 1947!

Why two different versions of the book of Isaiah? How can we explain these divergent texts? The incomplete copy, called 1QIsa^b, reflects Biblical Hebrew more accurately and conforms very well to our medieval copies. Thus we may consider this version to be very close to the "original" book of Isaiah. The complete copy, called 1QIsa^a, incorporates linguistic forms particular to Qumran Hebrew, a dialect that diverges considerably from standard biblical Hebrew, and the text has numerous linguistic updatings. One theory holds that 1QIsa^b was intended for reading, while 1QIsa^a was used for studying; to uncover the book's true meaning, one needed the assistance of a linguistically updated version. However, this view is highly theoretical. Later we will look at other biblical manuscripts from Qumran and will see that the other texts also are very fluid at this time. Scholars had long theorized that the process by which the biblical books reached us from ancient times was not as smooth as traditionally minded Jews and Christians have believed. ■

Essential Reading

Vermes, *The Complete Dead Sea Scrolls in English*, 26–48.

VanderKam and Flint, *The Meaning of the Dead Sea Scrolls*, 209–238.

Yadin, *The Message of the Scrolls*, 15–38, 73–89, 160–189.

Questions to Consider

1. Imagine yourself as Professor Sukenik in November 1947, with the first Dead Sea Scrolls in your hand, as the United Nations votes to create the state of Israel. What kind of emotions go through your mind as you connect the Jewish past with the Jewish present?

2. How would you go about, in systematic fashion, checking the two newly discovered Isaiah scrolls against a modern copy of the Bible in the original Hebrew?

The First Seven Scrolls
Lecture 2—Transcript

In this lecture, we take you back to the years 1947–1948, when the first Dead Sea Scrolls came to light as they emerged after their fortuitous discovery at the site of Qumran. We begin at once to read passages from the scrolls, imagining ourselves to be the first scholars who laid eyes on these ancient Hebrew texts. Two of them are copies of the book of Isaiah, five of them we have never before seen. We hardly know where to begin as we feast our eyes on this remarkable discovery.

But before we get to the reading of the texts, we need to revisit the story of their discovery, which I mentioned briefly in Lecture One, and which I now present to you in greater detail. Sometime in the spring of 1947, the local Bedouin—they are the only inhabitants of this region around the Dead Sea—were shepherding their flocks, comprised of sheep and goats, somewhere along the shore of the Dead Sea. One of the goats strayed from the herd and climbed up—goats being great climbers—on the cliffs above Qumran. The goat entered into one of the caves. The shepherd lad—smart young man that he was—did not climb up after the goat, but instead picked up a stone and threw it into the cave hoping to scare the goat out, and the goat would then return to the flock. Instead of the expected thud of a stone hitting the ground inside the cave, he heard a ping. Inquisitive, he took another stone, threw it into the cave, and heard another ping. This aroused his interest even more and so at this point, the Bedouin shepherd climbed up into the cave and there he saw two earthenware vessels—clay pots; tall, thin pots—opened them up, and inside he found the first seven Dead Sea Scrolls. We like to quip that at this point we lose track of the goat who's our real hero of the story, though most likely the goat safely returned to his herd.

The Bedouin kept these scrolls with them for a few weeks or so. The Bedouin typically are not able to read or write any language; they speak Arabic, and they certainly would not have been able to recognize the script or the language presented in the script of these seven ancient documents that they now held in their hands. On a regular basis, the Bedouin will visit the closest city—which in this case is Bethlehem—where they will do some trading. They will trade their own wares, which are typically from the goat herds and the sheep herds—goat skins, wool, milk products, and so on—and they will trade them for things that they need, perhaps a pot or another kind of vessel of some sort, or whatever they may need from the various little stores in the city of Bethlehem. The next time they made their way into Bethlehem, the Bedouin sold these scrolls to an individual named Kando. Kando was a shoe keeper—a shoemaker, a cobbler—in Bethlehem, and he also was an antiquities dealer on the side; and so they gave the scrolls to Kando for an agreed-upon sum of money. For reasons that we really don't know, Kando decided to divide the scrolls up into a group of three and a group of four. Kando, in turn, very quickly in July, 1947 sold four of the scrolls to an individual named Mar Samuel, the Metropolitan of the Syrian Orthodox Church in Jerusalem. Kando also contacted Professor Eliezer Sukenik of the Hebrew University of Jerusalem sometime in November, 1947, in order to determine whether Professor Sukenik was interested in purchasing the other three scrolls. Four of the scrolls Kando sold to Mar Samuel, head of the Syrian Orthodox Church in Jerusalem—we'll get back to his story in a moment—and the other three, he offered to Professor Sukenik to see whether he was interested in obtaining these scrolls.

I need to give you a little background of the time, not the time of antiquity that we have been talking about, but what was going on in Israel—specifically in Jerusalem—in 1947. During this time period, the British mandate in Palestine was still in place, although the British had handed over authority to the United Nations, asking the United Nations to come up with a plan by which a Jewish state and an Arab state could be created in the land of Palestine. It was a dangerous time period, and as a Jewish scholar living in predominantly Jewish Western Jerusalem, Professor Sukenik could not with any ease travel to Bethlehem to meet Kando to see these three documents that he was being offered for sale. What Professor Sukenik did—and as I said earlier, this does sound like a spy novel or a thriller from time to time—was dress up as an Arab, he walked from predominately Jewish West Jerusalem to predominately Arab East Jerusalem, and there he boarded a bus near the Damascus Gate outside the old city walls, and he took that bus to Bethlehem, a totally Arab city.

There Professor Sukenik, disguised as an Arab, meets Kando the shoemaker/cobbler/antiquity dealer, and he sets his eyes on the three scrolls. He buys them with money supplied by his home university, the Hebrew University of Jerusalem. Sukenik returns with the scrolls in his hand, and returns to his home safely where he begins to open these scrolls and read them carefully for the first time. In his diary, Sukenik noted the following coincidence: He was reading these texts on November 29, 1947 in his study; that was the same day that in New York City the United Nations General Assembly was voting to approve the United Nations plan that would establish an independent Jewish state in Palestine. As Sukenik himself said, the coincidence was as follows: He was holding in his hand documents written by Jewish scribes from more than 2,000 years ago, the last time that an independent Jewish political entity stood in the land of Israel, while listening to the radio as Jews throughout Israel and Jews around the world were doing in anticipation of the United Nations vote to establish a new Jewish state—an independent Jewish state—for the first time in more than 1,900 years, since the time when these scrolls were written. All of this Professor Sukenik describes in his diary. There you see the coming together of ancient history and somewhat modern history from the period immediately after World War II.

Sukenik, a few weeks or a few months later, was shown the other four scrolls by Mar Samuel. Keep in mind once more that they are both in Jerusalem—Sukenik again on the western half of the city; Mar Samuel in the eastern half of the city—and Mar Samuel hoped to sell these scrolls to Professor Sukenik when he learned, of course, that Professor Sukenik had bought the other three manuscripts directly from Kando. Needless to say, Professor Sukenik was excited about the prospects of buying these scrolls as well. As it turned out, however, the funding fell through and the Israeli War of Independence was now in full swing as Israel was fighting against a series of Arab armies so that travel between different parts of Jerusalem was now not only difficult but really impossible. Therefore, Professor Sukenik has his three scrolls, Mar Samuel has his four scrolls of the original seven found in Qumran, Cave One.

Mar Samuel, accordingly, turned to American and British scholars associated with an institution in East Jerusalem called the American Schools of Oriental Research, or ASOR for short. This is a venerable institution in East Jerusalem; I have visited the place a number of times on my own, enjoyed the company of the scholars there, used their excellent library, and so on.

Mar Samuel turns to the ASOR scholars present—Americans and Brits who were there at this time doing their research in Jerusalem—and he doesn't sell them the documents, but he grants them permission to publish these four documents. What you have here is Professor Sukenik publishing three documents and the ASOR scholars publishing four. One of those scholars associated with ASOR at that time in residence in Jerusalem was a man named John Trevor, and when Professor Albright—whom we referred to in Lecture One—found out about the scrolls, it was in a letter from Professor Albright to Doctor Trevor in Jerusalem where Albright announced that indeed this was the greatest manuscript discovery of modern times.

All seven scrolls, accordingly, were published as soon as possible with excellent photographs and transcriptions into Modern Hebrew typeface so that by 1951, scholars around the world could marvel at these unique documents. At a very early stage, scholars began to see correspondences between these Dead Sea Scrolls and the group of Jews from antiquity called the Essenes, whom we discussed in the previous lecture. In fact, Professor Sukenik himself had suggested such connections in one of his publications, though he did not develop the thesis fully. The full Essene hypothesis was developed by a French scholar named André Dupont-Sommer who published a monograph already in 1950 in which he posited connections between the Dead Sea Scrolls community and the Essenes as described by Philo and Josephus, our ancient 1st-century C.E. sources. A second edition of this book was translated into English in 1954 and it was entitled *The Jewish Sect of Qumran and the Essenes*; the title, as you can see, says it all: the connection between these two groups. As we saw in Lecture One, as I stated, the Essene hypothesis would become the dominant view of scholars, and it is an opinion with which we concur. I will present this course with that dominant view of scholars—the consensus opinion, we might call it—the Dead Sea Scrolls sect was a group of Essenes. We will talk about other opinions that have been offered by scholars from time to time, many of which have important things to say, but we will go with the dominant, consensus view: the Dead Sea Scrolls community and the Essene connection.

For the purposes of this lecture, let us pretend that we are the scholars in Jerusalem who are viewing these texts for the first time. The three scrolls obtained by Professor Sukenik: First, an incomplete manuscript of the book of Isaiah, resembling very closely, in wording, spelling, etc., the medieval copies of the book of Isaiah. This text resembles very closely in wording and in spelling the medieval copies of the book of Isaiah; and incidentally, our modern printed editions of biblical books—Isaiah and all the others—are actually based on these medieval copies. So Professor Sukenik has in front of him a copy of the book of Isaiah—about half of the book of Isaiah is preserved in this text—and it matches exceedingly closely our medieval copies and our modern printed editions. The second text that he has is called the Thanksgiving Hymns. It is a collection of hymns in praise of God, somewhat like the book of Psalms, which is a collection of hymns and prayers written by individuals in Ancient Israel. The collection called the Thanksgiving Hymns is a postbiblical document, a collection of similar hymns of praise to God. The third text that Professor Sukenik holds in his hands is called the War Scroll. It describes the conflict between the sons of light and the sons of darkness; those are the terms that the text actually uses. The text uses explicit and specific military terminology to detail the expected cataclysmic battle that will occur between the sons of light and the sons of darkness in which the former will defeat the latter, and this will usher in the messianic age. Those are three scrolls in Professor Sukenik's hands.

The four scrolls published by ASOR by the scholars at ASOR, John Trevor and his colleagues, are the following; these include the following four texts: A complete manuscript of the book of Isaiah; oddly, however, this one differs remarkably from our later medieval copies—different wording, different spelling—we'll come back and talk about these differences in just a few moments. But it is a complete copy of Isaiah, 66 chapters, and let me point out that Isaiah is the second longest book in the Bible, the only longer one is the book of Psalms. To have a complete copy of the second longest book of the Bible from more than 2,000 years ago, you can understand the scholarly excitement of this discovery of a complete Isaiah scroll in Qumran Cave One. The second text that the ASOR scholars publish is called the Community Rule. Actually, early on it was called the Manual of Discipline, although nowadays scholars more typically use the English title the Community Rule. This document lays out the basic theological underpinnings and the organization of the community, the community that scholars come to call more and more "the Qumran sect," and you'll hear me use that term as well. In the Community Rule, we see various rules that govern day-to-day life by the members of the sect. We'll be looking at this document, the Community Rule, in detail in our next lecture, Lecture Three.

The third text that the ASOR scholars have and publish is called Pesher Habakkuk. It is a commentary on the biblical prophetic book of Habakkuk; and we will talk about the term "Pesher" later on in our course, it's a specific genre to the Dead Sea Scrolls community. A fourth scroll is too brittle to open and read, though later efforts would reveal it to be a text called the Genesis Apocryphon; it's a misnomer, actually, as we'll talk about in a later lecture. This text is written in Aramaic and it provides expansive retellings of portions of the book of Genesis; the story of Noah and the Flood and the story of Abraham and Sarah, for example. But given its extremely poor state of preservation, this document—the Genesis Apocryphon—is very difficult to read. There you have the seven documents: three published by Sukenik, four published by the ASOR scholars.

The first question that we—as we assume ourselves now to be the scholars in Jerusalem back in the late 1940s—address is: How did these texts wind up in a cave above Qumran? The general consensus is the following: A community of Jews lived nearby, in the archaeological ruin known as Khirbet Qumran—mentioned in the previous lecture—easily visible from the cave; and even though the excavations there have not proceeded yet, we assume that there's a connection between the site and the caves, that a group of Jews lived at Khirbet Qumran and stored their documents in these caves. Why and under what circumstances would they have taken these scrolls and put them in the caves? These were their most valued possessions—obviously, their biblical books, sacred writings, and even their own compositions that they considered to be sacred—and what was going on in, let's say, 68 C.E.? This was the time that the Roman army was advancing throughout the region approaching the Dead Sea; eventually they would besiege Jerusalem and destroy it two years later in the year 70 C.E. One imagines that the Qumran community took these scrolls, hid them in the caves, and hoped that they would be there for safekeeping until they returned one day. History, however, had something else in store: These Jews never returned to these caves; almost undoubtedly the Jews of the region—the Qumran community and everyone else in the area—were caught up in the maelstrom of the Jewish revolt against Rome, which led to the destruction of Jerusalem in 70 C.E. and the fall of Masada in 73 C.E., never to return to the site of Qumran. There the scrolls remained until a goat strayed from the herd into the cave sometime during 1947.

We next ask ourselves: Why do we have two different versions of the book of Isaiah in front of us? How to explain these divergent texts? Does this mean that centuries after the biblical book of Isaiah was written there still was not a single canonical version? Let me mention here, by the way, that the book of Isaiah as we have it in the Bible is actually the compilation of two distinct works: I Isaiah, Chapters 1–39, dates to about 700 B.C.E.; while the second part of the book, Chapters 40–66, dates to about 540 B.C.E. Then the two were put together to create the single canonical book of Isaiah. But here we are in Qumran Cave One, 500–700 years after this material was written, and we still don't have a single version that all Jews could agree upon? That is to say, we have two different copies of Isaiah with different wording, different spelling, and so on.

The incomplete copy that Professor Sukenik published is now called by scholars 1QIsa[b], and it reflects biblical Hebrew very accurately, and we noted it conforms very well to our medieval copies. Thus we may consider this version to be very close to the "original" book of Isaiah. The complete copy published by the ASOR scholars, which comes to be known as 1QIsa[a], incorporates linguistic forms distinctive of Qumran Hebrew. I referred to this slightly in the end of Lecture One, and we will devote a lecture to Qumran Hebrew, a specific dialect that diverges considerably from standard Biblical Hebrew, later on. Plus the text has numerous linguistic updatings. To help you envision these two copies of Isaiah, let me present the analogy of a Shakespearean play. We have on the one hand the original text as written by Shakespeare, and we have a modernized version that is sometimes produced on the stage. If that's helpful to you, you can understand why we might have two different copies of the book of Isaiah in the same cave at Qumran.

Let me give you examples of some of the differences in wording that we see between these two copies of the book of Isaiah. In Isaiah 56:9, the archaic form of the word for "field" is used; that's the Hebrew word *saday*, and it's used in many biblical texts. In 1QIsa[a], in the complete scroll that has updated the language, it replaces the archaic form of the word *saday* with the standard form *sadeh* to make it more understandable for later readers.

As another illustration, I take the passage from Isaiah 47:2. A unique word occurs there, it occurs only in the Bible; the word is *shovel* and it means something like "skirt" or a type of garment. That appears in our medieval manuscripts and in any printed edition that you would pick up today. But in the 1QIsa[a] scroll, this word was probably no longer understood by the readers of this document, because, as I mentioned, it's a rare word—it's a unique word, it occurs only here in the Bible—and thus the scribe replaced it with a more common word, the word *shulayikh*, which happens to be a plural form and it also includes a second feminine singular pronoun attached to it so it means something like "your skirts"; but it's using a different word, a more common word, replacing the archaic word *shovel* which apparently was no longer understood.

One theory holds that 1QIsa[b] was intended for reading the "original" work (whatever that may mean at this point, the original work of Isaiah), while 1QIsa[a] was used for studying the book of Isaiah; in order to uncover the book's true meaning, one needed the assistance of a linguistically updated version to really make it understood to a community of readers 500 or 700 years after the text was actually written. Again, note the Shakespearean analogy that I provided for you earlier. We emphasize, of course, that this view is highly theoretical, and naturally we can neither prove nor disprove the point; we really do not know why we have two different copies. This is the standard operating hypothesis of scholars, why two different copies of the book of Isaiah in the same cave at Qumran. Later we will look at other biblical manuscripts from Qumran, and we will see that the situation that I have just described here for the Isaiah texts is also true of other biblical manuscripts, so that the text of the Bible at this point was still very, very fluid. It would take another couple of centuries probably before the Jewish community agreed on a single, canonical text of the Bible without the kind of variations that I've been describing for you just a moment ago.

Prior to the discovery of the Dead Sea Scrolls, scholars actually had theorized that the transmission process by which the biblical books had reached us from ancient times—from Ancient Israel—through the medieval period until the age of printing was not as smooth as traditionally-minded Jews and Christians have us believe; and indeed the Dead Sea Scrolls actually confirmed that for us very, very boldly because we have such variation in the documents from the Qumran corpus.

You've heard me use the expressions 1QIsa^a and 1QIsa^b; let me now describe for you what these sigla mean, and how we use these sigla to keep track of the 930 individual documents at Qumran. You'll recall from Lecture One that eventually scrolls were found in 11 different caves, so the number before the "Q" gives us the cave number; so all the texts that I've been talking about there are from Qumran Cave One, and therefore they begin with a "1," so "1Q" means "Qumran Cave One." Then you have Isaiah, 1QIsa, and because there were two different copies of Isaiah found in Cave One, we need to distinguish them so we refer to one as 1QIsa^a (with a superscript "a") and 1QIsa^b (with a superscript "b"). Other documents are similarly named and numbered. Once you get to Cave Four, you will recall, that there were more than 500 texts found in Cave Four, many of them fragmentary, and so we cannot associate them with a particular document readily—at least not at first glance—and so scholars used a numbering system. Eventually we will be talking about texts such as 4Q396. What does that mean? You know the system by now; Qumran Cave Four, Text 396. Essentially, scholars numbered them as they came out of the caves, tried to organize them as well as they could, and gave them numbers.

Some of the texts are so well-known that they actually get a letter attached to them; the biblical books, of course, get an entire name as we saw in 1QIsa^a or 1QIsa^b; other texts, some of the sectarian texts in particular, will actually get a name attached to them in addition to their number. For example, the Community Rule—which I've already referred to and which we will study in detail in our next lecture—is called 1QS. You may say, "Where does the "S" come from because "S" is not part of "Community Rule" or "Manual of Discipline"? "S" stands for the Hebrew word *serekh*, because the text actually begins—and we have the very beginning of this document—it actually has its own title, and the title that it presents is *Serekh ha-Yahad*, which means "The Rule of the Community" or something like that, and therefore we use the English expression "Community Rule," but we use the abbreviation 1QS. And so it goes with all of these Dead Sea Scrolls documents; it's a system by which scholars are able to keep track of the various texts. Eventually you'll hear me say things such as, "3Q15," and you'll all be up to speed, because you'll know "Qumran Cave Three, the 15th text that came out of that cave." Then you'll hear me say, "11QT," and you'll say, "That must be one of the important texts, because instead of a number it actually has a letter, and the letter there is "T." that's the Temple Scroll, and in Lecture One I referred to the Temple Scroll as one of the last documents to come to light in 1967, eventually published in 1977 (11QT, the Temple Scroll).

Here we have the seven scrolls before us, to summarize once more: three of them published by Professor Sukenik in West Jerusalem, four of them published by the scholars at ASOR in East Jerusalem, all of them well-published and well-distributed around the world so that scholars could read them—wherever you were sitting in any library, or in your own private study, or in your office on campus, a scholar could read these texts—the first time these documents have come to light since they were deposited in a cave almost 1,900 years earlier. Then they appeared in English translation very early as well so that the public at large was able to get a sense of what these documents contained.

Of these first seven scrolls found in Cave One, the one that attracts our attention most of all is the one I've referred to several times now: the Community Rule, 1QS. We will study this text in detail in our next lecture.

Opening and Reading the First Scroll
Lecture 3

The scroll known as the Community Rule or the Manual of Discipline (1QS) defines the Qumran group better than any other Dead Sea Scroll ever found.

In this lecture we survey a complete Dead Sea Scroll text: the Community Rule, also known as the Manual of Discipline. Its Hebrew name is *Serekh ha-Yahad*, with "*Yahad*" being the sect's self-designation. Upon reading this scroll, scholars immediately saw that the beliefs and practices presented in this text diverge from the rabbinic Judaism of the time. Some of these beliefs and practices correspond to those of the Essenes, including the initiation rites, the pooling of financial resources, and the eating of communal meals.

The Community Rule is divided into five sections.

- The Introduction, with an emphasis on community and covenant.

- The Tractate on the Two Spirits, presenting the essential dualism of the sect.

- The Statutes, a series of laws that governed the sect, including its communal lifestyle, organization, leadership, and so forth.

- The Rules for the Master, specific to the leader of the community.

- The Hymn of the Master, a poem in first person where the Master addresses God.

Let us examine some sample passages from the Introduction, found in the column 1, lines 9–17. "Sons of light" refers to members of the sect; "sons of darkness" refers to other Jews. Pagans and polytheists (Greeks, Romans, etc.) are beyond even talking about. One notes a vitriol that typifies religious sects, who see themselves as an oppressed minority. People are said to volunteer to be members of the *Yahad* and contribute their wealth to the group, thereby pooling their resources. This corresponds to Josephus's and Pliny's reports of the Essenes' communal pooling of wealth. The passage exhorts members "not to deviate in the smallest detail from any of the words of God." This is probably something that all Jews would have agreed to, but it is emphasized here in the Dead Sea Scrolls, not in other Jewish writings, and Josephus informs us that the Essenes were the strictest observers of Jewish law. Next the passage warns members not to alter the dates of holy days and festivals. Finally, the text speaks of initiation rites similar to those Josephus describes as the Essenes'.

The Tractate of the Two Spirits (3:12–4:25) presents the essential dualism of the sect and speaks about predestination. God has created spirits of light and darkness in each person. The text uses expressions such as "prince of lightness" and "angel of darkness," both very reminiscent of terminology from Zoroastrianism, an ancient Persian religion. It makes many comments implying belief in predestination, which reminds us of Josephus's statement that the Essenes denied free will and relied solely on the doctrine of predetermination or predestination.

There are no references to women in the Community Rule. This point confirmed for many interpreters that the sect was celibate.

The Statutes section presents the laws of the sect. The beginning refers to the supervision of the sect by priests called the sons of Zadok. The last line of the section makes mention of "the coming of the Prophet and the Messiahs of Aaron and Israel," a key passage, with two messiahs mentioned. The sect is said to "eat," "bless" (i.e., pray), and "advise" together—the communal aspects of the group in clear terms. Josephus notes that the Essenes lived a communal lifestyle. The statutes section includes punishment by confinement for various offenses.

The Community Rule refers to ritual immersion in a number of places, which was practiced by all Jews in antiquity for the removal of ritual impurity. But the Community Rule presents something new. 1QS 5:13–14 indicates that ritual bathing can remove not only ritual impurity but also sin and transgression. The setting of this passage is the initiation rite into the community. Thus, ritual bathing was a final act before one enters the *Yahad*. Together, these items are paralleled in the various books of the New Testament.

There are no references to women in the Community Rule. This point confirmed for many interpreters that the sect was celibate, and thus the linkage to the Essenes was made firmer, especially in light of Pliny. ∎

Essential Reading

Vermes, *The Complete Dead Sea Scrolls in English*, 97–114.

VanderKam, *The Dead Sea Scrolls Today*, 57–58.

Schiffman, *Reclaiming the Dead Sea Scrolls*, 97–112.

Yadin, *The Message of the Scrolls*, 113–127.

Supplementary Reading

Rendsburg, "*lśwh* in 1QS 7.15."

Questions to Consider

1. What is your reaction to the passage about "the Prophet and the Messiahs of Aaron and Israel" (1QS 9:11)? How does one begin to process this reference with its striking mention of two messiahs?

2. Notwithstanding the notice—by Philo, Josephus, and Pliny—that some Essenes were celibate, did scholars jump to too hasty a conclusion and make too much of the point that the Community Rule makes no mention of women?

Opening and Reading the First Scroll
Lecture 3—Transcript

In this lecture, we will survey a complete Dead Sea Scrolls text, namely, the Community Rule; when this text was first published, scholars were wont to call it an English Manual of Discipline, though nowadays the term the Community Rule is more in vogue. The Hebrew name is *Serekh ha-Yahad*, with "Yahad" being the Dead Sea Scrolls sect's self-designation ("Serekh," "rule"; "Yahad," "community"; the "Rule of the Community" or the Community Rule). Upon reading this scroll, scholars saw immediately that the beliefs and practices presented in this text diverge from the mainstream rabbinic Judaism of the times, though we will return to the issue of mainstream anything later on in our course. Moreover, some of these beliefs and practices correspond to those of the Essenes, whom we have already mentioned in our course, including the use of initiation rites to become a member of the group, the pooling of financial resources, and the eating of communal meals. It was for all of these reasons that the Community Rule was such a prime text for scholars when they first began to read the Dead Sea Scrolls back in the late 1940s. No other provides so much information about the nature of the sect, its beliefs, and its practices as the Community Rule; and so as we move into this part of our course, I elect to begin reading a Dead Sea Scroll by choosing the Community Rule as the document to read with you.

The Community Rule consists of 11 columns, and therefore it's a relatively long text, well-preserved, and it divides into the following five sections: an introduction (columns 1 and 2, and the first half of column 3), with an emphasis on the community (the "Yahad") and the covenant that exists between God and this group of people. Next, the second section is called the Tractate on the Two Spirits (taking up the rest of column 3 and all of column 4); this section of the text presents some of the dogmas and doctrines of the community, including the dualism that is inherent in the Dead Sea Scrolls sect; more on that in a moment. Next is the largest section of the Community Rule, the Statutes (comprising columns 5, 6, 7, 8, and half of column 9), a series of laws that govern the sect including its communal lifestyle, organization, leadership, and so on. The fourth part of the Community Rule is a small section (the second part of column 9 and the beginning of column

10) called the Rules for the Master, and these include various rules that are specific to the leader of the community. Finally, (most of column 10 and all of column 11), is the Hymn of the Master, a poem in first person as the Master addresses God in a series of prayers and requests of the deity.

We begin by looking at the Introduction to the Community Rule, and we will start and focus most of all on a series of texts that appear in column 1. The first text I want to read with you is 1:9–10, which states as follows: The community members are to, "love all the sons of light, each according to his lot in the council of God; and to hate all the sons of darkness, each according to his guilt, with the vengeance of God." First we note that the same phrases are used in the War Scroll. Earlier in our course, we saw that the words "sons of light" and "sons of darkness" are used in the War Scroll, and here they appear as well in the Community Rule. this was an important linkage for scholars as they began to read the Dead Sea Scrolls in those early years of Qumran scholarship because it showed that this was not a haphazard collection of documents, but the same phrases that were used in Text A are also used in Text B; and so the group of Dead Sea Scrolls together came to be seen (correctly so) as a collection of documents written by the same people with a singular purpose.

The "sons of light" refers to members of the sect, while the "sons of darkness" (we gather) refers to other Jews, other Jewish groups; and we've talked about the variegated Jewish life at this time. You may ask, "What about non-Jews; what about pagans and polytheists; the Greeks, the Romans, etc.?" Apparently they are beyond even talking about; so when you hear the expression "sons of light," we're talking about the sect itself—the sect uses that term to refer to their own—and the "sons of darkness" refers to other Jews. Those are their enemies; and the people beyond the Jewish umbrella—Greeks, Romans, and so on—are not part of the discussion of this text, or the other texts usually found among the Dead Sea Scrolls. Finally on this passage, one notes the vitriol: "with the vengeance of God." This typifies religious sects who see themselves as an oppressed minority; they very often see themselves besieged in this way, and thus they need to fight back, and the way to fight back is with strong words: "with the vengeance of God"; you were supposed to hate the sons of darkness.

A few lines later, in 1:11–12, we have the following passage: "And all who volunteer for His truth ["His" referring to God] shall bring all their knowledge and their strength and their wealth into the *Yahad* of God"; the "Yahad," the community. First, we note that people volunteer to be members of the group. Second, more importantly, we note that they contribute their wealth to the group, thereby pooling their resources. Josephus refers to the Essenes's communal pooling of wealth; and we also noted that this was in the passage of Pliny the Elder that we quoted in our very first lecture. You begin to see here a linkage between the Dead Sea Scrolls' own documents—that they are supposed to volunteer with all of their wealth—and the descriptions of the Essenes in our ancient sources, most importantly Josephus who talks about the Essenes's communal lifestyle and the pooling of their wealth.

Another text in column one, another couple of lines below, 1:13–14: The members are the sect are told "not to deviate in the smallest detail from any of the words of God." This is probably something that all Jews would have agreed to—no one would want to deviate from the word of God as laid out in the Torah and the other books of the Bible—but it is emphasized here in the Dead Sea Scrolls, and much more so here than in other Jewish writings. Josephus informs us that the Essenes were the strictest observers of Jewish law; and so when you see a text such as this—that one should not deviate from even the smallest detail of God's word—you can begin to connect this text once more with Josephus's description of the Essenes.

We're going to talk about the Jewish sects in greater detail in a future lecture; in a previous lecture I referred to the Essenes, along with the Sadducees and the Pharisees. We'll lay out all those differences, contrasts, and comparisons between and among the sects; but already now, as you can see, I need to present to you some basic information about the Essenes as detailed by Josephus, Philo, and to some extent Pliny so that we can begin to see how the Community Rule as a paradigmatic Qumran document fits into the Essenes hypothesis.

Later on in column one—again, another line or two below—we read that the community is "not to advance their holy times and not to postpone any of their festivals." Let me repeat that: "not to advance their holy times and not to postpone any of their festivals." When you see a prohibition such as this, you can be certain that there are people who are actually doing this. Here I need to provide for you a large amount of background material to make you understand what's important about this passage. Let me try to explain it in the following way: We know from the rabbinic practice, and we know from the rabbis' own texts, that they would adjust the calendar to make sure that the holiday of Yom Kippur, the Day of Atonement, never fell on a Friday or a Sunday. They needed to do that for the following reason: As everyone is aware, the Sabbath falls on the seventh day of the week, and the Bible in the Torah lays out various laws concerning the Sabbath. Among the things one cannot do: One cannot work, and one cannot kindle a fire; and as we know from the Jewish tradition—all Jews would have agreed on this—one cannot cook on the Sabbath (after all, it requires a lighted fire to cook). Therefore, Sabbath preparation, or the preparation of cooked food in particular, had to occur on Friday in advance of the Sabbath. What would happen if Yom Kippur fell on a Friday? Think—if it helps you—for a moment to consider the Christian calendar, especially the holiday of Christmas. Christmas can fall on any day of the week as it migrates with a particular date (December 25) from year to year, it could fall on a Monday, Tuesday, or Wednesday; and that's true of the Jewish holidays as well.

What happens with Yom Kippur falls on a Friday? The problem is that the Rules of Sabbath apply to the Day of Atonement as well; the Torah refers to this day as equal to a Sabbath, therefore anything that you can't do on the Sabbath you also can't do on Yom Kippur, the Day of Atonement, such as cooking. What happens if you need to prepare your Sabbath cooked food on Friday and Yom Kippur's on a Friday? It creates a difficulty; and therefore—as we know from rabbinic sources—the rabbis tweaked the calendar (I'll explain how in just a moment) to make sure that Yom Kippur could never fall on a Friday. What happens if Yom Kippur is going to fall on a Sunday? What's the problem? Here you have a slightly different problem: Because Yom Kippur, the Day of Atonement, is a fast day, one needs to fast for 24 hours, and one needs to eat a major meal of cooked food in advance of the fast that will happen in the late afternoon hours before sunset on the Day of Atonement. If Yom Kippur is a Sunday, the previous day is the Sabbath, and you have the problem in a different direction: You cannot now prepare your major meal before the fast of cooking food because it's the Sabbath day. This is a complicated subject; I hope I've laid out the problems for you.

What did the rabbis do? They ensured that Yom Kippur would never fall on a Friday or a Sunday. How did they do that? If the Torah states—which it does, very clearly in the book of Leviticus and elsewhere—that this holiday will fall on month seven, day 10, how does one deal with the problem of the calendar? You can't change what the Torah says; what you can do, however, is tweak the beginning of the month, and that's what the rabbis would do. They would assure that the sighting of the new moon occurred at a particular time, or that there was a two-day new moon festival that month instead of a one-day new moon; and so they would make sure that the holiday of the Day of Atonement did not fall on a Friday or a Sunday. It actually could fall on a Saturday and override the Sabbath; but they ensured that it would never fall on a Friday or a Sunday. Therefore the Qumran community in opposition to what other Jews were doing states in column one of this text not to advance the holy times and not to postpone any of the festivals; and by moving the Day of Atonement artificially from a Friday to a Saturday you are postponing it, or moving it from a Sunday to a Saturday you are advancing it. This was something that the Dead Sea Scroll community opposed in this text. A lot of background material to explain to you that single passage from column one of the Community Rule.

A few lines further down (still in column one), 1:16–17, we read: "All who enter the rule of the *Yahad* shall be initiated into the Covenant before God, to do according to all that He has commanded, and not to backslide because of any fear or terror." The text goes on to speak of the initiates being inducted into the Covenant, and there's a ceremony that takes place in which the priests and the Levites bless God and the initiates respond, "Amen, amen." Josephus, once more is very informative here, because he describes initiation rites that the Essene community partook in. No other Jewish community did this; but people volunteered to become members of this group and went through an initiation period with these rituals. Essenes of Josephus's description, initiation rites; Community Rule column 1, initiation rites: We have another nexus between the Dead Sea Scrolls sect and the Essenes.

The second section of the Community Rule, as I mentioned, is the Tractate of the Two Spirits (the second half of column three and all of column four). This section of the document presents the essential dualism of the sect and it speaks about predestination. Let's look at each of those items now.

Dualism: In the mindset of the Qumran community, God has created a spirit of light and a spirit of darkness and placed each in each person. The world is governed by entities that are referred to—alongside God—as the "Prince of Lightness" and the "Angel of Darkness." Both of these terms are very reminiscent of Zoroastrian terminology. Zoroastrianism was the religion of Ancient Persia, and its most characteristic trait was dualism. There were many religions of antiquity that were polytheistic, and of course Judaism developed as a monotheism. The Persian religion is somewhere in between. It countenances two deities—therefore we call it a "dualism"—the god of good, Ahura Mazda, and the god of evil, Angra Mainyu; and they see these two forces or entities always in battle and in conflict with one another. Zoroastrianism influenced other ancient religions, including Judaism—at least the brand of Judaism reflected in the Dead Sea Scrolls where this dualism is spoken of in very, very clear terms—and then there is similar influence from Zoroastrianism on early Christianity. This trait of dualism is central to the Dead Sea Scroll community; it is right here in column 3 of the Community Rule.

The same column three just a few lines further down gives us the clearest expression in any Dead Sea Scroll of the notion of predetermination or predestination. Let me read for you this text from 3:15–16: "From the God of Knowledge comes all that is and (all) that shall be. Before things come to be, He has prepared all their thoughts, so that when they do come to be, at their appointed times, according to His glorious plan, they fulfill their action, a destiny impossible to change." One could hardly ask for a clearer statement of predetermination or predestination. All of this reminds us of Josephus's statement that the Essenes denied free will and relied solely on the doctrine of predetermination or predestination. Once more, in a future lecture when we talk about the sects in greater detail, we'll lay out the differences between and among Pharisees, Sadducees, and Essenes concerning this very important doctrinal difference. But for here, you can see the predetermination of the Dead Sea Scroll community is spoken of in very, very clear terms: All that is and all that ever will be God has set in motion, and it is a destiny that cannot be changed.

We now move to the next section of the Community Rule, and that's the largest section in the middle, the section of the Statutes. These are rules that govern the community. At the beginning of the Statutes section (5:2), we have a reference to the supervision of the sect by the priests, and the priests here are called the "the sons of Zadok." Zadok was the high priest of the first Temple when Solomon first constructed it; he lived during the reigns of David and Solomon and he was the high priest in the Temple when it was first constructed. The term "sons of Zadok" is used by later Jews as if this meant the authentic priests, and it suggests that there is some debate here between this group and another group that may have seen the priests coming from a different priestly line. Regardless, this passage demonstrates an emphasis on the priesthood, and this has led some scholars to suggest a link with the Sadducees, since the name "Sadducees" derives from this very word "Zadok." In truth, very few scholars adhere to this view, but we will return to it in a later lecture in our course.

The last line of the Statutes section (9:11) has the following to say: It refers to "the coming of the Prophet and the Messiahs of Aaron and Israel," a key passage, with two messiahs mentioned here, a Messiah of Aaron and a Messiah of Israel. You can see why this fascinated scholars—scholars were just fascinated by this text time and time again—this passage coming near the end of the Community Rule most important of all. All of the Jews of antiquity would have agreed that there was a Messiah of Israel; that is to say, on the national level, the people of Israel awaited the coming of a messiah who, in their theology, was a descendent of King David who would restore kingship and glory to the people of Israel and lead the world into the Messianic Age. What you see nowhere else, however, is a reference to the Messiah of Aaron. This suggests that alongside the Davidic kingly or royal messiah, there is also a priestly messiah. Aaron was the first High Priest going back to the earliest time of Israel as the brother of Moses; and his investiture as High Priest, along with his sons, is described for us in the Torah in the books of Exodus and Leviticus. Here you have something unique to Jewish life that we did not know of before the Dead Sea Scrolls: a group that believes not only in the Messiah of Israel—that is to say, the Davidic Messiah—but also a priestly messiah, the Messiah of Aaron. There's an emphasis on priesthood here as we noted at the beginning of the Statutes section with the reference to the Sons of Zadok, and at the end of the Statues section with the reference to a Messiah of Aaron.

A key passage in the Statues section is 6:2–3. Very briefly; very succinct language: "Together they shall eat, together they shall bless (that is, pray), and together they shall advise." Here we see the communal aspects of the group in the clearest of terms, and once more we note a linkage because Josephus notes that the Essenes lived a communal lifestyle. When this document refers to the group as eating together, praying together, and deliberating together, that is a clear connection to the Essene group as described by Josephus. The Statutes section also includes punishment by confinement for various offenses in column seven. We don't know where this confinement would have taken place—did they have a small jail cell on the site? We simply don't know—but what we do see in this text is taking their responsibilities to the community as a whole very seriously. Let me give you some examples of why one would be punished by the Qumran community: for speaking foolishly (that gets you three months); interrupting another community member while speaking (that gets you 10 days); falling asleep during a meeting (three months); exposing one's nakedness in public (that's a more serious offense, that carries a punishment of six months confinement); and spitting during a meeting (don't do that, or you'll get 30 days in confinement).

Here I would like to share with you one of the contributions I have made to Dead Sea Scrolls scholarship. Another passage in column seven in this list of offenses occurs in 7:15, and it states: "He who draws out his left hand *lasuah* with it, he shall be punished ten days." Most translations render the verb "to gesticulate," but this leaves unanswered why only the left hand? I, a scholarly article that I published in 1989, investigated this rare verb *lasuah*, a Hebrew verb, which also occurs in the Bible on several occasions, and I determined that the word actually means "to urinate," perhaps also "to defecate." As I said, I published the results of my study in 1989. In addition, I showed how rabbinic texts refer to the use of the left hand for purposes of excretion, and that's why this Dead Sea Scroll text refers specifically to the left hand and that the word *lasuah* must mean "excrete," "defecate," "urinate," or something in that semantic field, and not "gesticulate" because it would leave unexplained why only the left hand? My little contribution to the world of Dead Sea Scrolls scholarship; I will refer to a few other items that I have contributed as our course proceeds through its end.

41

The Community Rule refers to ritual immersion in a number of places, though this would have been practiced by all Jews in antiquity; and here, once more, I need to give you a good amount of background information as to what this entails. In the Torah in the book of Leviticus 12–15 and also in Numbers 19, we have references to what we call "ritual impurity." What is ritual purity, and what is ritual impurity? According to the Jewish system as laid out in the Torah, a person is born in a state of ritual purity. Certain actions or states can move you, however, into the state of ritual impurity. These include, for example: childbirth, which obviously affects only women; various skin diseases; genital flows such as menstruation for women or signs of blood not at the time of their menstruation, and for men nocturnal emissions of semen; and most importantly—also as discussed in Numbers 19—contact with the dead, what we might call "corpse impurity," the most serious type of ritual impurity. Then the Torah goes on to describe how you remove your ritual impurity and it usually entails a waiting period, bathing, ritual immersion, and then a sacrifice that occurs upon which you are returned to the state of ritual purity.

You will notice that these have nothing to do with sin. For example, giving birth to a child is the fulfillment of a commandment: The first Commandment that God gives to the first human couple is to be fruitful and multiply; and nevertheless, a woman giving birth is rendered at this point impure. Or burying the dead: This renders you impure because you've obviously had to come in contact with a corpse; and yet this is one of the greatest things you can do, a great deed that you can do, for another human being, to provide the proper burial rituals and funerary practices that the society expected and demanded. Yet that, too, renders you impure; so this has nothing whatsoever to do with sin in the system that the Bible sets up.

But when we come to our Dead Sea Scrolls community, however, all of a sudden we see something very, very different, because in the Statutes section of the Community Rule, we are told that one must enter the water before one can touch the purity—that is, the pure food—"of the men of holiness; for they shall not be purified, unless they turn from their wickedness–for he is impure among all who transgress his word." Let's break down this passage and explain exactly what is entailed in this particular case. One needed to be in a state of purity before one could enter the table and eat of the pure food. You had priests who were offering sacrifices in the Temple, and they, of course, had to be very diligent in observing the laws of ritual purity; but so did anyone who wanted to enter into the Temple, and only then could you eat of the sacrifices. If you were in the state of ritual impurity, one could not do that. The Dead Sea Scrolls passage indicates that ritual bathing (ritual immersion), however, removes not only ritual impurity—which the Bible discusses—but that it also removes sin and transgression, and that one had to do this before they can eat of the holy food. As we will see in future lectures, the Qumran community actually did not participate in the rituals in the Temple because they considered the entire Temple complex to be polluted and impure since it was in the hands of other Jewish groups. But in their ideal, in their model, they believed that you still had holy food, you still had food that was as if it were sacrificial food in the Temple, and most likely all the food they ate in their community—in their own little sacred space that they had created—was of this type. Before you could eat such food, however, you had to ritually immerse to remove not only ritual impurity but also sin and transgression. This is a whole new feature of Jewish life that we don't get from our other sources that we do get in the Community Rule and in other Dead Sea Scrolls documents.

Taken together, these items are paralleled in the New Testament in the following way; and here, for the first time, we provide for you a nexus between the Dead Sea Scrolls community and the books of the New Testament: Consider, for example what one reads at the very beginning of the Gospel of Mark 1:4: "And so John came (John the Baptist), baptizing in the desert region and preaching a baptism of repentance for the forgiveness of sins." In Matthew 3:6: "Confessing their sins, they were baptized by him in the Jordan River." Again, if you go back to the biblical books of the Torah where this is laid out in Leviticus and Numbers, the baptism, the immersion, the ritual bathing has nothing to do with sin, it only has to do with the removal of ritual impurity that is brought on by things that are not sinful, things beyond your control like menstruation or an accidental emission of semen. Yet the Qumran community and the early Christian community have in common here that you can use this act of immersion in a body of water not only for the removal of ritual impurity but also for the removal of sin.

In the Community Rule, there are no references to women. This point confirmed for many interpreters of this text that the sect—the Dead Sea Scrolls community—was celibate; and thus we have another linkage here to the Essenes, especially in the light of the Pliny text that we quoted earlier, and also Philo and Josephus in their description of the Essenes tell us that some Essenes were celibate. Celibacy among the Essenes, or some of the Essenes, and the lack of any references to women in the Community Rule made the connection between this community and the Essenes firmer again. We do have to say, however, that this is qualified by the fact that another important document that we will look at in a future lecture called the Damascus document and other texts as well do refer to women, so one can only take this to an extent; but nevertheless, the point is made here by certain scholars early on in Dead Sea Scrolls scholarship connecting the lack of references to women in our Community Rule with the celibacy of some Essenes as revealed in our ancient sources.

One wonders, of course, whether other Jewish sects of the time also possessed documents such as this one—that is, their own community rules—but we have no way of knowing. Most likely, though, the answer is no, since the communal nature of the Essenes would have demanded such a document in a way that the Sadducee or Pharisee lifestyles would not have demanded; and therefore we probably do not have such documents from those groups and it is only from this group with its Essene connections that one sees in a text like the Community Rule.

As a final note, I want to say another word about the term "Yahad." As I have stated, this is the term that the sect itself uses to refer to its own community; and scholars, in turn, have adopted this term "Yahad" to refer to the sect in their own modern scholarly writings. This is especially true of those scholars who do not admit to the Essene identity of the sect, because if you call them only the "Yahad," you're using an objective self-designation without biasing which group this particular Yahad or community may have belonged to. But it is even true of those scholars such as myself who do identify the Qumran community with the Essenes; and in our course we shall follow suit so that at times, sometimes simply for the sake of variety, I will use the term "Yahad" to refer to the Qumran community.

The Historical Backdrop of Ancient Judaism
Lecture 4

Unfortunately, the Scrolls hardly ever refer explicitly to these events or individuals.

We begin with a basic review of the history of Israel during the biblical period. First came the premonarchic period (1400–1020 B.C.E.), including the era of the patriarchs, the time in Egypt, the Exodus, and finally the emergence of the nation of Israel through the period of the Judges. Next was the monarchic period, covering the reigns of Saul, David, and Solomon and the division of Israel into the kingdoms of Israel and Judah after Solomon's death. Finally came the late period, including the Babylonian Exile, the Persian period, the reconstruction of the Temple, and the conquest by Alexander the Great.

The empire of Alexander the Great (333–323 B.C.E.) stretched from Greece in the west to India in the east—the largest empire the world had ever seen. Greek culture spread via Alexander's conquests, and thus we call this the Hellenistic period. In the Near East, including Israel, Greek ideas, thought, and culture blended with native, traditional Middle Eastern ones. Many people, especially in the larger cities, began to speak Greek. While Hellenism had clear influences on Jewish life, the Temple in Jerusalem remained the main focus and the main locus for the worship of God. During the 1st and 2nd centuries C.E., when the biblical canon was established by Jewish sages, one criterion for inclusion was authorship during the pre-Hellenistic period, since many of the ideals of Hellenism were inimical to traditional Jewish values. Even as many Hellenistic ideas permeated Judaism, such as the immortality of the soul, the canonical boundary remained.

In 301 B.C.E., four successor kingdoms to Alexander's empire emerged with relatively well-defined boundaries. For this course, two are relevant: the Ptolemies and the Seleucids. The Ptolemies ruled Egypt from their capital in Alexandria, and their kingdom extended into Judea. As under Alexander, Jewish religious life, especially the Temple cult in Jerusalem, continued with little change. One important development during this period was the translation of the Bible into Greek. Sponsored by Ptolemy II, the resultant translation is known as the Septuagint. Septuagint fragments were found among the Dead Sea Scrolls, which indicates that even in the land of Israel, some Jews were reading the Bible in Greek translation. The Seleucids ruled in Antioch, in northern Syria/southern Turkey. The kingdom included all of Mesopotamia and Persia, so large numbers of Jews resided there as well. In 198 B.C.E., after the Battle of Paneas, the Seleucids gained control of all of Judea. Ptolemy territory was henceforth restricted to Egypt proper. Once more, Temple rituals continued unchanged in Jerusalem.

All of this changed with the ascension of Antiochus IV (r. 175–164 B.C.E.), who began to persecute the Jews. During this period, the high priest served as the de facto leader of the Jewish people, since the Jews were seen more and more as a religious community, rather than a nation. Two passionate Hellenizers, Jason and Menelaus, vied for the high priesthood, and Jerusalem began to look more and more like a Greek polis. Menelaus ascended to the role of high priest by outbidding Jason before Antiochus IV. Fed up with internecine Jewish fighting, Antiochus IV sought the total Hellenization of the Jews, and in fact Menelaus assisted him. The Jews were subjected to a royal decree that forbade Jewish modes of worship, forbade the observance of the Sabbath and the festivals, outlawed circumcision, and forced Jews to sacrifice pigs to Greek gods in the Jerusalem Temple.

Some Jews, called the Hasidim, or the pious ones, resorted to civil disobedience and therefore suffered martyrdom by the hundreds if not thousands; others took a more active role, in particular the Maccabees. The Maccabee patriarch was Mattathius, with his son Judah as the active military leader. Much to the surprise of everyone, the Maccabees defeated the Seleucids. This was the first war in the history of mankind fought for the sake of religious freedom. The first act of the victorious Maccabees was the purification and rededication of the Temple in 164 B.C.E., which led to the establishment of Hanukkah. Members of the Maccabee family established the Hasmonean dynasty and ruled until 63 B.C.E. Judea gained greater and greater independence from the Seleucids. Jonathan Maccabee assumed the role of high priest in 152 B.C.E. Many scholars believe that he is the Wicked Priest of the Dead Sea Scrolls.

It is easy to see why the Essene movement sprang up at this time. Even with the Temple purified and in Jewish hands again, the Essenes disapproved of the manner in which the Temple was governed. They disapproved of all the contenders for high priest. The Qumran community believed that only the "sons of Zadok" should serve as priests, and thus they saw all other priests as emanating from illegitimate priestly lines. One can understand the *Yahad* retreating from the general Jewish community to establish their center at Qumran.

The Hasmonean dynasty ruled until the coming of the Romans. Under John Hyrcanus (r. 134–104 B.C.E.), Judea expanded greatly; his conquests included Idumea (biblical Edom), whose people were forcibly converted to Judaism, and Samaria, where he destroyed the Samaritan Temple on Mount Gerizim. Aristobulus I (r. 104–103 B.C.E.) had a very short reign but was the first to call himself king. Alexander Janneus (r. 103–76 B.C.E.) fostered a close relationship with the Essenes, which may explain why a blessing to King Jonathan (his Hebrew name) has been found among the Dead Sea Scrolls (4Q448). The Maccabees revolted to oppose Hellenization, yet within decades, the Hasmonean rulers had stylized themselves more and more as Hellenized monarchs.

The Dead Sea Scrolls occasionally refer to the arrival of the Romans, though they use the code word Kittim.

When the sons of Alexander Janneus and Salome Alexandra, Hyrcanus II (r. 67–66 B.C.E.) and Aristobulus II (r. 66–63 B.C.E.) fought for the throne, they invited the Roman general Pompey to mediate. Pompey took control of Judea and Jerusalem, with Hyrcanus II as his puppet king (r. 63–40 B.C.E.). The Dead Sea Scrolls occasionally refer to the arrival of the Romans, though they use the code word Kittim (originally referring to Cyprus in the Bible). Antigonus (r. 40–37 B.C.E.) attempted to regain the throne independently, without the recognition of Rome. Herod the Great (r. 37–4 B.C.E.) claimed Hasmonean succession through his marriage, convinced the Roman Senate to declare him king of Judea, and then arranged for the execution of Antigonus. Interestingly, Herod is not mentioned in the Dead Sea Scrolls, either because the Qumran community had far retreated from public life by this time or because most of the documents antedate Herod. Within a decade or so after Herod's death, Rome came to rule Judea directly through a series of prefects, or governors, the most famous of whom is Pontius Pilate (26–36 C.E.).

The Zealot movement rose in opposition to Roman rule. It had both political and apocalyptic overtones. The first Jewish Revolt took place between 66 and 73 C.E. The Romans destroyed Jerusalem and the Second Temple in 70 C.E. Masada, the last Zealot holdout, fell in 73 C.E. A new Judaism developed, post-Temple. The synagogue rose as the locus of Jewish worship. The Jewish people migrated throughout Europe, Asia, and Africa, an event called the Diaspora.

The Second Jewish Revolt (132–135 C.E.), led by Simeon Bar-Kokhba, ended in disaster; the Romans forbade Jews from living in Jerusalem and its environs, and thus the center of Jewish life moved north to Galilee. ∎

Essential Reading

Schiffman, *Reclaiming the Dead Sea Scrolls*, 65–72.

———, *From Text to Tradition*, 1–176.

Supplementary Reading

Jaffee, *Early Judaism*.

Questions to Consider

1. What is your opinion of the Hasmoneans? Do you take a positive, negative, or indifferent view towards them?

2. Would you have joined the Zealot revolt? Or to word this differently, what Roman actions or policies would have been necessary to make you join the Zealot cause?

The Historical Backdrop of Ancient Judaism
Lecture 4—Transcript

Before proceeding further with the specific topic of the Dead Sea Scrolls, we need to consider the general history of the time. In this lecture accordingly, we begin with a brief outline of the biblical period in order to survey the history that preceded the time of composition of the Dead Sea Scrolls. We next turn to the postbiblical period, when Alexander the Great and his successors, the Ptolemies and the Seleucids, dominated the scene. Our narrative will focus on the reign of King Antiochus IV, the Maccabean revolt, and the establishment of the Hasmonean dynasty. We then move to such topics as the arrival of the Romans in Israel, the reign of King Herod, the life of Jesus, the Zealot uprising, the destruction of Jerusalem, and the fall of Masada. Unfortunately, the Scrolls hardly ever refer explicitly to these events or individuals; a notable exception is 4Q448, a prayer for the king, which mentions King Jonathan by name. Nonetheless, the historical background presented in this lecture is of crucial importance for understanding the world that produced the Dead Sea Scrolls.

We begin with a basic outline of the history of Israel during the biblical period before we reach the period of late antiquity from which the Dead Sea Scrolls come. In the biblical period, the first major period is the premonarchic period, about 1400–1020 B.C.E. The biblical tradition begins with the three Patriarchs: Abraham, Isaac, and Jacob. We then read of the experience in Egypt, with the highlights being Joseph, the Slavery, Moses, and the Exodus, all familiar narratives from the books of Genesis and Exodus. This period in turn is followed by what we call the emergence of Israel as a nation. Three shorter periods fit here: the wandering through Sinai, the settlement in Canaan, and the period of the Judges. We have only a few archaic poems from this period embedded into the books of the Bible such as Exodus 15 and Judges 5.

The next major epoch is the monarchic period. Israel moves to a monarchy in about 1020 B.C.E. with Saul as the first king of Israel. He is followed by kings David and Solomon whom we call the united monarchy, and this brings Israel's glory period. Upon the death of King Solomon, Israel splits into two kingdoms, what we call the period of the divided monarchy, with the kingdom of Israel in the north and the kingdom of Judah in the south. The great compilation known as the Torah—Genesis through Deuteronomy, or the Pentateuch—was written during this period, along with other biblical books such as Samuel and Kings, most of the Psalms, and the prophetic works such as Amos, Hosea, Isaiah, and Jeremiah.

Finally, there is the late period, or the post-monarchic period, closing out the era of biblical history. The Babylonian destroyed Jerusalem in 586 B.C.E., and they exiled the people to Mesopotamia. The Babylonian exile was short lived, however, because in 538 B.C.E., a new world power arose: the Persians. The Persian Period for Ancient Israel commenced with the Persian conquest of the Babylonians and the decree by their king, Cyrus the Great, to allow the Jews to return to Jerusalem and rebuild the Temple. This rebuilt Temple we call the Second Temple; the First Temple had been constructed by Solomon and lasted until 586 B.C.E. With the building of the Second Temple, allowed by the Persians when they permitted the Jews to return to Jerusalem, we commence the Second Temple period. The conquest of Alexander the Great in 333 B.C.E., when the Greeks defeated the Persians, brought an end to this era that we call biblical history. The period that follows is called either late antiquity or the postbiblical period. Biblical books written during this late period include Ezekiel, Zechariah, Ezra, Nehemiah, and Chronicles.

The empire of Alexander the Great stretched from Greece in the West to India in the East. It was the largest empire the world had ever seen, larger than the preceding empires of the Assyrian, Babylonian, and Persian. The realm includes such lands as Egypt, Anatolia, Israel, Mesopotamia, Persia, and much more. Greek culture spread via Alexander's conquests, and thus we call this period the Hellenistic period; in the Near East, including Israel, the main characteristic is a blend of Greek ideas, thought, and culture with native, traditional Middle Eastern ones. Greek cities, replete with a gymnasium, theatre, amphitheatre, hippodrome, and other such structures are built throughout the Near East during this period. Greek philosophy and science are introduced to the peoples of the Near East; let us recall that Alexander had been a student of Aristotle. Many people, especially in the larger cities—including in the land of Israel—begin to speak Greek.

While Hellenism has clear influences on Jewish life, by and large Jewish religious life continued apace, with the Temple in Jerusalem remaining the main focus of religious worship and the main locus where the sacrifices occurred for the worship of God. Centuries later, during the 1st and 2nd centuries C.E. when the biblical canon was established by Jewish sages, one criterion for inclusion in the canon was authorship during the pre-Hellenistic period. Since many of the ideals of Hellenism—such as the emphasis on the body as realized through nude statuary—were inimical to traditional Jewish values, books written during the Hellenistic period were by their very date of composition seen as suspect. At the same time, of course, many Hellenistic ideas permeated Judaism, even without the Jews recognizing such influence at times—we will discuss the immortality of the soul, for example, in our next lecture—but the boundary line remained, and no book written after the arrival of the Greeks in the land of Israel could bear the sanctity required for entrance into the canon when the canon was closed about a half a millennium later. Thus we note that the reign of Alexander the Great brings an end to the biblical period.

Alexander died young—he was only 33 years old in 323 B.C.E.—and for the next 22 years a general sense of chaos ensued as various generals strove to gain control of the huge realm that I described earlier. Finally, in 301 B.C.E., four successor kingdoms to Alexander's empire emerged with relatively well-defined boundaries. For our course, two of those kingdoms are relevant. The first of them is the House of Ptolemy: 13 different kings use the name Ptolemy during the period 322–30 B.C.E. The last dynast is the famous Cleopatra VII, the wife and sister of Ptolemy XIII. The Ptolemies ruled in Egypt with their capital in the newly-founded city of Alexandria (named for Alexander the Great, obviously). The Ptolemaic kingdom extended northward from Egypt into Judea—as the land of Israel was now called—at least until 198 B.C.E., so that many Jews lived within the Ptolemaic realm.

Again, as under Alexander, Jewish religious life, especially the Temple cult in Jerusalem, continued with little change under the Ptolemies. One important development during this period that we need to mention is the translation of the Bible into Greek; this is the first time in history that the Bible was translated from its original language (Hebrew, with the addition of a few chapters in Aramaic) into another language, the Greek language. This project was sponsored by King Ptolemy II, and the resultant translation came to be known as the Septuagint or LXX for short. Some LXX fragments were found among the Dead Sea Scrolls; that is to say, Greek biblical translations of the original Hebrew text were also found in the caves at Qumran. This indicates that even in the land of Israel some Jews were reading the Bible in Greek translation.

The second successor kingdom to Alexander that is relevant to our course is the Seleucid Empire, which ruled from 312–63 B.C.E. Seven kings in this dynasty used the name Seleucus among the several dozen kings during these centuries. The Seleucids ruled in Antioch in northern Syria to the north of Israel (though on the modern map this city is located in southern Turkey. The Seleucid kingdom included all of Mesopotamia and Persia, so that large numbers of Jews resides in the Seleucid Empire as well. In 198 B.C.E., the two kingdoms met—the Seleucids and the Ptolemies—in a battle called the Battle of Paneas (or Banias), a city situated in far northern Israel. The Seleucids at this time defeated the Ptolemies, and therefore gained control of all of Judea, as the Ptolemies retreated from the area that they had been ruling with their territory from this time forth restricted to Egypt proper. The first Seleucid kings to rule over the land of Israel were Antiochus III and his successor Seleucus IV. Once more in these early decades of the Seleucid Empire and the Seleucid rule over the land of Israel the Temple rituals continued in Jerusalem with no discernible changes. All of this would change, however, with the ascension of Antiochus IV to the throne. The years of his reign are 175–164 B.C.E.; and it was this king, Antiochus IV, who began to persecute the Jews.

Let's take time out for a moment from the historical chronology that I'm giving you to give you a more general sense of what was going on: how the Jewish people were ruled; how they governed themselves in Jerusalem in an autonomous fashion under the Ptolemies earlier or the Seleucids during this time period now. During this period, the position of high priest—the Jewish high priest—served as the de facto leader of the Jewish people since the Jews were seen more and more as a religious community in the Hellenistic world with no king of their own (obviously) in their home territory of Judea, and with Jews spread throughout both empires (both the Ptolemaic Empire stretching down into Egypt and the Seleucid Empire stretching north and east to places like Babylonia and Persia).

It was during the reign of Antiochus IV that two Jewish priests, Jason and Menelaus, vied for the high priesthood. Both of these individuals were passionate Hellenizers; that is to say, they wanted to modernize—in their terminology—Judaism and bring it more into line with the Hellenistic thought and Hellenistic ideas that we referred to earlier. Under these two influential leaders—Jason and Menelaus—Jerusalem began to look more and more like a Greek polis; for example, the first gymnasium was built in Jerusalem. The struggle between these two individuals was won by Menelaus, who ascended to the role of high priest by outbidding Jason before King Antiochus IV. Moreover, according to the book of Maccabees—which is a key source for this period—Menelaus was not even from a priestly family of the tribe of Levi, but rather belonged to a different tribe, the tribe of Benjamin. Let me make this clear: That is to say, that two Jews contended for the high priesthood—which typically was a hereditary priesthood passed down from father to son, by tradition going back all the way to Aaron as we discussed in the previous lecture—and of these two, Jason and Menelaus, the latter was not even a true priest according to the book of Maccabees. They ascended, one in turn after the other, to high priesthood via bribery to the Seleucid king, each one trying to be more Hellenistic than the other in order to curry favor with Antiochus IV.

Fed up with this internecine Jewish fighting, Antiochus IV sought the total Hellenization of the Jews; and, in fact, Menelaus—the new high priest in Jerusalem—assisted him in this program. Some scholars would go further and argue that the king did not wish to Hellenize the Jews so much, but rather denationalize them altogether so that the Jews would be no different from anyone else in the empire, since to this point the Jews represent the only monotheists in the world. Thus the Jews were subjected to the following royal decree instituted by King Antiochus IV. First, the Jews were forbidden to engage in Jewish modes of worship. Second, they were forbidden to observe the Sabbath and the festivals. Third, Antiochus IV outlawed the ritual of circumcision so central to Jewish peoplehood; indeed, it's the sign of the covenant between the people of Israel and God according to various passages in the Bible. Fourth, Antiochus forced the Jews to sacrifice pigs to the Greek gods, with idols set up in the Jerusalem Temple.

What was the Jewish reaction to all of these persecutions; these new decrees from King Antiochus IV, the Seleucid emperor that the Jews were now subject to? The result was the Maccabean rebellion. Some Jews, called the Hasidim—the Hebrew word for "the pious ones"—actually resorted to civil disobedience; they resisted peacefully, and our sources indicate that they suffered martyrdom by the hundreds if not thousands. Others, however, took a more active role, in particular, the Maccabees. They were a priestly family from the town of Modi'in to the west of Jerusalem, and they banded together to lead a guerrilla-style rebellion against the armies of Antiochus IV. The patriarch of this Maccabee family was Mattathius—or in Hebrew, Matitiyahu—and with his son Judah as the active military leader, the family led the Jewish rebels against the armies of Antiochus IV. Much to the surprise of everyone, the Maccabees succeeded in defeating the Seleucids against all odds.

I note the following very important point: This was the first time in the history of mankind—in our recorded history—that we have a war fought for the sake of religious freedom. When the Jews lived well under other sovereigns, be they Persians, Alexander the Great, the Ptolemies, the first two Seleucid kings even, the Jews were content to live without political independence as they were part of these larger empires as long as their religious freedom was not compromised. When Antiochus IV began to repress the Jewish religion, however, the situation was very different, and thus the Jews rebelled, successfully as we have seen. The first act, now that the Jews had their independence, was the purification and rededication of the Temple. All of the pagan elements, the pig sacrifices, and the remnants of all of the Hellenization of the Temple had to be done away with; and this act of purification and rededication was accomplished in 164 B.C.E. This led to the establishment of the holiday of Hanukkah. The word "Hanukkah" means "dedication," because the Second Temple had been rededicated now with all the pagan influences removed and the Temple purified once more for Jewish religious worship.

The early years of the Hasmonean Dynasty are our next subject. The members of the Maccabee family established this dynasty—the terms "Maccabee" and "Hasmonean," incidentally, are more or less interchangeable—and the Hasmonean Dynasty ruled the land of Israel until 63 B.C.E., with the area of Judea gaining greater and greater independence from the Seleucids, and, in time, more and more territory in Israel and surrounding areas coming under Hasmonean rule. One of the Maccabees, Jonathan Maccabee, assumed the role of high priest in 152 B.C.E., and here we can see a specific connection with our Dead Sea Scrolls: As we will see in a later lecture, one of the figures who was mentioned in the Dead Sea Scrolls not by name but by a term is an individual called the Wicked Priest; we will be discussing more about him later on. Many scholars believe that when the Qumran community refers to the Wicked Priest, they have in mind Jonathan Maccabee, the ruler in Jerusalem who assumed the role of high priest.

Josephus explains that the three major sects—which we already have referred to in our course—developed during this period. It is easy to see the Essene movement springing up at this time; for even with the Temple now purified and in Jewish hands again, the Essenes disapproved of the manner in which the Temple was governed. First, they disapproved of all the contenders for high priest; to be sure, Jason and Menelaus before the revolt, and then Jonathan Maccabee and other members of the Maccabee family after the revolt. As the Dead Sea Scrolls indicate, the Qumran community believed that only the "sons of Zadok" should serve as priests; and we refer to this in lecture three. The implication with their emphasis on the sons of Zadok specifically is that the Qumran community saw other priests as emanating from illegitimate priestly lines, Jonathan Maccabee, the new high priest, among them. To be sure, one can understand in the light of all this how the Yahad—the Qumran community—retreated from Jerusalem and from the general Jewish community to establish their own center at Qumran, out in the desert, isolated from the major developments of the time, to live their life of piety. Given the general situation, one understands how the Qumran community would have considered Jonathan Maccabee to be the Wicked Priest.

Let's return to our narrative of the Hasmonean Dynasty. The next king who rules is a king named John Hyrcanus. Under his reign, Judea expanded greatly, and John Hyrcanus conquered, in fact, other lands including Idumea (the old land of Edom, as it's called in the Bible); and these people (the Idumeans) were forcibly converted to Judaism under John Hyrcanus. It's actually the only time in history that the Jews ever conquered another people and converted them to their own religion. John Hyrcanus also conquered the area of Samaria to the north, at which point he destroyed the Samaritan Temple on Mount Gerizim. We will be referring to the Samaritans in our next lecture and at other points in our course as well. John Hyrcanus was succeeded by his son, Aristobulus I, who had a very short reign of just a year or two. But—and this is an important point—Aristobulus I was the first of these kinds to use the title "king." The previous Maccabees had not used this title, and for good reason: The use of the title "king" was heretical. The reason for this was as follows: According to the biblical tradition, a king of Israel must come only from the tribe of Judah and specifically descend from King David to hold the title "king." Since the Maccabees were priests and therefore came from the tribe of Levi, they could not possibly be called "king"; they were priests, they had assumed the high priesthood and were ruling the land, but they could not take the title "king." Aristobulus I takes the title "king," an act of heresy in the minds of anyone who knows the biblical tradition in which kingship must come from one tribe and priesthood must come from the other.

The next king in this dynasty is called Alexander Janneus (or in Hebrew, Alexander Yannai); he reigned from 103–76 B.C.E. Our sources indicate that this king fostered a close relationship with the Essenes, and so for this brief period we know that the Essenes and the Hasmonean Dynasty had some affinity for one another because of the nature of this particular king, Alexander Janneus. This will explain why a blessing to King Jonathan was found among the Dead Sea Scrolls; I mentioned it earlier, its siglum is 4Q448. You all know by now how this operates: This means that it was found in Cave Four and this was the 448th text to come out of that cave. Jonathan may sound as if it were Jonathan Maccabee whom we referred to earlier and whom many scholars believe is the Wicked Priest; but Jonathan was also the Hebrew name of Alexander Janneus. Accordingly, a blessing to King Jonathan found among the Dead Sea Scrolls matches our understanding of Alexander Janneus, whose Hebrew name is Jonathan; and therefore one is not surprised to see the Qumran community having a text that blesses this king who, in turn, understood the Essenes and enjoyed their company. By the way, the wife of this king, Alexander Janneus, is the famous Salome Alexandra, who actually ruled herself upon her husband's death as Queen of Judea.

As we saw, the Maccabean revolt arose due to opposition to the Hellenization imposed by Antiochus IV. Yet, within decades, these rulers of the Hasmonean kingdom began to stylize themselves more and more as Hellenized monarchs. When the sons of Alexander Janneus and Salome Alexandra—and their names, by the way, were Hyrcanus II and Aristobulus II; and I need to apologize for throwing all these royal names at you—contended back and forth for the throne in the years 67–63 B.C.E. with neither son achieving the kingship without the other one looking over his shelter, they invited the Roman general Pompey to mediate between them. Pompey at this time was campaigning in Syria, and so he was nearby. Pompey, of course—the Roman general—saw this as an opportunity to gain control of Judea and Jerusalem, which he did with Hyrcanus II as his chosen puppet king, though by now he was ruling solely by the grace of Rome. The Dead Sea Scrolls occasionally refer to the arrival of the Romans in the land of Israel—again, that year is 63 B.C.E.—though they use the code word Kittim. "Kittim" is a word that occurs in the Bible and originally relates to Cyprus; that is to say, a land out in the Mediterranean. The Dead Sea Scrolls community adopted this word Kittim as a code word for the Romans, who obviously sailed across the Mediterranean as well from their base in Italy to reach the land of Israel.

The last of these monarchs of the Hasmonean Dynasty, Antigonus, reigned for just a few years, down to 37 B.C.E. He actually attempted to regain the throne independently with no recognition of Rome, but I hardly need to add: this attempt failed.

The next name is the famous King Herod. Herod ruled 37–4 B.C.E. Let me tell you a little bit about the background of King Herod. He was of Idumean extraction; remember I mentioned that John Hyrcanus had conquered the Idumeans and had forcibly converted them to Judaism? Herod comes from that Idumean group that had converted to Judaism. Herod's father was a high official in the Hasmonean kingdom; so what this means it that Herod himself is not a member of the Hasmonean Dynasty, but there is a way to become one and that is to marry into the dynasty. And he does: He marries a woman named Mariamme, a Hasmonean princess who was the granddaughter of the previous king, Hyrcanus II. In this way, Herod gained some claim to dynastic succession. Herod was extremely loyal to Rome; he convinced the Roman Senate to declare him King of Judea, which they did in 37 B.C.E. He then, I might add, arranged for the execution of Antigonus who was ruling up until this time period.

Herod's massive building projects are to be seen everywhere in the land of Israel: in Jerusalem, where he greatly expanded the Second Temple; in Caesarea, a new city that he built, the great harbor city, as homage to his patron Augustus Caesar; and Herod built personal palaces in Jerusalem, Caesarea, Jericho, and Masada. The remains of all of these can be seen today; one is welcome to visit the archaeological sites throughout Israel and see the constructions of King Herod. Interestingly, Herod is not mentioned in the Dead Sea Scrolls; neither by name—as I mentioned earlier, almost none of these figures are mentioned by name—and neither by any coded language either, it appears. The reason for this is either because the Qumran community retreated more and more—restricted itself—from public life, and/or because most of the documents found at Qumran predate Herod. For either or both of these reasons, Herod, as famous as he is, is not mentioned in the Dead Sea Scrolls.

Within a decade or so after Herod's death, Rome came to rule Judea directly—there were no more kings, not even kings ruling with the grace of Rome as had occurred with King Herod—and instead, Rome rules the land directly with a series of prefects or governors. The most famous of these individuals is Pilate who governed from 26–36 C.E. (we're now in the 1st century C.E.); and, of course, Jesus lived at this time (Jesus died in 33 C.E.).

A few decades later, tired of Roman rule in the land, a new rebellious movement arose, and we call them the Zealots. They are described by Josephus, and we will talk about them in the next lecture. The Zealots had purely political overtones, sometimes with an apocalyptic message as well; and the Zealots rebelled against Roman rule. They led the revolt in 66 C.E., the first year of the revolt. The Romans, however, were able to quash this rebellion; it took them some time, more effort than they had expected, but the Romans defeated the Jews during what we call the Jewish Revolt of 66–73 C.E. in the course of the war, the Romans destroyed Jerusalem in 70 C.E., and with it destroyed the Second Temple. Since 70 C.E., no Temple has stood in Jerusalem down to the present day. The last Zealot holdout was Masada, also on the Dead Sea although far south of Qumran at the southern end of the Dead Sea; Masada fell in 73 C.E.

A new Judaism developed at this time: Post-Temple Judaism. It is characterized by the rise of the synagogue—and we'll have more to say about the synagogue later in our course—and there's also a developing Diaspora. Because of the conditions in the land of Israel, more and more Jews leave the land and begin to settle in other regions of the Mediterranean and into the east towards Babylonia and Persia. Eventually, there will be a Second Jewish Revolt in 132–135 C.E.; we're now well beyond the time of Qumran, but I need to complete this narrative for you. There was a Second Jewish Revolt as well, as I indicated, led by Simeon Bar-Kokhba, another disastrous attempt at independence. From this point on, the Romans forbid Jews from living in Jerusalem and environs, and thus the center of Jewish life began to move in the 2nd century C.E. away from Jerusalem north to the region of the Galilee.

The history of Judaism during the last two centuries B.C.E. and the 1st century C.E.—and if we move to the Bar-Kokhba rebellion, the Second Revolt, we also have the 2nd century C.E.—serves as the backdrop for our next lecture: the rise of Jewish sectarianism during late antiquity.

The Rise of the Jewish Sects
Lecture 5

The main sects of Judaism in the late antique period were the Sadducees, Pharisees, Essenes, and Zealots, although other groups such as the Samaritans and early Christians dotted the landscape.

Josephus was general of a Jewish fighting force in Galilee who surrendered his troops to the Romans in 67 C.E., after which he joined the Romans as a chronicler of events. In this role, he witnessed the fall of Jerusalem, the destruction of the Temple, and the fall of Masada. After the Jewish revolt, Josephus settled in Rome, where under the patronage of the Flavius family he wrote his important historical works, composed in Greek, to explain Jewish history and Jewish religion to a Greco-Roman audience.

At the beginning of the Maccabean, or Hasmonean, period, three main sects arose in Judaism: Sadducees, Pharisees, and Essenes. In the decades leading up to the Jewish revolt, a fourth group, the Zealots, or Sicarri, arose. They were a militant group who advocated independence from Rome. Josephus also mentions Jesus of Nazareth, though the passage was doctored by later Christian scribes. Josephus does not refer to the nascent Christian movement.

The Sadducees were the main priestly group, supported by the nobility and aristocracy of Judea. Their approach to Jewish religion was essentially biblical; they believed that sacrifices in the Temple, as laid out in the Torah, was the sole manner by which God could be worshipped. They denied the existence of angels and the immortality of the soul. They also denied the existence of the Oral Law, a concept developed by the Pharisees. On the question of fate versus free will, the Sadducees believed in free will only. They did not believe in the resurrection of the dead.

The Pharisees had the support of a broader segment of the population. They developed customs and practices not found in the Bible and transferred many customs associated with the Temple to the home. They believed in the

the existence of angels and the immortality of the soul. Most importantly, they developed the concept of the Oral Law, an amorphous collection of religious practices, equal to and parallel to the Written Law, or the Torah. In their conception, both were given by God to Moses at Sinai. On the question of fate versus free will, the Pharisees took a middle ground. The Pharisees are mentioned several times in the New Testament, but usually in a negative way as overly concerned with laws and rituals and with a self-righteous attitude.

The Essenes were separatists, living more to themselves, less involved in the Pharisee-Sadducee dichotomies. They lived communally, with no private wealth. They had a series of initiation rites. They had a stricter approach to Jewish law than the other groups. They agreed with the Pharisees concerning the immortality of the soul and the existence of angels. They denied free will and believed that everything is preordained or predetermined by God.

Pliny the Elder visited Israel (probably in the 60s C.E.) and mentioned the Essenes living without women and dwelling near the Dead Sea—almost undoubtedly referring to the community of Qumran. It is possible that Josephus's three groups had further subdivisions. As a parallel, today we speak about three major divisions within Christianity (Catholic, Orthodox, and Protestant), with further denominations beneath those. Perhaps the Qumran community fell under the Essene umbrella but did not match up with Josephus's Essenes. Thus some scholars prefer to speak of the community as an Essene-type group.

Other Jewish groups existed during this period, and thus some scholars prefer to speak of "Judaisms" in the plural, with a "common Judaism" uniting the disparate sects and movements. Early Christians can be subdivided into Judaizing Christians who wished to continue Jewish ritual practice and non-Judaizing Christians who believed that the Jewish rituals had no place in the nascent Christian movement. The Ebionites, mentioned by later church fathers, were

> **Some scholars prefer to speak of "Judaisms" in the plural, with a "common Judaism" uniting the disparate sects and movements.**

a Jewish Christian group who accepted Jesus as messiah but did not believe him to divine. The Therapeutae were an ascetic group in Egypt, mentioned by Philo. The Boethusians, an offshoot of the Sadducees, were mentioned in the Talmud, but we know very little about them. The Samaritans were an early offshoot of Judaism (c. 500 B.C.E.). The main issue separating the Samaritans from the Jews was the question of where to worship God: Mount Zion in Jerusalem or Mount Gerizim above Shechem. Samaritans also rejected the Davidic kingship and related traditions. The Qumran community was clearly within the Jewish orbit and had no links to the Samaritans, but some of the peculiar grammatical features of Qumran Hebrew occur in the Samaritan brand of Hebrew as well. Does this suggest a deliberate attempt to distance themselves from the Jerusalem authorities by both the Samaritans and the Qumran community?

Judaism was a very variegated religion during this period, something which we should have known all along, but something scholars did not fully perceive until the discovery of the Dead Sea Scrolls. ■

Essential Reading

Vermes, *The Complete Dead Sea Scrolls in English*, 49–66.

VanderKam, *The Dead Sea Scrolls Today*, 71–92, 99–118.

VanderKam and Flint, *The Meaning of the Dead Sea Scrolls*, 239–292.

Schiffman, *Reclaiming the Dead Sea Scrolls*, 72–81, 154–157, 249–255.

Questions to Consider

1. If you were alive in the 2nd and 1st centuries B.C.E., with which of the three main Jewish sects—Pharisees, Sadducees, and Essenes—would you most likely align? Why?

2. Given the variegated picture of Judaism painted in this lecture, do you think that scholars should speak of a single Judaism or multiple Judaisms?

The Rise of the Jewish Sects
Lecture 5—Transcript

The previous lecture provided the historical backdrop for our course material. In this lecture, we turn our attention to the rise of Jewish sectarianism in late antiquity. Our main source for this subject is the great Jewish historian Josephus, and then we get additional information provided by other sources: the Jewish philosopher Philo, the authors of the New Testament books, the later rabbis, and, as we've seen earlier in our course, the Roman polymath Pliny the Elder. The main sects are the Sadducees, Pharisees, Essenes, and Zealots, though other groups such as the Samaritans and the early Christians dot the landscape as well. Within this discussion, we also will analyze the mention of Jesus in Josephus's narrative; though to be sure, scholars debate the authenticity of this famous passage. We will explore the theological differences between and among these various sects, especially as presented by Josephus. A leading question in Qumran scholarship is: Which of these groups wrote the Dead Sea Scrolls? We already have mentioned the dominant theory which associates the scrolls with the Essenes, a topic that we will explore further in this lecture.

I want to begin with some basic information about our number one source, the great Jewish historian Josephus. I want to introduce you to his life and into his career and his writings. Josephus was a general of a Jewish fighting force in the Galilee who surrendered his troops early on during the first Jewish Revolt against the Romans in 67 C.E., after which Josephus joined the Romans not as a general, not as a fighter, but as a historian; as a chronicler of the events. In this role, Josephus witnessed the important events of the time including, and most importantly, the fall of Jerusalem and the destruction of the Temple in 70 C.E., as well as the fall of Masada, the last stronghold of the Jewish Revolt, in 73 C.E. Josephus was there for both of these crucial events.

After the Jewish Revolt, Josephus settled in Rome, where under the patronage of the Flavius family he wrote his important historical works, composed in Greek, with the aim to explain Jewish history and Jewish religion to a Greco-Roman audience. Josephus wrote four different works. First, *The Jewish War*: This is a detailed account of the events leading up to the Jewish Revolt, and the Revolt itself, 66–73 C.E. His second and largest work is called *Jewish Antiquities*: This is a narrative presenting the entirety of Jewish history based on the Bible and postbiblical sources. It retells everything we know about the people of Israel in the Bible, and then brings the story up to times closer to Josephus's own day in the latter half of the 1st century C. E. His third work, called *Contra Apion*, is a shorter work. It is written in response to anti-Jewish charges from the pen of a certain Greek named Apion, and Josephus responds, describing why Judaism is a religion of valor. His fourth work is his autobiography called *My Life*; and from this we learn that Josephus himself came from a priestly family in Jerusalem, and that he had spent time living among the different sects of the day including the Sadducees, Pharisees, and Essenes, so that when he describes them once more we are getting first person information since Josephus himself lived among these groups and experienced their lives.

The Jewish sects as presented by Josephus: How much material we get from Josephus really is so crucial to this discussion. From these works of Josephus, we learn that at the beginning of the Maccabean or Hasmonean period, three main sects arose in Judaism, marked mainly by what Josephus would call philosophical differences. Remember, he's writing for a Greco-Roman audience that reads philosophy, that reads philosophical material, and so Josephus uses the same kind of terminology when he's writing in Greek for this largely polytheistic audience explaining Judaism to them. He provides detailed accounts of the three sects—as I've mentioned, the Sadducees, Pharisees, and Essenes—but he gives the most attention of all to the Essenes. Josephus spends more time describing them than the other groups, probably because of his fascination with the "other," the sect most different from the others; somewhat like an anthropologist approaching the exotic.

When Josephus's account reaches the decades leading up to the Jewish Revolt, he informs us of a fourth group called the Zealots, a militant group who advocated independence from Rome as their sole cause. Josephus also mentions Jesus of Nazareth in his writings, though the passage has been doctored by later Christian scribes. We should point out here that Josephus's writings were not preserved in the Jewish tradition but were preserved by Christian scribes throughout late antiquity into the Middle Ages as a witness to the time period in which Jesus himself had lived. Therefore, the works of Josephus are crucial for early church history because he provides the background for the development of Christianity, and—as I'm mentioning right here—Jesus himself is mentioned in Josephus's writings as a person who lived in the early decades of the 1st century C.E. Josephus, however, does not refer to the nascent Christian movement; only a very short passage about Jesus, he does not refer to the developing Christian movement either among the Jewish followers of Jesus or among the Gentile converts to this new religious tradition.

Let us now detail the three sects and their characteristic traits as outlined by Josephus. We begin with the Sadducees: The Sadducees are the main priestly group; they gain their support from the nobility and aristocracy of Judea. Their approach to Jewish religion is essentially biblical; that is, they believe that the sacrifices in the Temple—as laid out in the books of the Torah, especially in Exodus and Leviticus—should serve as the sole manner by which God is to be worshipped. The Sadducees deny the existence of angels, and they deny the immortality of the soul. You may ask, "But don't angels appear in the Bible? How could they deny the existence of the angels?" The word "angel" appears—the Hebrew word there is *malak*—but typically the term has a different connotation in biblical texts, something more like a manifestation of God. In postbiblical sources it comes to mean something like the modern English connotation of the word "angel," some sort of intermediary between the realms of Heaven and Earth. The concept of the immortality of the soul is a new idea in Judaism; it is not mentioned in the Bible at all. In fact, it comes from the writings of Plato; and from Plato through the growing Hellenistic influence on Judaism during the last few centuries before the Common Era, immortality of the soul comes to be understood by some Jew, as we'll see, as a component of Jewish religion. The Sadducees, however, deny the immortality of the soul.

The Sadducees also deny the existence of the Oral Law. As we'll see in a moment, this is concept developed by the Pharisees; the Sadducees reject this totally. On the question of fate versus free will, the Sadducees believe in free will only. Human beings have free will, and this governs what happens in our lives; that is the Sadducee belief. We also learn from the New Testament (Mark 12:18) that the Sadducees did not believe in the resurrection of the dead, along with the other items they didn't believe in that I've just referred to such as the immortality of the soul and the existence of angels.

Our next group is the Pharisees. According to Josephus, the Pharisees had the support of a broader segment of the population. The Pharisees developed customs and practices that are not to be found in the Bible. In particular, they held that communal prayer is an equally appropriate mode of worship, and that the study of Torah itself is a sacred act equal to the worship of God. That is to say, not only the sacrifices in the Temple, which the Sadducees saw as the sole mode of worshiping God, but that other ways of worship were being developed by the Pharisees as well. Notice that the sacrifices in the Temple were conducted only by the priests, and therefore this was a monopoly of how to worship God in the Sadducee system. The Pharisees are democratizing in this fashion by allowing or promoting other modes of worship: as I mentioned, communal prayer and the study of the Torah. By the way, in the Bible, prayer is solely a private matter, as illustrated, for example, by the story of Hannah in 1 Samuel 1. The Pharisees now expand the use of prayer into the public domain: Congregational prayer (people praying together, not only privately), and the study of the Torah, as I mentioned.

In addition, many customs associated with the Temple itself are transferred to the home where people live. The best example of this is the custom of washing ones' hands before eating. The priests had to be in a state of ritual purity—as we've discussed earlier in our course—before they could enter the Temple and before they would offer the sacrifices in the Temple to God. A last act of purity was to have their hands washed by their Levitical assistants before they would actually then offer the animal on the altar and partake of that food. The Pharisees wanted to transfer this custom to the home where everybody could be doing this act as well; and therefore eating in the home becomes a religious act, and therefore one needs to wash one's hands before eating even in one's home. That would be the Pharisee system, analogous to what the Sadducees were doing; but for the Sadducees, led by the priest, it was simply located in the Temple. You can begin to see how a whole new breed of Judaism is being produced here by the Pharisees.

The Pharisees believe in the existence of angels—contrary to the Sadducees—and they adhere to the concept of the immortality of the soul;

and as I mentioned a moment ago, this is a fine illustration of how Hellenism takes root in Judaism, even when Jews are not necessarily conscious of the influence. Most importantly, the Pharisees develop the concept of the Oral Law, an amorphous collection of religious practices that, in their mind, were equal to and parallel to the Written Law embodied in the Torah. In their conception, both the written law—the Torah or the Pentateuch—or the Oral Law, which has been transmitted orally, were given at Sinai by God to Moses. In this Oral Law, within this oral tradition, are all sorts of practices among which I have just referred such as prayer, studying of Torah, washing of hands, and other similar rituals. On the question of fate versus free will, the Pharisees take a middle ground; or to use the scholarly philosophical term for this, they are "compatabilists"; that is, they see room for both ends of the continuum in different aspects of life. The free will view of the Sadducees, and—as we referred to earlier in our course and we will see in a moment just again—the predetermination or predestination view of the Essenes; the Pharisees took a middle ground here. The Pharisees are mentioned several times in the New Testament, though usually in a negative way, as overly concerned with laws and rituals and with a self-righteous attitude.

In a moment, we will see some possible connections between the early Christians and the Pharisees, which raises the question then: Why are the Pharisees portrayed so negatively in the Gospels? First, there is the rule of "minimal differences," whereby one group sees as its greatest adversary the group closest to it. We saw this earlier in our course with the Qumran community where it sees itself as the sons of light and the other Jews as the sons of darkness, without concern for peoples who were even further removed such as the polytheists of the greater Greco-Roman world. Similarly here, the New Testament authors polemicized against the Pharisees in particular, even though both the Jesus movement and the contemporary Pharisees were within the greater umbrella of 1st century C.E. Judaism. Secondly, and more importantly, scholars agree that the depiction of the Pharisees in the Gospels stems from the fact that the early Christian community sought to distance itself from the Jews, represented most of all by the Pharisees in the New Testament, especially in the years after the destruction of the Temple in 70 C.E. when most of the New Testament books were written.

Then we come to our third group: the Essenes. We've already introduced the Essenes in our course, because when we read the Community Rule together in Lecture Three we needed to talk about a variety of theological stances and practices that are mentioned in the Community Rule and how these relate to the Essenes. You've already been introduced to them; but now since we're discussing them in greater detail here, especially alongside the Pharisees and Sadducees, let's present our information that we gain from Josephus about the Essenes in more systematic fashion.

The Essenes were separatists; they lived more to themselves. They were less involved in the Pharisee-Sadducee dichotomies that we've outlined for you, and there were fewer Essenes than there were either Pharisees or Sadducees. Josephus describes them as living communally, with no private wealth—you've heard me say these things before—and with a series of initiation rites that one must pass in order to enter this particular group, the Essene group. Much of this, as I've said, we've talked about, especially in Lecture Three because of the connections between what I'm saying now and the Community Rule 1QS document. The Essenes had a stricter approach to Jewish law than the other groups. For example—and this may be hard to fathom—Josephus informs us that the Essenes did not defecate on the Sabbath; we will actually return to this very interesting item later in our course, but this gives you an idea how strict their application of Jewish law was. No defecation on the Sabbath day.

The Essenes agreed with the Pharisees concerning such matters as the immortality of the soul and the belief in angels, which we've already referred to. The Essenes—and you've heard this before now on several occasions—denied free will. They believed that everything is preordained or predetermined by God, and humankind can do nothing to change what is predestined. That is to say, the Essenes were at the other end of the continuum from the Sadducees on this important issue, with the Pharisees—as I've indicated—holding the middle ground. Some of the Essenes are celibate, according to Josephus, and this point was made by Philo as well; we've talked about that earlier in our course and we will continue to come back to it in future lectures.

Let's return to the comment of Pliny the Elder, which I've referred to several times in our course already. The great Roman polymath who visited the land of Israel and incorporated information about the Dead Sea region in his encyclopedic compendium called the *Natural History*, published in 77 C.E. Pliny mentions the Essenes, living without women (you'll recall the quote) dwelling near the Dead Sea—and now let me provide for you another piece of information that I have not mentioned earlier—*infra hos Engada*—those are the words that Pliny uses. The Latin word there for "below" is *infra*; *infra*, and then he uses the Latin version of the word of the place name: Ein Gedi. Where is Ein Gedi and why is this important? Ein Gedi is located about halfway down the shore of the Dead Sea; so if you have Qumran on the northern shore of the Dead Sea and Masada—which we referred to in the previous lecture—at the southern end of the Dead Sea, in between them is the site of Ein Gedi. If "below" means "to the south"—and this is the conclusion of most scholars who've read the Pliny passage—then almost undoubtedly Pliny is referring to the community at Qumran. If you traveled north of Ein Gedi along the shore of the Dead Sea—and I have done this numerous times in my life—you would reach no other spot other than Qumran; it is empty terrain north of Qumran, one reaches Jericho and then as you turn west from there you come to Jerusalem. But above Ein Gedi, north of Ein Gedi, there's simply nothing other than Qumran. This is a firm piece of information that for me and other scholars who adhere to the Dead Sea Scrolls/Essene connection apply this piece of information from Pliny and we make that connection here as well in this lecture.

We have mentioned the three main groups here. It is possible that Josephus's three groups represent umbrellas with further subdivisions. We can't be sure about this, but let's note a parallel: Today, for example, we speak about three major divisions within Christianity—Catholic, Orthodox, and Protestant—though only the Catholic Church is a unified whole since there are many eastern Orthodox churches and even many, many more Protestant denominations. It is possible that the Qumran community falls within the Essene group but does not match up with Josephus's Essenes all the time. This is why some scholars who doubt the Essene/Qumran connection look at Josephus's Essenes and say, "It doesn't always match 100 percent of the time, so maybe they really aren't Essenes"; this is the point I'm making here, of course, that perhaps the term "Essene" is an umbrella term that would include those whom Josephus describes and with some variation the Qumran community. Let me give you an example of where Josephus's Essenes and the Dead Sea Scrolls don't match up necessarily: One, Josephus does not mention the dualism that we saw in Lecture Three when we read the Community Rule together as part of the Dead Sea Scrolls belief system; and Josephus does not mention the apocalyptic element of the Essenes, though this is very much present in the Dead Sea Scrolls community. We haven't talked about the apocalyptic element in the Qumran scrolls yet, but we will return to that in a future lecture. Therefore, because of some of these items that Josephus doesn't necessarily mention, although scholars are willing to see the Dead Sea Scrolls community as Essenes, they will prefer to use the term an "Essene-type group." That's ok; I'm just giving you some of the scholarly information here, the scholarly debate, and how people come down to use terms in a slightly different fashion.

We also need to note that beyond these main groups that Josephus describes that we know that there were other groups that existed as well. The result is an extremely diverse Jewish people at the time, and thus some scholars prefer to speak of "Judaisms" in the plural, with a "common Judaism" uniting the disparate sects and movements. Let's refer to some of these other groups that Josephus does not include in his description beyond the Pharisees, Sadducees, Essenes, and as I mentioned at times he adds the fourth group, the Zealots. Who are these other groups that we see on the map in the area of the land of Israel at this time? First and foremost there are the Christians; and the Christians can be further subdivided into two groups: There are the Judaizing Christians. They are associated with James, the brother of Jesus, who wished to continue Jewish ritual practices such as circumcision and the dietary laws; those are the Judaizing Christians. The other group is the non-Judaizing Christians. They are led by Paul, who believed that the Jewish rituals should have no place in this new Christian movement.

One may note here that scholars debate the question: To which of the other Jewish sects did the early Christians have the closest links? On the one hand, the term "rabbi" is used in the Gospels to refer to both Jesus and John the Baptist, and we also learn that Paul was a student of the great rabbinic sage Rabban Gamaliel I; this is mentioned in Acts 22:3. Since the rabbis of later Jewish literature are the successors to the Pharisees—we will begin to talk about a Pharisaic-rabbinic continuum—and since you have this term "rabbi" used in the New Testament and Saul was a student of this great rabbinic sage, one would assume some connection between the early Christians and the Pharisees. On the other hand, as we will see repeatedly in our course, so much of Christian thought reflects Essene beliefs and practices that one also has to assume connections to the Essenes as well. That is where more scholars certainly come down on this—more scholars will see a Christian/Essene connection than they would a Christian/Pharisee connection—but I'm giving you a sense here of the complexity of the picture.

Then there are other sects as well: The Ebionites are mentioned by later church fathers, several centuries later, as a Jewish Christian group who accepted Jesus as the messiah but who did not believe that Jesus was divine. Yet another group mentioned by Philo—I've referred to them earlier in our course—is the Therapeutae, an ascetic group in Egypt. There may have been Therapeutae living in Israel as well—Philo, of course, living in Egypt speaks about them there—but there may have been Therapeutae in Israel, too, and, in fact, there was without a doubt a connection between the Therapeutae and the Essenes. The ascetic lifestyle of the Therapeutae as described by Philo links up in many ways with some of the ascetic components of the Dead Sea Scrolls community, too. Yet another group that we know from our ancient sources: the Boethusians, an offshoot of the Sadducees, mentioned in the later rabbinic compendium called the Talmud; though unfortunately we know very little about this group, but at least we have their name, the Boethusians, an offshoot of the Sadducees.

Then there are the Samaritans. The Samaritans were an early offshoot of Judaism; they split at a much earlier period, about 500 B.C.E. or 450 B.C.E. The main issue that separates the Samaritans from the Jews is the question of where God is to be worshipped. For Jews, the answer is Mount Zion in Jerusalem; for Samaritans, the answer is Mount Gerizim above the city of Shechem to the north of Jerusalem. Mount Gerizim and neighboring Mount Ebal are mentioned in the Torah, while Mount Zion actually is not; although, of course, Mount Zion and Jerusalem are mentioned in later biblical books where they become the focus of attention in books such as Samuel, Kings, Isaiah, Jeremiah, Ezekiel, and so on. But if you go back to the books of the Torah itself, one does not see Mount Zion and Jerusalem mentioned; one does see mention of the two mountains of the Samaritans, Mount Gerizim and Mount Ebal. Thus, while the Jews canonized all the biblical books—all the books that we come to know as the Jewish canon, the Jewish Bible—the Samaritans, by contrast, canonized only the five books of the Torah. They rejected those books such as Samuel and Kings that speak about the centrality of Jerusalem, and the entire Davidic kingship and all the relevant traditions; those are rejected by the Samaritans, they have only the Torah or the Pentateuch, the five books from Genesis through Deuteronomy. Those are the Samaritans.

The Qumran community is clearly within the Jewish orbit and has no links to the Samaritans, but it is interesting to note that some of the peculiar grammatical features attested in Qumran Hebrew—and we referred to this earlier and we will devote a later lecture to this subject in detail—occur in the Samaritan brand of Hebrew as well. Does this connection suggest a deliberate attempt to distance oneself from Jerusalem by use of a particular Hebrew dialect as used both by the Samaritans and the Qumran community? I raise the question; although naturally we have no firm answer for that question. Even within the Samaritan movement, one may see the following subdivisions: There is the main Samaritan group that we've described to you; and then there's and offshoot called the Dositheans. Unfortunately we know very little about this group, though possibly they were a gnostic group within the Samaritan movement. Then once more I want to mention the Zealots: not quite a religious sect, but a well-defined group within Judaism with the goal of political independence from Rome.

In short, Judaism was a very variegated religion during this period, something that we should have known all along, but something that scholars did not fully perceive until the discovery of the Dead Sea Scrolls and until Qumran research engaged this topic in the late 1940s and 1950s; and indeed it remains part of scholarly inquiry down to the present day. Let us list here once more the different groups we have mentioned, giving them to you all in a list at once so you get a sense, in a single moment, what we're talking about: Pharisees, Sadducees, Essenes, Zealots, Judaizing Christians, non-Judaizing Christians, Ebionites, Therapeutae, Boethusians, Samaritans, Dositheans, and perhaps other groups for whom we simply have no information, not even a name, that also may have existed in the land of Israel within the Jewish umbrella during this time period. Therefore I repeat what I said earlier: There were various "Judaisms," plural, during late antiquity—this is the way scholars now consider the question—with a single common Judaism. They would have agreed, all the Jewish sects, about certain things: the centrality of the Torah and the worship of God. But even certain issues such as where God should be worshiped caused divisions, such as when the Samaritans split off from Judaism; and then even if you do agree that God is to be worshiped in Jerusalem, how is that worship to occur? In the Temple alone, outside the Temple; all sorts of options for Jewish groups during this time period.

Once upon a time, scholars thought that Pharisees and the rabbis that succeeded them—the Pharisaic-rabbinical continuum—was the normative Judaism. We no longer can speak in such terms; however, given that there were so many different Jewish groups at this time, we no longer assume any kind of normative Judaism in late antiquity. The rabbinic movement was one such group, but it was not by any means normative in the light of all the different sects, groups, and denominations that we have presented in this lecture.

At this point in our course, after the previous lecture and the present lecture, both of which have presented broad swaths of material, it is time to refocus our attention on Qumran specifically. We do so in the next lecture, as we consider the excavations conducted by archaeologists at the site of Khirbet Qumran.

The Dead Sea Site of the Qumran Sect
Lecture 6

The archeological site of Qumran, near the Qumran caves, was first excavated shortly after the discovery of the Dead Sea Scrolls.

Before discussing the excavations at Qumran, let us look at its general area, including the topography of the Dead Sea region. If we take Jerusalem as our starting point, heading due east, we reach the desert right on the outskirts of the city. We travel 37 kilometers through the desert as the road descends precipitously all the way to the Dead Sea. Turning south, we reach Qumran about five kilometers away. It is almost impossible to describe the isolation and remoteness of Qumran, along with the loneliness that one feels there. Qumran is on flat land near the shore of the Dead Sea, while the caves are in the cliffs above the archaeological site. There is very little water around. The Dead Sea is salt water, undrinkable and unusable, but nearby flows a wadi, called the Wadi Qumran, and from here the Qumranites obtained their fresh water, diverting it into specially constructed channels that flowed to the site. This is the lowest spot on Earth, at 400 meters below sea level. The Dead Sea and entire Jordan valley are part of the great Syrian-African rift, which begins north of Qumran and extends south through the Red Sea, into Ethiopia and Kenya. In addition to its salt content, the Dead Sea contains minerals such as potassium, magnesium, and bromine. The result is that nothing lives in these waters—thus the name "Dead Sea," although in Hebrew it is called *yam ha-melah*, "the Salt Sea."

This is the lowest spot on Earth, at 400 meters below sea level.

Soon after the discovery of the Dead Sea Scrolls, scholars realized that they would need to excavate the site of Qumran, located about 1,000 meters away. Père Roland de Vaux of the École Biblique et Archéologique Française led the excavations, which were administered by the Dominican monastery in Jerusalem. De Vaux traced the period of settlement to c. 134 B.C.E.–c. 68 C.E., with a slight interruption following an earthquake in 31 B.C.E. Three vessels containing more than 500 coins were found, a major help in establishing the specific chronology of the site. Most are dated to the reign of the Seleucids. The fact that these coins were all found together suggests that this was the community treasury. In the early years of Qumran research, carbon-14 dating was brand new and thus little used. Subsequently, various organic materials, including some of the scrolls themselves, were tested, and a rough date of c. 100 B.C.E. was calibrated—confirming de Vaux's estimates. Major buildings were found, including a tower; a pottery-manufacturing area; a kitchen and pantry; a main meeting hall, which probably doubled as the dining hall; a scriptorium in which writing tables and ink wells were found; and an elaborate system of cisterns and *miqva'ot* (ritual baths) fed by an aqueduct leading from the nearby Wadi Qumran. Lacking were private homes and residences, which led de Vaux to see a the inhabitants living communally. The scriptorium and ink wells indicated that scribal activity was prominent, so once more a connection was made to the scrolls found in the nearby caves.

De Vaux and his colleagues interpreted their finds in the light of their own experiences as monks. Bolstered by Pliny's reference to the Essenes as dwelling without women and renouncing desire, de Vaux saw the Qumran community as a forerunner of Christian priestly orders. De Vaux may have been right, but the background for his interpretation needs to be noted nonetheless. Between 1948 and 1954, scholars systematically combed the caves in the area, with the assistance of the local Bedouin. In all, 11 caves yielded scrolls. Although the caves are situated in cliffs, note that their location is still about 250 meters below sea level. Most are natural caves, but some are man-made.

The caves were numbered in the order of discovery. Caves 1 and 2 are about one kilometer north of Qumran, and caves 3 and 11 are about another kilometer north. Caves 4–10 are only between 100 and 300 meters from the site. The mother lode was discovered in Cave 4, one of the man-made caves: more than 500 documents, though most were in a very fragmentary state.

The cemetery was excavated in 1966–1967, though only a small portion of the 1,100 graves were exhumed. Among them, however, were some women. The 1970s and 1980s saw off-and-on excavations by Pesach Bar-

Adon and his successor Vendyl Jones of a large cave near Cave 11, which yielded finds from the Hellenistic and Roman periods. In 1984–1986 and again in 1991, Joseph Petrach explored dozens of additional caves in the area, ranging from four miles south of Qumran to four miles north of Qumran, with archaeological remains from the Second Temple period found in 17 such caves. Between 1993 and 1996, Hanan Eshel and Magen Broshi thoroughly explored the area again and established a clear link between the caves and the archaeological site. They further posited that some members of the sect may have lived in tents beyond the excavation site as well as in the caves themselves.

Years after the first discoveries, scholars continued to study the initial finds. Jodi Magness has written the standard work, entitled *The Archaeology of Qumran and the Dead Sea Scrolls*. Among her findings are the following. About half of the clay of the Qumran pots was imported from Jerusalem. The cylindrical jars in which the scrolls were found are distinctive of Qumran. And since such jars were found both in the caves and at the site, we have another connection between the two locales.

As long as we are talking about these scroll jars, the following tales from antiquity may be of interest. The church father Origen (185–254 C.E.) reports that in his lifetime a scroll containing the book of Psalms in Greek was found in a jar near Jericho. A century later, the church father Eusebius (c. 260–340 C.E.) described the same text and mentions other Greek and Hebrew manuscripts found in a jar near Jericho. Finally, around 800 C.E., Timotheus I, a Nestorian patriarch wrote that the books of the Old Testament were found near Jericho. Were these discoveries from the Qumran caves? Probably not, but they inform us that other groups in the desert hid their scrolls in jars as well.

What happened to the Qumran community? The group clearly abandoned the area in 68 C.E., when the Roman legions were marching through Judea. Presumably they deposited their most valuable possessions, their scrolls, in the caves nearby, hoping one day to return. A copy of one particular Dead Sea Scroll, called Songs of the Sabbath Sacrifice, was found 48 kilometers to the south at Masada, leading scholars to conclude that some members of the sect sought refuge there. The disappearance of the Qumran community and other sects paved the way for the emergence of rabbinic Judaism. ■

Essential Reading

VanderKam, *The Dead Sea Scrolls Today*, 12–25.

VanderKam and Flint, *The Meaning of the Dead Sea Scrolls*, 20–54.

Schiffman, *Reclaiming the Dead Sea Scrolls*, 31–61, 395–397.

Yadin, *The Message of the Scrolls*, 53–67.

Supplementary Reading

Magness, *The Archaeology of Qumran and the Dead Sea Scrolls*.

Questions to Consider

1. To what extent do you think Roland de Vaux's status as a Catholic priest influenced his reconstruction of Qumran and the Dead Sea Scrolls, based on his excavation of the former and his reading of the latter?

2. Scholars continue to return to the caves in the general Dead Sea region in search of additional documents and treasures. To what extent do you think these activities are governed by true scholarly research versus the quest for glory, adventure, and publicity?

The Dead Sea Site of the Qumran Sect
Lecture 6—Transcript

Welcome back to our course on the Dead Sea Scrolls. Before proceeding to the specific topic of the excavations at Qumran, I thought that this would be a good time to say something about the general area, the geography, the lay of the land including the topography of the Dead Sea region. On several occasions I have mentioned the remote location and general isolation of Qumran, but I do not believe that I have emphasized that point enough. Let's ask the question, then: How does one reach Qumran? If we take as our starting point the city of Jerusalem, one heads due east, and, in fact, one reaches the desert already on the outskirts of Jerusalem; that is to say, if you're in the eastern part of Jerusalem and you start heading east, you reach the desert within a kilometer or two. One travels 37 kilometers through the desert on a continuous downward roadway, as the road descends precipitously at times, until one reaches the Dead Sea. En route, one passes a marker that indicates sea level, and from that point onward until you reach the Dead Sea you continue to head down below sea level until you reach the lowest spot on Earth. When you reach a T-junction at the end of that road, if one were to turn left and head north at this point and travel about 10 kilometers, one would reach Jericho, the largest city in the region, built around a series of large springs. But if you went to that T-junction and turned right to head south at that point and travelled about 5 kilometers, one would reach Qumran.

It is almost impossible to describe the isolation and remoteness of Qumran, along with the loneliness that one feels there. I have visited the site many times; I hardly ever travel to Israel without making the effort to visit Qumran, and no matter how times I have been there, I continue to marvel at this amazing location. On one occasion, I should tell you, I actually bicycled from Jerusalem to Qumran. This may sound like a feat of bravado, but in truth the trek is all downhill as one reaches speeds of 40 miles per hour heading down that hill towards the Dead Sea; and then I continued on that trek south of Qumran, past Ein Gedi, past Masada, to the southern end of the Dead Sea, one of the great experiences of my life in my explorations of the land of Israel.

As I have mentioned earlier in this course, Khirbet Qumran—that's the name of the archaeological site; let's remind ourselves. Qumran is the region, as we'll see in a moment there's also a Wadi Qumran, the site is called Qumran. Khirbet Qumran: "Khirbet" is the Arabic word for an archaeological ruin, and I'll use that term especially when talking about the excavations—as I mentioned, Khirbet Qumran is on the flat land, lying near the shore of the Dead Sea, while the caves are in the cliffs above the archaeological site. As you can imagine, there is very little water around. The water of the Dead Sea is totally saltwater; it's the saltiest water on the earth. It's eight times as salty as ocean water. It's totally undrinkable, it's totally unusable; you can't irrigate with it, you can't use it for your crops, your animals won't drink from it either. But nearby flows a wadi, called the Wadi Qumran. A wadi is a dried up riverbed during most of the year, especially during the summer months, but the occasional winter rain will fill the wadi with water; and from here the Qumranites obtained their fresh water as they diverted the waters of the Wadi Qumran into specially constructed water channels that then flowed to their homes.

In general we should note that in addition to the interest of archaeologists and historians in this area, geologists and naturalists, as you can imagine, continue to be amazed by the entire Dead Sea region. I should remind you, as I indicated a moment ago, that this is the lowest spot on earth: 400 meters below sea level. The Dead Sea and entire Jordan valley are part of the great Syrian-African rift, which begins to the north of our area and extends south through the Red Sea and into Ethiopia and Kenya. In addition to its salt content, the waters of the Dead Sea contain minerals such as potassium, magnesium, and bromine. In fact, I should mention here that since the Dead Sea is shared by the modern countries of Israel and Jordan, both nations have major mining operations along the Dead Sea shore in various places as they obtain the potassium, magnesium, bromine, and other minerals out of the Dead Sea shore and the Dead Sea waters. The result of all this is that nothing lives in these waters, thereby explaining the name "Dead Sea"; though in Hebrew, I should mention, this body of water is called *yam ha-melah* which means "the salt sea." That's its name already in the Bible, and that's the way it's continued to be referred to, to this day, in the modern Hebrew language. Is it any wonder that naturalists are so fascinated by this region, from Pliny the Elder 2,000 years ago to modern scientists today?

Now let's talk about those excavations at Qumran. Soon after the discovery of the scrolls in the caves, scholars realized that they would need to excavate the nearby site of Khirbet Qumran, located about 1,000 meters away from what we now call Cave One. The person who led the excavations was Père Roland de Vaux, a French scholar, a Dominican priest, who was housed and did his work at the École Biblique et Archéologique Française, administered by the Dominican monastery in Jerusalem. You'll recall earlier in our course I referred to ASOR, the American Schools of Oriental Research, where American scholars and some British scholars were housed? Many European nations and the United States as well had centers of academic research in Jerusalem: the Swedes, the Germans, the Brits, the Americans, and the French. In the case of the French, as I just mentioned, their center was under the administration of a Dominican group, the École Biblique et Archéologique Française; a remarkable place in the eastern part of Jerusalem, a place that I have visited a number of occasions and enjoyed their remarkable library, the best library for the study of the Bible and the antiquity in the entire world.

Let's review the main finds of de Vaux's excavations during 1951–56. De Vaux determined that the period of settlement at Qumran began circa 134 B.C.E. and continued until circa 68 C.E.—that's more than 200 years—with a slight interruption following the earthquake that occurred in this area in 31 B.C.E. Incidentally, this may be another reason why Herod is not mentioned among the Dead Sea Scrolls, or even hinted at via some coded language, since the site was mostly abandoned during his reign; Herod reigned 37–4 B.C.E., the earthquake occurred in 31 B.C.E. Three vessels containing coin were found by de Vaux and his colleagues in their excavations, and they contained more than 500 coins in total. These coins are a major help in establishing the specific chronology of the site since the coins typically are dated. Usually they are dated to the reign of the Seleucid ruler—for example, Antiochus VII and Demetrius II—both of whom reigned in the second half of the 2nd century before the Common Era.

It may seem odd for Jews to have in their possession Seleucid coins, rather than Hasmonean coins—this is the time of the Hasmonean kingdom—but I would not read too much into this practice, since coins of both types were in circulation in Judea during this time, and the Seleucid coins had greater value since they could be used in a much wider geographical area. The fact that these coins were all found together in these three vessels, all placed together, suggests that this represents the treasury of the Yahad, the Qumran sect, the place where individual members of the sect deposited their wealth upon joining the community. Remember our discussions previously that people did not own private wealth, but rather everything was contributed to a common treasury. Here you have three vessels filled with coins, which dovetails very nicely with what we know about the Essenes and what we know about this Qumran community specifically from its own Community Rule, the topic of our discussion back in Lecture Three. Otherwise, we might expect that these coins would be strewn all over the site—a little bit here, a little bit there, some here, some there—but no, that's not the case; all 500-plus coins were found together in three vessels.

You may ask about carbon-14 dating; but in the early years of Qumran research, carbon-14 was little used. The dating technique was only developed in about 1950, so that de Vaux, who's beginning his excavations in 1951 and the next five years, did not rely on this method that is now widely used in archeological research. To remind you what carbon-14 is all about, any organic material—anything that was once alive—contains carbon; and carbon-14, which is an isotope of carbon, is used by scholars in a laboratory test to determine when that organic material ceased to be alive. You can take wood, you can take linen, you can take a woolen garment; you can take anything that was once alive and date it by a carbon-14 test. Again, in de Vaux's day in the 1950s, this test was just being developed and it was really not very reliable. Subsequently, though, various organic materials from the Qumran area, both the site and the caves, including some of the Dead Sea Scrolls themselves—no, we didn't lose any words, we just took a little bit off the edges of the parchment and tested them in a carbon-14 lab test—and also some of the linen wrappings that were found in the caves have all been submitted to carbon-14 tests, not in de Vaux's day but in the decades since then, and the dates of 150 B.C.E., 100 B.C.E. are the dates that typically come up in the calibration of the carbon-14 test, exactly what one would expect given all the other evidence that we have amassed for the Qumran community in the 2nd and 1st centuries B.C.E., continuing into the 1st century C.E. as well.

Back to de Vaux's excavations, however: He found a number of major buildings, including a tower, probably to protect the site; a pottery manufacturing area with kilns and so on; a kitchen and a pantry; a main meeting hall, a large room that probably doubled as the dining hall (remember, they ate their meals communally); a scriptorium, in which were found writing tables and inkwells; and an elaborate system of cisterns, water channels and *miqva'ot* (the Hebrew term for ritual baths) fed by an aqueduct leading from the nearby Wadi Qumran, as I mentioned just a few moments ago. This system of water channels, cisterns, and ritual baths called *miqva'ot* in Hebrew: With all of this in place on the ground from the archaeological excavations, we may recall the emphasis placed on ritual bathing in the Dead Sea Scrolls for the removal not only of ritual impurity as the Bible prescribes, but also for the moral impurity, for the removal of sin that we talked about earlier in our course. Lacking from de Vaux's excavations, from his findings, were private homes and residences; and this led de Vaux to see the Qumran a group as living communally, exactly as we know about from the description of the Essenes by Josephus and from the Dead Sea Scrolls documents themselves. Of course, the scriptorium with the writing tables and the ink wells indicated that scribal activity was a prominent feature of life at Qumran, and once more a connection was made to the scrolls found in the nearby caves.

We need to mention here that de Vaux and his colleagues (and remember that de Vaux and his colleagues were Dominican priests) interpreted the finds at Qumran—they interpreted this archeological material that they found at the site and the contents of the Dead Sea Scrolls coming out of the cave at this time period as well—in the light of their own experiences as Dominican monks living in a monastery. Bolstered by Pliny's reference to the Essenes as dwelling without women and renouncing all desire, and given the references in both Philo and Josephus concerning celibacy in connection with some Essene groups, de Vaux (Father de Vaux) saw the Qumran community as an early forerunner of what would emerge as Christian priestly orders comprised of celibate monks. We know today that he certainly overstated the case, and different people approach the evidence in different ways; but this is an interpretation from the early days of Qumran that needs to be noted here nonetheless. It certainly set the stage for understanding the Dead Sea Scrolls community—the Qumran sect; the Yahad—as a forerunner of early

Christianity. Not totally wrong, because as we've mentioned before and as we will see repeatedly there are connections between the Essenes, the Dead Sea Scrolls community, and the early Christian movement.

Let me talk a little bit more here about the caves, which we discussed earlier in this course in Lecture One, and I want to now summarize some of that information and expand upon it. You'll recall that during the years 1948–1954—this is while de Vaux is excavating more or less the same time period at the site of Khirbet Qumran—other scholars are systematically, with the assistance of the Bedouin—combing the caves in the area. In all, you will recall, 11 caves yielded scrolls. The caves are situated on those cliffs above Khirbet Qumran; though given how low the region is (below sea level), we should note that these caves themselves are still very much below sea level, in fact, about 250 meters below sea level. Most of the caves are natural caves; some of them, in particular Cave 4, are manmade caves. The caves were numbered in the order of discovery, so that the first cave into which our heroic goat had strayed was called Cave 1, and the next cave that yielded scrolls Cave 2, Cave 3, so on, through Cave 11. Caves 1 and 2 are about one kilometer north of Khirbet Qumran, and caves 3 and 11 are about another kilometer north of there; but the other caves—numbers 4–10—are in very close proximity to the site, ranging from about 100 meters to about 300 meters away (the distance between Khirbet Qumran and the caves); though the cliffs naturally make the journey to and from the one to the other, from the site to the caves, more than an easy walk of just 100 meters or 200 or 300 meters. The mother lode was discovered in Cave 4—one of the manmade caves as I noted—which yielded more than 500 documents, though most of them in a very fragmentary state. You will recall that the scrolls in Cave 1, the first ones to be found, were kept in jars; this was not the case with those 500 documents in Cave 4 that were laid right on the surface of the cave and therefore deteriorated over the course of almost 2,000 years so that we read them now in very, very fragmented state.

Let me talk about the excavations at Qumran since de Vaux's day. Scholars have repeatedly returned to the site to see if they can learn more about the site of Qumran and the community of Jews that lived there. In 1966 and 1967, during that two-year period, scholars decided to excavate the cemetery that is lying very close to the site. I haven't mentioned the cemetery until now; but yes, there's a cemetery at Qumran as well. It contains about 1,100 graves. Only a small portion of these were exhumed, and among them, we should note, were found female skeletons. The idea that this was a celibate community, or that no women lived here—which, of course, is a conclusion that one could reach based on the evidence and based on Pliny's mention of this community as well—is not 100 percent accurate because indeed there are women here, and, as I've mentioned earlier and which we will revisit in this course in a later lecture, women are mentioned in a variety of the Dead Sea Scroll documents.

Off and on during the 1970s and 1980s, an Israeli archaeologist named Pesah Bar-Adon and his successor, an American named Vendyl Jones, decided that they would explore the caves further; perhaps something had been missed during the years when the Bedouin and the early scholars of the 1950s had explored these caves. They found a large cave near Cave 11; unfortunately, no scrolls were found—no written documents were found in this cave—but Bar-Adon and Jones did find in this large cave near Cave 11 (it doesn't have a number because no documents were found there), which yielded finds from the Hellenistic and Roman periods. Archaeological finds: all sites, all different kinds of things; pottery vessels, some coins, and so on and so forth. Both archaeologists, Bar–Adon and Jones, believe that this cave might be the one in which all the treasures mentioned in the Copper Scroll are buried. We haven't really talked about the Copper Scroll *yet*; this will be the subject of another lecture later in our course, and we will see there that this scroll mentions large amounts of treasures: gold, silver, and other precious items. Bar-Adon and Jones think that this large cave near Cave 11 might be the one that the Copper Scroll is referring to; although I have to add, they have not convinced most scholars, mainly due to the lack of evidence.

A little bit later on the in the 1980s, another archaeologist named Joseph Petrach explored dozens of additional caves in the area. He took an eight mile span of land—four miles south of Qumran to four miles north of Qumran—and he did find, of course, archaeological remains in these caves as well; 17 caves gave us more archeological material: pots and coins, and the kinds of things that archaeologists typically find. Again, no further written documents: all from the Second Temple period, all from the period during which Qumran was active; but again, no further written documents.

Finally, in 1993–1996, two Israeli archaeologists, Hanan Eshel and Magen Broshi, thoroughly explored the area once again; they entered all the Qumran caves. You can see what happens: Every 5 or 10 years, another archaeologist or two, or another team of several archaeologists, want to explore this area again hoping, hoping , to find something that perhaps the earlier explorers may have missed. They sought in particular to establish a clear link between the caves and the site of Khirbet Qumran; after all, everybody including de Vaux has been positing such a connection. But there have been scholars who've doubted the connection between the scrolls found in caves and the archeological site nearby; we'll talk about some of those voices that have been expressed by other scholars in a later lecture. Eshel and Broshi decided that there really needs to be firm archeological evidence that will unite the two, the caves and the site itself, and they found it. They found a path that connects the two; one can still see the path to this day, untouched by the sands of time—literally in this case the sands of the region—where the people would walk back and forth between the site and the caves. They found the path, and on this path along the way they would find occasional nails; these were nails that no doubt came loose from the bottoms of people's sandals. Magen Broshi and Hanan Eshel further posited, asking the question: Where did the Qumran community live? If there were no private homes at the site that were found, where did they live? They posited that probably members of the sect—some of them at least, maybe most of them—lived in tents beyond the excavation site, and may have, in fact, lived in the caves themselves.

Years after the first discoveries, scholars continued to study anew with fresh eyes the initial finds from de Vaux's day and from the succeeding excavations. Here I should mention the work especially of Jodi Magness of the University of North Carolina, who has written the standard book on the subject entitled *The Archaeology of Qumran and the Dead Sea Scrolls*, published in 2002. She summarizes a vast amount of evidence, some of which are her new interpretations, and let me share with you some of the comments that she makes in that book; some of the findings that she presents to the scholarly world and to the public at large. It's a very easily accessible book. Magness points out that about half of the clay of the Qumran pots is imported from Jerusalem. You may ask: How can we determine, if it's just a clay pot, where the clay comes from? This can be determined from another lab test known as neutron activation, and this allows us to see—this laboratory test; this is the world of chemistry—the trace elements in the soil that was used. Neutron activation is a new tool that archaeologists use. You cannot date pottery, you cannot date a particular item this way, but you can at least determine where it comes from. Let me tell you how they do this: You take soil samples from around the land of Israel, and in fact from the Mediterranean basin as a whole, and you can begin to analyze that soil through neutron activation and determine whether a pot was, for example, made in Jerusalem, or whether it was made at Qumran, or whether it was made at Caesarea on the coast, or perhaps imported from somewhere across the Mediterranean. This is what scholars are able to do today with this laboratory test.

By the way, in the world of biblical studies, this is an important tool; and in general in the trade of the ancient Near East. Let's say you have an Aegean pot found at a coastal site in the land of Israel. You want to know: Was this imported from the Aegean, or was this made locally by someone who knew Aegean-style pottery? We can now determine that through the neutron activation test; and so we can determine whether a pot found at an Israelite coastal city was locally produced with local clay, or whether it was actually imported from, let's say Crete or some other place in the Aegean.

But back to Qumran: Half of the pots, Magness tells us—half of the clay used for these pots—is from Jerusalem, which means either that the pots themselves were made in Jerusalem, or perhaps the clay was brought from Jerusalem because the clay there is better clay, or maybe there was some purity issue. We've talked about purity and impurity; what I haven't noted up until now is that it's not only human beings who can become impure, but actually vessels can become impure as well including earthenware made from the soil. The other half of the pottery from Qumran presumably is from the local clay of the Dead Sea region; and you'll remember that I mentioned a few moments ago that there was, in fact, a pottery manufacturing area found at Khirbet Qumran. The picture that Magness presents here comes together from a variety of perspectives.

The second specific main point that she makes about these pots is the special kind of pottery that is found at Qumran, and these are tall, cylindrical jars. These were the jars in which the first scrolls were found in Qumran Cave

One, and they are very distinctive of Qumran. These jars, with their lids, were found both in the caves and at Khirbet Qumran, the archaeological site, and so we have another connection between the two locations. These jars are not found elsewhere in the land of Israel; they are specific and distinctive to this community: tall, thin, cylindrical jars with a relatively wide opening at the top. Other vessels from the world of ancient Israel and throughout the Roman Empire typically were fatter—larger in that sense—but had a smaller opening in which a cork was placed or a sealing was placed. These jars are of a different shape. These jars, according to Jodi Magness, fit the Qumran community's needs very, very well. As I've just mentioned, they do not have a seal, and thus they could easily be opened on the Sabbath—that is, just by removing the lid—and thereby there would be no violation of the strictures imposed by the Essenes for Sabbath observance. We're jumping ahead a little bit, because we'll return to this subject in a future lecture when we talk about the Essene view of Jewish law and Sabbath observance in particular; but for now, let me just mention that they did not allow the opening of a closed seal, of a closed vessel, and by simply removing the lid of a vessel, that apparently was ok within their interpretation of the way the Sabbath should be observed according to their views of Jewish law.

The other thing about these jars, Jodi Magness goes on to tell us, is that one cannot pour from these jars very easily. The other kinds of jars have a smaller opening and you can just pour out of them; these jars with their larger opening make it a little bit harder to pour out of, and it is more likely that one dipped a ewer into the jar to extract the content, whether it be wine or olive oil, for example. This also relates to a discussion that we're still going to have in a future lecture: It relates to the manner in which impurity could be transferred from one vessel to another. This is all part of the arcane laws of Judaism dealing with impurity, and we'll revisit this question when we come to a text that deals with this specific issue. Let me just note at the present, however, that the Qumran view of Jewish law held that impurity could actually flow "upstream," as it were; so that if you were pouring from a larger vessel into a smaller vessel, and the smaller vessel turned out to be impure for some reason and you were unaware of it, the impurity would actually flow upstream into the larger vessel. If you have these large cylindrical jars from which you do not pour but rather dip a ewer into, this prevents any kind of impurity from traveling upstream if you were pouring from a vessel, and thereby this particular cylindrical jar shape is again specific to the Qumran community. Finally, these jars allow for the storing of scrolls; and again, the Dead Sea Scrolls were first found in these jars in Cave One, the first set of seven scrolls.

As long as we are talking about these jars, used for the storage of scrolls, the following tales from antiquity are of particular interest. I have three tales to share with you: First, the church father Origen, who lived in the 3rd century C.E., reports that in his lifetime a scroll containing the book of Psalms written in Greek had been found in a jar near Jericho. Second, about a century later, the church father Eusebius from the 4th century C.E. describes the same text—the same Greek Psalms text that Origen had mentioned—and Eusebius then mentions other Greek and Hebrew manuscripts also found in a jar near Jericho, and he actually dates the original discovery to the reign of Caracalla, who reigned 211–217 C.E. The third and final note on this is from centuries later, circa 800 C.E., Timotheus I, a Nestorian patriarch—that is, a leader of the Syrian Orthodox Church—wrote that the books of the Old Testament were found near Jericho; ancient scrolls of the Old Testament were found near Jericho. Here you have three episodes from antiquity describing the findings of scrolls—books of the Bible, in some cases found in jars—in the region of Jericho; and I described earlier that Jericho is really about 15 kilometers, quite close to Qumran; only 15 kilometers away. Were these discoveries from the first millennium C.E. from the Qumran caves specifically? Probably not, since otherwise it would be hard to explain why 930 documents were still present in these caves in the 20th century; but these earlier discoveries described to us by church fathers inform us that other groups in the desert also hid their scrolls in jars, exactly as was the practice of the Qumran community.

Let's then ask the question: What happened to the Qumran community? The group clearly abandoned the area in 68 C.E.—the last date for which we have evidence that there were people resident at the site—with the Roman legions marching through Judea at this time. Presumably the Qumran group deposited their most valued possessions, their scrolls, in the caves nearby, hoping one day to return. Some were placed in earthenware vessels in planned fashion, as in Cave One; others simply were placed on the ground, as in Cave Four. A copy of one particular Dead Sea Scroll, called the *Songs of the Sabbath Sacrifice,* was found at Masada, 48 kilometers to the south. Let me repeat that: A Dead Sea Scroll that we know from Qumran was also found at the excavations at Masada. This discovery leads scholars to conclude that some members of the Qumran sect may have fled southward and sought refuge with the Zealots at Masada.

The disappearance of the Qumran community and the other sects of this time paved the way for the emergence of rabbinic Judaism. In our next lecture, we will explore the rabbinic enterprise, which presumably began as a small movement within Judaism, one sect among many; though as we shall see, over time it surfaced as the most normative brand of Judaism, down to the present day.

The Emergence of the Rabbinic System
Lecture 7

The later rabbinic texts come from several centuries after the florescence of Qumran, but their traditions were likely present at the time the Dead Sea Scrolls were composed.

What became of the various Jewish sects of the period? Since the Sadducees' raison d'être was the worship of God in the Temple in Jerusalem and the Temple was in ruins, they eventually died out. Whether or not we accept that the Qumran sect is a group of Essenes, it is clear that the number of Essenes was never great. In times of great upheaval, as in 70 C.E., such small groups often die out as well. The war against Rome brought disaster and the destruction of Jerusalem, so the Zealots also faded away. The Christian community continued to develop, but it became less and less a Jewish phenomenon and more and more a Gentile one. For our present purposes, therefore, the Christian movement is not very relevant. The only group that bridged the Second Temple period and the period after the Temple's destruction are the Pharisees.

The term "rabbi" is encountered for the first time in the New Testament, used, for example, by both followers of Jesus and John the Baptist. The word means simply "master" (or more literally "my master"), but it seems to have been adopted most of all by the Pharisees as a title for their teachers, especially those who mastered the law. We do not have Pharisaic-Rabbinic texts from the period of the Dead Sea Scrolls or the New Testament. All we have are the voluminous rabbinic texts from about 200 C.E. onward.

The war against Rome brought disaster and the destruction of Jerusalem.

The rabbinic corpus of texts is as follows. For the purposes of our course, if not for all purposes, the most important rabbinic text is the Mishna. It is the earliest codification of Jewish law, or Halakah, and dates to about 200 C.E. The Mishna has six orders—Seeds, Festivals, Women, Damages, Holy

Things, and Purities—each of which in turn is divided into 8–12 tractates treating specific issues. A key question in the study of Judaism is, Did the Mishna innovate new law, or did it simply put into writing practices that had existed for centuries? We will assume the latter. The Tosefta—literally "supplement"—is a companion and contemporary to the Mishna and is organized along the same principles. The Talmud of the Land of Israel seeks to explicate the laws of the Mishna, as the sages of the next several generations discussed the legal process, the rationale for specific laws, and more. The project was not completed but simply came to an end around 400 C.E. The Babylonian Talmud, encyclopedic in nature, was produced by rabbinic sages in Babylonia. Once more, the succeeding generations of scholars debated and discussed the legal process and the rationales for specific laws. It also contains legends and folklore, expanding on many stories in the Bible. The final work is dated to about 500 C.E.

A striking linkage between the Pharisees as described by Josephus and the rabbinic movement as witnessed by their own texts is in the area of compatibilism. Compatiablism is the middle ground between free will and predetermination. In the Mishna tractate Avot, which contains maxims attributed to individual rabbis, Rabbi Akiba (d. 135 C.E.) is quoted as saying, "All is foreseen, but the authority is given"—which matches perfectly with the compatabilism of the Pharisees. It may not be surprising that the Pharisees and their rabbinic successors won out. Philosophical extremes frequently fall by the wayside, allowing the center to continue onward. We will need to keep these texts in mind throughout our course, particularly the Mishna, whose laws often stand in contrast to the practices attested among the Dead Sea Scrolls.

Previous generations of scholars believed rabbinic Judaism became the norm after the second Jewish revolt. Today, scholars believe that much of the variegated Jewish life we can reconstruct from the Dead Sea Scrolls and Josephus continued in the centuries following. ■

Essential Reading

Schiffman, *From Text to Tradition*, 177–269.

Supplementary Reading

Neusner, *Introduction to Rabbinic Literature*.

Questions to Consider

1. Why did the Sadducees and Essenes die out after the destruction of the Temple in 70 C.E.? What could they have done differently to ensure their continuation even after that major upheaval?

2. We noted that the Pharisees won out because they held a middle ground in a philosophical debate. Can you think of any other factors?

The Emergence of the Rabbinic System
Lecture 7—Transcript

One cannot proceed further into Dead Sea Scrolls scholarship without first gaining a thorough understanding of the later rabbinic texts dated to the 3rd century C.E., but with roots going back several centuries. That is to say, while these rabbinic texts come from several centuries after the florescence of Qumran, the traditions they embody most likely were present already at the time of the composition of the Dead Sea Scrolls. We'll explore that very important issue in just a moment; but here I want to pick up where we left off at the end of the previous lecture and suggest once more what became of the Qumran sect, but to put it into a larger discussion: What became of all the Jewish sects of the period?

Let's begin with the discussion of the Sadducees. Since their raison d'être was the worship of God in the Temple in Jerusalem through the sacrificial system as outlined in the Torah with the priests officiating, and with the Temple now in ruins—having been destroyed by the Roman armies in 70 C.E.—the Sadducee group eventually died out. Without a Temple, there is no way to worship God in the Sadducee system. The Essenes: Whether or not we accede to the majority position that holds that the Qumran sect is a group of Essenes, it is clear that the number of Essenes never was great. In times of great social and political upheaval, as clearly was the case in 70 C.E., such small groups often simply fade away and/or die out. Probably this happened to the Essenes, especially—as we shall see in a later lecture—if there was an apocalyptic component to their belief system. The Zealots: The war against Rome brought disaster with the destruction of Jerusalem; so this group also fades away, especially after 73 C.E. when Masada falls, their last holdout. True, there is a second Jewish revolt against Rome under Bar-Kokhba about 60 years later, but after that equally devastating defeat the Jews no longer contemplate military rebellion against Rome.

The Christian community continues to develop in fine fashion, but it becomes less and less a Jewish phenomenon and more and more a Gentile one; that is to say, the growing number of Christians in the world comes from the formerly polytheistic population of the Greco-Roman world and not from within the smaller Jewish community. For our present purposes, therefore, the Christian movement is less relevant. Thus the only group that is able to bridge the pre-70 C.E. Second Temple Period and the post-70 C.E. Destruction Period are the Pharisees. The Pharisees accordingly emerge as the dominant, if not the sole Jewish option, though we begin to refer to this group differently as it morphs into what we call rabbinic Judaism.

The term "rabbi" is encountered for the first time in the New Testament. For example, Peter calls Jesus "rabbi" in Mark 9:5; and John the Baptist's disciples refer to their teacher as "rabbi" in John 3:26. The word "rabbi" means simply "master," or more literally "my master"; but it seems to have been adopted most of all by the Pharisees as a title for their teachers, especially those who had mastered the law. As an aside, we note once more how interconnected early Judaism and early Christianity were during this period; though, to repeat, the two movements diverge very, very quickly.

Unfortunately, we do not have contemporary Pharisaic rabbinic texts from the time period of the Dead Sea Scrolls (2nd and 1st centuries B.C.E.) or the New Testament (1st century C.E.). All we have are the voluminous rabbinic texts—and we'll outline them for you in just a moment—from circa 200 C.E. onward; that is to say, two or three centuries after the period we are considering. As I said earlier, we assume that the traditions embodied in these rabbinic texts were present already earlier at the time of the New Testament in the 1st century and at the time of the Dead Sea Scrolls in the 1st and 2nd centuries B.C.E. What we get are Dead Sea Scrolls texts that seem to be speaking to the rabbinic texts, even though the rabbinic texts are from a later period; we'll explore that in a future lecture. In the New Testament, we see issues that we know about from the rabbinic corpus of texts from a century or two centuries later, and yet they seem to be referring to practices that are already present. We'll come back and revisit these questions throughout our course.

After the destruction of Jerusalem in 70 C.E., and certainly after the second Jewish Revolt of 132–135 C.E., the center of Jewish life migrates northward to the Galilee, the northern part of the land of Israel, especially the city of Sepphoris, or in Hebrew Zippori. The rabbinic corpus of texts—or the earliest texts to be sure—stem from the Jewish community in the city of Sepphoris (Zippori). The most important of these texts is the Mishna. This text is the earliest codification of Jewish law; or, to use the Hebrew term, *halakha*. Mishna is the earliest codification of Jewish law, *halakha*, dated to circa 200 C.E. It was compiled and redacted by a rabbi known as Judah Ha-Nasi; "Ha-Nasi" is the Hebrew title that means "the patriarch" or "the leader" because of his position in the Jewish community. Rabbi Judah Ha-Nasi redacts and compiles the Mishna, the earliest codification of Jewish law, at a crucial event in Jewish history in 200 C.E.

The Mishna is divided into six orders; these orders—I'm translating their Hebrew names—are: seeds (that refers to agricultural laws), festivals, women, damages (which we may call tort law), holy things, and purities; the six orders of the Mishna. Each of these orders in turn is divided into between 8 and 12 tractates, and each tractate treats a specific subject such as in the first order of agricultural laws called "Seeds," we will see subjects such as gleaning and the Sabbatical year. For those of you who know your biblical texts well, you may be familiar with the Bible's laws, with the Torah laws, that deal with this. For example, one is commanded not to harvest the edges of one's field and to allow poor people to come and glean so that they can gain food from you; that's a commandment of the Torah. There's an entire tractate in the Mishna that then gives you greater understanding of how this is to be practiced; what kinds of things one must do both as a landowner and as one who wants to glean. A law about the Sabbatical: The book of Leviticus, Chapter 25, describes how in every seventh year the land must lie fallow; what is permitted, what is not permitted, and so on, is outlined in greater detail now in a Mishna tractate devoted specifically to the Sabbatical year. Those are examples from the first order dealing with "Seeds," to use the Hebrew term or an English equivalent of the Hebrew term; agricultural laws.

In the second order that is the order that deals with "Festivals," you have long discussions of how Sabbath is to be observed and how Passover is to be observed. In the third order, "Women," you have laws of marriage and divorce. In the sixth order, for example, on "Purities" you have the laws dealing with menstruating women. I've referred to some of these issues throughout our course, and these will come up time and time again in future lectures.

Let me give you examples here as to how the Bible's laws in the Torah and the Mishna's expansion of these laws interrelate with one another. Let's give two examples: the Sabbath Law and the Divorce Law. What we learn from the Torah is that you're supposed to rest on the Sabbath day; no work is permitted. The only real thing that we learn is that one is not allowed to kindle a light on the Sabbath day; so that's basically all the Torah tells us. You'll notice it doesn't define what constitutes work; and so later generations of Jews would determine what was and what was not work, and in the Pharisaic rabbinic system, all of this emerges in the tractate dealing with Sabbath in the second order of the Mishna devoted to the festivals. There, for example, one finds a list of 39 individual actions that constitute work that are prohibited on the Sabbath. Many of these are things that deal with your daily life, depending on your occupation; so, for example, various issues dealing with building and carpentry—hammering and so on—this is prohibited on the Sabbath; or working with textiles, so sewing is not permitted; or if you are a farmer, various things dealing with harvest such as harvesting, sowing a field, winnowing, and these kinds of things, these are not permitted. That's in the list of 39 items that one is not permitted to do on the Sabbath. The biblical law is succinct—no work—and the Mishna gives you all of this information that further gives us an understanding how the Sabbath is to be observed.

My second example: Let me give you the divorce law. The Torah only mentions divorce in one place, in Deuteronomy 24, and it's a most unusual law. It tells us in the following set of circumstances: If a man and a woman are married, and the man decides he would like to divorce his wife, he writes her out a bill of divorce—we do learn that from the law there in Deuteronomy 24—and they become divorced. The woman then goes off to marry another man, her second husband either dies or divorces her as well, and the law then states that the woman cannot remarry her first husband. This is a most unusual set of circumstances; how often does this happen in life? Obviously marriages and divorces occur; but how often does it happen that a woman who divorced or was divorced by her first husband then remarried and her second husband divorced her or died and now she wishes to remarry her first husband. A complicated set of circumstances; and there the Torah tells us what the procedure should be. It is prohibited; one is not allowed to do that.

But the question is: What about a standard, normal, average divorce; what takes place? How does one legally implement a divorce? We learn from the Torah, as I've indicated, that there has to be a written bill of divorce—there has to be something in writing that is the concrete statement that the divorce has occurred—but all sorts of questions arise; for example: What are the grounds for a divorce? Can a woman divorce a man, or can a man only divorce a woman; who has the legal right, and so on and so forth? The Torah is silent on all of these basic issues; it only goes on to talk about a unique set of circumstances. Therefore, there must have been in ancient Israel, throughout the Biblical Period and into the postbiblical Period, a general knowledge, a general understanding, of how a divorce should be executed; how it was legally to be done. All of this information then gets codified in the Mishna of Rabbi Judah. You have this interrelationship between the biblical laws and the laws of the Mishna. You'll recall from a previous lecture that we talked about the Pharisaic system as continued by the rabbis as believing in an oral law, something that was rejected by the Sadducees. That oral law is all of the information I'm giving you right now. The rabbis believed that these ideas, these actual laws, went back to Sinai as well. The list of 39 items that is prohibited for Sabbath work, how a divorce is to be executed, and so on; all of this comes to be written down for the first time in the Mishna in 200 C.E. through the editorial work of Rabbi Judah. But the followers of this system—of the Pharisee-rabbinic way of understanding Jewish law—saw all of this as being much, much more ancient.

We, as scholars, actually agree by and large with that view. We agree that this material probably was in place centuries earlier in the life of Jews in the land of Israel. A key question in the study of Judaism is: Does the Mishna innovate new law, or does it simply put into writing practices that have existed for centuries? Scholars come down on either side of that question. In this course, as I've just indicated, we will assume the second route; we will assume that throughout ancient Israel's history, including the postbiblical Period, the laws of how to observe Sabbath, how to do a divorce, and all sorts of other things were known by the population at large. Even if we won't accede to the specific rabbinic theological construct that these laws go back to Sinai, we will accept the idea that they are more ancient; there are predecessors or precursors to this in the centuries before they actually come to be written down by Rabbi Judah. That is the Mishna.

A related text is called the Tosefta. The word means literally "supplement" it's a companion volume to the Mishna organized along the same principles with orders and tractates. It is unclear why certain specific laws are included in the Mishna while others are relegated, as it were, to the Tosefta; but this is another work from 200 C.E. So this is the great project of Rabbi Judah: the Mishna in particular, and the Tosefta as a companion volume.

What happens to this collection, especially the Mishna? The Mishna becomes the basis for study by the successive generations of Jewish scholars; the sages that come after the Rabbi Judah. Academies are set up in two different locations: one is in the land of Israel, although no longer in Sepphoris but in another city in the Galilee—in the northern part of Israel—called Tiberius; and there the successor generations to Rabbi Judah debate the legal issues of the Mishna, and eventually what emerges is a very large project called the Talmud. We call this the Talmud of the Land of Israel, and it is completed about 400 C.E., although to be more exact the project is never really completed; that is to say, it doesn't have a final editorial hand but simply comes to an end. More famous is the Babylonian Talmud; that is to say, Rabbi Judah's Mishna was taken to Babylonia where there were also academies of Jewish sages and rabbis who studied the Mishna and debated its contents as well. The Babylonian Talmud is an even larger work, encyclopedic in nature, produced by these rabbinic sages in Babylonia. This Talmud, the Babylonian Talmud, actually did receive a final editing more or less; it comes to an end in around 500 C.E. Interwoven with all of the legal discussions, by the way, are lots of legends and folklore expanding upon many stories in the Bible. But the two Talmud*im*—the Talmud of the land of Israel and the Babylonian Talmud—both have in common the Mishna as its base and an attempt to understand the legal principles behind the Mishna.

Let me give you a sense here of how Mishna and Talmud interrelate by giving you an analogy out of familiar American documents. The Constitution of the United States just simply presents what the law is; it tells us, for example, that a member of the House of Representatives shall serve two years, a senator shall serve six years, and a president shall serve four years. It tells us how the members of the House come to be and how the members of the Senate come to be, and so on and so forth, in very succinct details. We are not given the legal reasoning in the Constitution; why different terms, two, four and six years? That's the way the Mishna is as well. The Mishna just gives you the law: It tells you that sewing is prohibited on the Sabbath, it tells you these are the grounds of divorce; but it doesn't give you the legal reasoning for it. That was what the rabbis of the Talmud were doing in these academies, both in Israel and in Babylonia: producing these very, very large works as they debated what was the legal reasoning behind Rabbi Judah's decision, because Rabbi Judah left us only a very succinct work that tells us, "This is the law." The analogy to the Talmud in early America would be the *Federalist Papers*, because the *Federalist Papers*, written mainly by Madison and Hamilton, gives us the legal workings (rationale) for many of the decisions that are expressed in simple, succinct terms in the Constitution of the United States. The only difference is that the Constitution and the *Federalist Papers* come from the same group of individuals, whereas the Mishna and the Talmud are chronologically distinct: the Mishna first and the two Talmud*im* were produced by the succeeding generations. Hopefully this analogy helps you understand the relationship between these rabbinic works.

A striking linkage between the Pharisees as described by Josephus and the rabbinic movement as witnessed by their own texts is the following: You will recall the issue of free will versus predetermination. The Sadducees believed only in free will; the Essenes believed in predetermination; and the Pharisees held the middle ground, what scholars call—to repeat the term I used in an earlier lecture—compatibilism. In the Mishna tractate called *Avot*—*Avot* actually means "Fathers"; and it is the only tractate of the Mishna that does not present law, per se, but rather contains maxims and sayings attributed to the original rabbis, the fathers (and that's why it's called *Avot*)—we read the following statement from one of the rabbis, two generations before Rabbi Judah. His name was Rabbi Akiba; he died in 135 C.E. Rabbi Akiba's famous maxim is the following; I'll say it in Hebrew first just to give you a sense of the Hebrew language and then give it to you in English: "*ha-kol zafuy we-ha-reshut netuna*"; "All is foreseen but the authority is given." By the "authority" here what Rabbi Akiba means is free will, the authority for humankind to decide its own fate. "All is foreseen but the authority is given"; that is to say, what you see here are both sides of the continuum in the free will versus predestination debate among the various sects. "All is foreseen" speaks to the idea that everything is predetermined; "but the authority is given" speaks to the free will notion that we've seen as well. Within the two extremes, you have a middle ground expressed here by Rabbi Akiba—one of the rabbis who appear in the Mishna when Rabbi Judah includes this favorite statement of his—and it matches perfectly with the compatibilism stance of the Pharisees.

While it is true that, vis-à-vis the other main sects—the Sadducees and the Essenes—the Pharisees "won out" through their continuation as rabbinic Judaism, the picture is actually much more complicated than this. First, though, let's give some further definition to rabbinic Judaism by asking the question: What did it mean to follow the rabbinic system? With the Temple no longer standing, Jews, under the guidance of the rabbis, sought new expressions of religious worship. The synagogue had been in existence even before 70 C.E. while the Temple stood—we have both archaeological and textual evidence that supports this fact—but the role of the synagogue seems to have greatly expanded during the post-Temple period. We actually referred to the rise of the synagogue as an important component in Post-Temple Judaism towards the end of Lecture Four. In time, a more or less standard prayer service developed; and indeed, this prayer service is outlined in the first tractate of the Mishna, entitled *Berakhot*, the Hebrew word for "Blessings." The regular public reading of the Torah becomes a central part of the prayer service, especially on the Sabbath. In fact, two different systems were developed: One, an annual reading of the Torah that was in practice for most of the Jewish communities in the Diaspora—that is, the lands outside of Israel—and in the land of Israel a system by which the Torah was read over the course of three years, called the triennial system, was in place. Regardless of whether it was the annual system or the triennial system, the public reading of the Torah becomes a centerpiece of the synagogue religious worship service.

Dozens of synagogues from the 4th century onward—we're a little bit beyond the main part of our course, the main chronological point of our course—have been excavated in the land of Israel, especially in the land of Galilee, and their architecture includes a niche where the Torah scrolls were kept. The rabbis transferred many of the rituals that had been used in the Temple to the synagogue. Let me give you some examples: On the Jewish holiday of Rosh Hashanah, the Jewish New Year festival, the shofar (the ram's horn) was blown in the Temple through a series of blasts. This ritual is transferred to the synagogue. The Torah also speaks of the holiday of Sukkot; it's the fall harvest festival, and it also commemorates the wandering of the people of Israel through the desert when they left Egypt. According to Leviticus 23, on this festival one is commanded to bring four species of different trees, most prominently the palm branches; and this custom took place in the Temple while the Temple still stood. Again, after 70 C.E., this ritual is transferred to the synagogue so that the bringing of the palm branches and the waving of the palm branches becomes a synagogue ritual.

A third example: On the holiday of Yom Kippur, the Day of Atonement—and we've actually referred to this holiday earlier in our course—again, according to the book of Leviticus, the high priest on this day was supposed to enter the Temple, indeed enter the Holy of Holies on that day, and he would purge the Temple of any impurities that may have invaded the Temple during the course of the previous year; and this was a ritual by which you cleanse the Temple, purge the Temple, of the kind of ritual impurities about which we have spoken. Then the high priest would enter the Holy of Holies and he would ask forgiveness of God for the sins of the people. This ritual, again, can no longer be practiced after the destruction of the Temple in 70 C.E.; it gets transferred to the synagogue as well where now a verbal recitation of what used to transpire in the Temple on Yom Kippur, the Day of Atonement, becomes part of the liturgy of the synagogue to observe that holiday.

In addition, the rabbis also transferred many Temple rituals to the home. We've actually mentioned one of these earlier: Again, back in Lecture Four, we talked about the washing of one's hands before eating. Let me give you another example here, one that's very well-known: the Passover Seder. When the Temple stood the custom was—as per Exodus 12—to bring a sacrificial lamb to the temple on the holiday of Passover. This, again, could no longer be done after the destruction of the Temple in 70 C.E., and therefore a new custom arose: Families gathered in their homes to remember the Exodus of Egypt with a recitation of a whole series of prayers and biblical passages, and expansions upon these biblical passages; an elaborate home-based ritual. You have customs that are moving from Temple to synagogue and from Temple to home based on the new rabbinic system. All of this transforms Jewish life during this period under this new rabbinic system that we're describing here; and, indeed, all of this remains in place down to the present day in Judaism.

As I indicated above, though, the picture is more complex. First of all, although eventually Jews came to embrace this system—which I have just described—we cannot be sure how many Jews followed this system in the early post-Temple period. It may have taken centuries, until the 5th or even 6th century, for this system of rituals in synagogue and rituals at home to become normative and mainstream among the general Jewish population. Which is to say, it is possible that the rabbis had only a small following at first; that Rabbi Judah Ha-Nasi's Mishna circulated only among the small circle of rabbis who exerted little real influence over the population at large. We need to be careful not to retroject a later system—which is still in operation today—onto the scene of the 1st and 2nd centuries C.E., or even 3rd and 4th centuries C.E. Today, we associate rabbis as community leaders, with positions of authority in the synagogue. In late antiquity, however, quite possibly—even probably—such was not the case. The rabbis' authority may have been limited to their relatively proscribed centers of learning, their academies, or yeshivot (singular: yeshiva), to use the Hebrew term.

The best evidence in favor of such a view is the following: Many of the synagogues that I mentioned, excavated in the Galilee, have exquisite mosaic floors with the Zodiac as the centerpiece, portraying Helios on his chariot and the 12 constellations all around. How do we explain these synagogue mosaics? This is a class example of syncretism: using Greco-Roman, artistic, and, indeed religious motifs on the floor of a synagogue. Does this mean that the Jews who were responsible for the construction of these synagogues had some allegiance to this Greco-Roman system? Or was it simply the cultural rage and this was the artwork that was en vogue and the synagogue builders, architects, or artists placed these designs on the synagogue floor? It is possible that we may have here, as one scholar has suggested, a visual depiction of what we read in Psalm 19. The first half of Psalm 19 deals with God's creation of the world and it focuses in particular on the sun, and the second part of Psalm 19 talks about the role of Torah in the life of the people of Israel. You have these two halves of Psalm 19: creation with the sun and Torah for the people of Israel. Is that's what is going on here on these synagogue floors? That's one possible interpretation.

Let me give you what is perhaps a modern analogy to help you understand what I'm talking about here. As many of you know, Orthodox Jews and traditionally-minded Jews will wear a kippah, a skull cap, and typically these are of no specific design, they're just whatever color one may choose. But children in particular may wear—and you may have seen these—a kippah with their favorite Sesame Street character portrayed on the skull cap; or perhaps, as they get older and become teenagers, their favorite baseball team; I've seen them in the New York area with New York Yankees emblems or New York Mets emblems. That is an example of syncretism presumably; is there any religious statement being made here? No, of course not; but these are things that are en vogue, they're part of the cultural world of modern America just like the zodiacs were part of the cultural world of the Greco-Roman period.

In any case, it is hard to imagine any of these synagogues bearing the official endorsement of the rabbis who are responsible for the Mishna and the Talmud, because, as you know, the Torah prohibits the depiction of pagan images or even the image of the God of Israel, and the rabbis were quite strict in following this dictate of the Torah. If this is the case, as we have indicated, the rabbinic system may not have coalesced over all Jews, or the vast majority of Jews, for centuries.

We bring this conversation back to Qumran. As we proceed through our course, indeed starting with the next lecture, we will need to keep the rabbinic texts in mind at every turn, most importantly the Mishna, whose laws, as we will see, often stand in contrast to the practices attested among the Dead Sea Scrolls. That is to say, regardless of how many people followed the rabbinic system at any given time, one gains a better sense of the extraordinary nature of the Qumran community when one compares the Yahad to the rabbinic enterprise. We will make these comparisons time and again, especially when we consider the legal texts from Qumran: texts such as the Damascus Document, a composition known as the Halakhic Letter, and the Temple Scroll, all of which will be presented in detail in future lectures.

A Dead Sea Scroll from Medieval Cairo
Lecture 8

> During the 1890s, tens of thousands of Jewish manuscripts were discovered in the storeroom of the medieval Ben Ezra Synagogue in Cairo, Egypt. Among the texts were two copies of a previously unknown composition now called the Damascus Document.

During the 1890s, the greatest manuscript discovery in world history occurred when 200,000 documents were found in the storeroom of the Ben Ezra Synagogue in Cairo. Jewish law does not allow one simply to discard holy texts; they must be disposed of with honor and dignity. One system is burial, while another is deposition in a dedicated storeroom, known as a genizah. The Cairo genizah documents date to the Middle Ages and provide an extremely detailed picture of the life of the medieval Jewish community of Cairo.

The story of the discovery of the Cairo genizah also bears telling. Some scholars became aware of the existence of the Cairo genizah in the early 1890s, but travel to the Middle East was difficult, and thus access was very limited. Eventually, a pair of Scottish sisters named Mrs. Lewis and Mrs. Gibson came to England with Hebrew documents they obtained in Cairo. The sisters showed them to Solomon Schechter, a reader of Hebrew at Cambridge University, who immediately realized the importance of these medieval texts. With the assistance of authorities from Cambridge University, Schechter arranged for the purchase of 140,000 documents from the Cairo genizah, and they remain housed at the Cambridge Library to this day. Another 40,000 documents were obtained by the Jewish Theological Seminary in New York, and smaller numbers are housed in Manchester, England, and St. Petersburg, Russia.

Among the Cairo genizah documents are early manuscripts of the Mishna and the two Talmudim; the Hebrew original of the book of Ben Sira; new texts of Targum—that is, Aramaic renderings of the Bible; autographic letters and other texts signed by Maimonides; and perhaps the greatest surprise of all, a commentary by Saint Augustine on the Sermon on the Mount, as a palimpsest. Among the cache were two copies of a unique document, now called the Damascus Document. Although the manuscripts were medieval (10th and 12th centuries C.E.), the first scholars to work on them realized immediately that the composition itself was much older. Schechter published the text as Documents of Jewish sectaries, edited from Hebrew manuscripts in the Cairo genizah collection, now in the possession of the University Library, Cambridge, vol. 1: Fragments of a Zadokite work.

> **The Cairo genizah documents ... provide an extremely detailed picture of the life of the medieval Jewish community of Cairo.**

While Schechter incorrectly believed that the Damascus Document was associated with the Dositheans, a Samaritan sect, he properly understood the text's antiquity. Louis Ginzberg then produced the basic interpretation of the work under the title *Eine unbekannte jüdische Sekte* (*An Unknown Jewish Sect*). Ginzberg believed it was the product of a splinter Pharisee group—a bit more on-target than Schechter's view, but still incorrect. Four copies of the Damascus Document turned up in Cave 4, with two further fragment found: one in Cave 5 and one in Cave 6. Clearly, this was a seminal text for the Qumran community. While the aforementioned fragments are numbered in the usual manner of Qumran texts (4Q266, 4Q267, etc.), the text revealed by the Cairo manuscripts is known as CD (for "Cairo Damascus").

We can use the medieval manuscripts of the Damascus Document, which are virtually intact, to further our understanding of the ancient Qumran community. The title comes from the repeated mention of the sect's exile to Damascus (based on a reinterpretation of Amos 5:27), which presumably is a metaphor for the sect's removal from Jerusalem to Qumran. The document divides neatly into two halves: First, the Exhortation describes the founding of the community 390 years after the Babylonian destruction of Jerusalem, placing us within a few decades of the early Maccabean period. The text mentions a leader known as the Teacher of Righteousness (*moreh zedeq*), who is mentioned frequently in other Dead Sea Scrolls. Whereas the Bible sees the exile as a punishment by God for Israel's sins, the Damascus

Document turns this passage into a praiseworthy action and a promise for salvation. Certain strict legal positions are also taken, such as the prohibition against having more than one wife (indeed, this passage also may prohibit divorce) and the prohibition against uncle-niece marriage. The second half of the Damascus Document is the Statutes. Its most significant section is the Sabbath law, which in numerous places reflects a stricter Halakah than the rabbinic approach. Recall Josephus's description that the Essenes observed Jewish law in a stricter fashion than other Jewish groups.

We should emphasize here that all the Jewish groups could agree on one belief: The Torah is divine. The dividing point between and among them was the matter of interpretation. ■

Essential Reading

Vermes, *The Complete Dead Sea Scrolls in English*, 125–156.

VanderKam, *The Dead Sea Scrolls Today*, 55–57.

Schiffman, *Reclaiming the Dead Sea Scrolls*, 90–95, 273–287.

Questions to Consider

1. Imagine yourself as Solomon Schechter reading the documents as they emerged from the Cairo genizah. What kind of learning would you need to possess to be able to identify the Hebrew original of Ben Sira? Or to realize that the Damascus Document was an ancient composition, not a medieval one? Or to be able to identify still other documents in the cache?

2. For (especially American) participants in this course, the closest analogy to the interpretation of the Torah by its latter-day adherents is the interpretation of the U.S. Constitution by latter-day jurists. Can you think of specific examples (beyond the example of the Second Amendment) still debated to the present day where judges and legislators disagree over the interpretation of a specific passage in this foundational American document?

A Dead Sea Scroll from Medieval Cairo
Lecture 8—Transcript

In this lecture, we return now to a study of a particular Dead Sea Scroll, though first we need to turn back the clock about 50 years. During the 1890s—that is, 50 years before the discoveries at Qumran— tens of thousands of Jewish manuscripts were discovered in the storeroom of the medieval Ben Ezra Synagogue in Cairo, Egypt. Among the texts found in the Cairo genizah, as the storeroom is known, were two copies of a previously unknown composition known called the Damascus Document. The text was studied by the two leading Jewish scholars of the time, Solomon Schechter and Louis Ginzberg, both of whom concluded that while the copies were medieval, the composition itself was ancient and belonged to an unknown Jewish sect from long ago. During the 1950s, scholars found several fragmentary copies of the Damascus Document text in Qumran Cave Four. The discovery proved that a) Schechter and Ginzberg were correct in their assessment, and b) astonishingly, some group of Jews had continued to read, copy, and transmit this ancient text for over 1, 000, from the period of late antiquity into the Middle Ages. In this lecture, we will read selected passages of this important document, most importantly the section on the Sabbath law, but also some other passages related to marriage and divorce.

Let's detail the discovery of the Cairo genizah for you first. During the 1890s, the greatest manuscript discovery in world history occurred when 200,000 documents were found in the storeroom of the Ben Ezra Synagogue from medieval Cairo. We use the word *genizah*, the Hebrew term for a storeroom. Jewish law does not allow one simply to discard holy texts such as the Bible, but rather they must be disposed of with honor and dignity. One system is burial in a grave, while the other is deposition in a dedicated storeroom, again, the Hebrew word *genizah*. The former system (burial in a grave) seems to have been more common throughout Jewish history and remains in practice today. It is not clear to what extent the other system was used throughout Jewish history, which makes the Cairo Genizah all the more special and remarkable.

The genizah documents date to the Middle Ages and provide an extremely detailed picture of the life of the medieval Jewish community of Cairo, one with trade and other connections from Iberia in the west to India in the east, and all points in between. I repeat the number here: 200,000 documents, compared to 930 documents among the Dead Sea Scrolls. It is for this reason that one may question Albright's declaration, which we noted in Lecture One; though to be fair, Albright's full declaration is as follows: "The greatest manuscript discovery of modern times—certainly the greatest biblical manuscript find . ... What an incredible find!" Thus, first, Albright qualified what he meant by "manuscript discovery," adding "the greatest biblical manuscript find"; and second, it all depends on how one interprets Albright's use of the term "modern times" (the Dead Sea Scrolls 1947–1948; the Cairo genizah half a century earlier in the 1890s).

The details of the discovery of the Cairo genizah also are fascinating. Some scholars became aware of the existence of the genizah in the early 1890s, but travel to the Middle East was difficult, needless to say, so access was very limited. Eventually, though, two British travelers—the Scottish sisters named Mrs. Lewis and Mrs. Gibson—returned from Cairo to England with Hebrew documents that they had obtained in Egypt. The sisters showed them to Solomon Schechter, reader of Hebrew at Cambridge University, who immediately realized the importance of these medieval texts. With the assistance of authorities from Cambridge University, Schechter arranged for the purchase of 140,000 documents from the Cairo genizah, and they remain housed at the Cambridge Library until this day. Another 40,000 documents were obtained by the Jewish Theological Seminary in New York, and smaller amounts are housed in Manchester, England, and Saint Petersburg, Russia. I repeat: Scholars of the Middle Ages have at their disposal a treasure trove of documentation, with the bulk of the material coming from the 11th through the 13th centuries. On a personal note, I would add that I have visited the genizah collection in Cambridge, and since I live in the New York area, I've also visited the genizah collection at the Jewish Theological Seminary. Fascinating to have these documents, to look at them, and actually hold them on occasion.

I would like to mention just a few of these texts brings us to a place far removed from Qumran scholarship because I want to stay with you just for a moment in the Middle Ages; I cannot help but mention these because of the fascination that everyone has with these documents. Early manuscripts of the Mishna and the two Talmud*im* were found in the Cairo genizah, in many cases providing better readings than our later medieval manuscripts and early printed editions of these texts. The Hebrew original of the book of *Ben Sira* was found in the Cairo genizah; this is an ancient Hebrew composition from 180 B.C.E.—the 2nd century before the Common Era—not canonized by Judaism, but canonized by the Church and transmitted in Greek translation under the title *Ecclesiasticus or Sirach*. Also found were new texts of Targum; that's a new term for us in this course, it refers to Aramaic renderings of the Bible. We also have autographed letters and other texts signed by Maimonides, the greatest of all medieval sages, who lived in Cairo during the 12th century. And perhaps the greatest surprise of all, we have a commentary by Saint Augustine—the great Church father from the 4th and 5th centuries—on the Sermon on the Mount. The text is a palimpsest; that is to say, it was a document that somebody had, and the ink was scraped off and reworked—erased as best as possible—and then reused for a Hebrew text. We can read the Hebrew text clearly, and under it we can still see—that's what a palimpsest is—the document that is, I repeat, a commentary by Saint Augustine on the Sermon on the Mount. Presumably a Jewish scribe in medieval Cairo went to the marketplace to obtain some more paper, and he was able to find a piece of paper that was in use but he said, "I'll take it anyway"—nobody was reading it anymore, it was in the marketplace; second-hand paper, as it were—reworked the actual paper itself so he could write his new text on it. Through photography we're able to read not only the text that we have but actually Augustine's commentary beneath it; fascinating.

Our interest in the Cairo genizah, however—as fascinating as these medieval texts are—lies in the one specific text found in the genizah, as follows: Among the cache of these 200,000 documents were two copies of a unique document, now called the Damascus Document by scholars. Although these two manuscripts are medieval—one of them dates to the 10th century and the other to the 12th century, and we rely on handwriting experts to allow us to determine exact century from the Middle Ages these texts date from; one from the 10th, one from the 12th, these two copies—the first scholars to work on this document realized immediately, as I indicated earlier, that the composition itself was not medieval but in fact was much, much older. Solomon Schechter published the text under the title—a long title—*Documents of Jewish sectaries, edited from Hebrew MSS. in the Cairo Genizah collection, now in the possession of the University Library, Cambridge*, vol. 1: *Fragments of a Zadokite work*; that's a long title. You see there in the "vol. 1: *Fragments of a Zadokite work*" that again you have reference in this text to the priests of Zadok, which we referred to earlier in our course. Schechter believed that the Damascus Document was associated with the Dositheans, a Samaritan sect whom we mentioned earlier in our course. This turned out to be incorrect, but he properly understood— Schechter got this part right—that the text was ancient and belonged to an ancient sect of Jews. Louis Ginzberg then produced the basic interpretation of the work under the title (his German book) *Eine unbekannte jüdische Sekte*, published in 1922. The English translation did not appear until almost half a century later: 1970, *An Unknown Jewish Sect*.

Ginzberg believed that the Damascus Document was the product of a splinter Pharisee group; a bit more on-target than Schechter's view but still incorrect, as scholars came to realize once the Dead Sea Scrolls were discovered. The suspicion of these scholars turned out to be correct when four copies of the Damascus Document turned up in Cave Four at Qumran, with one further fragment found each in Cave Five and Cave Six. Clearly this was a seminal text for the Qumran community. While the aforementioned fragments follow the usual system of numbering of Qumran documents—4Q266, 4Q267, and so on—the text revealed by the Cairo manuscripts from the Middle Ages is known in scholarly parlance as CD. This equals Cairo Damascus; the "C" standing for the place it was found, Cairo (as opposed to the "Q" of Qumran), and "D," the title we give to this work, the Damascus Scroll or the Damascus Document). More importantly, we can use the medieval manuscripts, which are virtually intact, to further our understanding of the ancient Qumran community, since we only have fragmentary versions of this important text from the caves at Qumran. The title comes from the repeated mention of the sect's exile to Damascus; this is based on the sect's interpretation of a passage in Amos 5:27. We will return to this point in a moment; this use of Damascus here is presumably a metaphor for the sect's removal from Jerusalem to Qumran.

The composition the Damascus Document divides neatly into two halves: The first half is called the Exhortation. This section begins by describing the founding of the community 390 years after the Babylonian destruction of Jerusalem; the text actually says 390 years after the Temple was destroyed, the community was founded. If we do the math and we begin with 586 B.C.E. as our date for the destruction of the first Temple at the hands of the Babylonians, and then we add on the 390 years after that, we arrive at the date of 196 B.C.E. (the early 2nd century before the Common Era). While we do not take the 390-year figure literally, the resultant date (196 B.C.E.) places us within a few decades of the early Maccabean period—remember, the Maccabean Revolt is 164 B.C.E.—when all other evidence (the archaeological data, the textual data, and so on) indicates that the Qumran community started.

The Damascus Document text mentions a leader of the group known as the Teacher of Righteousness; the Hebrew expression is *moreh zedeq*. This individual is mentioned frequently in other Dead Sea Scrolls as well. We do not know who he is; no identity, no name given, just a title: *moreh zedeq*, Teacher of Righteousness, the leader of the community. A moment ago I mentioned Amos 5:27, a biblical passage; this passage is totally reinterpreted by the author of the Damascus Document in Column Seven. Whereas the biblical text actually refers to Damascus as a place of exile—the Israelites will be exiled beyond Damascus—as a punishment for Israel's sins, the Damascus Document turns this passage into a praiseworthy action and a promise for salvation. Let me explain: The original biblical text reads, "And I will exile you beyond Damascus, says the Lord," and this follows a passage in which the Israelites are condemned for worshipping foreign gods, including constellations associated with the ancient pagans. In the Damascus Document, however, one of these unusual words for "constellation" is replaced by the basic Hebrew word for "star" (*kokhav*), and this word in turn is understood to refer to a person who is *doresh ha-torah ha-ba' dameseq* (the one who interprets Torah, who comes to Damascus), with Damascus once more referring to the community outpost, presumably at Qumran.

This text includes certain very strict legal positions, and let us look at a few examples of this: The prohibition against having more than one wife—which is not encountered in the Bible at all, where polygamy is countenanced—and indeed this passage also may prohibit divorce. The prohibition against uncle-niece marriage is not included among the laws of incest in Leviticus 18. Let's read this passage for you from the actual text of the Damascus Document. The text starts out as follows, and we'll need to do some explication of this text; it begins at the end of Column Four: "They are caught in two: fornication, in taking two wives in their lifetime, though the principle of creation is: male and female, He created them," citing (quoting) Genesis 1:27. What we see here is that the author of this Damascus Document is castigating, chastising, those people who are caught in what he calls "fornication" by taking two wives in their lifetime; and he brings a prooftext that, in fact, says that we were created male and female, "he created them." What is being prohibited here? Clearly polygamy is being prohibited; but as I indicated, it's also possible that even divorce is being prohibited, as we'll explain in a moment.

The text continues at the beginning of Column Five, and it again cites a different biblical passage. Here, as a bolster to the argument that the author is trying to make: "And those who went into the ark, two by two they went into the ark," quoting Genesis 7:9, a reference to the flood story. Again, you can see that humanity is assumed to be—or in this case, the animal kingdom is assumed to be—paired up one male and one female; one husband, one wife. How did the author of the Damascus Document get around the idea that the Bible has all sorts of examples of individuals who had more than one wife: Abraham, Sarah, and Hagar; Jacob, Rachel, and Leah; and, of course, King David with multiple wives. Obviously the author of the Damascus Document knows his Bible; he has to deal with this issue right here and he does so as the text continues:

> But David had not read the sealed Book of the Torah, which was in the Ark; for it was not opened in Israel from the day of the death of Eleazar [that's the son of Aaron, one of the high priests] and Joshua and the elders who served the goddess Ashtoret [one of the pagan deities referred to in the Bible]. They buried it [the Torah]; it was revealed only when Zadok arose [Zadok, the high priest at the time of David and Solomon; so that David didn't realize that there was a prohibition against polygamy]. The deeds of David were all excellent, except for the murder of Uriah [you all remember the story of David and Bathsheba] for which God forgave him. They also defile the sanctuary for they do not separate pure from impure

according to the Torah, and they lie with one who sees her flowing blood [that is a woman during her menstrual period].

Here's our text: Our text is arguing against a whole series of issues related to what other individuals do in their religious practice concerning marriage; that is to say, "Other people engage in polygamy, we will not," and it actually even explains how the Bible actually really doesn't allow for polygamy in the manner that I've just explained here. Then it tags on, "We don't also don't like with any menstruating women; other people may be doing that." Again, of course, that is something prohibited in the Torah; menstruation is one of those things that brings you to ritual impurity.

Minimally, this text prohibits polygamy. It also, by the way, may prohibit divorce because, as it says in the beginning—let me repeat that passage—these individuals, the people who this text is speaking against, "take two wives in their lifetime." That may mean that you cannot divorce a woman and then remarry while the first woman is still alive. Minimally polygamy, maybe divorce also is being argued against here by this particular text.

Then the text goes on to talk about another prohibition that I have referred to just a few moments ago generally; now let me read that passage to you as well: "And they marry, each man the daughter of his brother and the daughter of his sister, although Moses said, 'Unto the sister of your mother you shall not draw near, she is the flesh of your mother.'" But the law of incest is written for males and applies also to females. Let me explain what's going on here: In the laws of Leviticus 18, there's a list of incest laws; and among the laws that are prohibited is the marriage between an aunt and her nephew, that kind of marriage is prohibited. The question is: Is uncle-niece, the reciprocal relationship, prohibited? The Torah never says that; and so, according to certain Jews, including the rabbis later on, uncle-niece marriage will be allowed. But according to the Qumran community, even though the Torah doesn't state this explicitly, only aunt-nephew marriage is prohibited, uncle-niece marriage also gets prohibited.

As we turn from this text to a relationship with Christianity, we note that Christianity also disdains polygamy and divorce. 1 Corinthians 7:2 reads, "Each man should have his own wife and each woman should have her own husband." 1 Timothy 3:2 reads, "Now a bishop must be beyond reproach, the husband of one woman." Jesus is quoted in the Gospels as follows: "Whoever divorces his wife and marries another, commits adultery against her" (Mark 10:11). Then the same prooftext of Genesis 1:27 is quoted Mark 10 as well. What you get here is a connection once more between the Qumran community and early Christianity, with a negative approach to polygamy and to divorce as well.

These last two discussions into which we have entered remind us that a text only means what its later interpreters would have it mean. That's an important point here; let me repeat that: a text only means what its later interpreters would have it mean. That is to say, Amos 5:27 in the context of the Bible is a threat of punishment, but for the Qumran community it is a motto of sort, even a badge of honor. Even though the Bible clearly refers to polygamy and refers to divorce as well—you will recall our discussion in a previous lecture about divorce and divorce laws—the Qumran community can interpret the text to mean exactly the opposite. Perhaps, as an analogy, we can use the debate among United States jurists and legislators regarding the meaning of the Second Amendment. Some would hold that the Second Amendment prohibits the right for individuals to bear arms, while others would hold that it allows for individuals to bear arms; so the debate goes on. A text means only what the interpreters bring to the text.

The second half of the Damascus Document is a whole section called the Statutes. In the exhortation section, some legal issues have been raised as we've just indicated, but as we turn to the second half of this composition we come to the Statues section. The most significant portion here is the Sabbath law, which in numerous places reflects a stricter *halakha* than the rabbinic approach. Remember the word *halakha*; we introduced it in a previous lecture: "Jewish law." The Damascus Document's Sabbath law is stricter *halakha* than the rabbinic approach. Examples: The rabbis permit one to walk 2,000 cubits beyond one's town on the Sabbath; the Qumran community imposed a 1,000 cubit limit. By the way, this discrepancy between the 1,000 and 2,000 cubits is based on a discrepancy that already occurs in Numbers 35 where both figures are given. But back to the point here: Can one walk 1,000 cubits or 2,000 cubits on the Sabbath beyond one's city limit? The point being: If you go beyond that you are no longer engaging in Sabbath observances, but presumably you have some sort of work to do or you now have moved beyond the idea of Sabbath rest and are now moving in some direction towards actual work. Again, for the rabbis, a more liberal opinion: they permit one to walk 2,000 cubits, and for the Qumran community, as this text makes clear, only a distance of 1,000 cubits.

Another example: The rabbis permitted the opening of vessels to remove food on the Sabbath; we talked about this earlier. For example, olives or dried figs from a jar, or anything that you might want to take out of a jar to eat on the Sabbath. The Qumran community held that all food preparation needed to be done in advance of the Sabbath; not just cooked food—as all Jews believe—but other food as well, including a simple a task as opening a vessel in order to remove uncooked food. As we saw in Lecture Six, the unique cylindrical jars found at Qumran may have allowed the community to remove food from a vessel, since its lid could be removed easily without a cork or seal needing to be broken. It's possible that the Qumran community, as we stated in that earlier lecture, may have used this as an end run around their own prohibition. We're not sure about that; I just mention that here as a possibility.

A third example where the Damascus Document presents a stricter application of *halakha* (Jewish law) than the rabbinic system: The rabbis allow for a non-Jew to do work for a Jew on the Sabbath; the Damascus Document, however, prohibits this action. Let me give you a modern analogy that might help you explain how this might be possible. If you were an observant Jew—somebody who observes the Sabbath—and you took your suit to the cleaners on Friday (assuming the cleaners is a non-Jewish operation, owned by non-Jews, and the workers are non-Jews) and expected it to be ready on Monday when you wanted to pick it up, there is a possibility (a strong possibility, in fact) that the suit will be cleaned on Saturday, especially if the cleaners is closed on Sunday. Are you allowed to do that? According to the rabbinic system, you are allowed to do that; it is a liberal view. According to the Qumran system, however, one cannot do what I have just described for fear that the non-Jew would do work on the Sabbath cleaning your suit that you've delivered to the cleaners, to use a modern example of how this could reverberate in daily life.

The Damascus Document includes other strict opinions as well, not just related to Sabbath—the contrast we've been presenting—but also regarding other items as well, other legal issues. For example, according to the traditional Jewish system, which is down to the present day, the animals that require ritual slaughtering are only those animals that were slaughtered in use for the altar in the Temple for the sacrifices. That includes land mammals and birds; because on the altar one would sacrifice bulls, rams, and so on, and one would also sacrifice pigeons and doves. Extrapolating from that, the rabbis and the main Jewish tradition determine that only land mammals and birds (fowl) require ritual slaughtering; that is to say, the third category of such creatures that come to mind are fish. Fish, which were never used in the Temple ritual, therefore do not require ritual slaughtering. But, according to the Damascus Document, fish also require ritual slaughtering by the fact that they also are animals like fowl and land mammals; they, too, require ritual slaughtering. That is mentioned in the Qumran text that we're referring to here, Damascus Document; that is another difference, another stricter opinion, of this community in contrast to the rabbinic system that we are using here as our point of comparison.

Then there was another issue where the Qumran community differs from the rabbinic system: the notion of sexual intercourse in the city of Jerusalem. Everyone would have agreed that sexual intercourse could not occur in the Temple (obviously; it would be disrespectful, needless to say) and especially since standard sexual intercourse rendered one temporarily impure, according to Leviticus 15—we keep on going back to these laws of ritual purity and ritual impurity—and therefore obviously no one in the Temple would have sexual intercourse. But to extend the prohibition to the city of Jerusalem as a whole in which the Temple stood is another example of how the Qumran community took a stricter view of *halakha*: no sexual intercourse in the city of Jerusalem. Was it any wonder that the group removed itself from the Temple and from Jerusalem; clearly, to their mind—to the mind of these Yahad community members—the entire city was impure. If they believed that you couldn't have sexual intercourse in Jerusalem and yet people who happened to live in the city were engaging in normal sexual intercourse, then obviously the whole city has become impure since sexual intercourse renders you impure and by the very nature of your surroundings becoming impure as well.

We recall Josephus's description that the Essenes observed Jewish law in a stricter fashion than other Jewish groups; and we are seeing that first-hand in one of their own texts, the Damascus Document. We should emphasize here that all the Jewish groups to whom we are referring in this course could agree on one belief: that the Torah was divine. The dividing point between and among all the groups was the matter of interpretation; we go back to that issue, how to interpret a text. Some (the Pharisees, the rabbis, their heirs) interpreting liberally; others (the Essenes) interpreted stringently.

In this lecture, we analyzed a text known from Qumran Caves Four–Six, but whose best copies are found in the documents of the Cairo genizah. In our next lecture, we turn to a detailed reading of another important Dead Sea Scrolls text, one of the original seven scrolls found in Qumran Cave One; namely, the Pesher Habakkuk text.

Pesher Interpretation—Prophecy Read Anew
Lecture 9

Pesher is a method of interpretation whereby the true message of a biblical book is understood to speak to present-day conditions, not the original historical setting.

Various forms of Bible interpretation have been found among the Dead Sea Scrolls, including retellings or paraphrases of biblical stories; an Aramaic translation of the book of Job; one plain-sense commentary on the book of Genesis; and, most important and most distinctive among the Dead Sea Scrolls, the *pesher* texts. *Pesher* (Hebrew plural *pesharim*) refers to a particular form and style of Bible interpretation. Typically a biblical passage is quoted, and then the text continues, "its *pesher* is ... " meaning "its interpretation is ... ." Then the text explicates the biblical passage. The *pesher* interpretation, however, takes the biblical book out of its historical context and reinterprets the passage for the present. The main *pesher* texts are of the prophetic books Isaiah, Hosea, Micah, Nahum, Habakkuk, and Zephaniah and the book of Psalms. In this lecture, we focus on Pesher Habakkuk, which covers all of chapters 1–2 of the biblical book, authored around 610 B.C.E.

Hab 1:5 states, "Behold the nations and see, marvel and be astonished; for I accomplish a deed in your days, but you will not believe it when told." The *pesher* then states, "This concerns those who were unfaithful together with the Liar, in that they did not listen to the word received by the Teacher of Righteousness from the mouth of God" (1QpHab 2:1–2). The Teacher of Righteousness was the leader of the sect. Of course, we gain no further information to his identity, no hint of his name, when he might have lived, and so forth. The teacher receives divine communication from God concerning the proper interpretation of scripture. We need to judge this statement against the later rabbinic statement that prophecy ended with Malachi. Scholars used to assume that the rabbinic statement was directed at Christianity, but it may have been directed at the Essenes.

Hab 1:6 refers to the Chaldeans (or Babylonians) as "that bitter and hasty nation." The *pesher*, however, interprets this phrase to refer to the Kittim, the Qumran code word for the Romans "who are quick and valiant in war, causing many to perish" (1QpHab 1:10–12). In other words, the Qumran text would have us believe that for about 600 years the text of Habakkuk was transmitted without anyone knowing the true meaning. People presumably took "Chaldeans" at face value, meaning the Babylonians, but the Pesher Habakkuk tells us they were wrong. Here we see the belief that a text only bears the meaning that its interpreter ascribes to it.

Hab 2:2 describes how God told Habakkuk, "Write down the vision and make it plain upon the tablets." For the *pesher* writer, the prophecy of Habakkuk speaks to the present day: "And God told Habakkuk to write down that which would happen to the final generation, but He did not make known to him when time would come to an end" (1QpHab 7:1–3). We see here an eschatological message inherent in this text, though one would be hard-pressed to read such a message in its original context. Hab 2:2 continues with the phrase "that he who reads it may read speedily," which for the *pesher* author "concerns the Teacher of Righteousness, to whom God made known all the mysteries of the words of His servants the Prophets" (1QpHab 7:4–5).

Hab 2:4 states, "But the righteous shall live by his faith," with the assumption being that the righteous person shall prosper by his own faith in God. But the *pesher* author states that the faith is directed through the Teacher: "This concerns all those who observe the Law in the House of Judah, whom God will deliver from the House of Judgment, because of their suffering and because of their faith in the Teacher of Righteousness." (1QpHab 8:1–2) This same passage of Habakkuk is quoted three times in the New Testament (Romans 1:17, Galatians 3:11, and Hebrews 10:37–38), as Paul sees this passage referring to Jesus and to the future life. We have uncovered, accordingly, a key nexus between the Dead Sea Scrolls and the New Testament; both the Qumran sect and the early Christians used Hab 2:4 as a key passage in their theology of a single individual through whom faith is to be directed.

Hab 2:15 reads, "Woe to him who causes his neighbors to drink, who pours out his venom to make them drunk that he may gaze on their feasts." The *pesher* text says "This concerns the Wicked Priest who pursued the Teacher of Righteousness to the house of his exile that he might confuse him with his venomous fury. And at the appointed time for rest, for the Day of Atonement, he appeared before them to confuse them, and to cause them to stumble on the Day of Fasting, their Sabbath of repose. (1QpHab 11:5–8) We learn here about the Wicked Priest, the opponent of the Teacher and of the Qumran community, undoubtedly to be identified with one of the Hasmonean high priests or kings. Many scholars believe that this is Jonathan Maccabee.

Incidentally, the phrase puns on the Hebrew term for "high priest," *kohen ro'š*, versus "the wicked priest" *ha-kohen ha-raša'*. We further learn that the Qumran sect must have used a different calendar than other Jews, for how else could the Wicked Priest have traveled on Yom Kippur? It must have been Yom Kippur in Qumran, but not in Jerusalem.

The Qumran sect must have used a different calendar than other Jews.

The *pesher* method of interpretation is found throughout the New Testament as well. The most famous examples are Matthew 1:23, which invokes Isaiah 7:14 to refer to the birth of Jesus to his mother Mary; and a host of passages that apply Isaiah 53 (the suffering servant passage) to Jesus's suffering. For hundreds of years, the Isaiah passages were transmitted by Jews with meanings unrelated to Jesus, but the Christian community now understood these verses as speaking for the present. This is exactly what we see in Pesher Habakkuk and the other *pesher* texts among the Dead Sea Scrolls. Habakkuk's original intent and original context are irrelevant.

This is perhaps a good time to take stock of what we have learned thus far in our course, vis-à-vis Essene–Dead Sea Scroll–Christian connections. We have identified six points. Dualism is seen in the Community Rule and the New Testament. Celibacy was practiced by some Essenes and was an ideal for early Christians. Divorce and polygamy were forbidden. Both believed in continued revelation beyond the books of the prophets, as indicated by statements concerning the Teacher of Righteousness and by the New Testament books. Habakkuk 2:4 is used in Pesher Habakkuk and in three New Testament verses. Both use the *pesher* method of interpretation. Does the Qumran sect have much in common with early Christianity? Yes, definitely, as this growing list of connections demonstrates. ■

Suggested Reading

Vermes, *The Complete Dead Sea Scrolls in English*, 478–485.

VanderKam, *The Dead Sea Scrolls Today*, 43–51.

Schiffman, *Reclaiming the Dead Sea Scrolls*, 117–121, 223–238.

Yadin, *The Message of the Scrolls*, 90–98.

Essential Reading

Horgan, *Pesharim*.

Questions to Consider

1. Notwithstanding the fact that Paul quotes Habakkuk 2:4 three times in his letters, on what grounds could you argue that too great an emphasis is placed on this presumed nexus between the *Yahad* and the Jesus movement?

2. How do you envision the Teacher of Righteousness? Do you think he was a single individual who founded the sect, or do you think that this may have been a title that was borne by consecutive leaders of the community?

Pesher Interpretation—Prophecy Read Anew
Lecture 9—Transcript

In Lecture Two, we referred to a text among the original seven scrolls found a Qumran that interprets the biblical book of Habakkuk. As more and more Dead Sea Scrolls came to light, it became apparent that this scroll belongs to a genre of texts known collectively as the Pesher commentaries. Pesher—that's the Hebrew singular, the plural form is *pesharim*—refers to a method of interpretation whereby the true message of the biblical book is understood to speak to present-day conditions, as opposed to the original historical setting centuries earlier. In this lecture, we will look at the most important of the Pesher commentaries, the Pesher Habakkuk to use the Hebrew pronunciation, or Pesher Habakkuk to use the more familiar English pronunciation of that biblical book, designated by scholars as 1QpHab (Qumran Cave One, "p" for Pesher," "Hab," the abbreviation for Habakkuk), clearly the most important of the compositions belonging to the Pesher genre. We will read about the Teacher of Righteousness—the leader of the sect whom we mentioned in the previous lecture—and we will be introduced to the Wicked Priest, the key opponent of the sect, though the exact historical identities of these two figures remain elusive. Finally, we will note that the Pesher system of interpretation is present in the New Testament as well.

Various forms of biblical interpretation have been found among the Dead Sea Scrolls, including some retellings or paraphrases of biblical stories, an Aramaic translation of the book of Job—and let us recall that every translation is to some extent an interpretation—one commentary that is a plain sense commentary of the book of Genesis (all of these will be explored in a future lecture), but most importantly and most distinctively among the Dead Sea Scrolls in the larger genre of biblical interpretation is the specific style known as the Pesher commentary.

Pesher—again, the plural: *pesharim*—refers to a particular form and style of Bible interpretation attested at Qumran. Typically a biblical passage is quoted, and then the text continues—"its *pesher* is"; or in plain English, "its interpretation is"—upon which the text explicates the biblical passage. The Pesher interpretation, however, takes the biblical book out of its historical context, and it reinterprets the passage for the present; the present day, when the author was writing, when the community was reading this text. The main Pesher texts are of the prophetic books Isaiah, Hosea, Micah, Nahum, Habakkuk, and Zephaniah—actually in all these cases, with the exception of Habakkuk, we only portions thereof; again, the fragmentary nature of the finds of the Qumran manuscripts—and then we also have one Pesher for the book of Psalms, again, only portions thereof, mainly Psalm 37 with tiny portions for other Psalms: 45, 57, 60, 68, and so on.

In this lecture we will focus, as I indicated, on Pesher Habakkuk, which covers all of Chapters One and Two of this biblical book, a book of prophecy authored circa 610 B.C.E. in the last few decades of the existence of the kingdom of Judah before the destruction of Jerusalem in 586 C.E. As scholars long have recognized, the poem in Habakkuk 3 is probably an appendix; it reads more like a Psalm, and it was attached secondarily to the prophetic book. Therefore, the community at Qumran interprets in its Pesher Habakkuk text only Chapters One and Two of the biblical books.

Let's begin with a few passages, read some of these passages, from the book of Habakkuk and then its interpretation in the Pesher commentary. Hab. 1:5 in the biblical text states as follows: "Behold the nations and see, marvel and be astonished; for I accomplish a deed in your days, but you will not believe it when told." The Pesher then continues as follows: "This concerns those who were unfaithful together with the Liar ["Liar," the person who lies, to whomever that may refer], in that they did not listen to the word received by the Teacher of Righteousness from the mouth of God." Let me repeat that: "in that they did not listen to the word received by the Teacher of Righteousness from the mouth of God." There's hardly any of this that would be indicative in the plain sense of the text of the biblical book of Habakkuk, but again it is being interpreted by the authors of this Pesher text. We learn once more from the text that we have just read that the Teacher of Righteousness—the *moreh zedeq*, the Hebrew expression—whom we met in our earlier lecture is the leader of the sect. Of course, we gain no further information, as I've indicated earlier, as to the identity of this original; no hint of his name, when he might have lived, we simply have the title.

We further learn in this text that the Teacher receives divine communication from God, with the proper interpretation of Scripture. Again, that passage:

"they did not listen to the word received by the Teacher of Righteousness from the mouth of God." We need to judge this statement in the Pesher Habakkuk text against the later rabbinic statement that prophecy ended with the prophet Malachi; the last of the prophetic books in the Jewish canon dated to approximately 450 B.C.E. Scholars used to assume that the rabbinic statement that prophecy ended with Malachi was directed at Christianity in the first few centuries C.E. when the rabbis were actively compiling their corpora of texts, since Christians saw the books of the New Testament as continuing revelation into the 1st century C.E. But we now need to countenance another view: that this statement is not directed at the Christians, but rather at sectarian Jews. That is to say, the Essenes; that is, the Yahad members, who saw—as you can see in this passage—the Teacher of Righteousness as one who received divine communication from God.

Our next text from this Pesher Habakkuk scroll: Hab. 1:6 refers to the Chaldeans as "that bitter and hasty nation," using an alternative term, Chaldeans, to refer to the Babylonians, as befitting the historical setting of the book—the prophet, Habakkuk—as I indicated, 610 B.C.E. when the Babylonians were the new world power, alternatively called the Chaldeans, and, of course, within a matter of a few decades they would destroy Jerusalem as we've indicated. The Pesher, however, takes none of this at face value; it ignores what the word, what the text might have meant 600 years earlier, and instead it reinterprets the word "Chaldean" (this phrase, "the Chaldeans") to refer to the Kittim, the Qumran code word for the Romans which we've discussed earlier. So it refers to the Chaldeans here as the Kittim "who are quick and valiant in war, causing many to perish"; there you have a great description, of course, of the Roman Empire: "quick and valiant in war, causing many to perish." Chaldeans in the biblical text referring to the Babylonians ignored essentially by the writer of our text who then sees the Chaldeans as the Kittim; we all know that the Kittim is a code word for the Romans. That's how this operates. In other words, the Qumran text would have us believe that for about 600 years the text of Habakkuk was transmitted by Jews, though no one quite knew the true meaning. People presumably, over the course of centuries, took Chaldeans at face value, meaning the Babylonians; but the author of this text tells us, no, the reference here is to the Kittim, who in turn are the Romans. We repeat what we stated in the previous lecture: A text only bears the meaning that its interpreter ascribes to it.

Another example from this fascinating document, Hab. 2:2 reads as follows: It describes how God told the prophet Habakkuk, "Write down the vision and make it plain upon the tablets." A common expression in the Bible that things are supposed to be written down; God just tells the prophet, "Write down the vision and make it plain upon the tablets." For the Pesher writer—and you now know how this operates—though, the prophecy of Habakkuk speaks to the present day. The text goes on and reads as follows: "And God told Habakkuk to write down that which would happen to the final generation, but He did not make known to him when time would come to an end." We see here in this text an eschatological message inherent here, though one would be hard-pressed to read such a message in the book of Habakkuk in its original context. We will return to the subject of eschatology in our next lecture, so I content myself here with simply pointing this passage out, and we will engage in a fuller discussion in the next lecture as I indicated.

Hab. 2:2 continues with the phrase, "that he who reads it may read speedily"; that's the biblical passage, "that he who reads it may read speedily." But for the Pesher author, of course, the text means something else. The Pesher continues as follows: "This concerns the Teacher of Righteousness, to whom God made known all the mysteries of the words of His servants the Prophets." Here you have, again, a connection, a reinterpretation, of a biblical text now being reinterpreted, and again with reference to the Teacher of Righteousness.

Next text as we continue to work through the biblical book of Habakkuk along with the Pesher interpretation attributed to the original text by our Dead Sea Scrolls author. Hab. 2:4, an extremely well-known passage; the biblical text reads: "But the righteous [meaning the righteous man or the righteous individual] shall live by his faith," with the assumption being that the righteous person shall prosper by his own faith in God, through his own faith. That the "his" there refers to the righteous; "but the righteous shall live by his faith," "his" is a pronoun, the antecedent to "his" in the plain sense of the Hebrew text is the righteous person mentioned earlier in the text. But the Pesher author states something differently; he states that the faith is directed through the Teacher (the Teacher of Righteousness). That is to say, the pronoun "his" doesn't refer back to the righteous individual at the beginning of this passage but rather refers to the Teacher of Righteousness. Let me read that passage for you; this is what the Pesher Habakkuk document says: "This concerns all those who observe the Law in the House of Judah, whom God will deliver from the House of Judgment, because of their suffering and because of their faith in the Teacher of Righteousness." You see it there plainly, I hope, that the word "his" is referring not to the righteous person I repeat, but that the "his" refers to the Teacher of Righteousness. Let me read it again: "This concerns all those who observe the Law in the House of Judah, whom God will deliver from the House of Judgment, because of their suffering and because of their faith in the Teacher of Righteousness." This passage—the original biblical passage, Hab. 2:4, "the righteous shall live by his faith"—is quoted three times in the New Testament, clearly an important passage to the Jesus movement. It is quoted in Romans 1:17, Galatians 3:11, and Hebrews 10:37–38 in the Letters of Paul, as Paul sees this passage referring to a) Jesus, and b) to the future life. Again, "the righteous shall live by his faith" in the New Testament context is faith through Jesus; and in the Qumran community context, it is faith through the Teacher of Righteousness.

Both our Essene group at Qumran and the New Testament epistles here are interpreting this passage in similar fashion: that the faith is through another individual; that is where salvation will come. We have uncovered, accordingly, a key nexus between the Dead Sea Scrolls and the New Testament; both the Qumran sect and the early Christians used Hab. 2:4 as a key passage in their theology of a single individual—whether it be the Teacher or Jesus—through whom faith is to be directed, as opposed to individuals addressing their worship directly to God.

Let's look at another passage now, Hab. 2:15. Again, let's read the biblical passage within the context of 600 or 610 B.C.E., and then we'll come back and look at how the Pesher text relates to this passage. Hab. 2:15: "Woe to him who causes his neighbors to drink, who pours out his venom to make them drunk that he may gaze on their feasts." This is the usual kind of prophetic indictment of the people of Israel who, apparently in this case according to the prophet Habakkuk, were drinking too much at the time of their festivals. Yes, wine, of course, is part of the culture of ancient Israel, but overdoing it—as you can see in a passage such as this—can have a negative effect in the minds of obviously the religious worshipers and the prophet calls the people of Israel on this very question at this point. What does the Pesher text do with this passage? I've just given you a basic understanding of this passage within the context of ancient Israel.

Now we're in the Postbiblical period and the Pesher author has this to say. The Pesher text reads as follows: "This concerns the Wicked Priest who pursued the Teacher of Righteousness to the house of his exile that he might confuse him with his venomous fury." It picks up on the word "venom" that occurred in the biblical text, that occurs there in Hab. 2:15, and it uses it here. You'll remember that in the biblical text, "who pours out his venom to make them drunk," that's the original text; and the Pesher author writes now, "This concerns the Wicked Priest who pursued the Teacher of Righteousness to the house of his exile [we'll get to that in a moment] that he might confuse him with his venomous fury." You can begin to see how the Pesher text relates back to the biblical text. Then it continues: "And at the appointed time for rest, for the Day of Atonement [Yom Kippur], he appeared before them to confuse them, and to cause them to stumble on the Day of Fasting, their Sabbath of repose." A little background information here that relates to something we talked about earlier in our course: The Day of Atonement, Yom Kippur, how does one atone, how does one fast? One fasts for the 24 hour period as an act of atonement, and therefore the holiday is referred to here as well as a Day of Fasting. Then the passage goes on and concludes by calling this day a "Sabbath of repose." You'll remember in a previous lecture we mentioned that the laws of Sabbath apply to the Day of Atonement as well; so you can see how all of this begins to fit together as our course proceeds from lecture to lecture.

What do we learn in this passage? We learn here about the Wicked Priest, the opponent of the Teacher of Righteousness and of the Qumran community. Almost all scholars agree that the Wicked Priest agree that the Wicked Priest is to be identified with one of the Hasmonean priests/kings, because you'll recall that the Hasmonean Dynasty begins really as a priestly family, the Maccabee family, and eventually takes on the title of "king" as well. But they were priests, and one of them, we assume, is the Wicked Priest referred to here in this text. As we saw earlier, many scholars believe that the Wicked Priest is to be identified with Jonathan Maccabee, one of the dynasts of the Hasmonean kingdom. Incidentally, the Hebrew phrase here puns, includes a very nice pun: The Hebrew term for "'high priest" is *kohen ro'š* and the phrase here for "the wicked priest" is *ha-kohen ha-raša'*; so you hopefully have heard the same sounds there. "High priest" would be *kohen ro'š*, a phrase that would be known to anybody who was active at this time, engaged in the life of Judaism in the Temple, outside the Temple, it didn't matter. People would know the term *kohen ro'š*. The Wicked Priest: *ha-kohen ha-raša'*; so you hear the same syllables there (*ro'š*, *ha-raša'*) and that's the play on words that is being used here by our author, and of course this term "Wicked Priest" appears in other Qumran texts as well.

We learn here that the Qumran sect must have used a different calendar in some fashion than the one in use in Jerusalem and by other Jews, for how else could the Wicked Priest have traveled on Yom Kippur from Jerusalem to Qumran? That is what the text implies. Let me read that again; it says here that "the Wicked Priest … pursued the Teacher of Righteousness to the house of his exile" and that he did this on Yom Kippur. We assume, we reconstruct from this, that the Wicked Priest, who was in Jerusalem, be it Jonathan Maccabee or somebody else, left Jerusalem on Yom Kippur and traveled to Qumran—referred to in our text as the house of exile of the Teacher of Righteousness—because as we've indicated, the Qumran community retreated from the religious life in Jerusalem and sought out its own self-imposed exile as it were in its small, remote, isolated community at the site of Qumran on the shore of the Dead Sea. This means that it must have been Yom Kippur in Qumran for the sectarians who were writing this text, but it could not have been Yom Kippur in Jerusalem for the Temple community and for the general Jewish community. Keep in mind, as I indicated, that the laws of Sabbath apply to the other holidays, including Yom Kippur, as well: Work is prohibited, and among the prohibitions clearly would be traveling from one locale to another. Obviously this would be well beyond the 1,000 cubits or 2,000 cubits beyond one's city limit that we referred to in a previous lecture; anything beyond that, of course, is travel such is prohibited.

So, Yom Kippur for the Wicked Priest and Yom Kippur for the Qumran sect were different days. Is this because other Jews—and you'll remember this phrase from the Community Rule—"advanced their holy days and postponed their festivals," according to the Qumran community. Is this the case where perhaps it was a Friday/Saturday/Sunday issue as we talked about with the fixing of the date of Yom Kippur; how it could not fall on a Friday or a Sunday in the rabbinic system or perhaps in the general Jewish system, but that it could do that in the Qumran community and therefore you had different days of Yom Kippur, one in Jerusalem and one here at Qumran. Or is this because the Qumran community had a different calendar altogether, so that even more was at stake than adjusting or tweaking the calendar here or there? We will return to this subject of the specific Qumran calendar in a later lecture, and we will see that indeed they did have their own calendar, different from the calendar that most Jews were using during this time period. You can see what can happen when the same holiday will be observed on different days depending on which calendar one follows and whether one adjusts or tweaks that calendar along the way as the days proceed through the year.

The Pesher method of interpretation is found throughout the New Testament as well. The most famous examples are Matthew 1:23—the very beginning of the New Testament, the first gospel in the canonical order—which invokes Isaiah 7:14 to refer to the birth of Jesus to his mother Mary. Another famous example is a host of New Testament passages such as Matthew 8:17 that apply Isaiah 53 (the "Suffering Servant" passage) to refer to Jesus's suffering. These are common examples; these are well-known examples, taking one Isaiah passage to refer to the birth of Jesus, another Isaiah passage to refer to the suffering of Jesus. For hundreds of years the Isaiah passages were transmitted by Jews with meanings unrelated to Jesus, but the Christian community now understands these verses as speaking for the present; the very present, the 1st century C.E. when Jesus lived and died. This is exactly what we see in Pesher Habakkuk and the other Pesher texts among the Dead Sea Scrolls. Habakkuk's original intent and the original context and how the original readers of that biblical book may have understood that message, all of that is irrelevant at this point when the Pesher writer or the New Testament writers apply biblical texts for meaning in their own day. I repeat: The text means only what the interpreter brings to the text; the text means only what the interpreter says it means. In the case we're looking at, it's the Teacher of Righteousness in the Pesher Habakkuk and the Qumran scrolls; or in the case of the New Testament authors, what the early Christian community believed the text means.

This is perhaps a good time to take stock of what we have learned thus far in our course, vis-à-vis Essene, Dead Sea Scrolls, and Christian connections. It is rather obvious, of course, that in our Dead Sea Scrolls material we are dealing with Jewish texts from the century or so before the life of Jesus, and all sorts of associations with other Jewish texts of the general timeframe arise naturally. We've been doing that throughout our course as we've looked at this community, these texts, in relation to other texts; the rabbinic texts, the Mishna, for example, most prominently. But what about Christian connections? By my counting, we already have identified six important areas where the Dead Sea Scrolls and the Essene community—as we know from Josephus—have points of contact with Christianity. Let's review those here. The first of these is dualism. We talked about dualism back in Lecture Three when we read the Community Rule together. Dualism is a major component of that text and the Dead Sea Scrolls community, the Yahad, and it appears in the New Testament as well. A second feature would be celibacy. Again, as we know from Josephus, Philo, and from Pliny the elder, celibacy was practiced by some Essenes, and it does become an ideal for early Christians as well, especially as monastic orders begin to develop in the first Christian centuries.

A third point of contact that we saw when we looked at the Damascus Document: The Damascus Document prohibits polygamy, and most likely, probably, or perhaps prohibits divorce. The early Christian community also takes a negative view on these two elements, polygamy and divorce. In this lecture, we saw a fourth point of contact between the Dead Sea Scrolls and early Christianity: the idea of a continued revelation beyond the books of the Prophets as canonized in the Jewish Bible, beyond those prophetic books as indicated by both the New Testament books, which are a revelation in the 1st century C.E., and by statements concerning the Teacher of Righteousness, which we see in this Pesher text, because the Teacher of Righteousness has gotten the revelation from God that allows him to understand to interpret these texts in the right manner according to this community. Continued revelation: another point of contact. The use of Hab. 2:4 in this Pesher Habakkuk text and in three New Testament verses: You couldn't ask for a more specific connection between the Dead Sea Scrolls community and the early Christian community. Hab. 2:4: a crucial passage with important theological meaning for both of these movements in late antiquity. Finally, generally speaking, the Pesher method of interpretation as we've been pointing out in this lecture. The Pesher system used at Qumran, and the Pesher system, as we saw, with the Isaiah texts applied in the gospels to the life of Jesus.

Hopefully this list allows you to see where our course is headed. Is the Yahad a proto-Christian group? No, definitely not, for reasons that we will explain as our course progresses. Does the Qumran sect, however, have much in common with early Christianity? Yes, definitely yes, as this growing list of connections demonstrates.

As we noted at the outset of our course, seven individual scrolls were found in Qumran Cave One. Pesher Habakkuk, which we have surveyed in this lecture, is one of those texts. Another one of these documents is the War Scroll. We will return to the War Scroll in our next lecture, and we will discuss the contexts of that text, of that important document, and the eschatology that is forthcoming from reading that document.

The War Scroll and Other Apocalyptic Texts
Lecture 10

> The War Scroll details a cataclysmic battle between the sons of light (the sect's self-designation) and the sons of darkness (all other Jews, apparently), using military techniques and maneuvers known from Roman sources.

The War Scroll is a major document found in Cave 1 in 1947. There are also eight additional fragmentary copies from Cave 4, indicating that this document was of prime importance to the Qumran community. The War Scroll provides a manual for the conduct of the war of the sons of light against the sons of darkness, with the former referring to the Qumran community and the latter referring to their enemies, also called "the army of Belial." All evil is to be destroyed at the appointed time, and God's rule will be established. We know that there must be an appointed time, because we already have discussed the Essene belief in predetermination. Included among the enemies are not only other nations such as the Kittim, but (perhaps more importantly) other Jews with whom they disagree over theological and doctrinal issues—that is, the sons of darkness. Once more we see the essential dualistic nature of the particular type of Judaism adhered to by the *Yahad*, with the world divided into good and evil. Later on, the text uses very strong language, including expressions such as "day of vengeance" (*yom naqam*, 1QM 7:5) and "war of God" (*milhemet 'el*, 1QM 9:5), making it very clear what kind of battle is described here. We also note a connection to the New Testament here, since the expression "sons of light" occurs in John 12:38 and 1 Thessalonians 5:5.

The War Scroll was one of the three scrolls purchased by Eliezer Sukenik from Kando in 1947. Sukenik's son was Yigael Yadin, both a leading general in the Israeli army and a leading historian and archaeologist. He combined his two interests to produce a detailed study of the War Scroll published in 1957.

The War Scroll divides as follows. Its introduction begins with reference to the sons of Levi, Judah, and Benjamin, the exiles in the desert [who will] return from the Desert of the Peoples to camp in the Desert of Jerusalem; and after the battle they will go up from there [that is, to Jerusalem to do battle]. (1QM 1:2–3) The General Rules of Battle include detailed descriptions of the trumpets, standards, weaponry, movements, and so forth, along with the duties of the priests and Levites who will accompany the troops. Scholars have concluded that the military arrangement and tactics described are based on the Roman legion. The Prophetic Description of the Final Battle demonstrates clearly that the sect saw this battle in apocalyptic terms—that is, "The purpose [actually *goral*, "fate"] of God is eternal redemption" (1Q15:1) and "destruction for all the nations of wickedness" (1QM 15:2). Incidentally, angels fight on both the sides: good and evil.

> We see the essential dualistic nature of the particular type of Judaism adhered to by the *Yahad*, with the world divided into good and evil.

Apocalyptic is a particular type of eschatological thought with a linear (as opposed to cyclical) view of time, a calendar element, and the notion of a cataclysmic battle. Apocalypticism was borrowed from Zoroastrianism and dovetails nicely with dualism. It filtered into Judaism especially in the last few centuries of the biblical period, exemplified most of all by the canonical book of Daniel. One finds apocalyptic in other postbiblical Jewish works as well, although the two apocalyptic movements best known to us are the Qumran community and the early Christians. In contrast to early Christian belief, the Dead Sea Scrolls are less focused on a messiah figure. The word "Christ" or "messiah" appears more than 500 times in the New Testament but only 32 times in the Dead Sea Scrolls.

In the War Scroll, "messiah" appears only once (1QM 11:7), and in the plural, just as we saw in the Community Rule. Another apocalyptic text found at Qumran is the Rule of the Congregation (or the Messianic Rule, 1QSa). This text provides "the rule for all the congregation of Israel in the last days" (1:1) and culminates in the communal meal, to be presided over by the messiah (2:20–21). Several scholars, including G. R. Driver of Oxford University and Chaim Rabin of the Hebrew University, believed that the presence of the War Scroll among the Dead Sea Scrolls indicated that the Qumran community belonged to the Zealot movement. This theory is not accepted today, but it is worth mentioning that the Zealot movement may have had apocalyptic beliefs attached to it. Josephus does not mention the apocalyptic view of the Essenes because he was writing for an educated Greco-Roman audience, under Roman patronage, and any hint of apocalypticism would be seen as subversive and treasonous.

Once more the Jewish nature of these texts is self-evident. However, it may be useful to consider Dead Sea Scrolls–Christian connections again. The War Scroll offers a major point of contact: the apocalyptic vision. ∎

Essential Reading

Vermes, *The Complete Dead Sea Scrolls in English*, 137–186.

VanderKam, *The Dead Sea Scrolls Today*, 64–67.

Schiffman, *Reclaiming the Dead Sea Scrolls*, 317–327, 329–339.

Yadin, *The Message of the Scrolls*, 128–143.

Supplementary Reading

Collins, *Apocalypticism in the Dead Sea Scrolls*.

Questions to Consider

1. What is the main attraction of apocalyptic thought in ancient times and in modern times?

2. Have we explained the absence of any mention of apocalypticism in Josephus's description of the Essenes correctly? Is any other explanation readily forthcoming? Is it possible that we are totally off-track, and if so, in what way?

The War Scroll and Other Apocalyptic Texts
Lecture 10—Transcript

The next lengthy document that we will consider is the War Scroll, one of the original seven documents found in Qumran Cave One. The War Scroll details a cataclysmic battle between the sons of light (the sect's self-designation) and the sons of darkness (the enemies of the sect) using military techniques and maneuvers known from Roman sources. Our reading of this scroll leads us to a consideration of apocalyptic belief among the Dead Sea sectarians, which very clearly links this group with the early Christian community once more. At the same time, however, we note that early on in Dead Sea Scrolls scholarship, the War Scroll suggested to some scholars that the Qumran community belonged to the Zealot movement, especially since Josephus made no mention of apocalyptic belief among the Essenes. We will consider these various views, though in the end we will set aside the opinion that the Qumran community was a Zealot group, and more importantly we will explain this apparent discrepancy in Josephus's description of the Essenes.

The War Scroll is designated in Qumran research as 1QM; and by now you know the system: 1, Cave One; "Q" Qumran; "M" stands for the Hebrew word for "war," *milhama*, a word that appears repeatedly in this scroll. Accordingly, we call it 1QM, or the War Scroll. This is another of the major documents found in Cave One in 1947. In addition, there are eight additional fragmentary copies from Cave Four, all of which get a 4Q designation, and this indicates with the eight fragments from Cave Four and the large scroll from Cave One that this document was of prime importance to the Qumran community. We assume the more copies attested among the corpus of Dead Sea Scrolls, the more importance can be ascribed to a particular document.

The War Scroll provides a manual for the conduct of the War of the sons of light against the sons of darkness; it's a battle manual. The phrase "sons of light" refers to the Qumran community, and the latter phrase, "sons of darkness," refers to the enemies. They are also called "the army of Belial"; we'll talk about this term (Belial) in a few minutes. There is only one way to introduce this text, which covers 19 columns, and that is to read from the outset of this document, near the beginning of column 1. I have a long quotation here for you; let me read it:

> A time of salvation for the people of God, and an end-time for the dominion of all the men of his forces, and an eternal destruction for all the forces of Belial. And there will be a great upheaval. ... The dominion of the Kittim shall come to an end, and wickedness shall be subdued, without a remnant, and with no escape for the sons of darkness. And the sons of righteousness shall shine over all the ends of the earth, continuing to shine until the appointed times of darkness are totally consumed. And at the time appointed by God, his exalted greatness shall shine for all time with peace and blessing, glory and joy, for length of days over all the sons of light.

The message could not be clearer: All evil is to be destroyed, at the appointed time, and God's rule will be established. We know that there must be an appointed time, because we already have discussed the Essene belief in predetermination: Everything is fixed; everything is predestined, including when this will occur. Indeed, the word for "forces" in the quotation that I just read, which has a sense of military forces in this context, is actually the Hebrew word *goral*, which literally means "fate"; as if to say, it appears, even what side of the battle one is on is due to fate, so that one's *goral*, one's fate, becomes one's force, which fighting force one is a member of. Included among the enemies are not only other nations such as the Kittim—and that refers to the Romans once more; you heard the word "Kittim" when I read this text aloud a moment ago—but, and perhaps more importantly, other Jews with whom they disagree over theological and doctrinal issues; that is, the sons of darkness. Once more we see the essential dualistic nature of the particular type of Judaism adhered to by the Yahad, with the world divided into good and evil. Later on, the text uses very strong language, including expressions such as "day of vengeance" (in Hebrew, *yom naqam*; that's in Column Seven), and "war of God" (*milhemet 'el*; that's in Column Nine), making it very clear what kind of battle is described here: A "day of vengeance," *yom naqam*; the "war of God," *milhemet 'el*. I hope you enjoy that I occasionally pepper these lectures with some of the Hebrew phrases, giving you a sense of what these scrolls sound like when they are read aloud.

We also note a connection to the New Testament here, since the expression "sons of light" occurs twice in the New Testament: It occurs in John 12:38 and it occurs in 1 Thessalonians 5:5. In the John passage, Jesus says, "As long as you have the light, believe in the light, so that you may become children of light," or the "sons of light" if we use non-neutral gendered language. The similarity of language again highlights the relationship between the Yahad community and the nascent Christian community.

I would like to add here a personal account, not concerning me personally, but the persons involved with the research into the War Scroll. In Lecture Two, we learned that the War Scroll was one of the three scrolls purchased by Professor Sukenik from Kando, the antiquities dealer in Bethlehem, in 1947. Sukenik's son was the famous professor Yigael Yadin, who made very important contributions to Dead Sea Scrolls scholarship. He was a leading general in the Israeli army—in fact, was one of the heroes of the Israeli War of Independence in 1948—and he was a leading historian and archaeologist. Professor Yadin combined his two interests to produce a detailed study of the War Scroll, published in 1957. By the way, if you're curious about why these two individuals, father and son, have different surnames: Sukenik, the father, was born in Russia, and emigrated to Israel in 1911, and he retained his Eastern European name; while Yadin, the son, born in Israel, adopted a Hebrew surname.

The War Scroll divides into three components. We begin with a discussion of the Introduction, which is essentially Column One; and I already read a long passage from Column One to you. The very beginning of the column, however, begins with the following passage: The reference here is to "the sons of Levi, Judah, and Benjamin, the exiles in the desert [who will] return from the Desert of the Peoples to camp in the Desert of Jerusalem; and after the battle they will go up from there," that is, to Jerusalem to do battle. Apparently, "the Desert of the Peoples" refers to their site in Qumran, in the middle of the desert. "The Desert of Jerusalem" is, of course, is also a reference either to their desert home as if they are in a Jerusalem removed from the actual Jerusalem, or it may refer here specifically in reality to the city of Jerusalem. That's how the text begins: "the sons of Levi, Judah, and Benjamin, the exiles in the desert [who will] return from the Desert of the Peoples to camp in the Desert of Jerusalem; and after the battle they will go up from there." That's one of the passages from the Introduction, and then I read for you a very long passage as well also from Column One earlier.

The largest chunk of this document comprises Columns 2–14, and here you have the General Rules for Battle, including detailed descriptions about everything you'd ever want to know about military array: the trumpets, the standards, the weaponry, the movements, etc.; all of us is detailed for us in this large chunk, Columns 2–14, of the War Scroll. Also in that section, we learn what the duties of the priests are, and the duties of the Levites, who will accompany the troops into battle. This is a religious experience, therefore the religious leaders—the priests and Levites—accompany the troops to do battle. Scholars have concluded that the military arrangement and the tactics described here are based on the Roman legion, as opposed, for example, to the Greek phalanx or some other options. It shows you to what extent the Qumran community, no matter how isolated they were—no matter how remote their dwelling may have been from the real world of Jerusalem, Caesarea, Rome, and all the other places in the Mediterranean—they were knowledgeable about the Roman legions and how the Roman legions operated, and then adopted that terminology and, of course, translated it into Hebrew equivalents in writing the War Scroll. Indeed, it was Professor Yigael Yadin who first demonstrated this point, as again, as I noted, he combined his careers as scholar/archaeologist on the one hand and military leader/general on the other to become one of the world's great experts on military history, especially in ancient times.

The third and last section of the War Scroll comprises the last five columns, Columns 15–19. This is the Prophetic Description of the Final Battle; this is what we've all been waiting for. Now that we have the battle array, and the trumpets, and the movements, and the tactics, and all that described for us in the middle chunk of this document, we now reach the description of the final battle, Columns 15–19. Here we get clear evidence that the sect saw this battle in apocalyptic terms. For example, in Column 15:1: "The purpose of God is eternal redemption"; and, by the way, the word "purpose" here is again that Hebrew word *goral* which, as I said earlier, means "fate," so it's a word that gets used in different ways in this document. *Goral*/fate: an important theological concept; fate, predetermination, one's lot in life, all of that is *goral*. It's used for the army, the forces of God as we saw earlier in Column 1; here in Column 15 it's the purpose of God. Of course, we have to translate this same word by the context, and it has a broad range of meanings. In any case, that statement again, let me repeat it: "The purpose of

God is eternal redemption"; and then the next line refers to the "destruction for all the nations of wickedness." That's in 1QM 15:2: "the destruction for all the nations of wickedness"; so everybody is going to be destroyed. Incidentally, both sides—the good and the evil; the sons of light and the sons of darkness—have angels fighting with them or on their behalf: the good angels with God and the sons of light, and the bad angels, or demons perhaps, with Belial and the sons of darkness.

A moment ago I used the word "apocalyptic," so let's take some time here to ask the question what is apocalyptic and to answer that question. We present here a history of eschatology. We start with the term eschatology—I used it in a previous lecture—and I want to say more about that general term and then something about the specific kind of eschatology called apocalyptic. In the Bible already, one sees passages with an eschatological view. Essentially, eschatology means "considerations about the end of time"; the eschaton—that's a Greek word—the end of days, the end of time, the end of history as we know it. This is based on a concept in ancient Israel that understood that time operates in a linear fashion. This is opposed to the way many of the peoples in the ancient world understood time as operating in a more cyclical fashion. That is to say, in the polytheistic world, you have gods who are associated with nature—you have a storm god and an earth goddess and so on—and the seasons of nature dictate time, so you go through spring, summer, fall, and winter. Time doesn't play out on a linear timeline, but rather plays out through nature's cycles, the natural cycles that we all understand in our daily lives. That's the cyclical view of time, which was the dominant way of understanding time in the ancient world.

The Israelites, by contrast, developed the linear view of time. In ancient Israel, God had a totally different trait about him: He was not associated with an element of nature—he wasn't a sea god or a desert god or a storm god as I mentioned, or anything like that—God was associated with history; he's a God of history. God manifests himself in history by intervening in human affairs. "I am the Lord your God who brought you out of the land of Egypt"; that's how the Ten Commandments begin. That's a historical event in the minds of the ancient Israelites, and God is responsible for it. If God operates in history, then time begins to gain a new understanding—or the Israelites bring a new understanding to time—and becomes a linear conception, not a cyclical one. It begins with Creation, and then we move into everything that is played out in the Bible—we have all sorts of stories that can be placed on a chronological timeline, as it were—and then we come to the idea of the eschaton. This linear time, this history as we know it, is not open-ended; it will reach an end point, and we will be vaulted into the eschaton. That's the way the Israelites developed the concept of eschatology.

Let me mention some biblical passages that are relevant to this discussion. Isaiah 2 and Isaiah 11 are the key passages in the Jewish Bible that talk about eschatology. Isaiah 2 states that nations shall never again know war, and they are supposed to take their weapons of war—their swords and their spears—and convert them into agricultural implements; into pruning implements, plowshares, and so on. All of that has to do with the world peace that is going to ensue with the coming of the eschaton. That's Isaiah 2. Isaiah 11 gives us a different understanding of it—actually the same understanding, although it uses the different metaphor—it uses the metaphor of the animal kingdom, and the animals that prey and the animals that are preyed upon will no longer engage in such actions; and so the wolf will lie down with the lamb, and so on. You all know these passages; they're quite famous, they are among the most famous of the biblical passages. Those are the eschatological passages of Isaiah.

Already in biblical times, and much more so in postbiblical times, a second or specific type of eschatology develops, and that's the apocalyptic view. The apocalyptic has the same ideas as the general eschatological view, but it adds two components: a) a calendar element; that is to say, we can determine when the end time will be. The general eschatological view leaves it open; in fact, Isaiah 2 simply begins, "In days to come," without telling us when that will occur. In the apocalyptic understanding, however, there is a calendar, and we can work out when this will occur, when time will end, history will end, and we will move into the End of Days, the eschaton, the Messianic Age. And b) the shift, the transition, from historical times to the eschaton will occur through a cataclysmic battle. That's the second component that apocalypticism brings to this. Apocalypticism originates with Zoroastrianism, by the way, and indeed it dovetails nicely with the dualism inherent in this ancient Persian religion that we spoke about in a previous lecture. From Zoroastrianism, this belief filtered into Judaism, especially in the last few centuries of the biblical period, exemplified most of all by the canonical book of Daniel. One finds apocalyptic in other postbiblical Jewish works as well, though the two apocalyptic movements best known to us are the Qumran community and early Christianity.

Connected to the eschatological thought and to the apocalyptic variety as well is the concept of the Messiah. We should add here, accordingly, that in contrast to the early Christian movement that is heavily based on a Messiah concept, the Dead Sea Scrolls are less focused on a single Messiah figure. To illustrate the point, we note that the word "Christ" or "Messiah" appears more than 500 times in the New Testament. *Mešiah*, the Hebrew word on which our English word "Messiah" is based means "the anointment one and Christ" is simply based on the Greek equivalent thereof. So this term appears 500 times in the New Testament. In the much larger Dead Sea Scrolls corpus, the Hebrew word *Mešiah* ("the anointed one," "the Messiah") appears only 32 times; 8 times in the Damascus Document, 1 time in the Community Rule—and we actually referred to that text when we studied that document in Lecture Three—and only 1 time in the War Scroll as well. Again, the Messiah concept is present; much more present in the New Testament: I repeat, 500-plus references in the relatively small corpus of New Testament books, only 32 times does the word "Messiah" appear in the much larger Dead Sea Scrolls corpus.

In the War Scroll, as I mentioned the Hebrew term *Mešiah* ("the anointed one" or "the Messiah") appears only once. It occurs in 1QM 11:7, and it reads as follows: "by the hand of your anointed ones [Messiahs, in the plural], those who discern testimonies, you have told us the end-times of the battles of your hands, to fight against our enemies, to bring down the troops of Belial." Once more we note the plural form "Messiahs," just as we saw in the Community Rule when we discussed that document in Lecture Three. Belial—you've heard me read that word several times now, let me explain that term for you—is a synonym of Satan, the devil figure, the leader of the forces of evil. For the Qumran community, as well as for the early Christians, Belial/Satan/the Devil was a very real figure.

Another apocalyptic text found at Qumran is a document known as the *Rule of the Congregation*; it is also sometimes called the *Messianic Rule*, so it goes by different names. Its designation in the numbering system is 1QSa. This text—and I'm going to give you the quote from the very beginning of that document—provides "the rule for all the congregation of Israel in the last days." Again, it's looking forward to this eschatological period; "the rule for all the congregation of Israel in the last days." Then it goes on—it's a short text of only a couple of columns—it culminates in the communal meal, to be presided over by the Messiah. In addition to 1QM, which is the focus of this lecture in which we get most of our eschatological information about this group, especially the apocalyptic type of eschatology, I did want to note that there was another text found in Cave One, this 1QSa text, which also fits into this. It's not a single document from Qumran, but, as you're seeing here, a second document and then scattered references in some of the other Dead Sea Scrolls as well. Very clearly, this was a group with this apocalyptic belief.

Now some more about the history of scholarship into these Dead Sea Scrolls: Early on in Dead Sea Scrolls research, there were two scholars who believed that the presence of the War Scroll among the Dead Sea Scrolls suggested that they were not Essenes but rather Zealots. These two scholar as, both very, very famous individuals, were G. R. Driver of Oxford University and Chaim Rabin of the Hebrew University in Jerusalem. They figured that if you have this document that lays out military terminology in such detail using all of that material that we know of from the Roman system of warfare, and if that's been adopted by this community—again, I refer to the standards, troop movements, trumpets, and all these kinds of things that we know about from our understanding of ancient Roman warfare—if this group is using this material, then they must have been the Zealots. Let's recall that the Zealots had only one goal, and that was independence from Rome; and they would lead a rebellion in 66 C.E. that culminated in the disastrous destruction of Jerusalem in 70 C.E. and eventually the fall of Masada, the final Zealot holdout, in 73 C.E. So Professor Driver and Professor Rabin, working someone independently, somewhat in tandem with each other, developed the Zealot hypothesis.

Today, most scholars reject this theory; this theory is simply not accepted. But it is worth mentioning here that the Zealot movement may have had apocalyptic beliefs attached to it. When we presented the sects earlier in our course and we talked about the Zealots, we did not mention this apocalyptic factor that is part of the Zealot mention. It's not clear to us, it's certainly not mentioned by Josephus in his description of the Zealots, so we can only take this so far; and we certainly don't have any explicit reference to this with the First Revolt. We do have explicit references concerning the Second Jewish Revolt. The Second Revolt, remember, was led by Simeon Bar-Kokhba in 132–135 C.E. This rebellion was supported by Rabbi Akiba. We mentioned Rabbi Akiba in an earlier lecture, in Lecture Seven, as giving the rabbinic expression to the Pharisaic view that there is room for both predetermination and free will in the Pharisaic/rabbinic conception of things. What I didn't say then—and I now want to say a little bit more about Rabbi Akiba—is that Rabbi Akiba actually supported the Bar-Kokhba rebellion and saw it in Messianic terms. We know of all this from our rabbinic sources, which talk about Rabbi Akiba's support of the Bar-Kokhba rebellion, and from other sources we get this sense, yes, there was an eschatological if not apocalyptic sense to the Second Revolt. So although we don't have explicit evidence for that for the First Revolt, we do have to contend with the possibility that there was to the Zealot movement an apocalypticism for the First Revolt as well. This doesn't mean that Driver and Rabin weren't correct that this scroll means that the entire Qumran community is a Zealot group, we still hold that they are Essenes; but I did want to situate that scholarship from the 1950s and 1960s by two prominent scholars into the larger picture of the Jewish revolts against Rome, and certainly the apocalyptic element in the Second Jewish Revolt.

All of this leads us to ask the question: If the Essenes do have an apocalyptic view built into their philosophy—which they clearly did based on the War Scroll and on the 1QSa text that I mentioned only briefly—if this is all clear from our documents, then why does Josephus not mention the apocalyptic view when he describes the Essenes? You'll recall that he spends more time talking about the Essenes than he does about the Pharisees or the Sadducees, and yet somehow he seems to omit any reference to the apocalyptic view of this group. The answer lies as follows: Josephus was writing his works for an educated Greco-Roman audience, writing in Greek for the general Mediterranean world, and he was writing under Roman patronage. Any hint of apocalypticism, which by definition means opposing or at least having no regard for the civil and/or imperial rule of Rome, would be seen as subversive and treasonous. Yes, the Essenes were apocalyptic as we can determine from the Dead Sea Scrolls, and we also can understand why Josephus omitted reference to this when he talks about the Essenes.

Once more, the Jewish nature of these texts is self-evident: They are written in Hebrew by a group of Jews in the pre-Christian period. Once more, however, as we did at the end of the previous lecture, it may be useful to consider Dead Sea Scrolls-Christian connections once more; and the War Scroll offers for us a major point of contact: the apocalyptic vision that characterizes both the Qumran texts and the New Testament books is a clear point of linkage. In the New Testament, the last book of the canon in the traditional canonical order is known as the Book of Revelation, or alternatively, the Apocalypse.

This lecture and the previous two lectures have been devoted to individual Dead Sea Scrolls texts: the important Damascus Document, the Pesher Habakkuk text, and now the War Scroll. Our detailed readings of these three scrolls have greatly increased our understanding of the beliefs and practices of the Qumran community in all areas: in theology, in religious practice, in *halakha*. Time and again, the close readings of these three texts have given us much information about the Yahad, the Dead Sea Scrolls community. In our next lecture, we will turn our attention away from the sectarian texts found in Qumran, and instead will consider the shape and the nature of the 230 biblical manuscripts that were found in the caves at Qumran.

Biblical Manuscripts at Qumran
Lecture 11

While none of the biblical Dead Sea Scrolls manuscripts can be considered anything like the "autographed original" of, say, Isaiah or Jeremiah, they nevertheless push our knowledge of the biblical text back to ancient times. In this lecture, we enter the arcane world of biblical textual criticism, a scholarly enterprise that attempts to establish the original text of the Bible. We discuss the scribal transmission of texts in antiquity, the oral reading tradition, ancient translations of the Bible, the Samaritan version of the Torah, and most pertinently the biblical manuscripts found in the Qumran caves.

In biblical times, texts were produced in two versions: oral and written. Scribes copied the text over and over again, while tradents transmitted the text orally from generation to generation (though most likely they held a text in their hands as a guide). Before the discovery of the Dead Sea Scrolls, we had evidence of divergent manuscript traditions, especially from the Septuagint. The Septuagint was the first translation of the Bible into any language, but other renderings would follow: Aramaic, Syriac, Latin, and so forth. At times, these translations reflect a different Hebrew text, known as the Vorlage. In the traditional Hebrew text, Exod 1:5 states that 70 Israelites (Jacob and his family) went down to Egypt. In the Septuagint, the text presents the number as 75 Israelites. In the traditional Hebrew text, Deut 32:8 states, "He [i.e., God] set the boundaries of the peoples [i.e., of the world], according to the number of the children of Israel," using the Hebrew phrase *bene yisra'el*. The Septuagint states, "according to the number of angels of God," using the Greek expression *angelôn theou*. The Samaritans had their own version of the Torah, though as all scholars agree, the divergences therein stem from linguistic updating of the older text during the Persian period and from ideological matters.

Before the discovery of the Dead Sea Scrolls, the only authentically ancient Hebrew text that we possessed was the Nash Papyrus, found in Egypt in 1898. A small piece of papyrus of 24 lines dated to about 125 B.C.E., it contains the Decalogue and the beginning of the Shema prayer. Otherwise, our oldest copies of the Bible in Hebrew are medieval manuscripts, in the form of great codices dated to around 900 C.E. (Aleppo Codex) and 1009 C.E. (Leningrad Codex). These works are known as the Masoretic Text, based on the Hebrew word *masora* ("tradition"). When the Dead Sea Scrolls were discovered, we obtained 230 copies of biblical books. Every biblical book except for Esther is represented among the scrolls. The only complete book that we possess is Isaiah, as presented in 1QIsa[a]. Recall that this is a linguistically updated version of the book of Isaiah and that it departs from the Masoretic Text.

The best represented of the biblical books are Psalms, Deuteronomy, and Isaiah, with 34, 27, and 24 copies, respectively. As another linkage to early Christianity, these are also the most cited books in the New Testament. Ranking next are other books of the Torah: Genesis, Exodus, and Leviticus (20, 13, and 9 copies, respectively), and then the 12 minor prophets and Daniel (with 8 copies each)—the latter attesting to the apocalyptic component prevalent in the Qumran sect. Furthermore, in the case of the Daniel manuscripts, dated to about 125–100 B.C.E., these documents were copied only several decades after the book (or at least its second part) was composed in 164 B.C.E., the year of the Maccabean revolt. Nine copies of books of the Torah are written in the paleo-Hebrew script. In other copies, the Qumran scribes wrote the four-letter name of God, YHWH in the ancient script, though the rest of the document is written in the newer script.

The Qumran manuscripts adhere to what would emerge as the Masoretic Text most of the time but diverge at others. We noted above a minor discrepancy between the Masoretic Text and the Septuagint concerning Exod 1:5. We posited that the LXX translators had a different Vorlage, a different Hebrew text, one that read 75, instead of 70—and then, among the Dead Sea Scrolls, we find 4QExod[a], which also reads 75! There is a discrepancy in Deut 32:8, with the Masoretic Text reading "according to the number of the children of Israel" and the Septuagint reading "according to the number of angels of God." The Septuagint translators must have had a Vorlage akin to these Qumran texts. In 1 Samuel 11, the Masoretic Text commences a story with no apparent background. 4QSam[a] supplies several verses before reaching 1 Sam 11:1, thereby providing the background of the story. Some of the manuscripts, such as 1QIs^{aa}, present a linguistically updated text, sometimes with features of Qumran Hebrew included.

When did all these variations in the actual text of the Bible die out? The answer is not long after the end of the Qumran period. Our evidence comes from other locations near the Dead Sea, including Masada and several caves in the vicinity of Ein Gedi. At Masada several biblical documents were found that all match the later Masoretic Text very closely. The caves near Ein Gedi are from the Bar Kokhba period also matching the Masoretic Text. All of this indicates that some time in the late 1st or early 2nd century C.E., variant texts no longer were countenanced by Jews. Does this have to do with the end of Jewish sectarianism? Scholars once thought so, but we cannot be so certain any more.

When did all these variations in the actual text of the Bible die out?

The biblical manuscripts found among the Dead Sea Scrolls teach us much about the transmission of the biblical text over the course of long periods of time. Notwithstanding some important differences from manuscript to manuscript, overall one is impressed by the degree of coherence between the Qumran copies and the medieval codices. ∎

Essential Reading

VanderKam, *The Dead Sea Scrolls Today*, 29–33, 121–141.

VanderKam and Flint, *The Meaning of the Dead Sea Scrolls*, 87–153.

Schiffman, *Reclaiming the Dead Sea Scrolls*, 161–180.

Shanks, *The Dead Sea Scrolls after Forty Years*, 56–73.

Abegg, Flint, and Ulrich, *The Dead Sea Scrolls Bible*.

Supplementary Reading

Tov, *Textual Criticism of the Hebrew Bible*.

Questions to Consider

1. Are any of the variants from text to text discussed in this lecture truly crucial?

2. Do you think the scribes and tradents of antiquity, especially those of ancient Israel and postbiblical Judaism, performed their tasks responsibly or sloppily?

Biblical Manuscripts at Qumran
Lecture 11—Transcript

As noted in the very first lecture of this course, approximately one-fourth of the 930 individual Dead Sea Scrolls documents are biblical manuscripts. These copies of the biblical books are approximately 1,000 years older than our next oldest copies, which date to the early Middle Ages. While none of these manuscripts can be considered anything like the "autographed original" of, say, Isaiah or Jeremiah, they nevertheless push our knowledge of the biblical text back to ancient times, and in some cases, we can aver that the copies found at Qumran date to only two or three centuries from the date of composition. In this lecture, we will enter the arcane world of textual criticism; that is, the scholarly enterprise that attempts to establish the original text of the Bible, or any other document or anthology. We will discuss the scribal transmission of texts in antiquity, the oral reading tradition, the ancient translation of the Bible into Greek known as the Septuagint, the Samaritan version of the Torah, and most pertinently the biblical manuscripts found in the Qumran caves. We will illustrate this entire process with key passages from books such as Exodus, Deuteronomy, and Samuel.

In biblical times, texts were produced in two versions: an oral and a written. The best evidence for this process comes from Exodus 17:14; this is the first time in the Bible that the word "write" is used, and the passage reads as follows: God is commanding Moses, "Write this (as) a memorial in a book, and place (it) in the ears of Joshua." What you see here from the two halves of this commandment by God is to write it down in a book, in a written document—the Hebrew word is *seper*, we translate it as "book" even though in reality "book" is a much later invention; it means a written document of any sort in its ancient context—"Write this (as) a memorial in a book, and place (it) in the ears of Joshua." What this means is that the text was written down using the 22 letters of the Hebrew alphabet—which, I must add, are only consonants; there are no vowels, we'll talk about the vowels in a few moments—so you write it down, the 22 letter alphabet provides you the consonants, and then you place it in the ears of Joshua.

What does that mean? What that means is that Moses, as the presumed author of whatever is being written here, needs to teach the reading of this text to the next generation, represented here by Joshua. Then, over time, scribes copied the text over and over again as necessary, as a particular written version or a particular copy became worn out or illegible; while another group of individuals—whom we call tradents, from our word "tradition"—transmitted the text orally from generation to generation. If we take the biblical text at face value, Moses writes it down; his copy, when it becomes worn is rewritten by some other scribe; and he teaches the reading of this text to Joshua. When Joshua gets old—this is not stated explicitly, but we're recreating; bear with me as I recreate this little world of the transmission of biblical texts in antiquity—Joshua, in turn, would teach the reading of this to the next generation of whoever is his successor. So it goes, being passed down in two forms: the written form by scribes, the oral form by the tradents. The tradents knew the proper reading of the text—the accentuation, the punctuation, all of this—though most likely they held the written texts in their hand as a guide, this text only had (I repeat) the 22-letter alphabet, all consonants, no punctuation marks, it doesn't tell you where to pause; all of that was known by oral tradition.

Before the discovery of the Dead Sea Scrolls, we had evidence of divergent manuscript traditions, especially from the Septuagint; or, as it's called for short, the LXX, based on the tradition that 72 Jewish scholars translated the Torah into Greek. This translation was accomplished by the Jews of Alexandria in approximately 250 B.C.E., and I referred to this in an earlier lecture: This enterprise was sponsored by King Ptolemy II in Alexandria. The other books of the Bible were rendered about a century later; so eventually the Septuagint, while strictly referring to the Torah or Pentateuch only, comes to be used for the entire Bible, translated into Greek by the Jews of the Greek-speaking city of Alexandria in Egypt. Eventually the Bible was translated into other languages as well, as Jews rendered the text into Aramaic—we used the word Targum in a previous lecture; these would be Targumim, Jewish renderings of the biblical texts into the Aramaic language—and then Christians also were translating the Bible, the biblical books, into Syriac and Latin, for example. At times, these translations—in Greek, Syriac, Latin, etc.—reflect a different Hebrew text, known as the Vorlage. "Vorlage" is a German word; it means literally "that which lies before." It refers to the Hebrew text that must have been lying in front of the translators when they sat down to render the text into, let's say, Greek in the case of the case of the Jewish translators in Ptolemaic Alexandria.

Let me present here two minor examples of where the traditional Hebrew text and the Greek translation part company. First one: In the traditional Hebrew text—and what I mean by that we'll explain in just a moment—Exod. 1:5 states that 70 Israelites (Jacob and his family) went down to Egypt. In the LXX, in the Septuagint, however, the Greek text presents the number as 75 Israelites. A minor discrepancy of no major theological value here, whether it's 70 or 75; nevertheless, a discrepancy in different versions of the text: Hebrew says 70, Greek says 75. A second example: In the traditional Hebrew text—and again, we will discuss what I mean by that in just a moment—Deut. 32:8 states, "He [the reference here is God] set the boundaries of the peoples [the peoples of the world], according to the number of the children of Israel," and it uses the Hebrew phrase *bene yisra'el* (the children of Israel). The Septuagint, however, states that God did this, "according to the number of angels of God"; not "according to the number of the children of Israel" as per the Hebrew text traditionally transmitted, but rather "according to the number of angels of God." The phrase at the end is changed: Instead of "children of Israel" (Hebrew: *bene yisra'el*), this Greek Septuagint text reads "the angels of God" using the Greek expression *angelôn theou*.

The Samaritans, by the way, had their own version of the Torah, though as all scholars agree, the divergences in the Samaritan Pentateuch stem from a) linguistic updating of the older text during the Persian period when the Samaritan group started; and b) ideological matters, such as the Samaritan insistence that God is to be worshipped on Mount Gerizim near Shechem. You'll remember that we talked about the Samaritans in a previous lecture.

Before the discovery of the Dead Sea Scrolls, the only authentically ancient Hebrew text that we possessed was a small papyrus called the Nash Papyrus, found in Egypt in 1898 (by the way, not connected in any way to the Cairo genizah, the subject of an earlier lecture). This small piece of papyrus, 24 lines, dates to approximately 125 B.C.E., and it contains the Decalogue (the Ten Commandments) and the beginning of the *Shema* prayer from the book of Deuteronomy, the central *Shema* prayer in Jewish ritual. Incidentally, the papyrus is named for a certain Mr. W. L. Nash, who obtained the fragment while traveling in Cairo and then donated it to the Cambridge University Library where it remains on display today.

Otherwise, our oldest copies of the Bible in Hebrew, before the discovery of the Dead Sea Scrolls and excepting the very small Nash Papyrus, are medieval manuscripts in the form of great codices—codices, the plural of codex; that is, the complete book versions. A codex is very similar to the book format that we're familiar with today—and these codices, the two major codices that we have, date to approximately 900 C.E. (that's called the Aleppo Codex; it was kept in Aleppo, Syria into the 20th century and then it's now housed in Jerusalem) and a second codex called the Leningrad Codex dated to 1009 C.E. It still bears the name of the former Soviet city Leningrad because this text was published when the city was called Leningrad; obviously the city is again today called Saint Petersburg, and one can find this text still housed in the Saint Petersburg library. These two works—these two major codices of the early Middle Ages, the 10th and 11th centuries—the Aleppo Codex and the Leningrad Codex, are known as the Masoretic Text, based on the Hebrew word Masora, which means "tradition," since these copies were handed down both orally and in writing in the traditional manner by Jews for hundreds of years in line with the process that I described earlier. These codices, moreover, from the early Middle Ages include the recently created written notation of the vowels, accentuation, and punctuation; remember I said that the original text, the format in ancient Hebrew, was to write with the consonants only without the vowels, no accent marks, no punctuate. All of that was created by a group of people called the Masoretes, and this collective process is called the Masora, the tradition created about 800 C.E. Writing down, the ability to now notate in writing, the oral reading tradition that had been passed down; and our medieval codices have all of those vowels and punctuation marks.

Then the Dead Sea Scrolls were discovered during the years 1947–54, revealing 230 copies of the biblical books. Every biblical book except for Esther is represented among the scrolls. This is probably not a coincidence, but rather stems from several facts: One, the book of Esther does not mention God; it's the only book of the Bible in which there's no reference to God. Two, the scene is in distant Persia as opposed to the land of Israel, and the

Qumran community may have just seen that too far removed geographically and culturally and therefore had no concern for the book of Esther. Three, for those of you who've read the book of Esther, you know that the story itself can be rather bawdy at times, and this may also have been somewhat off-putting to the Qumran community. For any variety of reasons, the book of Esther was not present in the mindset, and therefore among the documents, of the Dead Sea Scroll community. Incidentally, some ancient readers were disturbed by these aspects of the book of Esther—I should add this point here—and thus entire sections were added by later scribes that include prayers by the main characters, Esther and Mordecai, directed towards God. These additions were included in the Septuagint and eventually in the Latin version of the Bible called the Vulgate produced by Saint Jerome, and thus these additions to Esther are included in the Christian canon in the Orthodox and Catholic traditions, though these additions were never part of the Jewish canon, and they are also not part of the Protestant biblical canon.

The only complete book— back to Qumran now—that we possess among the Dead Sea Scrolls is the book of Isaiah, as presented in 1QIsa^a, which we discussed earlier in Lecture Two. You will recall that 1QIsa^a is a linguistically updated version of the book of Isaiah, and thus it departs from our Masoretic Text of Isaiah, which we believe to be more traditional, even though the copies are from the Middle Ages, in spelling, wording, and so on. You'll remember that I just used the expression "linguistically updated" a few moments ago in reference to the Samaritan Torah. The Samaritans were producing a Torah with linguistic updating, and at Qumran the Dead Sea Scrolls community was doing the same thing, at least with certain texts as we have with 1QIsa^a. As it is, it is the only (to repeat) complete copy of a biblical book in the Dead Sea Scrolls corpus.

The best represented of the biblical books at Qumran—which were the books they were reading the most, which were the books they were copying the most—are Psalms, Deuteronomy, and Isaiah; 34 copies of Psalms, 27 of Deuteronomy, and 24 of Isaiah, respectively. As another linkage to early Christianity, we note that these three books—Psalms, Deuteronomy, and Isaiah—are also the most cited books in the New Testament. Ranking next, incidentally, are other books of the Torah—Genesis, Exodus, and Leviticus, with 20, 13, and 9 copies respectively—and then what's called the Book of the Twelve, that is to say, the 12 minor prophets, which are considered a single book in Jewish tradition, and then the book of Daniel with 8 copies each. This attests to the very prominent apocalyptic component prevalent in the Qumran sect. In the case of the Daniel manuscripts, which are dated to circa 125–100 B.C.E., these documents were copied only several decades after the book—or at least the second part of the book of Daniel—was composed in 164 B.C.E., the year of the Maccabean revolt. Earlier I said that our biblical manuscripts at Qumran are centuries removed from the dating of these books, but in this case with Daniel we're only talking about a few decades, a half-century at the most.

Earlier in our course we noted that only those books written before the rise of Hellenism were included in the Jewish canon; and thus dating Daniel as I just did to 164 B.C.E. would seem to be a problem. However, since parts of the book of Daniel are set in the court of the Babylonian king Nebuchadnezzar, who reigned during the 6th century B.C.E., the later Jewish sages who read this book believed that Daniel was an older composition; they were not aware of the fact that it dates to the Maccabean period. Scholars have been able to determine that Daniel dates to the Maccabean period, though, based on its contents, along with the presence of several Greek words in the text. That's just a long footnote about the book of Daniel, written in the Maccabean Period, nevertheless entering the Jewish canon because the readers of the book of Daniel believed that the book was actually centuries older than we scholars today indeed know.

Nine copies of books of the Torah are written in the Paleo-Hebrew script. What is all that about? The Hebrew script changed over the course of time; there was an older script that was in use in ancient Israel, and we call that the Paleo-Hebrew script. If we find inscriptions in archeological excavations from Israel from the Biblical Period—and we do find such inscriptions—they are written in the Paleo-Hebrew script. Sometime during the Persian Period, in the 5th century B.C.E. let's say, Jewish scribes changed the script. It's the same 22 letters, but the forms were now altered—over the course of time letter forms change—and they started using what we call the more standard Hebrew script or the more standard Jewish script. A modern analogy if it helps you is the gothic script that once was used for the writing of German, although today German uses the Latin script. Of course, we can still see the gothic script in use occasionally as we can see in the *New York Times* masthead, for example.

At other times, the Qumran scribes would write the four-letter name of God—in Hebrew יהוה, the equivalent English letters would be YHWH; scholars reconstruct the pronunciation "Yahweh" for the name of God in antiquity—the entire text written is out in the newer Hebrew script, but the four-letter name of God is written in the ancient script, what we call the Paleo-Hebrew script; so the scribes were doing different things: by and large, using the new Jewish or Hebrew script, occasionally writing documents in the old Paleo-Hebrew script still, and occasionally just inserting God's name in the Paleo-Hebrew script into what was otherwise a document using the newer script.

As we noted earlier in our course, some of these manuscripts have been submitted to carbon-14 dating, and the results of these tests match the paleographic analysis. What is paleography? Paleography is the study of handwriting, and the experts who have analyzed the Dead Sea Scrolls have told us that the texts date to the 3rd, 2nd, and 1st centuries B.C.E.; obviously that's the main approach that we've been using in this course, dating these scrolls to the last few centuries B.C.E. Then you can actually test this in a laboratory once the carbon-14 test became available and became a more accurate laboratory test, and indeed a portion of 1QIsa^a—a tiny little fragment was taken off at the end, we didn't lose any ink or anything like that, anything with any writing on it; it was just a blank part of the parchment—was submitted to a carbon-14 test, and the carbon-14 test assigned the dates with a range of 202–107 B.C.E.; that is to say, in the 2nd century B.C.E., exactly where paleographic experts who inspected the manuscript before the carbon-14 test was performed had dated this very large document 1QIsa^a.

The Qumran manuscripts adhere to a great extent to what would emerge as the Masoretic Text—which we talked about as the great early medieval project of the Masoretes, the traditional Jewish transmission of the text—most of the time. This demonstrates that our medieval copies are accurate transmissions of the ancient text, since we now have manuscript evidence from the Dead Sea Scrolls approximately 1,000 years earlier than the Aleppo Codex or the Leningrad Codex, which can confirm the point I'm making here.

On the other hand, one must note, at times the Qumran manuscripts diverge from the medieval Masoretic copies. Let me present for you some examples: Earlier we noted a minor discrepancy between the Masoretic Text (MT) and the Septuagint (the LXX) concerning Exodus 1:5. The Masoretic Text reads 70, while the Greek version reads 75. We posited that the Septuagint translators had a different Vorlage, a different Hebrew text, in front of them when they set out to translate this portion of Exodus, one that read in Hebrew 75 instead of 70. Then, among the Dead Sea Scrolls comes a fragment of the book of Exodus that reads 75. We now actually have a Hebrew text that says 75. For those of you who like to keep track of the designations of these texts, that text is 4QExod[a].

Another example: Again, as we saw earlier, there is a discrepancy in Deut. 32:8, with the Masoretic Text stating "according to the number of the children of Israel" at the end of the verse, while the Septuagint states "according to the number of angels of God." Let me add here the beginning of that verse; let me read the beginning of that verse to you: "When the Most High apportioned the nations, when he divided humankind, he set the boundaries of the peoples, according to the number of the children of Israel," or "according to the number of angels of God," as per the Septuagint reading. Again, once more, we have evidence from Qumran to support the LXX reading. Indeed, two Dead Sea Scroll fragments, 4QDeut[j] and 4QDeut[q], read "sons of God"—the Hebrew expression there is *bene 'el*—not quite "angels of God" as per the Septuagint, but let me explain that point in just a moment. First, though, I just want to reiterate what I just said here: Did you notice the names of these texts? 4QDeut[j] and 4QDeut[q]. Remember I said that Deuteronomy is one of the best-attested books amongst the Dead Sea Scrolls; therefore, we're already down to the letter "q" in our alphabet as we keep track of all the Deuteronomy texts that come out of Cave Four.

Back to this expression *bene 'el*, literally "sons of God": The original connotation of the Hebrew phrase *bene 'el* was to the pantheon of old which numbered 70 deities, as we know from the Ugaritic texts from ancient Canaan, for example; and this number in turn, according to the author of Deuteronomy 32, matches the 70 nations of humanity which one can see presented in Gen. 10. So the 70 gods of the pantheon relate to the 70 nations of humanity. This was a somewhat polytheistic sense of the text obviously, but the people of ancient Israel were not too worried about this; and that's because in ancient Israel before the development of a pure monotheism, we actually have something called a monolatry: the worship of one god, but it countenances the existence of other gods at least; it doesn't deny their existence altogether which is what monotheism would do. We have the shift in the biblical period 6th century B.C.E. from monolatry to monotheism; so when this text in Deuteronomy was written at an earlier period, *bene 'el* simply meant "the gods," "the sons of god," which is a Hebrew way of saying the deities at large.

Later Jews could not countenance the idea, once they were monotheists, that there could be a reference here to other gods. The result was a shift in meaning of the expression *bene 'el* no longer meaning "sons of God" per se but now coming to mean "angels"; and therefore the Jewish scribes could continue the tradition of copying this text with the words *bene 'el*. That is to say, it no longer means the gods of old, the pagan pantheon, but can refer to the angels because there is a semantic shift in this text. Other Jewish scribes, however, didn't like the expression *bene 'el* because they had a sense that this referred to gods even if latter-day readers understood it as angels; and therefore they changed it to *bene yisra'el*, the children of Israel. In Deuteronomy 32:8 we don't have *bene 'el* in the Masoretic tradition, we have instead *bene yisra'el*. But at Qumran, there were still scribes who didn't want to alter the text; they kept *bene 'el* exactly as the text was transmitted to them, although clearly they understood it as "angels." Then when the Septuagint translators sat down to translate a Hebrew text that no doubt said *bene 'el*, they rendered it with the Greek equivalent, and that would be "the angels of God." A complicated story for you there, but it gives you an indication of what goes on in this arcane field of textual criticism as we compare and contrast different readings of the text and different translations of the text into other languages such as Greek.

Another example of where a Dead Sea Scroll diverges from the Masoretic Text; in this case, not in a particular word or phrase, but in a much larger way. 1 Samuel 11: The Masoretic Text here simply commences a story with no apparent background; but a very important document from Qumran, 4QSam[a], supplies several verses before reaching 1 Sam 11:1, thereby providing the background of the story. For example, in the Dead Sea Scrolls text, the character Nahash is introduced as "Nahash, king of the children of Ammon"—Ammon is a country neighboring Israel to the east—as befitting a first reference to this individual: Nahash, king of the children of Ammon. The Masoretic Text, by contrast, simply says "Nahash the Ammonite," not giving us a sense that he's the king. Clearly there appear to have been some verses that were missing beforehand in the Masoretic Text that 4QSam^a now provides for us; and the background is as follows: Nahash has oppressed the tribes of Gad and Reuben in Transjordan and had gouged out the right eyes of all the Israelite men; and only then did Nahash besiege of Jabesh-gilead, a city of the territory of Gad, which is what led the people of this city to propose a vassal treaty and service to Nahash. That's in the Bible, but without the background information of Nahash having done what he did to the people of this territory of Israel, we would not gain a sense of what's really going on in the story; and in this way, 4QSam^a provides for us very important information. in addition, some of the manuscripts are similar to 1QIsa^a in that they present a linguistically-updated text—so we may have a manuscript of Song of Songs that does that, or we may have a manuscript of Jeremiah that does that, for example—and sometimes these linguistic updating are features that are characteristic of Qumran Hebrew; and again, I keep talking about Qumran Hebrew in our course, I will devote a lecture to exactly what that means later on in our course.

You may ask: When did all these variations—70, 75, sons of God, angels of God, and so on—in the actual text of the Bible die out? The answer is not long after the end of the Qumran period. Our evidence comes from other locations near the Dead Sea, including Masada from the 1st century C.E. at the southern end of the Dead Sea, and several caves in the vicinity of Ein Gedi—Ein Gedi located in the middle of the Dead Sea along the western shore of it—from the 2nd century C.E. At Masada, several biblical documents were found; incidentally, the excavator of Masada is Professor Yigael Yadin whom we referred to in our lecture on the War Scroll, he's also the great archaeologist who excavated Masada, the last Zealot holdout in the First Revolt against the Romans. There, in Yadin's excavations he found biblical manuscripts including a fragment of Deuteronomy; and all of these manuscripts match the later Masoretic Texts very closely. Then, in the caves near Ein Gedi—in between, located between Qumran and Masada—these date from the Bar Kokhba period, and, in fact, these caves yielded letters written by the leader of the Second Revolt himself, Simeon bar Kokhba. From these caves, we also get biblical manuscripts.

In one cave, at a place called Wadi Muraba'at, archaeologists found an Exodus fragment that matches our later medieval codices 600–700 years later based on the Masoretic Text exactly, letter for letter. At another cave, at a place called Nahal Hever, archaeologists found a Greek version of the Minor Prophets—the book of the Twelve, Hosea through Malachi—but in this case the Greek translation does not follow the Septuagint anymore, but rather it adheres more closely to the Masoretic Text. That is to say, Jews in the land of Israel were reading the Bible in Greek, but they had altered the old Greek translation so that it now matched more closely the traditional Hebrew version. From the late 1st and early 2nd century, we seem to have now a uniform Hebrew text; the variants that we see at Qumran no longer were countenanced by Jews as far as our evidence demonstrates. Instead, the Jewish community had coalesced around a single text type for the Bible. Does this have to do with the end of Jewish sectarianism? Once upon a time, scholars may have thought so, but given what we said earlier in this course, we cannot be certain anymore; it may simply have been an independent thrust.

In short, the biblical manuscripts found amongst the Dead Sea Scrolls teach us much about the transmission of the biblical text over the course of long periods of time. Notwithstanding some important differences from manuscript to manuscript, overall one is impressed by the degree of coherence between the Qumran copies and the medieval codices, with about 1,000 years separating the two groups of texts.

Alternative Views of Qumran and the Scrolls
Lecture 12

We have presented the majority opinion concerning the Dead Sea Scrolls. To be fair, we must mention competing views.

We have proceeded on the assumption that Qumran was an Essene community that, in advance of the arrival of the Roman army, deposited their scrolls in nearby caves. But other scholarly opinions have been offered. Why is this? Generally speaking, in the academy, scholars are willing to go out on a limb to offer something truly original, even if it means (at times) stretching the evidence to the limit and then some. The fascination with the Dead Sea Scrolls, especially since these precious documents date to the cusp of the bifurcation of Judaism and Christianity, seems to have generated a public ready to consume any theory that somehow sounds new and innovative. Because we have so much new evidence, sometimes pointing in different directions, and because prior to the discovery of the scrolls so little was known about the 1st century B.C.E. in this area, in many ways there was room for any individual scholar to spawn a new theory.

Returning to Golb's view: Although I (along with the vast majority of scholars) do not accept it, Golb has forced those who adhere to the Essene opinion to focus our argument a bit better. It is quite clear that the scrolls present Essene beliefs and practices in many places. There is also the manner in which key phrases repeat in the scrolls: "Sons of light" (Hebrew *bene 'or*) and "sons of darkness" (Hebrew *bene hošek*) occur in both the War Scroll and in the Community Rule; "Teacher of Righteousness" (Hebrew *moreh zedeq*) appears in the Damascus Document, the Pesher Habakkuk, and 4Q171 = 4QpPs[a], 4Q173 = 4QpPs[b], and 4Q172 = 4QpUnid. "Wicked Priest" (Hebrew *ha-kohen ha-raša'*) appears in Pesher Habakkuk and again in 4Q163 = 4QpIsa[c] and 4Q171 = 4QpPs[a].

To my mind, these and other examples demonstrate that the documents cohere as a corpus, or at least a significant number of them cohere as sectarian documents. Of course, Golb is correct that not all the documents belong to the single sect, since many of the texts (about 250) belong to a common Judaism of the time. But this number is outweighed by the 350 "sectually explicit" texts. In short, Golb has issued an important challenge to the majority opinion, but his counter-approach does not bear up to scrutiny.

Alternative Interpretations

- When the scrolls first were discovered, Solomon Zeitlin went against the scholarly consensus by proclaiming that the scrolls were of medieval origin. This idiosyncratic view had no followers.

- G. R. Driver and Chaim Rabin believed that the Dead Sea Scrolls community had Zealot connections. They have found latter-day adherents in Michael Wise and Robert Eisenman.

- Norman Golb believes that the scrolls have no connection to the nearby archaeological site nor to the Essenes. He opines that the scrolls represent the library of the Jerusalem Temple, which was brought to the caves in the months before the Romans entered Jerusalem.

- Robert Eisenman believes that many if not most of the scrolls date to the 1st century C.E. In addition to positing Zealot connections, he identifies James the Just, the brother of Jesus, as the Teacher of Righteousness. (None of this can be correct based on the carbon-14 dating of the scrolls.)

- Barbara Theiring also believes that the scrolls originate in the 1st century C.E., with specific connections to early Christianity, though she goes even further by claiming that the Teacher of Righteousness is John the Baptist and that the Wicked Priest is Jesus.

- Jose O'Callaghan believed that 7Q5, written in Greek, is a copy of Mark 6:52–53. In truth, the only complete word in this tiny Greek fragment is the word *kai* ("and"), from which one cannot build an entire theory.

- Yizhar Hirschfeld, Yitzhak Magen, and Yuval Peleg deny a connection between Khirbet Qumran and the scrolls in the caves. They believe that the archaeological site is first and foremost a fortress, with some farming and trading in the area.

- Lena Cansdale believes that Qumran was an important commercial center on a north-south trade route through the Jordan Valley and the Dead Sea, with a spur to Jerusalem.

- Robert Donceel and Pauline Donceel-Voute posit that Qumran was a villa or manor house, inhabited by wealthy individuals.

- Jean-Baptiste Humbert has developed a hybrid view. He agrees with the Donceels that Qumran began as a villa rustica but believes that the Dead Sea Scrolls sect later occupied the site.

Finally, Lawrence Schiffman believes that the sect originated within the Sadducee movement. He bases this judgment on several important connections between various Halakhic views expressed in the scrolls and the same views attributed to the Sadducees in rabbinic texts. ■

Essential Reading

VanderKam, *The Dead Sea Scrolls Today*, 23–26, 92–97.

VanderKam and Flint, *The Meaning of the Dead Sea Scrolls*, 311–320.

Shanks, *The Dead Sea Scrolls after Forty Years*, 1–17.

Golb, *Who Wrote the Dead Sea Scrolls?*

Questions to Consider

1. Why are there so many divergent views concerning Qumran and the Dead Sea Scrolls? What is it about this subject that generates so many different opinions?

2. Has the argument presented at the end of this lecture sufficiently responded to Norman Golb's challenge?

Alternative Views of Qumran and the Scrolls
Lecture 12—Transcript

Until this point, we have presented the majority opinion concerning the Dead Sea Scrolls: The scrolls were written at Qumran by a Jewish sect identified with the Essenes. With the advance of the Roman army in 68 C.E. the members of the sect hid the scrolls in the nearby caves for safekeeping. To be fair, however, we need to mention other competing views. Norman Golb of the University of Chicago, for example, believes that there is no connection whatsoever between the site of Khirbet Qumran and the documents found in the caves; instead, he holds that the documents represent the library of the Temple in Jerusalem, brought to the caves during the war against Rome for safekeeping. A group of Israeli archaeologists, most notably Yizhar Hirschfeld, believes that Khirbet Qumran represents a fortress, once more with no connection to the scrolls found in the nearby caves. Yet a third view is advocated by a Belgian academic couple, Robert Donceel and Pauline Donceel-Voute: They reconstruct a wealthy villa from the ruins of Qumran. A hybrid view is proposed by Jean-Baptiste Humbert: In his view, Qumran began as a villa rustica, after which the Essenes arrived and inhabited the site. Then there are those who propose connections with other Jewish sects, including the Sadducees and Zealots. All of these will be surveyed in this lecture as we bring our course to its halfway point.

Let us now proceed to a detailed presentation and analysis of these and other views. As you obviously realize, we have presented the material in this course based on the assumption, following the dominant scholarly hypothesis as I've just noted, that the archaeological site of Khirbet Qumran was the site of an Essene community who, in advance of the arrival of the Roman legions, deposited their precious scrolls in the nearby caves in the cliffs above. We should note, however, that other scholarly opinions have been offered, concerning both the nature and origin of the scrolls and the nature and origin of the archaeological site. Before listing these alternative views, perhaps we should explain why so many opinions have been proffered by scholars. First, generally speaking, in the academy, scholars are willing to "go out on the limb" to some extent to offer something truly original, even if it means at times stretching the evidence to the limit and then some. Second, the fascination with the Dead Sea Scrolls in particular, especially since these documents date to the century before Jesus at the cusp of the bifurcation of Judaism and Christianity, seems to have generated a public ready to consume any theory that somehow sounds new and innovative. Finally, because we have so much new evidence, sometimes pointing in different directions, and because prior to the discovery of the Scrolls so little was known about the 1st century B.C.E. in particular, in many ways there was room for any individual scholar to spawn a new theory.

Now to these different theories, many of which are idiosyncratic to a single scholar. First, when the scrolls first were discovered in the late 1940s and early 1950s, Solomon Zeitlin of Dropsie College, located in the city of Philadelphia, went against the scholarly consensus by proclaiming that the scrolls were not ancient but rather were of medieval origin. This idiosyncratic view had no followers. Zeitlin, incidentally, was clearly one of the greatest scholars of Second Temple Judaism; and, in fact, his book entitled *The Rise and Fall of the Judean State: A Political, Social and Religious History of the Second Commonwealth*, published in 1962, was for many years the standard treatment of our subject. Let me add a personal note: Zeitlin was one of my teacher's teachers. That is to say, my main mentor was Professor Cyrus Gordon, one of the greatest biblical scholars of the 20th century, and one of his main teachers way back in the late 1920s when Professor Gordon was a university student was Solomon Zeitlin.

A second view, which we've already referred to in our course, earlier in Lecture 10: G.R. Driver and Chaim Rabin believed that the Dead Sea Scrolls community had Zealot connections. They have found latter-day adherents to this theory in Michael Wise of the University of Chicago and Robert Eisenman; we'll return to Robert Eisenman in just a moment. Norman Golb of the University of Chicago, as I mentioned at the outset, believes that the scrolls found in the caves have no connection to the nearby archaeological site, or to the sect of the Essenes. Instead, Golb believes that the scrolls represent the library of the Jerusalem Temple, representing a host of Jewish views that were brought to the caves in the months before the Romans entered Jerusalem. Golb first expressed his view in two articles written in 1980 and in 1985, but only upon the publication of his article entitled "The Dead Sea Scrolls—A New Perspective," which appeared in the journal *The American Scholar* (volume 58, published in Spring 1989—the journal is published by the Phi Beta Kappa society—did Golb's opinion reach the public discourse and thereby elicit responses from scholars devoted the Essene hypothesis. Golb then developed this view further in his book entitled *Who Wrote The Dead Sea Scrolls?: The Search For The Secret Of Qumran*, published in 1996. I should point out that Professor Golb comes to the subject as an outsider. He is an authority in Jewish history of the Middle Ages, working mainly on Judeo-Arabic materials, including documents from the Cairo genizah; plus he has written an important history of the Jews of Normandy. We will return to Professor Golb's ideas later in this lecture.

I return now to Robert Eisenman, whom I mentioned earlier. He teaches at California State University in Long Beach. Eisenman believes that many, if not most, of the scrolls date to the 1st century C.E. In addition to positing Zealot connections—which I referred to just a moment ago—Eisenman identifies James the Just, the brother of Jesus, a character known from the New Testament, as the Teacher of Righteousness referred to in the Pesher Habakkuk and other Qumran documents. As such, according to Eisenman, the Dead Sea Scrolls have a very direct link to early Christianity. None of this, however, can be correct, because the carbon-14 dating of the scrolls—which we also addressed in a previous lecture—provides dates in the 2nd and 1st centuries B.C.E.; that is, too early to have any direct relation to the Jesus movement in the 1st century C.E. Of all the documents that have been submitted to a carbon-14 analysis, the only one that comes close to the 1st century C.E., or that can be dated to the 1st century C.E., is the Thanksgiving Hymns, the Hodayot Scroll known as 1QH. We referred to it early on in our course, and we will devote a forthcoming lecture to the Thanksgiving Hymns. It dates, according to the carbon-14 test, to 21 C.E. plus or minus 40 years, which means it can go from either 21 B.C.E. as late as 61 C.E. But apart from this one document, all the other scrolls—I repeat—that have been submitted to the carbon-14 test that gives us a relatively accurate dating fall into the 1st and 2nd centuries B.C.E.; again, far too early to have any direct connection to the Jesus movement or to James the Just in particular as Eisenman would have it.

Yet another scholar, Barbara Theiring, an independent researcher in Australia, also believes that the Dead Sea Scrolls originate in the 1st century with specific connections to early Christianity; though Theiring goes even further by claiming that the Teacher of Righteousness—that key figure whom we have met in a number of Dead Sea Scrolls—is to be identified with John the Baptist, and that the opponent of the teacher, known as the Wicked Priest, is Jesus. Again, a very idiosyncratic view to Barbara Theiring; and again, the same issues concerning Professor Eisenman's approach are true here as well: The carbon-14 dating of these scrolls do not allow connection to 1st century C.E. material.

Another scholar: Jose O'Callaghan, a Spanish Jesuit. He looked at a single text that we call 7Q5; and again, you all know the scholarly parlance by now: This means a text found in Qumran Cave 7, text number five. It is one of the Greek documents that emerges from Cave 11 in Qumran; you will recall earlier on in our course that we referred to the fact that while the vast majority of material is written in Hebrew, there also are texts in Aramaic, and a small number—about 20 of them—written in Greek. Father O'Callaghan believes that this small fragment, only a few centimeters wide and a few centimeters high, is a copy of Mark 6:52–53, thus connecting at least one of the scrolls very directly to the New Testament. But it is an extremely tiny fragment, and in truth, the only Greek word that can be read in this tiny little text is the word *kai*, the Greek word for "and"; clearly one of the most common words in any lexicon in any language. Only by reconstructing all the broken words along the edges of this small fragment can Father O'Callaghan justify his claim that this is a portion of Mark 6. Clearly all scholars agree that this is far too little material on which one can build an entire hypothesis.

We now come to some of the archaeologists who've approached the material. As I've surveyed these different opinions—those that are different from the majority view—I've been talking until now about people who've looked at particular scrolls and made connections between scroll this or that and item or century or personage this or that. Three Israeli archaeologists working together—Yizhar Hirschfeld, Yitzhak Magen, and Yuval Peleg—deny a connection between Khirbet Qumran, the site that they have investigated, and the scrolls in the caves. Again, these three individuals are field archaeologists; they study the material culture that comes out of the excavation, they do not read the texts. Regardless, they believe that the archaeological site—as they look at it through their scientifically trained archeological eyes—is first and foremost a fortress with some farming and trading in the area. You'll recall that when we surveyed the buildings that Father de Vaux excavated back in the 1950s, one of them was a defense tower; and from that finding, which everyone agrees to, these three archaeologists—Hirschfeld and his colleagues—build the theory that the site of Qumran was a fortress. Apparently, they would explain the presence of the scrolls in the caves in a manner similar to Professor Golb.

Hirschfeld in particular has been excavating a site on the cliffs above Ein Gedi; Ein Gedi, you will recall, is further south down the Dead Sea shore, south of Qumran on the road to Masada, about halfway down the coast of the Dead Sea. He believes his site on the cliffs above Ein Gedi is indeed the Essene settlement visited by Pliny the Elder; we keep going back to that important text by Pliny. Pliny's words were *infra hos Engada* ("below this is Ein Gedi"); after Pliny has talked about his Essene community that he encountered in his travels in the Dead Sea region, he then says, "Below this is Ein Gedi." We have interpreted that to mean "south of this community is Ein Gedi," but Hirschfeld interprets it topographically, not directionally; and that "below this community is Ein Gedi" means literally on the cliffs above is the Essene community that Hirschfeld believes he has found, and below it is Ein Gedi. Again, other archaeologists who have looked at the material do not agree; nevertheless, this is another theory in the panoply of opinions dealing with Qumran and the archeology of Khirbet-Qumran and the Dead Sea Scrolls.

Another idiosyncratic view, in my opinion, comes from Lena Cansdale, another independent scholar from Australia. She believes that Qumran was an important commercial center on a north-south trade route that ran through the Jordan Valley down to the Dead Sea region, with a spur heading westward to Jerusalem. Again, this is a view to which most scholars—or I should say almost all scholars—do not adhere.

Another archeological viewpoint is forthcoming from two Belgian scholars, the husband and wife team Robert Donceel and Pauline Donceel-Voute. They posit—again, they've looked at the archeological remains of de Vaux's excavations and of succeeding excavations, expeditions, and explorations in the area—that Qumran was a villa or manor house inhabited by wealthy individuals. Thus, for example, the tables that de Vaux identified as writing tables found in a room that he called the scriptorium, this archaeological team interprets these tables not as writing tables but as dining tables in a triclinium. We know of the triclinium and of Roman villas throughout the Mediterranean world, including a superb exemplar from several centuries later at the city of Sepphoris (Hebrew: Zippori) in the Galilee. We actually mentioned this city earlier in Lecture Seven because it was the center of rabbinic activity in the 3rd, 4th, and 5th centuries C.E. One wonders, of course, how Cansdale or the Donceels would explain the 1,100 graves in the cemetery at Qumran; again, we referred to this earlier as well. If it was a trading post, or if this was a villa, why are there 1,100 people buried in a cemetery adjoining the site? On the other hand, many scholars believe that some of the skeletons found in this cemetery date to a later period, probably from Bedouin over the course of the centuries.

Jean-Baptiste Humbert, a French archaeologist, has developed a hybrid view; he's taken some of the preceding information that I've presented and brought it together in the following way: Humbert agrees with the Donceels that Qumran began as a villa rustica, but that the Dead Sea Sect then came and occupied the site. We should note that Roland de Vaux never published his field notes from his excavations in the 1950s; you've heard me refer to his excavations throughout our course, but he never published what's called a final field report. Instead, all of his notes remained in a manuscript form as he left it housed in the library of the École Biblique. De Vaux did produce several articles in the way of a preliminary report, and then he wrote a popular book summarizing the data published in French in 1961, and then revised and expanded and translated into English under the title *Archaeology and the Dead Sea Scrolls* published in 1973. Humbert is the official successor to de Vaux, though, at this point, only after decades have passed. Humbert produced two detailed volumes based on de Vaux's excavations and his own interpretation of the data, these two volumes published in 1994 and 2003; again, 40–50 years later after de Vaux does his excavations. As one can see, Humbert reached a very different conclusion from analyzing the data inherited from de Vaux via his field notes. Incidentally, Humbert and the Donceels actually cooperated at first, though they later separated, apparently after coming to different conclusions about the archaeology of Qumran.

Finally, Lawrence Schiffman of New York University; a very important scholar, we'll be talking more about Professor Schiffman as we progress through our course. He believes that the sect originated within the Sadducee movement. He bases this judgment mainly on several important connections between various Halakhic views expressed in the Scrolls—that is, issues related to the greater subject of Jewish law, *halakha*—and the same views that are attributed to the Sadducees in rabbinic texts. We will return to this presentation of Professor Schiffman when we discuss this issue further of the *halakha* of Qumran in Lecture 16. As I indicated, and I hasten to add here, Professor Schiffman is the leading scholar of the Dead Sea Scrolls in the U.S.; and thus he stands clearly in the mainstream of Qumran scholarship, unlike some of the above individuals, whom I mentioned, have very idiosyncratic views. Schiffman's book, *Reclaiming the Dead Sea Scrolls*, published in 1994 as an example of what I'm suggesting here about this work is, to my mind, the best overview of the Qumran community available, and I commend to you this volume. As I said, we'll continue to engage with Professor Schiffman's views in the lectures ahead.

For the nonce, let us mention that the predestination concept, so strong in the Dead Sea Scrolls, to my mind and the mind of those scholars who do not follow Schiffman, rules out the Sadducees automatically. You'll recall that according to Josephus, the Sadducees held that only man's free will dictates what is to occur.

I want to return now to Professor Golb's view. Although I—along with the vast majority of scholars—do not accept his view, I believe that we all agree that Professor Golb has forced those who adhere to the Essene majority opinion (myself included) to focus our argument a bit better. Let me attempt to do so here: It is quite clear from all that we have said in our course that the scrolls present Essene beliefs and practices in many places. Most importantly, perhaps—the issue to which I was just referring—is the predetermination or predestination position, mentioned by Josephus as a dogma of the Essenes, and which we have seen in the Dead Sea Scrolls documents on several occasions. Then there are several practices, including the initiation rites and the communal lifestyle, both described in the Community Rule found at Qumran that, again, coheres nicely with the description of the Essenes in Josephus's writings.

At this point, however, I wish to present something else—internal to the Dead Sea Scrolls—without consideration of Josephus's presentation of the Essenes, and that is the manner in which key phrases repeat in the Scrolls; and I will use this approach to counter the argument of Professor Golb that the texts from Qumran are the Jerusalem Temple library expressing all different kinds of opinions presumably by all different kinds of Jews in the umbrella that we have referred to as "common Judaism." I already referred to one such item earlier in our course back in Lecture Three: The expressions "sons of light" (in Hebrew, *bene 'or)* and "sons of darkness" (the Hebrew expression is *bene hošek*) occur in both the War Scroll and in the Community Rule (1QS). As I said in the earlier lecture, this point demonstrates a linkage between two key documents. The expression "sons of light" also occurs in two other texts—just to give you their names and numbering according to the way that Qumran scholars refer to these texts; bear with me as I do this for you here and in just a moment with some other texts—the two other places where the expression *bene 'or* or "sons of light" occurs, one of those texts is 4Q177, which we call 4QCatena[a], a string of passages strung together from Psalms, Isaiah, and other biblical books, and with some commentary with it; exactly as the word "Catena" is used in later Christian writings. The second text from Qumran is 4Q510, also known as 4QShir[a]; manuscript a, "Shir" being the Hebrew word for "song." This text is a song of praise. In both of these texts—4QCatena[a] and in 4QShir[a]—you have the expression "sons of light" exactly as you have it in the War Scroll and in the Community Rule. All of this begins to cohere: You take some texts from this cave and texts from this cave, and you begin to see the same expressions occurring in them.

Another example: The phrase "Teacher of Righteousness"—Hebrew: *moreh zedeq*—appears both in the Damascus Document and in the Pesher Habakkuk text; we've addressed these two important texts in earlier lectures as well. The same expression—"Teacher of Righteousness"—again occurs in three texts from Cave Four (fragmentary texts like all of our texts from Cave Four are) and they are 4Q171 and 4Q173; both of those are the same document, different manuscripts. It is a Pesher to the book of Psalms—you'll recall the Pesher system of commentary—so we have 4QpPs[a] and 4QpPs[b]. In that text, in both copies that we have from Cave Four, we have the same expression, *moreh zedeq*, Teacher of Righteousness; and in a third text from Cave Four,

173

4Q172, which is a Pesher of some sort as well, although unidentified which biblical book it is commenting upon, therefore we call it 4QpUnid.

Another example still: The opponent to the Teacher of Righteousness, known as "the Wicked Priest"—again, the Hebrew term, we mentioned it earlier: *ha-kohen ha-raša'*—this expression occurs in the Pesher Habakkuk, the commentary to the biblical book of Habakkuk which we addressed in Lecture Nine), and again in two other texts, 4Q163, which is a Pesher on the book of Isaiah, and again in 4Q171, the Pesher on the book of Psalms that I mentioned just a moment ago. Again, apologies for throwing all sorts of numbers at you—4Q this and 4Q that—but that's the way we refer to our texts, and it gives you a sense of how these terms appear in the different documents.

To my mind, these and other examples—which could be multiplied if we looked at the entire corpus of documents, the 700 non-biblical documents from Qumran—appearing in Text X and Text Y and Text Z and so on, different phrases, demonstrate to my mind that the corpus as a whole, these documents, cohere as a corpus, or at least a significant number of the texts cohere as sectarian documents. This would be my response to Professor Golb in his view which is that they are a representation of the Temple library without any connection to a particular group, a particular sect, or a particular denomination under the umbrella of Judaism in late antiquity. Of course, Golb is correct about one thing, and that is not all the documents belong to the single sect, presumably the Essenes according to the majority opinion; but we've noted this point from the outset of our course, beginning, in fact, in Lecture One. We mentioned that many of the texts, approximately 250, belong to common Judaism. But this number is outweighed by the 350 "sectually explicit" texts; you'll recall that I used that expression back in Lecture One as well. There are far more texts that relate and correlate to a particular viewpoint assigned to a particular group than to, let's say, a panoply of views expressed in the corpus of the Dead Sea Scrolls.

In short, Professor Golb has issued an important challenge to the majority opinion; and we take his view seriously, but his counter approach to the majority opinion does not bear up, in my mind and the mind of most scholars, to the scrutiny based on the kind of information that I have presented to you here. Earlier in this lecture, I mentioned that Professor Golb comes to the field as an outsider; that his work is mainly in medieval Jewish history, both in the world of Islam and in the world of Christendom. I don't intend that, incidentally, in any way as a criticism. In fact, it is wonderful that a scholar can bring his intellect and his acuity to a subject from the outside. This happens time and again in the world of scholarship, and it helps those of us who are working with these texts to frame our questions and frame our answers differently. So in this sense, we can at least commend Professor Golb for entering the fray of Dead Sea Scrolls scholarship.

In our next lecture, we will continue to explore the world of Qumran research and Dead Sea Scrolls scholarship by introducing you to still other personalities who have left their mark on the subject beginning with the early years of the 1940s and the 1950s down to the present day.

Stops and Starts En Route to Publication
Lecture 13

> All seven original scrolls from Cave 1 are on display at the Israel Museum. The vast majority of the documents were taken to the Palestine Archaeology Museum, now the Rockefeller Museum, where a team of international scholars transcribed and translated them.

We return to the fascinating narrative of how the scrolls came into the hands of scholars and how scholars published the scrolls. Recall that Mar Samuel allowed scholars to view, photograph, and publish the four scrolls from Cave 1 he had obtained, but he did not sell them right away. Samuel moved to the United States in 1949 to become the Syrian Orthodox Church's patriarchal vicar to the United States and Canada. In 1954, Samuel placed an ad in *The Wall Street Journal*, looking to sell the four scrolls. By coincidence, Yigael Yadin was in the United States at the same time. Yadin—via an intermediary—purchased the scrolls on behalf of the Hebrew University. These scrolls were thus reunited with the three remaining Cave 1 scrolls. Together, they formed the basis for the Shrine of the Book, a special pavilion at the Israel Museum built in 1965, which displays these seven scrolls and additional Qumran finds.

At first, the Dead Sea Scrolls were mainly the subject of scholarly interest. This changed in May 1955, when literary critic Edmund Wilson first published an essay in *The New Yorker*, and later that year a book, called *The Scrolls of the Dead Sea*.

Mar Samuel's ad in *The Wall Street Journal*.

The great majority of the Dead Sea Scrolls were found in 1948–1954 during the systematic exploration of the caves of Qumran while that part of Israel was under Jordanian rule.

The scrolls were taken to the Palestine Archaeology Museum in East Jerusalem. There the Jordanian Department of Antiquities created a team of international scholars—though it should be noted no Jewish scholars were included. J. T. Milik, a Polish-born priest, was, according to most experts in the field, the most brilliant member of this team and, according to at least one accounting, published more texts than anyone else. Individuals were assigned to transcribe and translate particular scrolls. Their scholarly efforts were published by Oxford University Press in a series called Discoveries in the Judaean Desert. Some scholars, such as John Allegro, performed their task with alacrity, while others, such as John Strugnell, tarried for decades. These delays led to controversies.

One of the great tales from this period is the relationship between Roland de Vaux (then at the École Biblique in Jordanian-held East Jerusalem) and Yadin (at the Hebrew University in Israeli West Jerusalem). The two archaeologist-scholars—with offices only four kilometers from each other—had to correspond via Geza Vermes, a colleague living in England.

In June 1967, Israel captured East Jerusalem (as well as the rest of the West Bank territory held by Jordan) during the Six-Day War. The Israel Antiquities Authority gained control of the scrolls but left the original team of scholars intact. By sheer coincidence, during the war, a selection of the Dead Sea Scrolls kept in the Palestine Archaeology Museum were on temporary exhibit in the Amman Archaeology Museum—and there they remain to this day! Because of the politically charged name "Palestine," the Israeli authorities changed the name of the museum to the Rockefeller Museum, since the project had been funded by John D. Rockefeller II. As another result of the Six-Day War, Israel gained control of the West Bank, including Qumran itself and the city of Bethlehem.

During the late 1950s and early 1960s, rumors abounded that another lengthy Dead Sea Scroll had been found and was still in private hands, most likely Kando's. Yadin, serving once more as a general in the Israeli army, sent his troops to "liberate" the scroll from Kando's shop in Bethlehem. The shopkeeper had been keeping the scroll in a shoebox under his floorboards, and thus some of the scroll had deteriorated. Fortunately, most of the text still was legible. Yadin spent the next 10 years working on the scroll, which, at 9 meters long and 67 columns, is the longest by far of the Dead Sea Scrolls. The document deals with Temple rituals, and thus Yadin labeled the text the Temple Scroll (11QT). Its discovery and publication would forever change Dead Sea Scrolls research.

> **Rumors abounded that another lengthy Dead Sea Scroll had been found and was still in private hands.**

In the very international world of Dead Sea Scrolls scholarship, one country not mentioned until now is Germany. Two German scholars are particularly worth noting. Otto Betz, mainly a New Testament scholar, suggested that John the Baptist was an Essene, perhaps with very direct association with the Qumran community. Hartmut Stegemann developed a unique way to correlate fragments by comparing not their contents but rather their physical properties. He was able to help scholars match thousands of Cave 4 fragments. ∎

Essential Reading

VanderKam, *The Dead Sea Scrolls Today*, 187–193.

VanderKam and Flint, *The Meaning of the Dead Sea Scrolls*, 55–81, 381–403.

Schiffman, *Reclaiming the Dead Sea Scrolls*, 21–31.

Yadin, *The Message of the Scrolls*, 39–52.

Wilson, *The Scrolls of the Dead Sea*.

Questions to Consider

1. Can you excuse the scholars who delayed and prolonged the publication of the texts assigned to them, or are the delays inexcusable?

2. Do you consider the 10-year span from Yadin's obtaining the Temple Scroll until its publication with extensive commentary to be an acceptable period of time? Or do you think that he should have published this text more quickly (presumably without commentary)?

Stops and Starts En Route to Publication
Lecture 13—Transcript

In the previous lecture, we presented a series of alternative views and theories offered by scholars who do not follow the mainstream approach, the one which I and the majority of Dead Sea Scrolls scholars are following, which is to say that the texts relate to the Essene community. Those scholars, who we referred to in the previous lecture, gave interpretations and analyses of the data. In this lecture, I want to return to the fascinating narrative of how the scrolls came into the hands of scholars back in the 1940s and '50s, and as we will see into the 1960s, and how these scholars published the scrolls. As such, the scholars that we will be looking at in this lecture were on the front line, actually publishing the texts and bringing them out for the scholarly world to read.

Do you remember in Lecture Two we mentioned Mar Samuel? Let's return to the story of Mar Samuel, who was the metropolitan of the Syrian Church in Jerusalem who had obtained four of the original seven scrolls from Cave One from Kando. You will recall that Mar Samuel allowed scholars to view, photograph, and publish those four scrolls, but that the possession, the ownership of the scrolls, remained in his hands; he did not sell these documents to anyone. As late as 1954, they were still in his possession, seven years after he obtained them from Kando. In the meantime, he had moved, in 1949, to the United States, to take up the position of Patriarchal Vicar to the United States and Canada, centered in Hackensack, New Jersey. From 1957 onward, until his death (I believe) in 1995, Mar Samuel achieved even a higher rank: He served as Archbishop of the newly created Archdiocese of the United States and Canada. As one can see from this little biography of Mar Samuel, he became a very influential religious leader in North America as the head of the Syrian Orthodox Church.

But back to our story: In 1954, as I noted, Mar Samuel still personally owned the four scrolls, and he sought to sell these scrolls. How would you go about selling four Dead Sea Scrolls? Would you follow the approach of Mar Samuel? He placed an ad in *The Wall Street Journal*, looking to sell the four documents. The ad read as follows—it appeared in the "Miscellaneous for Sale" section—and here is what it said: "The Four Dead Sea Scrolls:

Biblical Manuscripts dating back to at least 200 B.C. are for sale. This would be an ideal gift to an educational or religious institution by an individual or group. Then the address: Box F 206, The Wall Street Journal." I am not making this up; Mar Samuel placed an ad in the *Wall Street Journal* seeking to sell the four Dead Sea Scrolls documents still in his possession. By coincidence, Yigael Yadin—do you remember that we also referred to Professor Yadin at the Hebrew University in a previous lecture? One of the great scholars associated with Dead Sea Scrolls research for decades—was in the United States at the same time on a lecture tour. Someone called the ad to his attention, and Yadin, via an intermediary, purchased the scrolls from Mar Samuel on behalf of the Hebrew University. Thus, the four scrolls that his father, Eliezer Sukenik—I hope you're recalling all these names, these people to whom we referred in previous lectures—had been shown by Mar Samuel back in 1947–1948, but which Professor Sukenik could not purchase due to a) the lack of funds, and b) the outbreak of the Arab-Israeli war of 1948 now came into his son's hands seven years later in 1954. Alas, Professor Sukenik had died about 16 months earlier.

The intermediary, by the way, was called Mr. Green, a pseudonym, though his identity became known soon thereafter. Let me explain to you why Professor Yadin needed an intermediary to do the transaction on his behalf. Yadin, of course, was an Israeli scholar; Mar Samuel was living in the United States, but the Syrian Church from which he came, you'll remember, was in East Jerusalem, now under Jordanian control. He wanted to be safe, and therefore he did not want to deal with an Israeli directly; and the Israeli Professor Yadin, of course, knew this as well, and therefore sent an intermediary who used the false name Mr. Green. It was revealed only a short time later that this individual was, in fact, Harry Orlinsky, professor of biblical studies at Hebrew Union College, a seminary for the training of rabbis in the reform movement in New York City. Again, a personal note: I knew Professor Orlinsky exceedingly well in the last years of his life because when I was doing my PhD at New York University, Hebrew Union College actually relocated its New York City campus from further uptown to Greenwich village; and so Professor Orlinsky and I became very, very close and I remember him very fondly, and he loved to tell the story of how he posed as Mr. Green.

All of this—this entire tale: the ad, Yadin, Orlinsky, Mr. Green, all of it— is described in very poignant fashion by Yigael Yadin in his personal account published only a few years later, *The Message of the Scrolls* (1957). Thus all seven of the original Cave One scrolls came into the possession of the Hebrew University in those early years between 1947 and 1954 due to the efforts of the Sukenik-Yadin father-son team. These seven scrolls formed the basis for the establishment of the Shrine of the Book, a special pavilion at the Israel Museum in Jerusalem, built in 1965, which still today displays these seven scrolls, along with additional Qumran finds.

We should note here that, perhaps not surprisingly, at first the Dead Sea Scrolls were mainly the subject of scholarly interest. After all, we're looking at ancient documents written in Hebrew, Aramaic, to some extent in Greek. We've dealt with the arcane subject of textural criticism, as far as the biblical scrolls are concerned; and to read the sectarian scrolls, you need to know Philo, Josephus, and so on and so forth as we've shown in this course. It was mainly a scholarly interest, the subject of the Dead Sea Scrolls. All of this changed, however, in May, 1955, when the famous literary critic Edmund Wilson published an essay in *The New Yorker* magazine that then was expanded into a book that appeared later that year, *The Scrolls of the Dead Sea*, published by Oxford University Press, and a second edition appeared still later, in 1969. Wilson's essay and the book vaulted the subject of the Dead Sea Scrolls into the public domain starting in the mid-1950s, and it has remained there ever since.

The great majority of the Scrolls, as we have said several times in this course, were found in the years 1948–1954 during the systematic exploration of the caves of Qumran. During this period, that part of the land of Israel was under Jordanian rule following the events of 1947–1948, namely the United Nations partition of Palestine, the Israeli War of Independence, and Jordan's annexation of the West Bank that included all sorts of sites to which we have referred: Qumran, Bethlehem, Jericho, and the eastern half of the city of Jerusalem. As the scrolls came out of the caves under Jordanian administration, they were taken to the Palestine Archaeology Museum— PAM for short, later renamed the Rockefeller Museum, as I will explain in a minute—located in East Jerusalem; the museum is a stone's throw from two leading scholarly institutions that we have mentioned already in our course:

the École Biblique, the French school of biblical studies in eastern Jerusalem, and the American Schools of Oriental Research, the American center for biblical archaeologists who want to investigate the land of Israel. There at the PAM (the Palestine Archaeology Museum) a team of international scholars was created, consisting mainly of French, British, and American scholars; though, it should be noted, given the control exercised by the Jordanian Department of Antiquities, no Jewish scholars were included on the team. More on this in a later lecture.

I should mention here that while the team was mainly French, British, and American scholars, one person who deserves special highlight was J. T. Milik, a Polish-born priest who was living and working in Jerusalem in those days. I single Milik out because first, according to most experts in the field, Milik was the most brilliant member of the team; and second, according to at least one accounting, he (Milik) published more texts than anyone else, especially the very fragmentary material from Cave Four. Indeed, *Time* magazine heralded him in 1956 as "the fastest man with a fragment." By the way, Milik left the priesthood in 1969, he married, and he moved to Paris, though he continued to work on the Dead Sea Scrolls until his death in 2006. I single Milik out because no course on the Dead Sea Scrolls should neglect to mention him and the important work that he contributed to our subject, even if he is not associated with any of the major scrolls from Cave One or elsewhere that we are discussing in our course.

Individuals were assigned the task of transcribing and translating the scrolls, and thus at any given time scholars were at work in the "scrollery," as the name of the room at the PAM came to be called where all the scrolls were kept, under glass, for easy reading and preservation, including all those literally thousands of fragments from Cave Four comprising, as we know, more than 500 documents. These scholarly efforts by the publication team set up—all the individuals that I had been referring to, Milik and the others—these reconstructions of the texts, the publications of the text, all of this appeared in the standard academic series dedicated to this work entitled *Discoveries in the Judaean Desert* (DJD for short), published by Oxford University Press. Some scholars, such as John Allegro of the University of Manchester, performed their task with alacrity; while others, such as John

Strugnell of Harvard University, tarried for decades. These delays led to controversies, as we shall see in a later lecture.

It is almost impossible to mention the name John Allegro without referring to the great controversy that he stirred with the publication of his book *The Sacred Mushroom and the Cross* in 1970, in which Allegro proposed that the roots of Christianity are to be found in ancient fertility cults, especially those attached to hallucinogenic mushrooms. For example, when Jesus says to Peter, "You are Peter, and upon this rock I will build my Church," everyone recognizes the pun between Peter's name and the Greek word *petra*, meaning "rock." Allegro, however, saw here the Aramaic word *pitra*, meaning "mushroom"; to this day, in Modern Hebrew the word for "mushroom" is *pitriya*. One hardly needs to add that Allegro fell into great disfavor by the Church upon the publication of his book *The Sacred Mushroom and the Cross*, and indeed he was ostracized by virtually all scholars after the publication of this book. Truth be told, I have heard all versions of the story: that Allegro published the book tongue-in-cheek, and that Allegro was very serious in this scholarship. The bottom line is we simply don't know, and of course Allegro has now passed away. On the other hand, scholars must admit, regardless of his controversial book, that of all the individuals who were granted responsibility for publishing Dead Sea Scrolls back in the 1950s, only Allegro published the documents assigned to him with dispatch and in toto. Strugnell, in the meantime, is another story altogether, and we will return to that narrative later in our course.

One of the great tales from this period is the relationship between Father de Vaux (Père Roland de Vaux), whom I've mentioned so many times in our course located at the École Biblique in Jordanian-held East Jerusalem and Yigael Yadin at the Hebrew University in Israeli West Jerusalem, with a wall separating them. East Jerusalem and West Jerusalem was a divided city during this period. The two archaeologist-scholars, de Vaux and Yadin, both working on Qumran and the Dead Sea Scrolls with offices about 4 kilometers from each other could not correspond directly with one another; there was no postal service across that wall. Instead, they corresponded via the intermediation of Geza Vermes of Oxford University, who would repost de Vaux's and Yadin's mail to one another. De Vaux would send a letter from East Jerusalem to Oxford to Vermes, Vermes would repost it with Yadin's address from England and it would go to Yadin in West Jerusalem; and back the other direction: Yadin to Oxford, Professor Vermes reposting it to Father de Vaux in East Jerusalem.

We have not mentioned Vermes since long ago in Lecture One, so perhaps we can refer once more to his standard translation entitled *The Complete Dead Sea Scrolls in English*. By the way, Vermes's personal story is yet another captivating narrative; allow me to digress to share his story with you. As his name suggests, he was born in Hungary; his parents converted the whole family to Roman Catholicism when Vermes was seven years old. His parents nonetheless died in the Holocaust, while the son Geza survived. After World War II, he became a Roman Catholic priest; but then he left the Church in 1957 and he reasserted his Judaism, now as an adult. Eventually, Geza Vermes made his way to England and he became professor of Jewish Studies at Oxford, from which he is now retired; another one of the great names of Qumran scholarship with another remarkable tale that I share with you here.

In June, 1967, Israel captured East Jerusalem as well as the West Bank territory that I described earlier including Bethlehem, Qumran, Jericho, and much more; in the Six-Day War of June, 1967, Israel conquered that territory from Jordan. The Israel Antiquities Authority now became the official authority—it's an arm of the Israeli government, just like the Jordanian Department of Antiquities is an arm of the Jordanian government—controlling the scrolls, but they respected the original team of scholars set up by the Jordanian authorities, and thus at first no changes in the administrative structure were made. As we shall see, this would change at some point; back to that in a future lecture. By sheer coincidence, during the Six-Day War (June, 1967), a selection of the Dead Sea Scrolls kept in the PAM (Palestine Archaeological Museum) were on temporary exhibit on the other side of the Jordan River in the Amman Archaeology Museum in the capital of the kingdom of Jordan, and there those texts remain to this day. They're not all in Jerusalem; there is a handful in Amman, and among these documents these documents located in Amman is the famous Copper Scroll. That will be the subject of a forthcoming lecture as well.

Because of the politically charged name Palestine, the Israeli authorities changed the name of the museum from the Palestine Archaeology Museum (PAM) to the Rockefeller Museum, since the project had been funded by John D. Rockefeller II back in the 1930s; though to be fair, I should add that the institution was popularly called the Rockefeller Museum throughout those decades even before the Israelis changed its official name. We should note, though, that to this day the official photographs of the Scrolls go by their PAM numbers, since the photographs all were taken in the late 1940s and early 1950s as the documents first emerged from the caves.

These two stories, the one about Yadin purchasing four of the original scrolls via an ad in *The Wall Street Journal*, and the history of the Six-Day War, serve as appropriate segues to the story about the obtaining of the Temple Scroll, the next key document that we will study in our course. During the late 1950s and early 1960s, rumors abounded that another lengthy Dead Sea Scroll had been found in one of the caves and was still in private hands, most likely in the hands of Kando, our friend from Bethlehem, the shopkeeper/shoemaker/cobbler-cum-antiquities dealer. As a result of the Six-Day War, Israel gained control of the West Bank, as I mentioned, which had been claimed by Jordan, and now it was the Israeli Army in that territory. Yadin—you'll recall that he'd been a general in the Israeli Army in the War of Independence in 1948; he was serving once more as a general now in 1967—sent his troops to "liberate" the scroll from Kando's shop in Bethlehem. The shopkeeper had been keeping the scroll—where do you think?—in a shoebox under his floorboards, and thus some of the scroll had deteriorated. Fortunately, however, most of the text still was legible. Apparently somewhere Kando informed Yadin that the manuscript had been found in Cave 11. Not to worry, eventually Kando was compensated with more than $100,000.

Yadin then spent the next 10 years working on the scroll, which, at nine meters long; let me repeat that: nine meters. That's 10 yards, for those of you who are football fans, the equivalent of a first down. That's the longest of the Dead Sea Scrolls by far, consisting of 67 columns. The document deals with the Temple rituals, and thus Yadin labeled the text the Temple Scroll and with the information supplied by Kando from his Bedouin informants apparently, presumably, that it came from Cave 11, its scholarly siglum is

11QT. As we shall see, the discovery and publication of the Temple Scroll would forever change Dead Sea Scrolls research. As we have intimated, the direction of scholarship from the outset was towards theological issues. The Temple Scroll, along with the Halakhic Letter text—we'll talk about this in a future lecture, too—that came to public attention even later, focused everyone's attention now on the Halakhic issues, those issues of Jewish law that were at stake among the Dead Sea Scrolls documents for the Dead Sea Scrolls sect; something we should have known all along, but this only came into focus now with the Temple Scroll.

In the very international world of Dead Sea Scrolls scholarship, one country that I have not mentioned until now is Germany. I would, accordingly, like to mention here the work of two scholars from that country. The first one is Otto Betz. He was mainly a New Testament scholar, and he became a leading proponent of the John the Baptist-Dead Sea Scrolls connection. To be sure, he does not engage in the idiosyncratic view of Barbara Theiring—you'll remember from the previous lecture—that John the Baptist is the Teacher of Righteousness; Betz does not go there whatsoever, but he does note some very important connections between John the Baptist as revealed in the gospels in the New Testament and our Dead Sea Scrolls texts. First, some of the obvious correlations, for which see Matthew 3, which is paralleled in Mark 1: For example, John the Baptist preached repentance of sins through ritual bathing; that's something we've seen in the Community Rule, document 1QS, in an earlier lecture. There's a connection, therefore, between John the Baptist and the Qumran sect. John was active in the Judean wilderness near the Jordan River, which is where he would take people to baptize them. This places him very close to the vicinity of Qumran, probably within 10 kilometers or so.

Now Betz's contribution: The Gospels invoke a passage from the book of Isaiah, Isaiah 40:3, to refer to John the Baptist's work in the wilderness. The Hebrew text reads (in translation): "A voice calls, 'In the wilderness, clear the way of the LORD; make level in the desert a highway for our God.'" Incidentally, this is one of those verses where different punctuation can affect the sense of the text. Do you remember in an earlier lecture we talked about the oral reading tradition and how and where to punctuate a particular text? In fact, this passage is quoted in the New Testament slightly differently: "A voice calls in the wilderness, 'Prepare the way of the Lord, make his path straight.'" This same biblical text is invoked in 1QS (the Community Rule) 8:14 and 9:20—twice in that very important document—in the context of the Yahad. That is to say, of all the hundreds or thousands of passages in the Bible, both the Gospels and the Dead Sea Scrolls use Isaiah 40:3 as a key text, with reference to activity in the Judean desert.

In the Matthew version of John the Baptist's activity, the text continues with the description of a group of Pharisees and Sadducees approaching, which leads John to call them a "brood of vipers" (Matthew 3:7). In the Thanksgiving Hymns document, still to be studied in a later lecture, we read the expression "works of the viper" (Hebrew: *ma'ase 'eph'eh*), in 1QH (that's the designation) 11:17, to refer to wickedness; "brood of the viper," "works of the viper." Since the Greek word used in Matthew is *gennema*, derived from a root that means "to make," or "to produce," and then it comes to mean "to give birth," thus a "brood," the expression bears some resemblance to the Hebrew phrase that is based on the Hebrew word that means "to make" or "produce." All of this suggests to Professor Betz that John the Baptist was an Essene, perhaps with very direct association with the Qumran community.

The second scholar from Germany whom I would like to introduce to you is Hartmut Stegemann, also mainly a New Testament scholar, who developed a very unique way to correlate all of the fragments, especially those from Cave Four, with one another. Stegemann paid special attention not to the contents so much, but rather to the physical properties of the texts, of the documents, of the parchments. In this way, he was able to help scholars match the thousands of Cave Four fragments so that one could determine which pieces of the puzzle went with which other pieces. Most scholars will look at handwriting obviously; but Stegemann would look at other physical properties, such as looking at erosion trends, both those caused by animals— and, indeed, insects and rodents did eat away some of the parchment—and also erosion by the occasional exposure to moisture; even in these caves in a very arid part of the world, you will occasionally get a drip of water. In one famous instance, a French scholar named Maurice Baillet published a text called the *Song of the Sage*—it's 4Q510 and 4Q511—consisting of over 200 fragments, one of the most fragmentary of all of our documents from Cave Four. It included many, many, many tiny fragments, some of which contained just a few letters. Then Stegemann wove his magic, and he was able to produce—again, based on the physical properties of the text, not necessarily the words—a more coherent document with a now widely-recognized, widely-accepted by scholars sequence of individual songs in this one document, or perhaps stanzas belonging to one long song.

The last two lectures, this one and the previous one, highlight the manner in which different academic personalities have played key roles in the developing story of Dead Sea Scrolls research. Already in Lecture One, I stated that our course would move back and forth between such narratives as the ones presented in these two lectures on the one hand, and our actually reading and studying the contents of the documents on the other. After this hour-long excursion along the former path, it is time now to return to the latter route. We turn, accordingly, in our next lecture to a detailed examination of the Temple Scroll, which we have introduced to you in this lecture; we've described the discovery and the publication of this text, and the true importance of the Temple Scroll—the longest, once more, of all of our Qumran documents at 67 columns—we will discuss all of this in our next lecture.

The Qumran Vision for a New Temple
Lecture 14

Did the Qumran community consider the Temple Scroll a text of revelation?

The Torah includes three separate legal collections in Exodus, Leviticus, and Deuteronomy. Some topics are discussed in all three, with differences between and among the sources. The author of the Temple Scroll composed a single long text to bring all these sources into conformity with one another. The order of presentation is based mainly on Deuteronomy, with the legal material from Exodus and Leviticus (especially the latter) inserted and discussed where appropriate.

The main subjects covered include the Covenant between God and Israel; the Temple, especially the architectural layout of the inner chambers (this portion of the manuscript is badly damaged); the sacrifices, both for daily worship and for the festivals; various items in the outer courtyard of the Temple; purity laws concerning not only the Temple itself, but the city of Jerusalem and other cities in the land of Israel; and various laws concerning idolatry, vows, oaths, apostasy, and so forth. There were also laws concerning the king, conduct of war, criminal law, incest, and other topics.

Most striking is the manner in which the Temple Scroll speaks in the first-person voice of God, in contrast to the first-person voice of Moses in the book of Deuteronomy with God referred to in the third person. More than 20 times in Deuteronomy, Moses

Model of the Second Temple, in the Israel Museum.

refers to the worship site as "the place that YHWH will choose to set his name" or similar, understood by later readers to refer to Jerusalem. In the Temple Scroll the phrase is "the place upon which I choose to set my name" (11QT 52:16). About a dozen times in Deuteronomy, Moses refers to the land of Canaan as "the land that YHWH your God gives to you to inherit" or similar. In the Temple Scroll, it is "the land that I give you to inherit" (11QT 51:16). In the Torah, Numbers 30:2 states, "If a man makes a vow to the LORD … ," whereas the Temple Scroll states, "If a man makes a vow to me … " (11QT 53:14). The shift to first-person address suggests that the Temple Scroll is to be seen as a book of revelation from God to the people of Israel. Again, we repeat the connection with early Christianity, which sees the New Testament books as revealed scripture. Recall that later rabbinic tradition claimed that prophecy ended with Malachi. This claim was seen as a polemic against Christianity, but in light of the Dead Sea Scrolls, we now must consider this as an equal critique of other Jewish sects of late antiquity.

While in some Dead Sea Scrolls the divine name YHWH is written in older paleo-Hebrew script, in the biblical scrolls, it is in the contemporary script. This latter system is followed in the Temple Scroll, indicating that for the Qumran sect—or certainly this particular scribe—it was the equivalent of a book of the Bible, indeed a Torah from God.

The Halakah of the Temple Scroll is much stricter than that of the rabbis.

The Halakah of the Temple Scroll is much stricter than that of the rabbis. The scroll argues that only hides of animals that were slaughtered in the Temple could be used to transport wine and other products to the Temple. The rabbis took the position that sacrificing a pregnant animal does not violate the law of Leviticus 22:28, but the Temple Scroll states that it does. (One needs to realize here the economic hardship that the more stringent view creates.) Given these strict views, it is clear that the Qumran sect considered the actual Temple in Jerusalem to be impure and polluted. In his description of the Essenes, Josephus marvels at the fact that they did not defecate on the

Sabbath. We have evidence from the Temple Scroll and the Qumran site that confirms this practice.

As long as we are treating the issue of the Temple and Jerusalem, we need to discuss the enormous size of the Temple as described by the Temple Scroll. It is square, in contrast to all other descriptions of the different Temples in the Bible, including the First Temple built by Solomon, the vision of Ezekiel concerning the rebuilt Temple, and then the actually constructed Second Temple. It is 1,600 cubits (or about 0.45 mile) on each side, which amounts to about 160 acres! This would be the size of all of Jerusalem during the Maccabean or Hasmonean period. By comparison, Solomon's Temple was 60 cubits long.

Our last point concerns the law of the king as presented in the scroll. The basis for this is Deuteronomy 17:14–20. The king is not to multiply wives, not to multiply silver and gold, and not to engage in horse trade with Egypt. He is also to have a written copy of this law (Hebrew *tora*), which is to be read to him regularly.

1 Samuel 10:25 informs us that Samuel wrote down the law (Hebrew *mišpat*) of kingship in a book. One can imagine later generations of Jews wondering, where is this book? It is possible that all of this forms the background for the lengthy section concerning the king in the Temple Scroll. No surprise in light of our earlier discussion about polygamy and divorce, or the lack thereof, that the king is to have but one wife. We also learn that the king should have a council consisting of 12 priests, 12 Levites, and 12 nonsacerdotal leaders of the people.

Finally, we should contemplate the larger picture emerging from our study of the Temple Scroll, with two notable points. We cannot emphasize this document enough, especially since it showed Dead Sea Scrolls researchers how important legal/Halakhic issues were, with the Qumran sect stricter at every turn. Clearly, the Qumran community was very Temple focused, even though the *Yahad* members had elected to stop participating in the Jerusalem Temple cult. Naturally, much of the contents of the Temple Scroll is but an ideal, since the Qumran community never controlled the operations of the actual Temple in Jerusalem. ■

Essential Reading

Vermes, *The Complete Dead Sea Scrolls in English*, 190–219.

VanderKam, *The Dead Sea Scrolls Today*, 58–59.

Schiffman, *Reclaiming the Dead Sea Scrolls*, 257–271.

Questions to Consider

1. Could the Qumran community really have adhered to the practice of not toileting on the Sabbath?

2. If the Essenes distanced themselves from the Temple, how can we explain the presence of such an extraordinary document such as the Temple Scroll among the Dead Sea Scrolls?

The Qumran Vision for a New Temple
Lecture 14—Transcript

This lecture presents the Temple Scroll, also known as 11QT, in detail. This remarkable text is a reworking of the laws of the Torah, using Deuteronomy as its base with incorporations from the book of Leviticus and other books. One of the most noteworthy features of this text is the shift from the original third-person wording in Deuteronomy, where Moses appears as the speaker and God is referred to in the third person, to first-person wording in the Temple Scroll; that is, this text presents the voice of God as speaker. This raises the question: Did the Qumran community consider the Temple Scroll a text of revelation? Did the Essenes believe in an ongoing revelation in their day? How does this link up with early Christianity? Given the Temple Scroll's focus on temple rituals and other religious practices, we include in this lecture a consideration of the role of the Jerusalem Temple in ancient Jewish life. We also will note, once more, that where comparison is possible, time and again Qumran *halakha* (Jewish law) presents the stricter opinion than rabbinic *halakha*.

We will get back to these points in a few minutes, but as background information I need to present first a whole array of data, starting with the fact that the Torah includes three separate legal collections in the book of Exodus, in the book of Leviticus, and in the book of Deuteronomy. Some topics—for example, the Jewish holidays—are discussed in all three of these books, with differences between and among the various sources, as occurs perhaps most famously in the case of Passover. Some further background here: The books of the Torah—the setting of the books of Torah—is the wandering through the desert as the Israelites left Egypt and they journeyed en route to the land of Canaan. The sanctum, the holy site, that the Israelites had at this point was called the Tabernacle, a portable tent shrine; so that when the sources of the Torah—whether they be Exodus, Leviticus, or Deuteronomy, and also the book of Numbers we should mention here too—sensed the sanctum, when they have in mind what this holy place would have looked like, they understood it as the portable tent shrine known as the Tabernacle.

Eventually, the Israelites settled down in the land of Israel, and, of course, eventually Jerusalem became their capital city, established by King David. A generation later, Solomon built the First Temple in the city of Jerusalem. All the rituals that are described in the books of the Torah are now transferred to the Temple; that is to say, whatever occurred in the Tabernacle—for example, that's where the Ark of the Covenant was housed—was now transferred to the Temple. In the innermost sanctum, the Holy of Holies of the Temple, that's now where the Ark of the Covenant goes. The sacrifices that occurred in an altar in an outer courtyard of the Tabernacle now occur on an altar at the Jerusalem Temple. As Judaism continued to develop throughout the centuries, the role of the Jerusalem Temple expanded and expanded and became larger and larger in the mindset of the people. It is impossible to overstate the centrality of the Temple in Jewish life. This is true of all the Jewish groups of antiquity: the Essenes, the Sadducees, the Pharisees; whoever we are describing, all of them understood the Jerusalem Temple as the centerpiece of their religious life, the way they expressed themselves religiously in the worship of the single God. That, as background to the Temple Scroll.

The author of the Temple Scroll, composed in the 2nd century B.C.E., early on in the Qumran period—and again I repeat, this is the single longest text found among the Dead Sea Scrolls, 67 columns, nine meters in length—tried to bring all those sources of the Torah, with differences of opinion and different statements and different formulations from time to time, into conformity with one another. The order of presentation is based mainly on Deuteronomy, with the legal material from Exodus and Leviticus—especially the latter, especially the book of Leviticus—inserted and discussed where appropriate. Let me give you an example of one of the issues; just one out of literally dozens that I could present as way of illustration. The case here is the case of the blood of an animal. It is permitted to eat meat, specifically those animals that are permitted by the dietary laws presented both in Leviticus 11 and in Deuteronomy 14; but the blood of an animal is forbidden to be eaten. That's because in ancient Israel, as is described in a number of places including the book of Genesis, blood was seen as the symbol of life; and therefore eating blood was not allowed. Numerous biblical passages, numerous passages in the Torah and other biblical books, all refer to the not eating of blood, that point is clear.

Let me give you two of the formulations. In Leviticus 17:13, we read: "And he [meaning the individual who is engaging in the eating of meat or in the slaughtering of the animal] shall spill [or pour out, however you wish to translate the Hebrew verb there] the blood, and he shall cover it with dirt." In Deuteronomy 12:24, same prohibition—no eating of blood—but the formulation is different. Here we read: "You shall not eat it [referring to the blood], upon the earth you shall spill it [again, or pour it; the same verb] like water." Did you notice the difference? So which is it? Is spilling or pouring the blood out sufficient, which is implied in the Deuteronomy version? Or does one need to cover the blood with dirt, which is what the book of Leviticus commands? 11QT (the Temple Scroll) 52 (that is to say, it's towards the end of our very long 67-column book):11-12 reads, following mainly the Deuteronomy wording—that's the way the text is organized, as I said—but adding the Leviticus phrase, it reads as follows: "But you shall not eat the blood: upon the ground you shall spill it [or pour it; it's that same verb over and over again] like water, and you should cover it with dirt." What our Temple Scroll text has done is to take some of the wording from Leviticus, some of the wording from Deuteronomy, and bring it together in a single passage.

The main subjects of this very long Temple Scroll are the following; and I'm going to give you a list of nine items here, just to give you a survey very quickly of all of the subjects in 11QT, the Temple Scroll, and then we'll go back and discuss many of these in detail. First, the text begins (columns 1 and 2) with the material that one would expect at the beginning: the Covenant between God and Israel. This, of course, is to be found in many, many biblical passages; it is all summarized here at the beginning of the Temple Scroll, just as it occurs at the beginning of the book of Deuteronomy, the fifth and last book of the canonical Torah. Next, columns 3–12, the description of the Temple itself, especially the architectural layout of the inner chambers including the Holy Place and the Holy of Holies further inside the Temple, though this portion of the manuscript (columns 3–12) is badly damaged. Next, the text goes on to describe the sacrifices, both for daily worship and for the festivals. That's a large chunk, from column 13–29. The list also includes, by the way, some new holidays; new festivals not mentioned in the Torah, in any of the sources, but that do appear here in the Temple Scroll. We will discuss those in a future lecture as well.

Next, the Temple Scroll goes on to describe the various items in the outer courtyard of the Temple (columns 30–35), items such as the laver. That's the large object that contains water where the priests would wash their hands as one final step of purifying themselves just in case any impurities remained that had not been removed. The laver's in the outer courtyard, that's an example of what's being described in this next section of the Temple Scroll; then, the outer courtyard as a whole (columns 36–45) with its many, many gates and subdivisions. Next, the Temple Scroll goes on (columns 46–51) to describe the purity laws, concerning not only the Temple itself but the city of Jerusalem as a whole, and even other cities in the land of Israel. We've talked about purity in this course before; we will continue to come back to this subject time and again in our exploration and discovery of the Dead Sea Scrolls. Then (column 51–55): various laws concerning idolatry, vows, oaths, apostasy, and so on.

Then there's a relatively large section for one subject: Four columns (columns 56–59) deal with the laws relating to the king of Israel; we'll come back in a few minutes in this lecture and talk in greater detail about that section of the Temple Scroll. Finally, the last seven columns (columns 60–66): various laws concerning other topics such as the conduct of war, criminal law, incest, all of these are woven in, and then only a tiny little bit at column 67, the last of the columns of this, as I keep on repeating, the longest of all Dead Sea Scrolls documents.

Most striking is the manner in which the Temple Scroll speaks in the first-person voice of God. This is in contrast to the first-person voice of Moses in the book of Deuteronomy, with God referred to in the third person. Let me give you examples to illustrate this shift from third-person references to God to first-person references to God. First example: More than 20 times in Deuteronomy we encounter Moses referring to the worship site as "the place that Yahweh will choose to set his name," with all sorts of minor variations of this basic language. "The place that Yahweh will choose to set his name"; God is referred to in the third person, both by his proper name Yahweh and by the pronoun "his." This was understood, by the way, by all later Jewish readers to refer to Jerusalem obviously; the Samaritans, as we discussed earlier, saw this as a reference to Mount Gerizim where their temple stood to the north of Jerusalem. In the Temple Scroll, the phrase is changed; here we read "the place upon which I choose to set my name." god is now clearly the speaker: "I choose to set my name"; that passage is 11QT 52:16.

Another example: About a dozen times in Deuteronomy, we encounter Moses referring to the land of Canaan as "the land that Yahweh your God gives to you to inherit"; again, with some variations in the specific language, and again with Yahweh referred to in the third person using the proper name of God. In the Temple Scroll, the phrase is altered; we now read "the land that I give you to inherit." God is the speaker; that passage 11QT 51:16. Or to use a less familiar example—the two phrases I've just given you are well known from the book of Deuteronomy; they repeat over and over again as one works through the book of Deuteronomy in the book of Torah—from the Torah with its reworking in the Temple Scroll: Numbers 30 is a chapter of the Torah that deals with vows, and Numbers 30:2 states, "If a man makes a vow to the LORD ..."; again, God referred to in the third person, that is to say, Yahweh. "If a man makes a vow to the LORD ..." In 11QT (the Temple Scroll) 53:14 states, "If a man makes a vow to me ..." God is the speaker, "If a man makes a vow to me ..." Then the next verse in the book of Numbers treats the female: "If a woman makes a vow to the LORD ..." whereas the 11QT 53:16 states—and you can predict this already—"If a woman makes a vow to me."

The shift to first-person address suggests that the Temple Scroll is to be seen as a book of revelation; this is God speaking directly to the people of Israel. Did the Qumran community believe in on-going revelation; that is, beyond the great revelation at Sinai and the additional oracles from God to the prophets? Is there something beyond that? The Temple Scroll clearly implies this; and, of course, we actually discussed this earlier in Lecture Nine when we treated the Pesher Habakkuk, the commentary text on the biblical prophetic book of Habakkuk. Again, we repeat here the connection with early Christianity, which sees the New Testament books as revealed Scripture, coming from a period far beyond the time of Moses and the biblical prophets. Here we may add a specific reference from the New Testament itself, 2 Peter 3:1: "I want you to recall the words spoken in the past by the holy prophets and the command given by our Lord and Savior through your apostles." It's ongoing revelation.

Once more, we emphasize the point made earlier: Later rabbinic tradition claimed that prophecy ended with Malachi, the last of the prophets (450 B.C.E.); and this claim by the rabbis has traditionally been seen as a polemic against Christianity, though in the light of the Dead Sea Scrolls, we now must consider this as an equal critique of other Jewish sects in late antiquity. How the Essenes, how the Qumran sect understood the Temple Scroll vis-à-vis the Torah, that's a question that I have wondered about and I honestly don't know the answer to. That is to say, they still had the Torah obviously; we have multiple copies of the Torah, of all these books of the Torah—Genesis, Exodus, Leviticus, Numbers, Deuteronomy, especially Deuteronomy—amongst the Dead Sea Scrolls biblical manuscripts. Did they understand the Temple Scroll was actually going back to the time of Moses as well? Did it supplement, did it replace, did it stand next to? These are questions that we cannot answer; I've considered them in my own mind, I simply don't know. But I raise the issue, this little bit of speculation, as how the community itself might have realized the Temple Scroll and its relationship to the Torah.

I add here another point as a way of refining our earlier discussion concerning the manner in which the divine name Yahweh is written. In Lecture 11 we discussed this, and now I want to say something further. I mentioned there that in some scrolls, the divine name is written in the older Paleo-Hebrew script. This typically occurs, however, only in the non-biblical scrolls; for example, in the Pesher Habakkuk, which we just mentioned. The text is written in the newer Hebrew script; the divine name occurs in the older script. Another text, just to mention one that we haven't studied: 1Q14; it's a commentary; it's a Pesher, on the book of Micah. Same thing happens: The text is written in the newer script but the name of God is written in the older script. In the biblical scrolls, however, the Tetragrammaton—that's the technical name for the four-letter name of God—is written in the regular newer script. That was the script that was in vogue, and they did not change the name of God back to the older Paleo-Hebrew script. This latter system is followed in the Temple Scroll, with Yahweh—the four letters, which in Hebrew are יהוה, corresponding to the English "YHWH"—they are written in the regular letters just as if this were a biblical manuscript, indicating, as we've implied, that for the Qumran sect, or certainly for this particular scribe, the Temple Scroll was the equivalent of a book of the Bible, indeed a Torah in and of itself from God.

The *halakha* of the Temple Scroll is much stricter than the *halakha* of the rabbis. For example, within the discussion of the purity laws in column 47, the Temple Scroll argues that only hides of animals that were slaughtered in the Temple could be used to transport wine and other products to the Temple. The rabbis, on the other hand, in the Mishna several centuries later, held that hides of animals that were slaughtered anywhere could be used to transport items to the Temple. Let me explain what I mean here, the difference between these two issues: the Temple Scroll approach and the rabbinic approach. Let's say you live in the Galilee, in the northern part of the land of Israel, and you want to bring some wine or some olive oil to the Temple for one of the sacrifices; how are you going to transport it there? A big vessel is way too heavy; but you can transport it in a small skin bottle, sometimes used for water but also for other liquids. Where does that skin come from? That skin comes from an animal that's been slaughtered, most likely a goat. So if you live in the Galilee, according to the rabbinic system you slaughter your goat, you have some water skin bottle in your household, you fill it up with the wine or the olive oil, you bring it to the Temple, you present it to the priest, and you're fine. But according to the Temple Scroll, this would violate the sanctity and the purity of the Temple. According to the Temple Scroll, I repeat, you could only bring sacrifices in skins that were slaughtered in the Temple. That means you have to go to Jerusalem, you have to obtain an animal skin bottle that was made from an animal that was slaughtered as a sacrifice in the Temple, then bring the skin back to the Galilee, load it up, fill it up with your olive oil or your wine, and now bring it back to the Temple. You can see how difficult this would be; but that's the law of the Temple Scroll.

Another example: Leviticus 22:28 states that one must not sacrifice a mother and its young on the same day, presumably because this would be insensitive to the animal. What happens when you sacrifice a pregnant animal? By mistake, you sacrifice an animal, you start cutting it up, and you realize it was pregnant. The rabbis took the lenient position, ruling that sacrificing a pregnant animal does not violate the law of Leviticus, and that's expressed in the Mishna; that is to say, a pregnant animal does not violate the law of sacrificing a mother and its young—a living, viable young unto itself—on the same day. But the Temple Scroll states that it does violate the biblical law. A pregnant animal, in the mind of the Qumran community, violates the law of sacrificing an animal and its young on the same day. One needs to realize here the economic hardship that the more stringent view creates. Given these strict views of laws pertaining to the Temple ritual, it is clear that the Qumran sect considered the actual Temple in Jerusalem to be impure and polluted, beyond repair, as it were, in its present condition; and thus they renounced Temple sacrifice for the present, at least until they could gain control of the Temple cult and implement their own system.

One last example of a strict Halakhic stance pertains to toileting practices; I mentioned this far early in our course, we now reach the details of this issue. In his description of the Essenes, Josephus marvels at the fact that the Essenes did not defecate on the Sabbath. We now have evidence to confirm this point, though first we need to provide the context. According to Deuteronomy 23, in the desert, the Israelites were to defecate outside the encampment; remember they're journeying on the way to the land of Israel. The reason for this is that the entire camp was seen as a sacred place, both the Tabernacle in the middle, and the tribes arrayed around the edges. Not that excrement creates impurity—there's no indication of this in Leviticus or elsewhere—but rather merely that urine and feces are unseemly. The Qumran community considered all of Jerusalem—the city in which the Temple stood—to be the equivalent of the ancient encampment; thus, defecation in the city of Jerusalem as a whole—not just in the Temple; equivalent to the Tabernacle sanctuary of the Torah—was accordingly forbidden. Josephus refers to one of the city gates as the Essene Gate—and we know of this only from Josephus—and he indicates its location to the west of Jerusalem near a place called Betsoa, which, in fact, is the Hebrew expression for "latrine" or "lavatory," literally "house of excrement." There must have been a special gate for the Essenes to leave Jerusalem—those who lived in the city—so they could attend their bodily needs outside the city.

The Temple Scroll 46:15 states that the latrines must be 3,000 cubits removed from the city; referring to Jerusalem, in principle, although since these Essenes are no longer living in Jerusalem—the ones who've left us our Dead Sea Scrolls documents—and they have removed to a community in exile (Qumran, let's say); nevertheless, the latrine had to be 3,000 cubits removed from the city, whatever the city meant, whether Jerusalem, the real city that they would have loved to have been in control of, or their community in exile, and it needed to be to the northwest of the city. As we saw in the Damascus Document, however, back in Lecture Eight, the Qumran community imposed a 1,000 cubit limit on the distance one could walk on the Sabbath. Therefore, the latrines were beyond the Sabbath limit—the latrines were located 3,000 cubits away, but one could walk only 1,000 cubits—and therefore we can confirm the information presented by Josephus that this group did not defecate on the Sabbath. Do not ask me, please, for the anatomical or physiological way that this happened; I present to you only what the texts say, and we have a very exact correlation now between our Dead Sea Scrolls documents and the writings of Josephus.

Two scholars, James Tabor of University of North Carolina-Charlotte and Joseph Zias of Jerusalem announced in 2006 that they had discovered the latrine of Qumran at a distance of about 500 meters—that is to say, 1,100 cubits—northwest of the site. So while this is closer than the 3000-cubit statement that one gets in the Temple Scroll, it does conform to the same passage's directive that the latrine should be situated northwest of the city; and again, it places the latrine beyond the 1,000 cubit limit for the Sabbath.

As long as we are treating the issue of the Temple and Jerusalem, we need to discuss the enormous size of the Temple, as conceived by the Temple Scroll. First, we note that its shape is square, in contrast to all other descriptions of different Temples in the Bible, including the First Temple built by Solomon, the vision of the Prophet Ezekiel concerning the imagine rebuilt Temple, and then the actually constructed rebuilt Second Temple. All of those temples in the Bible are rectangular in shape, but our Temple Scroll envisions a square temple. Then the size: 1,600 cubits on each side. That's 2,400 feet, almost half a mile, 730 meters; it amounts to 160 acres. This would have been the size of all of Jerusalem during the period under discussion, the Maccabean or Hasmonean Period, and/or approximately the size of the old city of Jerusalem today within the walls constructed by the Ottoman Empire in the 16th century. An enormous Temple, 1,600 cubits on each side; by comparison, Solomon's Temple was 60 cubits long, 20 cubits wide. The Temple to Horus at Edfu, one of the largest of all the Egyptian temples in southern Egypt, was 140 meters long, 40 meters wide. At its greatest expansion, the Second Temple as expanded by Herod, which was not yet built at the time of composition of our text, was 200 meters long, 80 meters wide, and this was the largest construction in the known world. In short, a structure, even an entire complex such as the Temple as envisioned in our scroll, with sides of 1,600 cubits on each side is far beyond any conceivable reality.

One last point concerns the law of the king, as presented in columns 56–59. The basis for this is Deuteronomy 17:14–20, a seven-verse passage. We learn there that the king is restricted from doing the following: He's not to multiply wives, he's not to multiply silver and gold, and he's not to engage in horse trade with Egypt. We also learn that the king of Israel is to have a written copy of this law—Hebrew: *tora*, this *tora*—which is to be read to him on a regular basis. Then there's another passage in the Bible (1 Samuel 10) that informs us that Samuel wrote down the law—the Hebrew term here is a different word: *mišpat*—of kingship in a book, but we have no further information about that book that Samuel wrote. One can imagine later generations of Jews wondering: Where is this book? It is possible that all of this forms the background for the lengthy section concerning the king in the Temple Scroll, columns 56–59; four columns devoted to the single subject of the King of Israel. In fact, at the beginning of this section of the Temple Scroll, column 56 states, "they shall write for him this Torah in a book, before the priests"; and then at the top of the next column, 57:1, it continues, "This is the Torah," Then there's a broken section, though probably we can restore "which they wrote for him before," until the word "priests" is the next word that we can read there. "This is the Torah concerning the king" is what the Temple Scroll is telling us, presumably linking it back to the passage in Samuel and to the much, much shorter section—only seven verses—in Deuteronomy 17.

No surprise: In light of our earlier discussion, that polygamy and divorce are not allowed for the king; the king is to have but one wife. We also learn that the king should have a council consisting of 12 priests, 12 Levites, and 12 non-sacerdotal leaders of the people.

Finally, we should contemplate the larger picture that emerges from our study of the Temple Scroll, with two points to be noted: We cannot emphasize this document enough, especially since it showed Dead Sea Scrolls researchers how important legal/Halakhic issues were, with the Qumran sect demonstrating a stricter approach to Jewish law at every turn. Of course, we saw this in the Damascus Document, too, but the issue was not fully realized by scholars who were still on the theology path, especially in light of Josephus's description of the three sects. Clearly, the Qumran community was very Temple-focused—that's the second point I want to make here—even though the Yahad members had elected to no longer participate in the Jerusalem cult. After all, this longest of all the Dead Sea Scrolls focuses on the Temple rituals; and then there is the enormous size of the Temple; and then the council of the king with its 12 priests; and on and on it goes in the Temple Scroll. In addition, we have these other texts like the Community Rule that refer to the importance of priests. While we have not accepted the main conclusion of our colleague Lawrence Schiffman, we should note that the Temple Scroll is a major component of his argument. Any group that would write a text such as the Temple Scroll would, by definition, have a major focus on the Temple; and the Sadducees, of course, were the most Temple-centered of the Jewish sects of late antiquity.

Naturally, in the end, though, much of the contents of the Temple Scroll are but an ideal, since the Qumran community never did control the operations of the actual Temple in Jerusalem. With that, we segue into our next lecture, which, by contrast, describes what the Yahad members actually did do on a daily basis.

Daily Life at Qumran
Lecture 15

How did the Qumran community go about its daily life? It is important to remember that the sect members at Qumran were real people with real lives beyond our precious documents.

At Qumran, Roland de Vaux identified a tower, a pottery-manufacturing area, a kitchen and pantry, a meeting hall, a scriptorium, and an elaborate system of cisterns and *miqva'ot* (ritual baths). Lacking were private homes and residences. This led de Vaux to see at the Qumran group living communally. The scriptorium and ink wells indicated that scribal activity was prominent. There is a path that connects the site and the caves, suggesting a true linkage between the two main foci of our course.

I base much of my reconstruction of daily life at Qumran on two essays from *A Day at Qumran*: "From Dawn to Dusk among the Qumran Sectarians" by Adolfo Roitman and "A Day in the Life of Hananiah Nothos: A Story" by Magen Broshi. Where did the Qumran community members live? Tents have been proposed. Such shelters would have left little or no trace. Another option is that they lived in the caves, which did yield artifacts of everyday life. It is possible that individuals slept in the main site, perhaps in dormitory style.

> **Lacking were private homes and residences. This led de Vaux to see at the Qumran group living communally.**

Both Josephus (in his description of the Essenes) and various Dead Sea Scrolls (the Community Rule, for example) speak of the community rising at dawn to recite the morning prayers. And of course we note in the Community Rule passage that evening prayer also was recited. Both Philo and Josephus describe the Essenes as engaged in agricultural activities (though naturally this would be true of the vast majority of any population in ancient times). One is not surprised to find evidence for such activity at Qumran. Some members of the community engaged in the manufacture of baskets from palm fronds and reeds, textiles from wool and linen, parchment—necessary for producing the scrolls—from animal skins, and pottery vessels for ordinary cooking and food storage as well as those for storing scrolls.

Plenty of coins were found at Qumran, which may suggest some contact with the outside world via trade and commerce, or it may suggest a *Yahad* treasury, accumulated when individuals joined the sect and surrendered their personal wealth.

The practice of communal meals is discussed in the Community Rule and in other scrolls. Josephus explains that the Essenes perform their daily labors and occupations until the fifth hour, at which point they assemble for ritual bathing and communal dining, with blessings before and after the meal. After this, Josephus notes, the Essenes return to their labors for the remainder of the day.

How many people lived at Qumran at any one time? It was a small community; the scholarly consensus is about 150–200 people at any given time. Researchers arrived at this number by looking at the general size of the place, the number of graves in the cemetery, the amount of food that could be produced in an out-of-the-way inhospitable climate such as this, the amount of water provided by the rain collected in the Wadi Qumran and then channeled to the water cisterns, and so on. We cannot know how many of the residents were men, women, or children. A survey of the skeletons buried nearby reveals that most of those buried there died young. This may be due to the harsh conditions. Most likely, as people got older, they left Qumran, unable to handle the harsh conditions, and thus returned to Jerusalem to live among the Essenes there or in other communities perhaps. This would explain the relative youth of the people buried at Qumran.

The first interpreters of the scrolls and the archaeological site of Qumran believed that the group was celibate. They noted, correctly, that there are no references to women in the Community Rule. Pliny said the Essenes whom he encountered lived without women and renounced love, and Philo and Josephus noted that some among the Essenes were celibate. This view has largely been discredited, however, because of references to women in the other texts, including the Damascus Document, the War Scroll, and the Messianic Rule. The cemetery at Qumran has also revealed some female skeletons.

A unique document found at Qumran is an ostracon (inscribed piece of pottery). Unearthed in 1996, it was published by Frank Moore Cross and Esther Eshel. This text is a deed of gift, indicating the transfer of property (house, fig trees, and olive trees) of a certain Honi to the *Yahad* via an individual named Elazar ben Nahmani. We thus gain confirmation of the process indicated in the Community Rule whereby members donated their personal property to the community. Interestingly, the text also refers to Honi's slave, Hisdai. According to both Philo and Josephus, the Essenes did not own slaves. But we do have a reference to slaves in the Damascus Document: "A man should not provoke his male-slave or his female-slave or his hired-hand on the Sabbath." Unfortunately, the ostracon is badly broken, especially where the slave is mentioned, so we cannot be sure about Hisdai. Was he freed if Honi joined the sect? Was he given some responsibility for Honi's property at this stage? ■

Essential Reading

Schiffman, *Reclaiming the Dead Sea Scrolls*, 127–143.

Supplementary Reading

Roitman, *A Day at Qumran*.

Questions to Consider

1. To what extent should issues of daily life be important to our reconstruction of the Qumran community? Is it worth devoting an entire lecture to this subject, especially since the *Yahad*'s greatest legacy are the 930 documents they copied and authored?

2. From the evidence presented, do you believe that the Qumranites were celibate?

Daily Life at Qumran
Lecture 15—Transcript

Although the main focus of our attention in this course—as it is in every course on the Dead Sea Scrolls—is the collection of documents found in the caves at Qumran, from time to time we have turned our attention to the archaeological evidence as well. If we combine these two elements, what scholars call the written remains on the one hand and the material culture on the other, we are able to address a different question: How did the Qumran community go about its daily life? Accordingly, we take time out from our reading of the individual scrolls and from a discussion of major theological issues to speak about the quotidian. After all, although many of the sectarians may have been busy copying scrolls and studying the ancient texts, clearly daily life goes on. In this lecture, we shall use an integrative approach— that is, one based on both the texts and the archaeological data—to explore such questions as the sect's daily routine, social structure, economy, farming, food production, and more.

We begin by repeating some of the information presented in Lecture Six devoted to the archaeology of Qumran. The excavations at Qumran were conducted early on by Père Roland de Vaux in the 1950s, and then we also presented then some information about more recent archaeological explorations at the site of Khirbet Qumran, the caves, and the region in general. De Vaux identified the following major buildings or rooms at Qumran: a tower; a pottery manufacturing area; a kitchen and a pantry that contained literally hundreds of cooking vessels and dining utensils; a main meeting hall that probably doubled as the dining hall; a scriptorium, in which were found writing tables and inkwells; and an elaborate system of cisterns and *miqva'ot* (ritual baths) fed by an aqueduct leading from the nearby Wadi Qumran. Again, here we recall the emphasis placed on ritual bathing in the Dead Sea Scrolls for the removal of not only ritual impurity but also moral impurity. Lacking, according to de Vaux, were private homes and residences, which led de Vaux to see at Qumran a group living communally, as indicated by the scrolls and by Josephus's description of the Essenes. And, of course, the scriptorium: The writing tables and inkwells indicated that scribal activity was prominent at the site, and once more a connection was made to the scrolls found in the nearby caves. More recent excavations have identified a latrine as discussed in the previous lecture, beyond the 1,000 cubit limit from the site. Then there is the path that connects the site and the caves, suggesting a true linkage between the two main foci of our course: the archaeological site and the documents found in the caves at Qumran.

I base much of my reconstruction of daily life at Qumran for this lecture on the two main essays that appear in a book entitled *A Day at Qumran*, published in 1997, edited by Adolfo Roitman, curator of the Shrine of the Book. You'll recall I mentioned the Shrine of the Book as the special pavilion at the Israel Museum dedicated to the display and preservation of the Dead Sea Scrolls. This book in turn is based on an exhibit at the museum presented in that same year, 1997, to mark the 50th anniversary of the discovery of the first Dead Sea Scrolls. The first essay in the book is by Roitman himself, and it is entitled "From Dawn to Dusk among the Qumran Sectarians." The second one is a very delightful and creative essay by Magen Broshi, another Israeli scholar, Roitman's predecessor as curator of the Shrine of the Book, now retired; and Broshi's essay is called "A Day in the Life of Hananiah Nothos: A Story."

The name of the protagonist, Hananiah Nothos, comes from a unique Dead Sea Scroll document; again, it's fragmentary, as is all so often the case with the Cave Four material. This one is called 4Q477; it includes a list of individuals, mentioned by name—we finally get the names of individuals, something we hardly ever see in the Dead Sea Scrolls—in this case, individuals mentioned by name who were rebuked by the overseer of the community for various perhaps minor infringements. In the case of Hananiah Nothos, while the text is broken at this point—again, it's a Cave Four fragment—we can read that he was reproved by the leader, by the overseer, for doing something to "disturb the spirit of the community." We recall from the Community Rule, 1QS 7 there appears there a list of infractions and punishment by confinement for the offenses; and here you have a correlation between that important Community Rule document and this small fragmentary text from Cave Four giving us some names, including one person who disturbed the community.

We will discuss a whole variety of subjects related to the quotidian—to daily life at Qumran—in this lecture. Let's begin with the topic of shelter: Where did the Qumranites actually live and sleep? We ask this question especially because, as noted, the excavations revealed no private domiciles. One option proposed is that the members of the *Yahad* lived in tents, and we simply have no remains of those tents which are biodegradable material. Another option is that they lived in the caves. The exploration of the caves yielded not only the scrolls most famously, but also evidence of everyday life: pottery shards, combs, mats, ropes, some textiles, pieces of leather, two document-type items called *tefillin* and *mezuzot*—we'll explore these later on in Lecture 19—and even some remains of food. Some of these things were found in the very caves in which the documents were found; some of these were found in other caves in which no texts were found. Then is perhaps there a third option: Individuals slept in the main site, perhaps in dormitory style in one of the large rooms.

Regarding the notion that people lived in the caves, again we recall the discovery by Eshel and Broshi—referred to in a previous lecture—of a main path with some side paths leading from the site, from the community center if you will, to the caves. Along this path were found pottery shards once more and, more importantly, more than 60 sandal nails. That is nails that were used in the manufacturing of sandals—we know of these from all over the Roman Empire from antiquity—which would come loose as people would walk on a stony path. The fact that there are more than 60 of these nails, this find informs us that people were constantly walking back and forth from the site to the caves; as opposed, for example, to simply using the caves for the storing of documents as necessary on an occasional basis.

The next topic I want to explore as we go through the daily life of the community at Qumran is morning prayer. Both Josephus in his description of the Essenes and the various Dead Sea Scrolls—the Community Rule, for example—speak of the community rising at dawn to recite the morning prayers. Let me read you a passage from Josephus: "And as for their piety towards God, it is very extraordinary; for before sunrise they speak not a word about profane matters, but offer certain prayers, which they have received from their forefathers, as if they made a supplication for its rising [the rising of the sun]." They face east, they face the sun; before sunrise, before they've spoken—I'm paraphrasing Josephus here—they offer prayers in the morning. This is Josephus in his important work, *The Jewish War:*

Book 2. Now, a quotation from the Community Rule; this is what 1QS 10:13–14 says: "When I first extend my hands and my feet, I will bless his name [obviously referring to God]. When I first set out or come home, to sit or arise, or to lie on my bed, I will praise him and I will bless him, with the offering of what comes forth from my lips." To paraphrase once more, when I first extend my hands and my feet—that, of course, means in the morning upon arising—I will bless him with prayer; in the words of this text, "the offering of what comes forth from my lips." Morning prayer would include the use of *tefillin*; I mentioned them a moment ago, I mention them here again. This is traditionally translated as "phylacteries"; we'll come back to the discussion of *tefillin* found at Qumran in a future lecture. Of course, we also note in the Community Rule passage that I just read that evening prayer also was recited.

Among the Dead Sea Scrolls are various prayer texts, though in most cases we cannot associate a particular document with a particular time for prayer—be it morning or evening, daily, Sabbath, festival in most cases; in some cases we can be more specific—and in any case, most of these prior texts are very (you guessed it) fragmentary. However, the one large text we have—1QH, the Hodayot Scroll, the Thanksgiving Hymns; we've referred to it several times—we'll come back to that in a future lecture; we'll see those hymns that are prayer-like or psalm-like hymns to God. We'll talk about that text again in a future lecture. All of this was true—the morning prayer, the evening prayer, and the use of *tefillin*, the phylacteries—of the later rabbis as well and most likely the Pharisees, who were contemporary to the Essenes. But for the Essenes we have explicit information: both Josephus's description, who mentions morning prayer for the Essenes; and, again, the Community Rule.

Next topic of discussion: agricultural work. Both Philo and Josephus describe the Essenes as engaged in agricultural activities; though naturally this would be true of the vast majority of the population, both Jewish and general, in ancient times. One is not surprised to find evidence for such activity at Qumran. Philo's description is worth citing. He writes:

For there are some of them [the Essenes] who are devoted to the practice of agriculture, being skilful in such things as pertain to the sowing and cultivation of lands; others again are shepherds, or cowherds, and experienced in the management of every kind of animal; some are cunning in what relates to swarms of bees.

Here you get all sorts of activities being referred to by Philo: growing crops, raising animals, even beekeeping.

What do we learn from Qumran? First, barley was grown in an area above the cliffs where it flattens out. There is a small valley called the Hyrcania Valley, flatland, and that allowed for the growing of barley and we have evidence for the growing of the barley there in this period. More importantly, the Qumran community ran an agricultural station at a place that today is called Ein Fashkha; that's the local Arabic name, still called using the term that the Bedouin in the region call it, Ein Fashkha. It's a natural spring three kilometers to the south of Qumran; not the freshest of water because it's very close to the Dead Sea, but there's a little bit of fresh water and a little bit of the saline water. In any case, there's enough water there to allow for crops to be grown, and the most important crop appears to have been dates. In Pliny's words—we keep going back to Pliny—the Essenes whom he encountered had "(only) palm trees for company." Charred dates and date pits have been found both at the site of Qumran and in the caves. Animal bones, especially sheep bones, have also been found at Qumran, which indicates that some people were engaged in animal husbandry. Sheep, naturally, are a ready source of milk for dairy products and wool for clothing.

Mention of the date pits leads to me a tangential discussion. Date pits also were found at Masada, far to the south, during the excavations conducted there by Yigael Yadin and his associate and successor Ehud Netzer, another Israeli archaeologist. In 2005, an Israeli botanist named Elaine Solowey asked Professor Netzer if he had any ancient date seeds, and he said, "Yes, I've been keeping some in my drawer that I found at Masada." Doctor Solowey experimented by planting three of the seeds provided to her by Professor Netzer in 2005; and indeed one plant has germinated. It now stands about four meters high, and it has sprouted a dozen fronds. As of this taping, it is still a bit too early to determine whether or not the tree is a female—and yes, with date palms, there is sex; there are male trees that do not give fruit, and there are female trees that obviously do give fruit—if it is, it should yield fruit when mature. I have visited this little wonder, this date palm, twice in recent years—in 2006 and in 2007—at the Arava Institute for Environmental Studies located at Kibbutz Ketura in the far south of Israel, where the "old new palm" has become something of a tourist sensation, a botanical phoenix. Access is limited given the delicate nature of this experiment, but if you ask permission you should be able to get to see this palm tree. What an exciting development from a date seed, a date pit, found at Masada.

Back to Qumran: Handicrafts, another subject I want to address with you. Other members of the community engaged in the manufacturing of baskets from the palm fronds and the reeds that one can find in the area. They made textiles, not only from wool, but also from linen (they must have been obtaining flax from some source), and parchment from their animal skins, and they, of course, were necessary for the many scrolls that they were copying. Then, of course, there was also the most common find in any archaeological excavation: pottery vessels; and again you'll recall that de Vaux an area where pottery was manufactured. Again, I want to cite a passage from Philo as he continues in his description of the Essenes. He writes as follows: "Others [among the Essenes] are artisans and handicraftsmen, in order to guard against suffering from the want of anything of which there is at times an actual need; and these men omit and delay nothing, which is requisite for the innocent supply of the necessaries of life." That is to say, these individual Essenes—and we are, of course, assuming that our Qumran community are Essenes—appear to be self-sufficient; they make everything that they could possibly need as I've indicated here for you: pottery, parchment, clothing. From whatever sources they were able to manufacture everything because there were members of the community who were expert in these various handicrafts. As indicated earlier, plenty of coins were found at Qumran, which may suggest some contact with the outside world via trade and commerce, though we also theorized in an earlier lecture that the horde of coins represented the *Yahad* treasury, accumulated when individuals joined the sect and surrendered their personal wealth.

We now turn our attention to the communal meal; we've mentioned this several times in the course, how the community deliberated together and ate together, and did all sorts of things together. Let's focus on that community meal; though first I want to cite, in this case, Josephus at length. After the quotation that I gave you earlier about the morning prayers, Josephus next explains that the Essenes perform their daily labors and their occupations until the fifth hour of the day, at which point (and here's this long quotation from Josephus):

> After which they assemble themselves together again into one place; and when they have clothed themselves in white veils, they then bathe their bodies in cold water. And after this purification is over, they every one meet together in a building of their own, into which it is not permitted to any of another sect to enter; while they go, after a pure manner, into the dining-room, as into a certain holy temple, and quietly set themselves down; upon which the baker lays them loaves in order; the cook also brings a single plate of one sort of food, and sets it before every one of them; but a priest says grace before meal; and it is unlawful for any one to taste of the food before grace is said. The same priest, when he has dined, says grace again after meal; and when they begin, and when they end, they praise God, as he that bestows their food upon them.

Again, from *The Jewish War: Book 2*, a long text from Josephus that describes for us the communal meal that the Essenes eat together. This accords well with the description in 1QS, the Community Rule, especially with the priest conducting the blessing. Let me now read this passage to you from 1QS 6: "When they have set the table for eating, or the new-wine for drinking, the priest will send forth his hand first to bless the first-portion of the bread or the new-wine to drink. The priest will send forth his hand first to bless the first-portion of the bread and the new-wine." That is not a mistake on my part, that's how the text reiterates, rewords, restates the fact that the priest needs to be the first one to send forth his hand, "first to bless the first-portion of the bread" and "the new-wine." Later in Column 6 of the Community Rule, we read that initiates to the sect may not "touch the pure-food of the group" until the period of their initiation is completed; that is, once their spirit has been inspected—I'm paraphrasing what the text says there—and they are now deemed to be acceptable to the other members of the sect. This also accords with what Josephus wrote in the quotation that I read aloud to you. Finally, Josephus notes that after the meal and the blessings after the meal, the Essenes return again to their labors for the remainder of the day until sunset.

Another major activity of the group clearly was the study of the religious texts and the writing and copying of the texts. As we can see from all of the Dead Sea Scrolls, from this large corpus, this must have been a major component of their regular life. Indeed, as we learn from, again, the Community Rule (staying in Column 6) that community members studied Torah and other texts for one-third of the night—that is, after dark; during the dark hours—every night of the year. That's actually stated in the Community Rule; clearly this was part of their daily, or in this case nightly, regimen. No doubt the parchment for the writing of these texts was obtained from their own flocks, and, of course, this entails an entire process from killing the animal, skinning the animal, tanning and preparing the leather, and so on; the whole procedure just to obtain the writing materials for the writing of their texts. The ink has been analyzed and it has been found to be a combination of soot, resin, oil, and water. Four of the scrolls—only 4 out of the 930—in some places use red ink and this was extracted from the mineral cinnabar. No writing utensils have been found at Qumran, though presumably the scribes used either pens made of sharp reeds or hard metal. By the way, some leather strips were also found in the caves along with the documents, most likely used to keep the scrolls closed when the scrolls were rolled up.

An important question, not addressed up until this point in our course: How many people lived at Qumran at any one time? Clearly this was a small community; the scholarly consensus is that about 150–200 people lived at the site of Qumran at any given time. Researchers arrive at this number by looking at the general size of the place, the number of graves in the cemetery adjacent to the site of Qumran, the amount of food that could be produced in an out-of-the-way inhospitable climate such as this—even including the site of Ein Fashkha, three kilometers to the south, where they did, in fact, grow food as I mentioned—the amount of water that is provided by the rain collected in the Wadi Qumran and then channeled to the water cisterns, and so on. All of these factors are taken into account by scholars in an attempt to get a very rough estimate of how many peopled lived at Qumran at a single time; and again, I repeat, 150–200 individuals, a tiny community within the much larger world of Jewish life in the ancient land of Israel. How many of these people were men, women, and children we simply cannot know.

A survey of the skeletons in the cemetery reveals that most people died young. This may be due to the harsh conditions of the site, of this location; remote, isolated, as we've described. Most likely, though, as people got older they left Qumran, unable to handle these harsh conditions, and thus they returned to Jerusalem to live among the Essenes there; or perhaps they went to other communities. This would explain the relatively low ages of the people who died and were buried at Qumran.

Now we come to the question of women at Qumran; we've discussed this several times, we've had a few things to say about it, let's now put it into one larger, systematic treatment. As we have seen, the first interpreters of the scrolls and the archaeological site as well, such as Father de Vaux, believed that the group was celibate. In particular, they noted (correctly) that there are no references to women in the key Community Rule document, the most important of the first seven scrolls to be found and published; and, naturally, they relied on the comment by Pliny that the Essenes whom he encountered lived without women and renounced love, plus there are references in Philo and Josephus to the fact that some among the Essenes were celibate. This view has been largely discredited, though, especially since there are references to women in other texts, including three that we have mentioned already in our course: the Damascus Document, the War Scroll, and the *Messianic Rule*; all of those have references to women. The cemetery at Qumran has revealed some female skeletons, I should add, though the picture is not as clear as one would hope. We do not always have the distinctive bones—namely, the pelvic bones—to determine male from female in these skeletons. Some of the burials also may date from a more recent time; they actually may be local Bedouin who may have used this cemetery, we simply can't be sure. Further complicating the matter is the fact that the skeletons in the cemetery do not contain enough collagen—that's the protein found in bones and tissues—which allow for a reliable carbon-14 dating. Then there's the issue of scholars wishing to be sensitive to the issue of exhuming human remains and submitting the bones to a carbon-14 test in the first place. All of these are issues involved in examining, analyzing, and interpreting the skeletal remains from the cemetery.

A unique document found at Qumran is an ostracon unearthed in 1996. An ostracon is an inscribed piece of pottery, a shard of pottery that was used to write down a text. Obviously, the 930 documents of Qumran are written almost all on parchment and some of them on papyrus; here we have a rare find: an inscribed piece of pottery, an ostracon, found in 1996, subsequently published jointly by Frank Moore Cross of Harvard University and Esther Eshel of Bar-Ilan University. The former, Professor Cross, is a member of the original scrolls team to whom was entrusted the publication of many of the biblical scrolls—those were handed over to Frank Cross back in the 1950s—while Esther Eshel, I add, represents the best of the younger generation of Dead Sea Scrolls scholars. This text on this ostracon is a deed of gift, indicating the transfer of property—and specifically three items are listed: a house, fig trees, and olive trees—of a certain person named Honi (the text breaks off, so that we do not know his father's name) is handed over via this document to the *Yahad*, transmitted to an individual named Elazar ben Nahmani (Elazar, the son of Nahmani) who apparently is the overseer or bursar of the *Yahad* at this point. We thus gain from this unique find, from this ostracon, the confirmation of the process indicated in the Community Rule (1QS) whereby members donated their personal property to the community.

Interestingly, the text also refers to Honi's slave named Hisdai from the city of Holon. According to both Philo and Josephus, the Essenes did not own slaves; but we do have a reference to slaves in the Damascus Document in Column 11 in the Sabbath law: "A man should not provoke his male-slave or his female-slave or his hired-hand on the Sabbath." Unfortunately, the ostracon is badly broken, especially where the slave is mentioned, so we cannot be sure about Hisdai. Was he freed if and when Honi joined the sect? Was he given some responsibility for Honi's property at this stage? Again, questions without definitive answers.

This lecture reminds us that while scribes were active on a regular basis at Qumran in the copying of texts, the daily life of people continued regardless. There are real people with real lives behind our precious documents, and hopefully we have given you some insight into how they went about their daily lives. Once upon a time, history was about texts, major events, rulers, and armies. Today, the study of history has shifted to include the quotidian, what people ate, their work utensils, the role of women, the life of the family, and much more. As this lecture indicates, using both the findings of the archaeologists and the contents of our ancient texts, we are able to reconstruct much of this even for a remote desert outpost such as Qumran.

The Halakhic Letter—Rituals Define the Sect
Lecture 16

The publication of this Halakhic Letter changed Dead Sea Scrolls scholarship in major ways.

The Halakhic Letter was found in 1954 but remained unpublished into the 1980s. John Strugnell, who was first assigned the scroll, was joined in his work by Elisha Qimron, who announced the letter's existence at an academic conference in Jerusalem in 1984, using "the Halakhic Letter" as its working title. The text was published under their joint authorship in 1994, with the scholarly designation 4QMMT based on the text's own title *Miqsat Ma'aseh ha-Torah* ("Some Precepts of Torah"). As far as we can determine, the very existence of this scroll was known only to Strugnell for 30 years.

The text was the basis for a lawsuit in an Israeli court in 1993. Hershel Shanks of the Biblical Archaeology Society obtained a copy of the text, which he then published in *Biblical Archaeology Review*. Qimron sued Shanks for copyright violation and won.

Why is this text so important? Before its publication, scholars followed Josephus, assuming that the major issues that differentiated the Jewish sects of late antiquity were theological. This letter, however, showed that the major issues were Halakhic ones. Six different copies were found in Cave 4, indicating that this was a foundational text for the sect. Unfortunately, all six copies are in fragmentary condition. The author presents about 20 individual legal matters, which form the basis of disagreements between the sect and its opponents. The letter speaks about "we," "you," and "they," indicating three different groups, which scholars reconstruct, respectively, as the Essenes (that is, the Qumran community), the Sadducees (the addressees of the letter), and the Pharisees (the "they"). Some of the issues are the same ones indicated in the Temple Scroll.

The question of "continuous streams" is one of the main issues of contention featured in the letter. When a liquid is poured from a pure upper vessel into an impure lower vessel, the rabbis declare that both the upper vessel and its contents remain pure. The Halakhic Letter, on the other hand, declares both vessels and their contents impure. Again, note the economic hardship here, disposing of an entire large vessel of olive oil or wine. This view of impurity moving upstream as well as down is also mentioned in the Mishna as the view of the Sadducees. This suggests that there might be some ultimate link between the Qumran community (and perhaps the Essenes in general) and the Sadducees, at least in the area of Jewish law.

Another featured issue is the case of what the rabbis call a *tevul yom*, one who has immersed in a *miqveh* (ritual bath) during the daytime to remove his impurity, even though sunset is still some hours away. Is this person pure or impure? Must one wait the full time until sundown? The Halakhic Letter argues that only on sundown is one ritually pure. The rabbis, as we know from the Mishna, allowed such a person to be in a state between true purity and true impurity. This discussion demonstrates that the later rabbinic principle (from the 2nd century C.E. Mishna) was already in place in the 2nd century B.C.E.

In hindsight, scholars should have known that Halakhic differences separated the sects from one another, since such issues have been at the heart of movements throughout the history of Judaism. By and large, though, the scholars were blind to this extremely important point. Throughout the 1950s, 1960s, and 1970s, and indeed into the 1980s, most of Dead Sea Scrolls research was in the hands of Christian scholars who were not necessarily knowledgeable about Jewish legal texts. The scholars focused on the doctrinal issues that separated the sects, as outlined by Josephus, for such have been the foci of debates within Christian religious history. We conclude that Josephus did not present Halakhic issues to his Greco-Roman audience because such minute practical distinctions would not have been understood by his readers. Now we have confirming evidence for Josephus's comment that the Essenes were the strictest of the late antique Jewish sects.

We have used the word "Halakah" throughout our course, defining it as Jewish law. The word comes from the verb *halak*, which means "go," as if to say every path that one follows in life is governed by Halakah. Among rabbinic texts, we had evidence for the word only from later compositions, the Mishna and the Talmud. Now from Qumran comes evidence that the word existed earlier.

Finally, we need to address an issue that has been implied in our course already but has not been stated explicitly: The Pharisees were not the only sect to survive the events of 70 C.E. The Essenes apparently survived as well, for one of their key texts was still read in the 10th and 12th centuries in medieval Cairo. The Sadducees may have survived as well, emerging 800 years later as the Karaites. This finding forces us to examine the texts, ideas, history, and any other evidence we may have at our disposal from these sects all the more closely. ∎

Essential Reading

Vermes, *The Complete Dead Sea Scrolls in English*, 220–228.

VanderKam, *The Dead Sea Scrolls Today*, 59–60.

Schiffman, *Reclaiming the Dead Sea Scrolls*, 83–89.

Supplementary Reading

Polliack, *Karaite Judaism*.

Questions to Consider

1. Can you think of some supposedly minor or insignificant differences in our own culture that, like the Halakhic issues here, serve to separate groups, sects, denominations, or political parties?

2. How do you think the Damascus Document continued to be read and copied for more than a millennium—that is, the time span separating our different textual witnesses (the Cave 4 fragments and two Cairo genizah manuscripts)? Can you reconstruct the continued existence of the Essenes deep into the Middle Ages? Similarly, do you think there is

a direct link between the Sadducees of late antiquity and the Karaites of the medieval period? Let your historical imagination guide you, as if, perhaps, you were writing a historical novel about the persistence of the Essenes and Sadducees in history, even when unattested.

The Halakhic Letter—Rituals Define the Sect
Lecture 16—Transcript

The publication of this crucial text, the Halakhic Letter, or 4QMMT, was delayed for years. It was discovered in Qumran Cave Four in 1954, but was not published until 1994, 40 years later. Once more we will narrate the tale of discovery and publication, including how the six fragmentary copies were pieced together to create a coherent whole; but more importantly we will delve deeply into the contents of this foundational text for the Qumran community. The document, known by its Hebrew name, *Miqsat Ma'aseh ha-Torah* ("Some Precepts of Torah," 4QMMT is its siglum), or more simply, in English, the Halakhic Letter, is a treatise written by the leader of the sect in which he refers to 20 points of *halakha*, Jewish law. These legal matters, we learn, differentiate the sect (referred to as "we" in the text; that is the Essenes) from the addressee (referred to as "you" in the text, understood as the Sadducees) and a third group (referred to as "they" in the text, understood as the Pharisees). Quite astonishingly, we learned that the issues that divide the groups are relatively minor matters of *halakha*, and not the larger dogmatic issues such as belief in angels, belief in an afterlife, and so on as noted by Josephus.

The publication of this text changed Dead Sea Scrolls scholarship in major ways. The text was found in 1954 and was assigned to John Strugnell, but it remained unpublished into the 1980s. Strugnell was joined in the enterprise of publishing this text by Elisha Qimron, an Israeli scholar from Ben-Gurion University, who announced its existence at an academic conference in Jerusalem in 1984, using the working title the Halakhic Letter. Finally, the text was published under their joint authorship—Qimron and Strugnell—in 1994 with the scholarly designation 4QMMT, using the initials "MMT" based on the text's own title, the Hebrew phrase *Miqsat Ma'ase ha-Torah* ("Some Precepts of Torah"). Yes, no matter how hard to fathom, as far as we can determine the very existence of this text was known only to Strugnell for 30 years, and even then scholars needed to await an additional 10 years before they could actually read the text. Once more I include a personal note here for you: Elisha Qimron showed me a copy of MMT in 1985, in the early years of his research into this document, though naturally I had to agree not to share the contents of this text with anyone else.

This text, by the way, was the basis for a lawsuit in an Israeli court in 1993. Hershel Shanks of the Biblical Archaeology Society is a major player in the story of the Dead Sea Scrolls, and we will talk about Hershel Shanks still to come in a later lecture. Shanks was able to obtain a copy of the text—we will explain how in that later lecture—which he then published in his journal, *Biblical Archaeology Review*. Qimron sued Shanks for copyright violation and he won.

Why is this text so important? Before the publication of the text, scholars followed the lead of Josephus in assuming that the major issues that differentiated the Jewish sects of late antiquity were theological ones: belief in angels, immortality of the soul, free will versus predetermination; these are the questions that Josephus presents that distinguish Pharisees, Sadducees, and Essenes. MMT, however, showed that the major issues were Halakhic ones. MMT is a letter written by the leader of the sect to his opponents. Six different copies were found in Cave Four, indicating that this was a foundational text for the sect. Their official designations are 4Q394–399; and when the six copies are put together we get 4QMMT. Unfortunately, all six copies are in fragmentary condition; nonetheless, Qimron and Strugnell succeeded to produce a coherent text.

Let me give you an analogy to explain how these two scholars went about their work. Imagine if you had six copies of a particular document; it could be a newspaper article, or a book, or whatever it might be, but keep in mind that they're not six copies that have been printed but rather six copies in different handwritings, as is always the case in Dead Sea Scrolls. So what they did: They had the beginning of the text in one copy, they had the end of the text in another copy, they had bits and pieces scrapped from the middle of the text, and hopefully they would have some overlap; so in the fragment that goes at the beginning of the text, they might have a couple of sentences where the text breaks off which is then in another fragment, and eventually they piece the whole thing together in this fashion to produce a single, continuous text out of these six fragments. These tiny scraps that emerged from Cave Four: Quite a bit of important work, baseline work in this field, done mainly by Elisha Qimron brought on board by John Strugnell to complete the task of reading, publishing, translating, and commenting on the MMT text.

In the letter, the author presents about 20 individual legal matters that form the basis of disagreement between the sect and its opponents. The letter speaks about "we," "you," and "they," indicating three different groups, which scholars reconstruct, respectively, as the Essenes, that is, the Qumran community, the "we"; the Sadducees, the addressee of the letter, the "you"; and the third group, referred to as the "they," the Pharisees. Many of the Halakhic issues may be considered very minor ones, but such is the phenomenon of Jewish sectarianism to debate these specific, from our vantage point, minor issues. Some of the issues are the same ones indicated in the Temple Scroll, such as the question of animal hides used in the Temple and the sacrifice of pregnant animals, which we discussed in a previous lecture.

Let us recall what those two topics are about: Do you remember our discussion about the animal hides? If you lived far from Jerusalem, the rabbis—as we know from a later period, the Pharisees—allowed you to bring your offerings, your liquid sacrifices, in an animal skin bottle from wherever that animal skin might have been obtained, presumably locally from a local tanner or from your own flock, perhaps; and you could bring its contents to the Temple where it could be sacrificed. But the Qumran community, as we learned from the Temple Scroll, disapproved of such a practice. For them, anything that came into the Temple had to have the purity of the Temple from the outset; and therefore, only an animal skin produced by an animal that was sacrificed in the Temple could be used to convey other materials to the Temple. Similarly, in the case of pregnant animals: Whereas the rabbis permitted the sacrifice of a pregnant animal and held that it did not violate the law in Leviticus that prohibits the sacrifice of a mother and its young on the same day, the Qumran community, as we learned in the Temple Scroll, prohibits such a practice. A pregnant animal cannot be sacrificed because it violates the law of slaughtering a mother and its young on the same day. Those were two texts in the Temple Scroll; we now learn from the MMT text that these are two of the 20 Halakhic issues that the sect saw as representing their own legal perspective in opposition to other Jewish groups of the time. As I said, the rabbis later on explicitly permit both of these; the Qumran community explicitly forbids them.

Obviously, with the publication of the Temple Scroll in 1977, we already knew of these Halakhic stances, which I've just summarized for you once more. In the Temple Scroll, however—remember, an exceedingly long document, 67 columns—these legal opinions are embedded within this very long text, so there is no way of really knowing which of the many laws presented in the Temple Scroll (dozens, hundreds in fact) serve as bones of contention between the sect and its opponents. Indeed, for all we would know, the doctrinal issues found in the Community Rule (for example, predetermination), or in the War Scroll (for example, apocalypticism), these might have been the major bones of contention; after all, this is the conclusion one would reach from reading Josephus. MMT, on the other hand, spells this out very clearly. The legal issues that separate the sect from its opponents are these specific items that they themselves saw as distinguishing them from the other groups.

An additional important example of 1 of the 20 issues of *halakha*—again, which we may consider a very minor legal issue—is the question of what we call "continuous streams." When a liquid is poured from a pure upper vessel into an impure lower vessel—I'll explain what that means in a moment—the rabbis declare that both the upper vessel and its contents remain pure; that occurs in the Mishna. The MMT text, on the other hand, declares that both the lower vessel and the upper vessel, along with the contents of both vessels, are now impure. Let me explain, in some greater detail, what this means and some of the background for it. We have spoken about purity and impurity throughout our course. We've talked about the issues that make someone impure; you'll recall: childbirth, contact with the dead, specific skin diseases, a nocturnal emission of semen, vaginal blood during menstruation; those are examples of what causes a human to become impure. Impurity is communicable, however; you can convey it to another person by touching a person. If you are in a state of impurity and you touch another person, that person becomes impure. Impurity can also be conveyed to vessels, to inanimate objects; vessels of pottery and glass and metal and so on. so yes, a vessel can become impure; and then by definition, its contents become impure as well.

Imagine a scene such as the following: You are a priest in the Temple in Jerusalem. You have a large vessel of olive oil or wine that you're going to use in the sacrifice; a big pithos, for example, a large piece of pottery in which you have the liquid contents. You can't carry that huge jug to the altar to use, so you're going to pour some of it off into a smaller vessel; and you can understand how pouring requires an upper vessel and a lower vessel. Unbeknownst to you, however, the lower vessel that you have chosen was impure. It was just sitting there, and as you grabbed it and then started pouring from the upper vessel to the lower vessel to then convey the contents in the lower vessel—a small amount; however many ounces of olive oil or wine you were then going to bring to the altar in this smaller lower vessel—as you're doing this, another priest says, "Don't; don't use that one, that one's impure." It happens to be lying over there, it'll have to be destroyed somehow or rendered in some other way pure; if it were a metal vessel this could have been done for example, or a glass vessel. But while you're doing this, it's already too late; you've started the process of pouring from the large upper vessel into the smaller lower vessel without realizing that the lower one was impure. I hope you're all following this; this is a major issue for the sect and its opponents.

What happens? As I said, the rabbis would declare—everybody would agree—that the lower vessel, which was to begin with impure, and its contents are now impure; and your olive oil or your wine cannot be used now for the sacrifices in the Temple. The question is: What happens with the large upper vessel? The rabbi stated that the large upper vessel—it could be a huge vessel, by the way—and its contents remain pure. But the Qumran community, we learn from our MMT text, held that the upper vessel is also now impure since impurity—like salmon, let's say—can travel upstream. Again, note the economic hardship here: One would now have to dispose of an entire large vessel of the liquid, be it the wine or the olive oil, according to this stringent legal opinion forthcoming in the MMT text.

The view of *MMT* is also mentioned in the Mishna as the view of the Sadducees. We learned from reading the Mishna that this was indeed one of the issues that separated the rabbi successor of the Pharisees from the Sadducees. That is to say, the rabbis alone held that the upper vessel remained pure; while the Qumran community, the Essenes, and we also learned from the Mishna the Sadducees as well held that the upper vessel was now impure.

This suggests that there might be some ultimate link between the Qumran community and the Essenes in general, and the Sadducees, at least in the area of Jewish law; and here we have to refer once more, importantly, to the view of Professor Lawrence Schiffman.

Another issue is the case of what the rabbis call a *tevul yom*—this was another one of the Halakhic issues raised in the MMT text—one who has immersed in a *miqveh* (or a ritual bath) during the daytime to remove his impurity, even though sunset is still some hours away. The book of Leviticus, throughout the Torah, the implication is one waits until sunset, bathes, and then is ritually pure once more. But the rabbis allowed for an individual to do this during the daytime, and then wait until sunset. Is this person pure or impure? Must one wait the full time until sundown? The MMT text argues that only upon sundown is one ritually pure. The rabbis, as we know from the Mishna—there is an entire tractate called *Tevul Yom* ("one who has immersed in the daytime" would be the English equivalent of that expression, *Tevul Yom*) devoted to this subject in the sixth and final order of the Mishna called the *Tohorot*, which means "purities"—and the rabbis allowed such a person to be in a state between true purity and true impurity. For example, if such a person touched regular food, the food could still be eaten. If he touched holy food—that is, food that was going to be sacrificed—the food could not be eaten, but the food itself did not transmit any further impurity to someone who might touch that food. Again, a small, minor legal issue from our vantage point; but for the sect and the other sects of antiquity, these were the debates of the day, 2nd and 1st centuries B.C.E., and 1st and 2nd centuries C.E.

This discussion demonstrates that the later rabbinic principle of *Tevul Yom*, as we know from the 3rd century C.E. Mishna, already was in place in the 2nd century B.C.E.—almost half a millennium earlier—since the author of MMT is debating the issue at this point. In hindsight, scholars should have known all along that it was Halakhic differences that separated the sects from one another, since such issues have always been at the heart of distinctive Jewish movements throughout the history of Judaism. We already have discussed the Samaritans in contrast to the Jews. Both performed the Torah's sacrificial rituals in essentially the same manner, with priests offering animals on the altar. The only question was whether this should occur in Jerusalem, as per the Jews, or on Mount Gerizim, as per the Samaritans.

The Mishna frequently records differences of opinions between and among the rabbis, and the issues are almost always relatively minor legal ones. They are all within the same rabbinic, that is to say, continuation of the Pharisaic movement, but even amongst the rabbis one can find minor differences of opinion on Halakhic legal issues. For example: Based on Deuteronomy 6:7, all Jews agree that the central *Shema* prayer should be recited each morning and each evening. But individual rabbis held diverse views on the exact time of recitation, especially regarding the question: Until what time at night could one recite the evening *Shema*? The opinions recorded in the Mishna are: First, until the first third of the night; second, until midnight; third opinion, until dawn. That's the Halakhic question.

Another example of where Halakhic issues separate Jewish sects: During the early Middle Ages, a new offshoot of Judaism arose called Karaism, based on the view that only the Bible, and not the Mishna and the Talmud, should dictate Jewish law; the Karaites reject the oral law that the rabbis held so dearly. This schism also led to Halakhic differences, such as the question of whether or not it is permissible to have a light that was kindled in advance of the Sabbath to burn during the Sabbath; or the question of whether sexual intercourse was allowed on the Sabbath. In both cases, the Rabbis said yes, while the Karaites said no. Which is to say, traditionally Jews have allowed differences in belief—in the Middle Ages, for example, one could be a neo-Aristotelian or a neo-Platonist or even a mystic, following the Kabbalah (Jewish mysticism)—but differences of Halakhic practices typically served to divide communities.

By and large, though, scholars were blind to this extremely important point for the following reasons: Throughout the 1950s, '60s, and '70s, and indeed into the 1980s, most of Dead Sea Scrolls research was in the hands of Christian scholars; and while there is no reason that Christian scholars could not have been adept at Jewish legal texts such as the Mishna, generally throughout this period, such was not the case. Instead, Christian scholars focused on the doctrinal issues that separated the texts, as outlined by Josephus, for such have been the foci of debates within Christian religious history throughout the ages. Consider, for example, the Protestant Reformation, with its major doctrinal stance *sola fide*, "by faith alone." Or within the Protestant movement, one notes relatively minor doctrinal issues that separate the innumerable denominations; in the United States alone there are over 50 different Baptist sub-denominations, for example.

We also conclude that Josephus did not present these Halakhic issues in his presentation of the three sects to his Greco-Roman audience since such minute practical distinctions—such as whether such-and-such liquid transmits impurity or not—would not have been understood by his readers. But philosophical differences, such as whether free will rules or whether predetermination rules, were very much at the heart of educated Greco-Roman readers, accustomed to reading Plato, Aristotle, the Stoics, the Epicureans, and others. While you may think that whether the soul is immortal or whether the dead will be resurrected are the truly important issues in life, for the Dead Sea sect it is clear that the questions of animal skins, slaughtered pregnant animals, and continuous liquid streams were much more significant.

Now for one of the major conclusions of our course; one of the most important findings from our study of the Dead Sea Scrolls: Before this course, if I had asked you, were the rabbis lenient or strict in their application of Jewish law, most likely you would have said strict, based on the hundreds and indeed thousands of rulings in the Mishna and the later Talmud, with every possible arena of human life legislated. We now learn, however, that time and again the rabbis offered the most liberal legal ruling possible. The Essenes were the strict ones, as Josephus indicates; and now we have confirming evidence for Josephus's comment.

I want to spend a minute at this point in the lecture discussing the word *halakha*. We have used the word throughout our course, defining it as Jewish law. It is a well-established term, especially in the history of rabbinic Judaism. As for its etymology, the word comes from the verb *halak*, which means "to go," as if to say, "Every path that one follows—wherever ones goes in life, from cradle to grave, as it were—is governed by *halakha*; literally "the going." We have evidence for the word *halakha* only from our later rabbinic texts; it occurs in the Mishna, the Talmud, and so on, corpora to which we continue to refer throughout our course. Now from Qumran, however, comes evidence that the word existed earlier, even though the word itself is not attested in our Dead Sea Scrolls corpus. Let me explain: Three times in the our documents—once in the Damascus Document in Column 1 and twice in the Thanksgiving Hymns, still to be discussed in a future lecture, in Column 10—the enemies of the sect are referred to as *doreše (ba-)halaqot*, literally "seekers of smooth things," and "smooth things" is not very good (compare the English expression "smooth-talking"). So the enemies of the sect three times in our corpus of documents are referred to as *doreše halaqot*, "seekers of smooth things." But the phrase clearly puns on the word *halakha—doreše halaqot*; *halaqot, halakhot*, the plural of *halakha*—even though our word *halakha* is attested only from four centuries later, this demonstrates that the term was in existence during the heyday of the Qumran community.

The first part of this phrase, incidentally—*doreše halaqot*—comes from the verbal root *daraš*, which also is used in rabbinic parlance as a term for interpretation; interpretation of a text. If you know the word Midrash, often incorrectly translated as a "legend" or a "folklore," but more properly it means "interpretation"; this word comes from the same verbal root, this verb comes from the same 'legend, folklore', this word comes from the same verbal root, *daraš*. If the Dead Sea Scrolls authors are using the expression, then clearly the term *halakha* must have existed in Hebrew already, especially as used by the sect's opponents; and since we have seen time and again that the opponents of the *Yahad*, from the perspective of Jewish law, are the Pharisees, we once more have evidence, indirect in this case, for the Pharisaic-rabbinic continuum.

Finally, we need to address an issue that has been implied in our course already, but which we have not stated explicitly. We have seen that the Damascus Document existed at Qumran in the form of Cave Four fragments, and it existed in the Middle Ages in the form of the two manuscripts from the Cairo genizah. How did the text span the more than 1,000 years from our documents in Cave Four of Qumran to our two manuscripts from the Middle Ages in the Cairo genizah? Clearly, scribes must have continued to read, copy, and study this text in some form; though without a single mention that this was going on in the vast rabbinic corpus of texts at our disposal from the intervening millennium. Let us recall the size of the rabbinic corpus: The Mishna and the Tosefta together are about the size of the Bible. The

Talmud of the Land of Israel comprises approximately 750,000 words. The *Babylonian* Talmud comprises about 2,500,000 words. Then there are the other rabbinic collections, including large collections of Midrash. All told, we have the size of several encyclopedias; and yet not a word from the rabbis that anyone else who was not part of their tradition was reading, studying, and copying the Damascus Document. We know this only through two modern chance discoveries: one the Cairo genizah, the other the Dead Sea Scrolls.

This leads us to another point, adumbrated earlier: A few moments ago, I referred to the Karaites, a medieval sect that denied the existence of the Oral Law, and instead insisted only on the Bible itself to determine religious practice. This sounds very much like the view of the Sadducees, as we discussed long ago in our course back in Lecture Five; though once more, there is a long span of time (in this case, about 800 years) separating the two groups: the Sadducees of late antiquity, the Karaites of the early Middle Ages. Scholars used to assume a coincidence here; but now historians of Judaism must consider the possibility that a Sadducee stream continued to exist post-70 C.E. throughout the early rabbinic period, only to surface in our texts (our Karaite documents) once again in the 8th and 9th centuries C.E. The result of this investigation is nothing less than staggering. Indeed, what I taught earlier in the course is incorrect; well, not quite incorrect obviously. I was giving you the standard approach that one will find in all the standard textbooks. But we now need to nuance that just a little bit. The Pharisees are not the only sect to survive post-70, which is what I had stated earlier, eventually materializing as the rabbis and indeed over the course of centuries emerging as mainstream, normative Judaism, again, with all the necessary caveats implied in that term.

The Essenes apparently survived as well—earlier I said they ceased to exist after 70, but now we have to correct that—for one of their key texts, the Damascus Document, was still read in the 10th and 12th centuries, the dates of our two copies in medieval Cairo. The Sadducees, too, may have survived; earlier I said they ceased to exist in 70, the whole temple worship that was the focus of their devotion to God could no longer occur after the destruction of the Temple in 70 C.E.; but here you have Sadducee ideas emerging 800 years later in the form of our Karaites. This is indeed a staggering consideration, but such is the drama of scholarship, with unexpected findings forthcoming from new discoveries. Frankly, the possibility that all this is true takes my breath away.

In fact, this finding that the different sects of late antiquity may not have been flash in the plan movements but rather groups with a continuity deep into the Middle Ages, forces us to examine their texts, their ideas, their history, whatever evidence we might have, all the more closely. Let us, accordingly, return to an inspection of additional Dead Sea Scroll texts in our next lecture, specifically documents related to our Bible, including some compositions that are on the cusp of entering the Bible; though, as we shall see, even the term "Bible" is amorphous at this period. We will ask such questions as: What books were the Jews of late antiquity reading? Which did they consider sacred? Do they or do they not make it into the official canon, whatever that term may mean? All of these questions will be addressed in our next lecture, even if definitive answers are not always forthcoming.

The Qumran Biblical Canon
Lecture 17

> The Genesis Apocryphon provides a retelling of portions of the book of Genesis, including the stories of Noah and Abraham.

When the Qumran community was flourishing, the biblical canon had not yet been fixed. Clearly the Jews had canonized the Torah and the Prophets, and no doubt the Psalms were seen in the same way. This is indicated explicitly in one copy of the Halakhic Letter, in a reference to "the book of Moses, the books of the prophets and of David." A similar reference occurs in the Greek preface to the book of Ben Sira, composed around 130 B.C.E. It refers to the Torah, the books of the prophets, and "the others that followed." The remainder of the canon still was open-ended.

At Qumran, it seems that the books of Enoch and Jubilees were seen as canonical. Eleven copies of Enoch, all in Aramaic, were found in Qumran Cave 4, with a smattering of other Aramaic copies found in caves 1, 2, and 6. Enoch is based on the statement in Genesis 5:24 that Enoch did not die but God simply took him. Since he is still alive, Enoch is able to tell the history of the world, including events that have yet to pass. The book of Enoch dates to the 3rd century B.C.E. and thus predates the Qumran sect. Eventually Enoch was translated into Greek (only fragments remain, found in Egypt) and then into Ethiopic (Geez). The Qumran manuscripts afford us four of the five parts of the book in the original Aramaic.

Eighteen copies of the book of Jubilees, written in Hebrew, were found in a series of Qumran caves (1, 2, 3, 4, and 11). Jubilees retells Genesis and Exodus 1–14, presented as a revelation by the angels to Moses while he was on Mount Sinai. The text reframes the biblical narrative into a series of jubilee (50-year) periods, based on the jubilee-year system presented in Leviticus 25. The book dates to the 2nd century B.C.E. and may predate the formation of the Qumran sect. This work was also translated into Greek and Latin, though only fragments remain, and then into Geez. The Qumran manuscripts afford us at least some of the original Hebrew work.

We also find fragments of other works known from late antiquity that were previously preserved only in Greek or other ancient languages, not in their Hebrew originals. Tobit and Ben Sira were canonized by the Eastern Orthodox and Roman Catholic churches. Portions of the Testament of the Twelve Patriarchs were preserved by various early Christian groups but did not achieve canonical status. Ben Sira's Hebrew original was found in the Cairo genizah. Additional manuscripts were found at Masada, so that we now can reconstruct a large portion of the Hebrew original. To give a sense of how open-ended the canon was, the rabbis in the Talmud continued to cite Ben Sira as if the book were canonical.

The so-called Genesis Apocryphon was among the first seven scrolls found in Cave 1. Some very tiny fragments from Cave 4 may also be Genesis Apocryphon material. The Cave 1 text is called 1QGenAp ar. (The "ar" means Aramaic). The text retells some of the Genesis stories, covering the span from Lamech (father of Noah) to Abraham. Among the most expansive passages is a long and detailed description of Sarah's beauty, evoking the language of the Song of Songs but based on the terse passages in Genesis 12. Other Dead Sea Scrolls texts also retell biblical stories, sometimes as paraphrases or in summary fashion.

Dead Sea Scrolls texts retell biblical stories, sometimes as paraphrases or in summary fashion.

The next text that interests us is a relatively well-preserved scroll of the book of Psalms from Cave 11, called 11QPs^a. Many of the canonical Psalms occur here but in a different order. Included at the end are about five additional Psalms, some of which were known previously only via Syriac translation. The end of the scroll contains a passage describing the Psalms as revelation to David. In all of this we see the ever-growing David tradition, culminating in Judaism's contention that the Messiah will be an offspring of David.

The Qumran community preserved a translation of the book of Job into Aramaic. The only previous translation of the Bible into another language is the Septuagint, which is in Greek. We know of Aramaic translations, called Targumim, produced by Jews in the centuries to follow, but this Dead Sea Scrolls rendering of Job represents our oldest such translation. Interestingly, the Tosefta preserves a tradition that the famous sage Rabban Gamaliel I (1st century C.E.) once banned a translation of Job into Aramaic (Tosefta Shabbat 14:2). Could our Dead Sea Scrolls text be that version?

Three of the texts referred to in this lecture were written in Aramaic: Enoch, Genesis Apocryphon, and Targum to Job. Clearly there is a pattern here. Aramaic was becoming more and more the language of the Jews during this period. Aramaic originated in the area of modern Syria, stretching from Damascus in the south to the Upper Euphrates River in the north. It became the language of a series of empires (Assyrian, Babylonian, and Persian), thereby becoming a lingua franca of the ancient world. There is a debate as to when Hebrew died out as a living language. Some say as late as 300 C.E., while others believe that this had occurred already in the 1st century C.E. Jesus, for example, spoke Aramaic, as we can determine from his words in the Gospels. All told, the Aramaic texts from Qumran provide linguists with an new corpus of texts by which to examine the Aramaic language as used during this period. Eventually, much of both Talmudim would be written in Aramaic.

Recall that during the 1st century B.C.E., and even into the 1st century C.E., the biblical canon was not fixed. Josephus mentions only 22 books in the canon, while the rabbis eventually settled on 24. We know from rabbinic literature that there were debates concerning Qohelet and Song of Songs specifically. Probably Esther elicited debate as well, and apparently Ben Sira was on the margins of canonicity. Thus, while all Jews agreed to the canonical status of the Torah, the Prophets, and the book of Psalms, there were differences of opinion concerning the various books mentioned here.

In the end, many books did not enter the normative Jewish canon as transmitted by the rabbis. But various Jewish groups clearly considered works such as Enoch, Jubilees, and Tobit to be canonical, and thus many of these works were included in the list of sacred books as organized by various early churches. Fortunately, among the Dead Sea Scrolls we have early textual exemplars of these works. ■

Essential Reading

Vermes, *The Complete Dead Sea Scrolls in English*, 301–307, 446–447, 448–459, 507–510, 513–517.

VanderKam, *The Dead Sea Scrolls Today*, 34–43, 142–157.

VanderKam and Flint, *The Meaning of the Dead Sea Scrolls*, 154–205.

Schiffman, *Reclaiming the Dead Sea Scrolls*, 181–195, 217–218.

Yadin, *The Message of the Scrolls*, 144–155.

Questions to Consider

1. Why, do you think, did some Christian groups eventually canonize (or at least copy and read) books such as Enoch and Jubilees, especially if Jewish groups no longer read these compositions?

2. In what ways do you think a text such as 4Q422, a summary of the Ten Plagues narrative, may have been used, either at Qumran or among Jews elsewhere?

The Qumran Biblical Canon
Lecture 17—Transcript

As we have seen throughout these lectures, numerous Dead Sea Scrolls provide interpretations of biblical texts. We have discussed the Pesher commentaries specifically in Lecture Nine, for example; at this point we turn to additional material. In Lecture Two, we referred to one scroll—one of the original seven—that was too brittle to unroll. As time passed, scholars accomplished this task, revealing a text now known as the Genesis Apocryphon, though it is a scholarly misnomer. This document provides a retelling of portions of the book of Genesis, including the story of Noah and the story of Abraham. The latter portion of this text, for example includes an elaborate description of Sarah's physical beauty, moving from her hair to her face and her breasts and beyond, all developed from the concise biblical statement that Sarah was beautiful (Gen. 12). We will look at this document, we will read other retellings of biblical stories—for example, the book of Exodus—and we will discuss the presence of copies of the book of Enoch and the book of Jubilees among the Dead Sea Scrolls. These latter two books were written in the postbiblical period with an eye towards a retelling of portions of the Torah. While they were not canonized by Judaism, they were preserved by the Ethiopian Church.

At the time of the floruit of the Qumran community, the biblical canon had not been fixed yet. Clearly, Jews had canonized the Torah and the Prophets, and no doubt the psalms were seen in the same way. This is indicated explicitly, in fact, in the Halakhic Letter, MMT (the subject of our previous lecture), copy D—that is 4Q397, in line 10; one of those fragments to which we referred—where we have reference to "the book of Moses, the books of the prophets and of David," "the book of Moses," the Torah; the books of the prophets, self-explanatory; the book of David, obviously the Psalms. But the remainder of the canon still—2nd century B.C.E., 1st century B.C.E., even into the 1st century C.E.—was open-ended. We get a similar reference in the Greek preface to the book of Ben Sira, written by the translator, the grandson of the author, circa 130 B.C.E.

Let me tell you a little bit about the book of Ben Sira. It is a collection of proverbial wisdom written approximately 180 B.C.E., modeled to a great extent after the biblical book of Proverbs, presenting very similar information, presenting maxims, sayings by an ancient Jewish sage named Ben Sira. His grandson translated the book into Greek, added the preface, and there in the preface the grandson translator refers to the Torah, the books of the prophets, and "the others that followed." That is to say, two divisions are present—Torah and prophets—and then a third category, "the others that followed," presumably referring to psalms and other biblical books including, for example, the book of Proverbs.

At Qumran, it seems that the books of Enoch and Jubilees were seen as canonical. Let's address each of these. The book of Enoch: 11 copies of the book of Enoch, all written in Aramaic, were found in Qumran Cave Four, with a smattering of other copies, also in Aramaic, found in Caves One, Two, and Six. I hardly need to tell you: all fragmentary; but altogether we have these sections of the book of Enoch now written in the original Aramaic amongst the Dead Sea Scrolls. The book of Enoch is an exceedingly long composition; it is divided into five separate parts and it is based on the statement that occurs in Gen. 5:24 that the biblical character Enoch did not die per se, but rather God simply took him and he walked with God. This occurs in the genealogy of individuals in Gen. 5 who occur— the 10 generations—from Adam to Noah; each of them lives an exceedingly long life, a lifespan, Methuselah being the longest of all. But with Enoch it says that he did not die, rather he "walked with God"; accordingly, he must still be alive, and therefore Enoch is able to tell the history of the world, including events that have yet to pass. An author in the postbiblical period accordingly stylizes a book of Enoch based on this biblical character. The book dates to the 3rd century B.C.E., and thus predates the formation of the Qumran sect.

Eventually this work was translated into Greek, although only fragments remain—they've been found in Egypt—and then from the Greek translation, the work was translated in its entirety into the Ethiopic language, the classical variety of Ethiopic that we call Ge'ez. The book was canonized only by the Ethiopian Church, so that we possess the entire work in its Ethiopic (Ge'ez) translation, though now—as I indicated—the Qumran manuscripts afford us at least some of the original Aramaic work. As I mentioned, there are five parts to the book of Enoch; four of those five sections are represented among these various fragments of the Aramaic Enoch amongst the Dead Sea Scrolls.

The book of Jubilees: 18 copies (18, I repeat) of this book written in Hebrew were found in a series Qumran caves: Cave 1, Cave 2, Cave 3, Cave 4, and Cave 11. Another long composition; this book, the book of Jubilees, is a retelling of the book of Genesis and the first 14 chapters of the Exodus, which takes us to the exodus from Egypt and the splitting of the sea of reeds, all of which is presented as a revelation by the angels to Moses while Moses was still on Mount Sinai. The text reframes the biblical narrative of Genesis and the early parts of Exodus into a series of jubilee periods—that is, 50-year periods—based on the jubilee-year system of 50-year segments that is presented in the Torah, specifically in Leviticus 25. The author uses that as the historical basis for retelling much of the early biblical narrative.

The book of Jubilees dates to the 2nd century B.C.E., and may predate the formation of the Qumran sect, which occurs in the middle of that century. This work also was translated into Greek and into Latin, though, again, only fragments remain; and then from the Greek translation it was further translated once more into the classical Ethiopic language, Ge'ez. As with Enoch, this book also was canonized only by the Ethiopian Church, so that we possess the entire work of Jubilees also only in Ethiopic translation, though now the Qumran manuscripts afford us a look to at least some of the original Hebrew of this composition. We will return to the presence of copies of Enoch and Jubilees—these two books—among the Dead Sea Scrolls in our next lecture which is devoted to the Qumran calendar. Incidentally, we've talked about the Temple Scroll at a variety of junctures in our course; 11QT, the Temple Scroll, is similar to Enoch and Jubilees in the sense that it is also a retelling of the Torah. Enoch and Jubilees are much more focused on the narrative, on the story that is being told, as a new story is woven and created by the authors of those two books. As we've seen, the Temple Scroll is also a retelling of a portion of the Torah, specifically the legal material using Deuteronomy as its base and inserting into the base texts from Deuteronomy other material from Exodus and Leviticus. There is a similarity here between and among these three works: Enoch; Jubilees—which were known prior to the discovery of the Dead Sea Scrolls through the Ethiopic translation—and the Temple Scroll, which, of course, came to light in Cave 11 at Qumran.

We also find fragments of other works known from late antiquity, other Jewish compositions, that were preserved only in Greek translation or into translation of other languages, though their Hebrew originals died out over the course of centuries and millennia. Here I may mention, for example, the book of Tobit and again the book of Ben Sira that I alluded to earlier. These are two books of the apocrypha; that is to say, Tobit and Ben Sira were canonized by the Eastern Orthodox and Roman Catholic churches, though they were not included in the Protestant canon or in the Jewish canon. Also found at Qumran: We get portions a work called the Testament of the Twelve Patriarchs. This document, this text, was also preserved by various early Christian groups, even though it did not achieve canonical status. The Testament of the Twelve Patriarchs is a text that purports to be the deathbed testaments—the last will and testaments—of the 12 sons of Jacob; and a postbiblical author, again, stylizes what it must have been like for Ruben, Simeon, Benjamin, or any of the brothers including Joseph to provide for their offspring their last will and testament; a book that we knew about in translation into these other ancient languages. Fragments, again, of this found at Qumran.

We mentioned Ben Sira before, whose Hebrew original was found in the Cairo genizah; I actually talked about that in Lecture Eight. Additional manuscripts were found also at Masada, so that we now can reconstruct a large portion of the Hebrew original, mainly from the Cairo genizah material, and the Masada material, and—as I mentioned—some fragments at Qumran. For those portions of the book of Ben Sira that we do not possess in Hebrew, we continue to rely on the Greek translation. To give a sense of how open-ended the canon was during this period, in fact, centuries later, the rabbis in the Talmud—3rd, 4th, and 5th centuries C.E.—continued to cite the book of Ben Sira as if the book were canonical, even though we know it never makes it into any official Jewish canon, and it is not transmitted beyond the Talmudic period as a canonical book. That is to say, the rabbis would occasionally cite a passage from the book of Ben Sira, and when they did, they used the expression "as it is written." That is an expression that the rabbis use when they cite a biblical book if they take a passage from Exodus, Deuteronomy, Jeremiah, or whatever book it would be as it is written. They use that as well when they introduce a passage from the book of Ben Sira. It is on the margins of canonicity, one may say; and as I indicated, it never does quite make it into the canon. Still pliable through the centuries, although it was being read in the Middle Ages, as we know from our manuscript in the Cairo genizah.

Another text: the Genesis Apocryphon. This was among the first seven scrolls found in Cave One, though only after some additional effort was the text unrolled and read; it was extremely brittle, eventually scholars figured out a way to open it up to ensure that it would not be destroyed and that the writing would be preserved. Some very tiny fragments from Cave Four may also be part of the Genesis Apocryphon, but those fragments are so tiny, it's hard to tell. No doubt you want to know the official siglum of this text. The Cave One text is called—ready for this—1QGenAp ar. "1Q," Qumran Cave One; "GenAp," Genesis Apocryphon; then a space, then "ar," with "ar" standing for "Aramaic." This text is in Aramaic, and it retells some of the Genesis stories covering the span from Lamech (the father of Noah) to Abraham. Among the most expansive passages is a long and detailed description of Sarah's beauty, evoking the language of Song of Songs, the biblical book of love poetry. All of this is based on a very concise passage in Gen. 12 that occurs both in verse 11 and verse 14, which mentions Sarah's beauty in the tersest terms. The only way for me to convey to you this section of the Genesis Apocryphon is to read it aloud. Let me read for you at some length here the description of Sarah in the Genesis Apocryphon:

How [pleasant] and beautiful is the image of her face, and how [pl]easant and how fine is the hair of her head. How lovely are her eyes; how pleasing is her nose and all the radiance of her face. How lovely are her breasts, how beautiful all her whiteness! Her arms, how beautiful! Her hands, how perfect—and delectable every visage of her hands! How beautiful are her palms, how long and delicate all her fingers! Her legs, how beautiful! How perfect are her thighs! No virgins or brides who enter the bridal-chamber surpass her beauty. Above all women is her beauty supreme, her beauty far above them all. And with all this beauty, great wisdom is with her, and all that she has is pleasant.

The Genesis Apocryphon, in Aramaic; that's from Column 20:2–8, the description of Sarah. All of that, a retelling, an expansion based on, I repeat, a very short expression in the biblical book of Gen. 12, which tells us simply that Sarah was beautiful.

Other Dead Sea Scrolls texts also retell the biblical stories, sometimes in paraphrases or in summary fashion. An example: 4Q422 relates the entire narrative of the Ten Plagues which comprises four chapters in the biblical book of Exodus—chapters 8–11—but in this Dead Sea Scrolls document, the whole story is condensed into a single column of 15 lines. Moreover, this text omits the sixth plague of boils and then changes the order of the later plagues by placing darkness, which is the ninth plague in the book of Exodus, before the seventh and eighth plagues of hail and locusts. Why the text does this, we don't know; I'm just presenting for you the data from this one document. Incidentally, this is also true of two psalms in the canonical Bible: Psalm 78 and Psalm 105 also include retellings of the plagues from the book of Exodus, the plagues against Egypt. Interestingly, in these two psalms the sixth plague of boils is also missing from Psalm 78 and Psalm 105; is it coincidental that it's missing from 4Q422, the retelling found amongst the Dead Sea Scrolls? Again, a question for which we cannot provide an answer.

The next text that interests us is a relatively well-preserved Psalms scroll from Cave 11; it's called 11QPs^a—which is to say, yes, there is a second Psalms scroll from Cave 11—but this is the one that interests us the most. It's a relatively long text, preserving a good amount of the canonical book of Psalms, 11QPs^a. First of all, many of the canonical psalms occur in this copy in a different order. Second, included at the end—we have the end—are about five additional psalms, some of which were known previously only via Syriac translation in a text called the *Peshitta*. Syriac is a dialect of Aramaic used by the early Christians of the Near East; still used today by the Syrian Orthodox Church. You'll remember Mar Samuel who has been a player in our story throughout our course. In the *Peshitta*, the Syriac translation of the Bible, we have these additional psalms that appear at the end of the 150 psalms in the Jewish canon.

Finally, after the addition of these additional psalms, there comes a description of the entire document in something like a colophon, which gives us a little bit of information about the author. In this case, of course, the author is assumed to be David; and it tells us that David wrote 3,000 psalms and 364 songs, one for each day of the year. In the Bible, 150 psalms; according to this text right here, 3,000 psalms David wrote, and then the statement 364 songs, one for each day of the year—we'll come back to that in our next lecture about the calendar as well—then some other documents giving us a total of 4,050 compositions from the pen of the famous, the great King David. Then this statement, the summary statement: "All these he [meaning David] spoke through prophecy, which was given to him by the Most High," which means that once more we are dealing with revelation beyond the biblical sense of prophecy. In all of this, we see the ever-growing David tradition, culminating in Judaism's contention that the Messiah will be an offspring of David, which to Christians is fulfilled in Jesus Christ.

Finally, we note that the Qumran community preserved a translation of the book of Job into Aramaic. Up until this point, the only translation of the Bible into another book was the Septuagint—the translation of the Bible—into Greek; that was the subject of an earlier lecture in our course. We know of Aramaic translations produced by Jews known as Targumim—singular Targum, plural Targumim—in the centuries that would follow ($1^{st}, 2^{nd}$, and 3rd centuries C.E., and so on), but the Dead Sea Scrolls rendering of the book of Job into Aramaic represents our oldest such translation. Interestingly, in the rabbinic collection known as the Tosefta, there is a tradition preserved that the famous sage Rabban Gamaliel I, who was active in the 1st century C.E., banned a translation of Job into Aramaic. Could our Dead Sea Scrolls text be the document, the text, which Rabban Gamaliel banned? As we noted earlier, this Rabban Gamaliel I is mentioned in the New Testament on two occasions: Acts 5, we learn that Rabban Gamaliel, famous rabbinic and Pharisaic sage, was tolerant of the early Christians; and in Acts 22, we learn that Paul was a student of this great sage. Why did Rabban Gamaliel ban this Aramaic translation? Was there something heretical contained in it? Probably not, but rather he simply wished for his students to read the Hebrew original of the book of Job, difficult as it is; and indeed, it is a difficult book of poetry. He may have been opposed to any translation.

You will have noticed that three of texts referred to in this lecture are written in Aramaic: Enoch, the Genesis Apocryphon, and the *Targum to Job*. Clearly there is a pattern here: Aramaic is becoming more and more the language of the Jews during this period. Aramaic originates in the area of modern Syria, stretching from the region of Damascus in the south to the area of the Upper Euphrates River in the north. It became the language of a series of empires—Assyrian, Babylonian, Persian—thereby becoming a lingua franca of the ancient world. We have documents in Aramaic stretching from as far east as Afghanistan and as far southwest as Aswan in southern Egypt. Incidentally, Aramaic is an example—a rarity in the world—it is the language of the conquered, not the conqueror. The Assyrians, the Babylonians, the Persians all swept up the Aramaeans into their empires, and yet the Aramaic language emerged as the lingua franca of the Near East during this period. Then the Jews participated in this trend and also began to use the Aramaic language more and more.

There is a debate among scholars as to when Hebrew died out as a living language. Some say as late as 300 C.E., while others believe that this occurred already in the 1st century C.E. Clearly in some areas, Aramaic was replacing Hebrew as the mother tongue of many Jews. Jesus, for example, spoke Aramaic, as we can determine from his words that appear in the Gospels; not in Greek translation per se, but a representation of Jesus's words as he spoke them, they are Aramaic. All told the Aramaic texts from Qumran that we're talking about here—Enoch, the *Translation of Job*, the Genesis Apocryphon—provide linguists with an entire new corpus of texts by which to examine the Aramaic language during this period. Eventually, much of both of the Talmud*im*, incidentally, would be written in Aramaic centuries beyond the period we are talking about.

We repeat what we stated at the outset of this lecture: During the 1st century B.C.E., and even into the 1st century C.E., the biblical canon was not fixed. Josephus, writing in the last few decades of the 1st century C.E., mentions 22 books to the canon, while the rabbis eventually settled on 24 books. Note, incidentally, that these numbers correspond to the number of letters in our ancient alphabets: Josephus's 22 books correspond to the 22 letters of the Hebrew alphabet; the rabbi's 24 books correspond to the 24 letters of the Greek alphabet. This may not be a coincidence; it may have been a scheme by which one could keep track of the number of books, which created a canon, a corpus. Incidentally, there are also 24 books to the *Iliad* and 24 books to the *Odyssey*. Yes, the rabbis knew Homer; they quote Homer as well in the rabbinic literature.

We know from the rabbinic corpus of text that there were debates into the 2nd and 3rd century C.E. concerning certain books like the book of Qohelet or Ecclesiastes, and the book of Song of Songs. Were they sacred? Were they to be canonical or not? Probably the book of Esther elicited debate as well; remember, no copies of Esther found at Qumran, and that probably also was being discussed in other sects of the time, including the Pharisaic-rabbinic continuum. Apparently, as we indicated, the book of Ben Sira was on the margins of canonicity, too. As for the book of Song of Songs, I can tell you that it was only through the effort of Rabbi Akiva—the Mishna gives us this statement explicitly—Rabbi Akiva, whom we've mentioned several times in our course, held that the Song of Songs was akin to the Holy of Holies; that if the works of the Bible were holy, than the Song of Songs was the Holy of Holies. Thus while all Jews agree to the canonical status of the Torah, the Prophets, and the book of Psalms, there were differences of opinions concerning the various books that we have mentioned here, those which eventually found their way into—or were excluded from—the division known as the *Ketuvim*, the Writings section that would become the third large grouping of books in the Jewish canon.

In the end, many books did not enter the normative Jewish canon as transmitted by the rabbis; but various Jewish groups clearly considered works such as Enoch, Jubilees, and Tobit to be canonical, and thus many of these works were included in the list of sacred books as organized eventually by various early churches. Fortunately, amongst the Dead Sea Scrolls we have early textual exemplars of these works.

Several times during our course I have stated that a text means only that which its interpreter or interpreters say it means. I want to unpack that statement a bit for you, which clearly is overstated. I say that because I believe in the idea of authorial intent and original meaning as understood by an original audience; that is to say, an author writes a text with a specific intent and for a specific audience, and his original audience understands what it means. But over the course of time, as we move to the period of interpretation of a text, in that case, yes, a text means only what its interpreter says it means. Let's go back to Song of Songs: Song of Songs is exquisite love poetry, on a par with ancient Egyptian love poetry with only one minor reference to God. Clearly the people of ancient Israel adored this book; and we know from the Mishna that people would sing the songs, the various stanzas of the Song of Songs, in the marketplace, for example. But not Rabbi Akiba: Rabbi Akiba saw the entire text of Song of Songs as an allegory for the love between God and the people of Israel. For example, the two breasts of the female lover in the love poem of Song of Songs, as it was intended by its original author, an exquisite description of the female body; the two breasts, in Rabbi Akiba's allegorical reading, refer to Moses and Aaron, the two brothers who are the foundations for early Israel in the books of the Torah. Then the Church used the same interpretative technique, reading the Song of Songs as the allegory for the love between Jesus and the Church. thus, in general, so it was for the Qumran community. Not that we have much of the Song of Songs attested among the Dead Sea Scrolls, only a few fragments; and not that the sectarians ascribed any significance to this book as far as we can tell; but insofar as they interpreted biblical texts as they saw fit, the Qumran community was part and parcel of a tradition of interpretation by all the sects of our period: the Essenes, the Christians, the rabbis, and others.

There is one major issue that separates the Jewish sects of late antiquity that we have not yet addressed in our course: the calendar. In our next lecture, we turn out attention to this extremely crucial matter.

The Qumran Calendar
Lecture 18

The standard calendar had lunar months with necessary adjustments to the solar year, whereas the Qumran calendar was strictly solar

The standard Jewish calendar that has dominated for millennia is a luni-solar calendar whose origins go back to the Babylonian calendrical system. The annual calendar is comprised of 12 lunar months, totaling 354 days. Since this falls 11 days short of a solar year, and since the harvest festivals (Passover, Shavu'ot, Sukkot) need to occur at the appropriate time of year, the calendar adds a leap month approximately once every three years. Since neither the 354 days of the regular year nor the 383 or 384 days of the leap year is divisible by 7, holidays fall on different days of the week, year after year.

An alternative calendar, based strictly on the solar cycle, developed in late antiquity. This system has 52 weeks, each comprised of 7 days, for a total of 364 days. Since 364 is divisible by 7, the holidays occur on the same day of the week each year. Of course, a 364-day system means that each calendrical year falls 1.25 days short of the actual solar year. We have no idea how this system compensated for the difference over time. No leap day is possible, since this would upset everything.

The solar calendar is reflected in the books of Enoch and Jubilees, and the Qumran community used this calendar as well. This explains why many Dead Sea Scrolls texts castigate the sect's opponents for celebrating the holidays on the wrong dates. The most telling passage is from Pesher Habakkuk, where we learn that the Wicked Priest attacked the Teacher of Righteousness on Yom Kippur (1QpHab 11:5–8). The passage can be explained only by assuming different days for the observance of the holiest day of the year. Note that according to the Qumran calendar, Yom Kippur always falls on a Friday, while according to the standard system, especially as manipulated by the rabbis, Yom Kippur can never fall on a Friday.

The one festival in the Torah without a specific date is Shavu'ot, the Feast of Weeks (Leviticus 23:15–16). The Torah instructs one to count seven weeks from a particular day associated with Passover and thereby arrive at the festival of Shavu'ot. Different interpretations led to different groups of Jews counting the seven weeks in different fashions. A plain reading of Leviticus 23:15–16 suggests that one should wait until Passover is over, then wait until the next Sabbath, and then one begins counting. This is how many ancient Jews observed this commandment, including the Qumran sect, the Boethusians, most likely the Sadducees, and then later the Karaites. Later rabbinic Judaism (and presumably their Pharisaic predecessors) held that one begins counting the seven weeks on the second day of Passover, thereby interpreting the word "sabbath" in Leviticus 23:15 as the first day of Passover.

The Qumran sect included festival days in its annual calendar that were not mentioned in the Torah.

The Qumran sect included festival days in its annual calendar that were not mentioned in the Torah. The Halakhic Letter begins with a calendar, laying out the weeks of the year and the holidays and mentioning a festival unknown from the Torah. The Temple Scroll and other texts also provide for additional festival days: the wine festival 50 days after Shavu'ot; the oil festival 50 days after the wine festival; and the wood festival, occurring immediately following the oil festival. All of this may sound awfully confusing and highly mathematical, but as students of calendars and time keeping have noticed, there have been innumerable systems in use by different cultures around the world throughout history. One can see how confusing it would have been for a single umbrella group, such as Judaism, to have different calendars operational in different subgroups. Some scholars have argued that this was one of the hot button issues that separated the sects. A strong argument in favor of this view is the presence of the Qumran calendar at the beginning of the Halakhic Letter. Some have considered the placement of the calendar here a matter of convenience; others consider the placement part of the polemic.

The differences between the two calendar systems may clarify a discrepancy in the Gospels. According to Matthew, Mark, and Luke (what scholars call

249

the synoptic Gospels), the Last Supper occurred on Passover. But according to John, the Last Supper occurred on the day before Passover. Could it be that the different New Testament writers were using different calendars? Most scholars would explain the discrepancy differently—namely, John (the last of the Gospels to be written) consciously redated the Last Supper so that Jesus would be presented to his readers as the equivalent of the Passover sacrifice, per Exodus 12:6. Nonetheless, it is interesting to note how a major issue in Dead Sea Scrolls research potentially could solve an issue in New Testament scholarship.

Let us discuss the meaning of the names of our three sects. The term "Sadducee" is derived from Zadok, the high priest of the First Temple under Solomon. "Pharisee" derives from a Hebrew term meaning "those who separated," or "separatist," though it is unclear to what or from what this group separated. The real quandary is the term "Essene," for which no convincing etymology has been suggested. The *Encyclopaedia Judaica* offers no fewer than six suggested etymologies. An old theory identifying the Boethusians with the Essenes is traced to one of the most remarkable scholars of all time, Azariah dei Rossi, a true Renaissance man, a Jewish savant of 16th-century Italy. Dei Rossi was the first to write a critical history of the Jews in ancient times, using all available sources, including classical historians such as Herodotus and Livy and church fathers such as Eusebius, Jerome, Augustine, and Clement.

While later Jewish scholars knew of the Pharisees and the Sadducees, since both are mentioned in rabbinic texts, they had lost knowledge of the existence of the Essenes. "Essene" is used by Philo and Josephus in their Greek writings and by Pliny in his Latin writing, but since these texts were not read by Jews, any awareness of the Essenes was lost to Jewish readers. In the Renaissance, Christian scholars in Italy rediscovered the great Greek and Roman classics. Dei Rossi, even though he was Jewish, was part of that world. His Latin was excellent, and while his Greek was weak, he was able to read the ancient Greek writings via Latin translations. It was from reading Philo and Josephus—he was, perhaps, one of the first Jewish scholars to do so—that dei Rossi proposed that the Essenes described by these two ancient Jewish writers were the Boethusians mentioned in Talmudic sources. This opinion was mainly a curiosity for centuries until it was recently revived by Yaakov Sussman. ∎

Essential Reading

Schiffman, *Reclaiming the Dead Sea Scrolls*, 301–305.

Supplementary Reading

Abegg, "The Calendar at Qumran."

Talmon, *The Importance of the Qumran Calendar in Early Judaism*.

Questions to Consider

1. To what extent do you think that different calendars served to separate Jewish groups in late antiquity? That is to say, if the sects had more in common with each other but still adhered to distinct calendars, could they have found common ground for dialogue and cooperation?

2. How could the *Yahad* have observed festivals not even mentioned in the Torah? On what grounds could this practice possibly be countenanced?

The Qumran Calendar
Lecture 18—Transcript

As we have noted already in our course, the Dead Sea Scrolls reveal that the Qumran community utilized a different calendar from other Jews at the time. While the standard calendar was a luni-solar one—that is, lunar months, with necessary adjustments to the solar year—the Qumran sect utilized a strictly solar calendar. The latter calendar, to solar one, is also reflected in the postbiblical books of Enoch and Jubilees, both of which are well-represented among the Qumran manuscripts, as we saw in the previous lecture. On practical terms, this means, for example, that the holidays mentioned in the Torah would be celebrated on different days of the year by different Jewish groups, analogous, for example, to the different dates for Christmas and Easter in the eastern and western branches of Christianity. In addition, the MMT text and the Temple Scroll mention other festivals celebrated by the sect that are unknown from our other Jewish sources, biblical or otherwise. In addition to a detailed presentation of the evidence, in this lecture we will consider how these calendar differences may have affected the sectarian nature of Judaism during this period.

I want to stand out with a discussion of the standard Jewish calendar, the one that has dominated for millennia; and again, I use the word "standard" cautiously. It is a luni-solar calendar, whose origins go back to the Babylonian calendar system. The annual calendar is comprised of 12 lunar months, which amounts to 354 days. Let's do the math: A lunar month is 29 ½ days approximately, therefore 6 months of the year we'll have 29 days (that's 174 days total) and 6 months of the year we'll have 30 days (that's 180 days total); you add the two together and you arrive at a 354-day year. Since this year of 354 days falls 11 days short of a solar year, and since the harvest festivals (the holidays of Passover, Shavu'ot, and Sukkot) need to occur at the appropriate time of the year—obviously if you're celebrating harvests, you have to ensure that the holidays are occurring when the appropriate crops were being harvested from the fields—the calendar needs to add a leap month when necessary. If the year falls 11 days short of the solar year every year—the difference between 354 and 365—then approximately once every 3 years you need to add an additional leap month; I hope you've been able to follow the math here. That's the standard Jewish calendar, the one that has been in practice from antiquity down to the present day. Since neither the 354 days of the regular year nor the 383 or 384 days of the leap year—depending on whether one adds a 29-day month or a 30-day month—is divisible by 7, this means that the holidays will fall on different days of the week, year after year. Thus, for example, Passover may commence on a Sunday one year, a Thursday another year, and so on.

An alternative calendar, based strictly on the solar cycle, however, developed in late antiquity. This system has 52 weeks, each of which is comprised of 7 days; 52 times 7 gives you a total of 364 days. Apparently there were 12 months of 30 days each, not connected to the lunar cycle, for a total of 360 days, with an additional day added for each of the four seasons, bringing the total to 364 days. Again, I hope you're following the math; it's quite complicated, but hopefully I'm simplifying it here for you. With this system, since 364 is divisible by 7, this means that the holidays will always occur on the same day of the week each year. For example, Yom Kippur (the Day of Atonement), the Torah tells us it occurs the 10th day of the 7th month (Leviticus 23:27); if you use the system I'm describing now, the Day of Atonement will always occur on a Friday. The first day of Sukkot (the Feast of Booths), a 7- or 8-day festival also described in Leviticus 23, which commences on the 15th day of the 7th month, this holiday of Sukkot will always occur on a Wednesday; and so on. Most interestingly and quite logically, the Jewish New Year according to this system, the holiday of Rosh Hashanah, occurs on a Wednesday. Why a Wednesday? Because the sun and the moon—go back to Genesis 1 in the Creation account—were created on day 4, a Wednesday: "and they shall be ["they" refers to the sun and the moon] for times and seasons, for days and years." That is to say, the biblical text in Genesis 1 recognizes that we use the sun and the moon not only to illuminate the sky by day and by night, but also to keep track of time. Accordingly, in this system—in the strictly solar calendar that we are describing right now—Rosh Hashanah, the New Year, will begin on day 4 when the sun and the moon are created. Before that, we couldn't keep track of time; the New Year festival on a Wednesday.

Of course, a 364-day system means that each calendar year falls 1¼ days short of the actual solar year, which we all know to be 365 ¼ days. We have no idea how this system compensated for this small difference of a day and a quarter; in any given two- or three-year span of time, this would have been only a very, very slight difference—Passover would still be falling in the springtime commemorating the spring harvest of barley, Shavuʻot would still be in the early summer commemorating the wheat and the first fruits, and Sukkot, the great fall harvest, would still be in the fall—but over the course of decades, over the course of much longer spans of time, that 1 ½-day difference would have amounted to a considerable difference with such passing of time. In addition, in this system no leap day is possible, since this would upset the entire system. Where would Sabbath fall if you inserted an extra day? One would need an 8-day week at some point presumably—obviously an impossibility—and all the holidays would be off; so you cannot insert a leap day.

The solar calendar that I've been describing to you is reflected in the book of Enoch and the book of Jubilees; and, as we learn from the sectarian documents among the Dead Sea Scrolls, this same calendar is used in Qumran as well. This will explain why many Dead Sea Scrolls texts castigate the sect's opponents for celebrating the holidays on the wrong dates. A key passage, for example, is found in the Damascus Document: "They shall keep the Sabbath day according to its exact interpretation, and the feasts and the Day of Fasting according to the finding of the members of the New Covenant in the land of Damascus." That's from the Damascus Document 6. The most telling passage, however, is from Pesher Habakkuk, where we learn that the Wicked Priest attacked the Teacher of Righteousness on Yom Kippur (1QpHab 11). As we commented when we read this text in detail, no matter how wicked the priestly opponent and the pursuer of the Teacher of Righteousness may have been, as a priest, he clearly would have been officiating in the Temple in Jerusalem on Yom Kippur. The passage can be explained only by assuming different days for the observance of the holiest day of the year (Yom Kippur, the Day of Atonement), with the mainstream of Judaism—again, I use that expression cautiously—with most Jews at the time apparently marking the holiday on one day, and with the Qumran community and perhaps others (Essenes, whomever) marking the holiday on another day.

As an analogy: Note, for example, the different dates for Christmas in the Western Christian tradition (Catholics and Protestant), and in the Eastern

Christian tradition (Greek Orthodox, Russian Orthodox, and so on). Note, by the way, that according to the Qumran calendar, Yom Kippur always falls on a Friday, as I mentioned; while according to the luni-solar calendar—let's call it the standard system—especially as manipulated by the rabbis, Yom Kippur can never fall on a Friday. Again, we discussed that earlier in our course.

By the way, this devotion to the solar calendar may be related to a passage from Josephus that we read earlier when we explored the topic of daily life at Qumran. Let me read that passage for you again now; the passage from Josephus, it's from *Jewish War* 2. He writes: "And as for their piety towards God, it is very extraordinary; for before sunrise they speak not a word about profane matters, but offer certain prayers, which they have received from their forefathers, as if they made a supplication for its rising," with the "its" referring to the sun. do you remember when we read this earlier? I didn't make the comment then, but let's do it now: Look at the emphasis on the sun; they were making supplication, as it were, for the sun to rise. That ties in, in my estimation, to the whole concept of using a solar calendar.

There is one festival in the Torah without a specific date. Earlier I was giving you some of the dates: Yom Kippur, month 7 day 10; the holiday of Sukkot, the fall harvest festival known as the Feast of Booths, month 7 day 15; and so on. The one festival in the Torah for which there is no specific date given is the holiday of Shavu'ot; that's the Hebrew word for "week," so we can call this the Feast of Weeks. Leviticus 23:15–16 is the key passage. this holiday commemorates the wheat harvest and the harvest of first fruits—I mentioned that a few moments ago when I was talking about the harvest nature of some of these festivals—and eventually the holiday of Shavu'ot also serves in Jewish tradition to commemorate the giving of the Torah at Mount Sinai; the revelation of the Torah from God at Mount Sinai, that becomes part of the celebration of this holiday as well. But no specific date is given as to when it is to be observed; instead, the Torah instructs one to count seven weeks from a particular day associated with Passover, and thereby arrive at the festival of Shavu'ot, and that's how we get the name of this holiday: It's called Shavu'ot (weeks) because one should count seven weeks from a particular day associate with Passover.

But which day associated with Passover? Different interpretations led to different groups of Jews counting the seven weeks in different fashion. Let me read for you now that text, Leviticus 23:15–16:

And you shall count for yourselves, from the morrow of the Sabbath [from the day after the Sabbath; a key passage, we'll come to it in a minute], from the day that you bring the sheaf of elevation [that's a grain offering], seven weeks, complete-ones they shall be. Until the morrow of the seventh week you shall count, fifty days; and then you shall bring a new grain-offering to the LORD.

A plain reading of this text suggests that one should wait until Passover is over, then wait until the next Sabbath, and then on the next day, the morrow of the Sabbath—that is to say, the day after the Sabbath, which occurs after Passover; that would be a Sunday obviously—and then one begins counting the seven weeks. This is how many ancient Jews observed this commandment, including the Qumran sect as indicated in our calendar texts amongst the Dead Sea Scrolls, as well as another group to whom we have referred earlier in our course—a small sect about whom we know very little—the Boethusians (the rabbis in the Mishna actually refer to the Boethusians here as celebrating Shavu'ot on a different day and calculating it in the manner that I've just described), and most likely the Sadducees (though we cannot be sure, but since the Boethusians and Sadducees had close connections), and then at a later time the group called the Karaites that we have also introduced to you in this course from the Middle Ages. All those groups followed the system that I've just described; they waited until after the seven day festival of Passover, waited for the next Sabbath, and then on the morrow of the Sabbath (a Sunday) began counting their seven weeks to arrive at the date for the celebration of the holiday of Shavu'ot.

Later rabbinic Judaism, however, and presumably their Pharisaic predecessors, had a different interpretation: They held that one begins counting the seven weeks on the second day of Passover, not waiting for the entire seven-day festival to be over but to count from the second day of Passover. They did this by interpreting the word "Sabbath" in Leviticus 23:15 Shavu'ot, which I've just read to you, as the first day of Passover; and while this is a most unusual elucidation of the word "Sabbath"—for nowhere else in the Bible does it mean a festival day per se; it means the Sabbath day, the weekly Sabbath day, but nowhere else does it ever refer to a festival day—this is how the rabbis interpreted the passage here: The Sabbath is the first day of Passover regardless of when during the week (on a Thursday or whenever) Passover may have fallen. Therefore they started counting their seven weeks from the second day of Passover. This is a quite peculiar interpretation to my mind, to be honest, but this is the one that the rabbis used. Remember, it is not always the most facile reading that is accepted by a tradition, rather it is the interpretation of a text that counts, and that interpretation can swerve considerably from the plain reading.

We also note that the Qumran sect included additional festival days in its annual calendar that are not mentioned in the Torah. Leviticus 23 is the place to look—it's the chapter that I've referred to several times here—for the holidays that the Torah presents. Those holidays are all the ones we've mentioned, the five of them: the harvest festivals, Passover, Shavu'ot, Sukkot; the holidays of Rosh Hashanah and Yom Kippur. Those are the five holidays mentioned in Leviticus 23, along with the Sabbath that, of course, occurs on a weekly basis.

Before proceeding to the points of Halakhic disagreement—which we've talked about earlier when reading the MMT text, the Halakhic Letter—that document actually begins with a calendar. I mentioned the 20 points of dispute between the author of the text and the addressee of that document; what I didn't mention when we read our text earlier is that it is preceded by something like a preamble, there's actually a chart there of a calendar. That calendar lays out the weeks of the year and the holidays, and there it mentions certain festivals unknown from the Torah. In addition, the Temple Scroll, along with a few other texts—Jubilees, 4Q327 (it's a calendar text from Qumran Cave Four)—these documents also provide for additional festival days.

What holidays are we talking about? What are these holidays occurring in the Qumran calendar that do not occur in the Torah? First, a wine festival: This occurs on month 5, day 3; it occurs on a Sunday; it occurs exactly 50 days after Shavu'ot. Just like Shavu'ot is 50 days after Passover (you're supposed to count seven weeks, add an extra day and you get to 50 days between Passover and Shavuʻot), you now count an additional 50 days according to the Qumran calendar system, to arrive at a wine festival (month 5 day 3) in which you celebrate the ripening of the grapes, the processing of the grapes into wine, and the dedication of the wine for the libation in the Temple. A holiday not known from the Torah or anywhere else in the Bible occurs here in our Dead Sea Scrolls documents. Then another festival that we have not encountered in any of our sources elsewhere: You then count another 50 days; from the wine festival you begin another 50-day count and you arrive at month 6, day 22 (also occurring on a Sunday) and you get to the oil festival, the festival of the olive oil. The olive are now ripening, they are being pressed into olive oil, and olive oil is now being brought to the Temple; that needs to be commemorated as well.

Then a third festival mentioned in our documents: the wood festival. For those of you who like to keep track of these things it's month 6, days 23–28; it's a 6-day festival, it commences on a Monday, and it occurs immediately following the oil festival. The bringing of wood to the Temple as an offering is mentioned in the biblical book of Nehemiah 10 and 13—in two passages in Nehemiah—so clearly this festival has its roots in early Second Temple period Judaism; the date of Nehemiah is approximately 450 B.C.E. The idea was that wood used on the altar for the burning of the sacrifices would always be abundant, was necessary, and one therefore would bring wood and celebrate the bringing of the wood to the Temple. This wood festival is also mentioned in other postbiblical Jewish texts in this case, unlike the wine and oil festivals that we only know from Qumran; at least in this case we do know of the wood festival from Nehemiah and then postbiblical texts such as Josephus in the *Jewish War* 2.425 (he mentions this festival, though without a clear date), and then it's actually also referred to in a rabbinic text from later on (a tractate called *Taʻanit*), and in that text the rabbis do recognize the wood festival though their date is different from the one here at Qumran, their date is month 5, day 15.

All of this may sound awfully confusing and highly mathematical; but as students of calendars and timekeeping have noticed, there have been innumerable systems in use by different cultures around the world throughout history. Even to this day we, in North America, for example, are able to live with a standard civil calendar, though with different Thanksgiving feasts in the United States and in Canada. If we consider the United States only, we note a civil calendar working side-by-side with different religious calendars: a Christian calendar, a Jewish calendar, a Muslim calendar, a Hindu calendar, because people from of all of those religions are resident here in the United States. Even within the Christian sphere, as I've noted, the dates of key holidays such as Christmas and Easter will vary depending on which division of Christianity one belongs to.

Transfer all of this to the world of the ancient Jewish sects, and one can see how confusing it would have been for a single umbrella group, the religion of Judaism, to have different calendars operational in different subgroups within the umbrella. In fact, some scholars have argued that this issue, the different calendars in use in late antiquity, was one of the "hot button" issues that separated the sects. One can clearly see why this is the case; after all, if different factions cannot agree even on what day to observe the holidays, holidays whose dates—with the exception of Shavu'ot—are stated clearly in the Torah, then there is very little room for accommodation, cooperation, and coexistence. A strong argument in favor of this view, that the use of different calendars among the Jewish sects was one of the major issues leading to the rift between and among the groups, is the presence of the Qumran calendar at the beginning of the MMT text. Some have considered the placement of the calendar here simply a matter of convenience, but the majority of scholars consider the calendar to be part of the polemic of the MMT document. Before proceeding to the 20 issues of *halakha*, which we surveyed when we treated the Halakhic Letter in a previous lecture, the scribe presented the calendar first as a reminder to the addressee, as if to say, "Our calendar (and not yours) is the proper one." Given the emphasis placed on calendar issues in other Dead Sea Scrolls texts, such as the Damascus Document and the Community Rule, to my mind, yes, the calendar served as a true "hot button" issue to factionalize the different sects. How could the *Yahad*, after all, even begin to participate in the Temple cult if the authorities in Jerusalem were celebrating the festivals on the wrong days; wrong, of course, according to the Qumran community and their strictly solar reckoning system?

One final point on the calendar issue: The differences between the two systems may clarify a discrepancy in the Gospels. According to Matthew, Mark, and

Luke, what scholars call the synoptic Gospels, the Last Supper occurred on Passover. But according to the gospel of John, the Last Supper occurred on the day before Passover. Could it be that the different New Testament writers were using different calendars? This has been theorized by some scholars, though naturally there is insufficient evidence either to prove or disprove the point. Most scholars would explain the discrepancy differently; namely, that John, the last of the Gospels to be written, consciously re-dated the Last Supper so that Jesus would be presented to his readers as the equivalent of the Passover sacrifice, for the lamb was slaughtered on the day before Passover, as per the biblical command in Exodus 12:6. Nonetheless, it is interesting to note how a major issue in Dead Sea Scrolls research potentially could solve an issue in New Testament scholarship.

I want to add a discussion here, which until now we have not presented: the meaning of the names of our three sects. Actually, we mentioned in passing that the term "Sadducees" is derived from Zadok (Hebrew *Zadok*), the high priest of the First Temple under King Solomon. The term "Pharisee" derives from a Hebrew term meaning "those who separated" or "separatist," even though it is unclear to what or from what this group (the Pharisees) separated; if anything, of course, the Essenes would be more separatist. The real quandary is the term Essene, for which no convincing etymology has been suggested. As evidence thereto, consulting the *Encyclopaedia Judaica*— that's the 16-volume standard reference work for the field of Jewish studies: Jewish history, Jewish philosophy, Jewish thought, Jewish everything—reveals no less than six suggested etymologies in the entry on "Essenes."

Recently, Professor Yaakov Sussman of the Hebrew University in Jerusalem has revived an older theory that proposes that the Boethusians, mentioned as a sect within rabbinic texts, are the Essenes. The former term (Boethusians) is to be analyzed as *bet 'issin*, with Hebrew *bet* meaning "house," and *'issin* meaning "Essenes," regardless of what the term actually connotes. Here we note a Boethusian-Qumran connection, the date of Shavu'ot. Since we know that the Boethusians are an offshoot of the Sadducees, which we mentioned earlier in our lecture on Jewish sectarian, we are able to present here additional fodder for Professor Schiffman's theory: there is a connection between the Qumran community and the Sadducees, whether we accede to Schiffman's approach or not. Of course, it matters not that rabbinic sources refer to the Boethusians centuries after 70 C.E., since, as we saw in the prior lecture, we now can trace the continuation of the Essenes well beyond the destruction of the Temple, into the Middle Ages, in fact. Can any or all of this be accurate? As with everything else, we need more texts. But the great authority of Professor Sussman, one of the leading experts in Talmud in the world, lends a major voice to the discussion.

A moment ago, I stated that Sussman revived an old theory in identifying the Boethusians with the Essenes. I would like to expand on that now. The theory is traced to one of the most remarkable scholars of all time, Azariah dei Rossi, a true Renaissance man, a Jewish savant of 16th century Italy, the first to write a critical history of the Jews in ancient times using all available sources, including classical historians such as Herodotus and Livy, and Church fathers such as Eusebius, Jerome, Augustine, and Clement. We should note that while later Jewish scholars knew of the Pharisees and the Sadducees, since both are mentioned in rabbinic texts such as the Mishna, they had lost knowledge of the existence of the Essenes. Recall that the term "Essenes" is used by Philo and Josephus in their Greek writings, and by Pliny in his Latin writing. But since these texts were not read by Jews—remember, Philo and Josephus were preserved by the Church, not by Jews—since they were not in Aramaic or in Hebrew, any awareness of the Essenes was lost to Jewish readers over the course of centuries, in fact, more than a millennium, even for those Jewish scholars capable of reading the difficult texts like the Talmud.

Then came the Renaissance, when Christian scholars in Italy rediscovered the Greek and Roman classics. Dei Rossi, even though he was Jewish, was part of that Italian Renaissance world. His Latin was excellent, and while his Greek was weak, he was able to read the ancient Greek writings—such as Philo and Josephus—via Latin translations that had been made over the centuries. It was in the course of reading Philo and Josephus—he was, perhaps, one of the first Jewish scholars to read this material and to incorporate their writings into his own research—that dei Rossi proposed that the Essenes described by Philo and Josephus were the Boethusians mentioned in Talmudic sources. This opinion was mainly a curiosity for centuries, until it was revived by Professor Sussman recently.

The calendar, naturally, is very much tied to the question of Jewish ritual practices; for example, when are the holidays mentioned in the Torah to be observed? The issue of the calendar serves as a nice segue to our next lecture, which will delve further into Jewish rituals, both in the broader Jewish community of late antiquity and at Qumran specifically.

Jewish Scholars and Qumran Ritual Practices
Lecture 19

> One would think that one's religious affiliation would not matter in scholarship, especially as scholars study ancient texts seeking objective truth without theological or denominational bias. Unfortunately, however, such is not the case. We saw, for example, that de Vaux and his colleagues understood the Qumran community as an early celibate monastery. ... By and large, scholars of Jewish law and Talmud tend to be Jews. ... Christian scholars paid most attention to the theological and doctrinal issues present in the text ... [but] Jewish scholars ... paid more attention to the Halakhic material.

With the passage of time in Qumran scholarship, more and more Jewish scholars became involved in primary research. When the international committee was established to publish the scrolls in the official Discoveries in the Judaean Desert series, Jewish scholars were excluded. Israeli scholars such as Yigael Yadin worked on the texts as they were published, and they continued to study anew the seven texts from Cave 1 obtained by Eliezer Sukenik and Yadin, but otherwise they could not contribute to the primary research. When Israel gained control of East Jerusalem in 1967, the Israeli authorities allowed the previously established committee to continue its work without interference. But delays in publication continued. Some were understandable, given the very fragmentary condition of the Cave 4 manuscripts, but this could not explain the exceedingly slow process of preparation and publication of the official volumes. Only a trickle of new texts were published throughout the 1970s and 1980s.

Part of the problem was that the scholars wanted to have essentially the "final word" on their texts. They wanted to make sure that they had found every parallel variant in every possible version (Greek, Latin, Syriac, Ethiopic, Georgian, Armenian, whatever it might be!), lest they be criticized for missing something. Note that none of these delays were due to pressure from the Vatican to withhold publication of the Dead Sea Scrolls. Such rumors abounded in popular culture, but there is no truth to them whatsoever. Finally, in 1991, frustrated by the lack of progress, the Israeli Antiquities Authority appointed Emanuel Tov head of the project.

At the same time, there were other developments in the United States. In September 1991, Ben Zion Wacholder and Martin Abegg announced that they had broken the lock of the international scholarly committee by using a privately distributed concordance of the scrolls. The Wacholder-Abegg volume was published by the Biblical Archaeology Society headed by Hershel Shanks, which also took up the campaign of agitating for the release of the entire corpus of scrolls. Two weeks after the appearance of the Wacholder-Abegg volume, William Moffet announced that the Huntington Library possessed a full set of photos of the scrolls and that it would allow any qualified scholar access to these photographs. In short, the cartel had been broken. Back in Israel, meanwhile, Tov began to expand the official publication committee by adding younger scholars, including Jewish ones, from Israel, the United States, and elsewhere.

Texts that had languished in the hands of older scholars for decades went to the younger scholars eager to publish them. By 2001, an additional 25 volumes had appeared, most devoted to the documents from Cave 4. In 2002, Tov published DJD 39, an introduction to the entire series with indices, marking the occasion of the publication of all the Dead Sea Scrolls.

One of the most amazing finds at Qumran are 20 tiny scrolls, some with cases, that are the oldest surviving examples of tefillin. The New Testament refers to these objects, worn on the head and the arm, as phylacteries, the Greek word for "amulets," or "protective devices" (Matthew 23:5), even though Jews have never considered them as such. Since the word "tefillin" derives from the Hebrew word *tefilla* (prayer), perhaps it is better to refer to these items in English as prayer accoutrements. The practice derives from a literal interpretation of Exodus 13:16 and Deuteronomy 6:8 and 11:18. We know that the Pharisees and rabbis interpreted these biblical passages in such fashion, and now we know that the Qumran community (and perhaps all Essenes) did likewise. While we do not have explicit evidence thereto, we assume that the Sadducees would have understood the passages metaphorically and therefore did not wear tefillin. This is certainly the case with the later Karaites. The rabbinic tradition records different opinions as to the order of the four passages (two from Exodus, two from Deuteronomy) to be written on the separate tiny scrolls and then placed in the tefillin case. The Qumran tefillin present yet another ordering.

A related phenomenon in Jewish tradition is the use of mezuza, a tiny scroll placed on the doorposts of one's house, in accordance with Deuteronomy 6:9 and 11:20. The later rabbinic tradition held that a single scroll including Deuteronomy 6:4–9 and 11:13–21 is to be placed on the doorpost. But some sectarians included the Ten Commandments in their mezuza scrolls. Strikingly, the Qumran mezuza texts have the Ten Commandments included. Another example of such a scroll is the Nash Papyrus, found in Egypt, dated to c. 125 B.C.E., which places the Ten Commandments and the Shema prayer on a single scroll. The Samaritans also take this commandment literally, though their mezuzot took the form of plaques above the doorway and also contained the Decalogue.

The Qumran texts refer to the blessing of food both before and after eating, with a priest performing the task. From a period several centuries later than the Dead Sea Scrolls, we possess the specific language of grace after meals as created by the rabbis. Moshe Weinfeld identified 4Q434 fragment 2 as a precursor to the rabbinic formulation, with a special focus on the expression "to eat of its fruit and of its goodness." A Deuteronomy manuscript found at Qumran (4QDeut^n) includes a space between verses 8 and 9 of chapter 8. This space is not included in our later medieval biblical manuscripts, but Weinfeld was able to divine its purpose here. The later rabbis decreed that only after eating bread is one required to recite the complete grace after meals. After eating other food, a much shorter prayer is recited. Deuteronomy 8:8 refers to grapes, figs, pomegranates, olives, and dates; then mentions bread in verse 9; and verse 10 states, "and you shall eat and be satiated, and you shall bless the LORD your God for the good land that he has given to you." The rabbis thus deduced that the full grace after meals is required only after eating bread. By placing the space between verses 8 and 9, the Qumran scribe anticipated the centuries-later rabbinic decision.

Before the discovery of the Dead Sea Scrolls, we knew about the practices discussed in this lecture from the Mishna, dated to the early 3rd century C.E. A scholarly debate arose as to whether practices mentioned in the Mishna but not specifically indicated in the Torah were innovations of the rabbis of the 2nd or 3rd century C.E. or whether the Mishna simply codified practices that had existed for centuries. The evidence of the Dead Sea Scrolls tilts the scales in favor of the latter opinion, which now should serve as the default position. Unless we can say with certainty that the rabbis of the Mishna innovated a particular custom or ritual, we may assume that practices incorporated therein, such as the use of tefillin and grace after meals, come from centuries earlier.

The scrolls came to be seen as more connected to Judaism than to Christianity.

As Jewish scholars began to focus their work on the topics described in this lecture, the research paradigm shifted, so that the scrolls came to be seen as more connected to Judaism than to Christianity. It is for this reason that Lawrence Schiffman called his book *Reclaiming the Dead Sea Scrolls*. ■

Essential Reading

VanderKam, *The Dead Sea Scrolls Today*, 193–200.

Schiffman, *Reclaiming the Dead Sea Scrolls*, 305–312.

Questions to Consider

1. If you were in the position of Martin Abegg and Ben Zion Wacholder, able to produce a preliminary edition of the scrolls based on a privately circulated concordance, what would you have done: share it with the scholarly community or hold onto it privately?

2. How and why do you think rumors about the Vatican's suppression of the scrolls got started and continued to be fueled?

Jewish Scholars and Qumran Ritual Practices
Lecture 19—Transcript

In this lecture, we will present a series of Jewish ritual practices reflected in the Dead Sea Scrolls, including the use if *tefillin* and *mezuza*—I'll explain what those terms mean in just a moment—and the recitation of the Grace after Meals. As with so many other aspects of Dead Sea Scrolls scholarship, these important discoveries extend our knowledge of these practices to a period centuries earlier than previously known. Typically as we have seen, numerous elements of the Qumran lifestyle and belief system were at odds with the later rabbinic Judaism that eventually emerged as normative in Jewish society and culture. In the cases just mentioned, by contrast, we will see major points of commonality between the two groups. Before proceeding to these discussions, however, I first wish to present information about the increased involvement of Jewish scholars in Dead Sea Scrolls research.

We recall that when the international committee was established to publish the scrolls in the official DJD series (Discoveries in the Judean Desert), Jewish scholars were excluded from the process. Israeli scholars such as Yigael Yadin worked on the texts as they were published in the DJD series, and they continued to study anew the seven texts from Cave One obtained by Sukenik and Yadin; but otherwise, they could not contribute to primary research on the texts from the other caves, especially as the more than 500 documents emerged from Cave Four. To repeat what was stated earlier in our course, when Israel gained control of East Jerusalem in 1967 during the Six Day War, the Israeli authorities allowed the previously established committee to continue its work without interference. But more and more delays in publication continued. Some of the delays were understandable given the very fragmentary condition of the Cave Four manuscripts; but this could not explain the exceedingly slow process in preparation and publication of DJD volumes. Thus, only a trickle of new texts was published throughout the 1970s and 1980s.

As an indication thereof, notice that DJD 1 appeared in 1955, with Volumes 2–6 appearing in the years following. But DJD 7 did not appear until 1982, and DJD 8 did not appear until 1993. At the same time, into the 1980s, many of the original committee members had retired, were elderly, had encountered illness, or even had died. Part of the problem is that scholars, when given the assignment of a particular text, wanted not only to publish the text, but to have essentially the final word on the text. If they were publishing a biblical manuscript, with variants to the *Masoretic Text*, they wanted to make sure that they had found every parallel variant in every possible ancient version—the Greek, Latin, Syriac, Ethiopic, other languages to which we have not referred: the Georgian translation, the Armenian translation, something known as the Old Church Slavonic translation, whatever it might be—lest they be criticized by other scholars for missing something. If they were publishing a non-biblical Dead Sea Scrolls document, the scholars wanted to make sure that they had found every possible parallel thought or comment or reference in the vast literature that we have surveyed: Enoch, Jubilees, Philo, Josephus, the New Testament, the Mishna, the Talmud, and on and on it goes; perhaps even a relatively obscure Church father or a medieval Jewish biblical commentator who may have had something to contribute to the subject.

I may mention here two names already presented in our lectures as way of illustration. Father J. T. Milik—you'll recall him as the "fastest man with a fragment"—he published more material than anyone else from the original team that was assembled in Jerusalem; he also was one with whom texts lingered for decades. Clearly he was assigned too many documents, and he could not complete the herculean task of assembling all the fragments, making sense of the text as a whole, translating, commenting upon the text, and then preparing all of this for official publication in the DJD series. At one point, his fellow priest, Father Joseph Fitzmyer of Catholic University, approached Father Milik, asking him to release some of the texts so that Father Fitzmyer could publish them—all he wanted to do was help—though to no avail.

Then Frank Cross whom we mentioned earlier as well, of Harvard University; to him were assigned many of the biblical fragments. But let us remember that Professor Cross was busy with a fulltime teaching load; in his career he supervised more than 100 dissertations at Harvard. And, of course, he had a real life with a wife and a family, and everything else that all of us have to contend with on a daily basis. So some of the delays are understandable; and in Cross's case, I am happy to report that he distributed many of the texts assigned to him—he was very generous—to his doctoral students, who then worked on these documents as their dissertation projects, and then they were allowed to present their results of their research in the DJD series.

None of these delays, we hasten to add, were due to pressures from the Vatican to withhold publication of the Dead Sea Scrolls over fears that the texts would have embarrassing consequences for Catholic thought, as if there was material in the Qumran texts that would undermine fundamental Catholic dogma. Such rumors abounded in popular culture throughout the decades, and then became the subject of a book entitled *The Dead Sea Scroll Deception* published in 1991, written by two British authors, Michael Baigent and Richard Leigh, with the alarming subtitle *The Explosive Contents of the Dead Sea Scrolls and How the Church Conspired to Suppress Them*. But there is no truth to these claims whatsoever. Incidentally, as an aside, Baigent and Leigh also wrote another book entitled *The Holy Blood and the Holy Grail* in 1982, from which they claim that Dan Brown took many of the ideas for his book, *The Da Vinci Code*, published in 2003, the international bestseller. The two authors sued Dan Brown for copyright infringement, but lost in a British court.

By this point, John Strugnell of Harvard University—the youngest member of the original team—was now the head of the international committee. To his credit, he had brought Elisha Qimron on board to help him publish 4QMMT (the Halakhic Letter), but progress still was very slow. Finally, in 1991, frustrated by the lack of progress, the Israeli Antiquities Authority removed Strugnell from his position—it also didn't help that he gave a very controversial interview with an Israeli newspaper with some charges of anti-Semitism that were forthcoming from that interview—and the Israeli Antiquities Authority replaced Professor Strugnell with Emanuel Tov of the Hebrew University as the new head of the committee.

At the same time, there were other developments happening here in the United States. In September, 1991, Ben Zion Wacholder and Martin Abegg, both of Hebrew Union College in Cincinnati—the former, Professor Wacholder, a professor at that institution; the latter, Abegg, then a graduate student—announced that they had broken the lock of the international scholarly committee by using a privately distributed concordance of the

Dead Sea Scrolls, a concordance that had been produced by the original team of scholars in the 1950s for their personal, internal use, and then they used that concordance to reconstruct previously non-published texts. Let me explain to you how Wacholder and Abegg went about their work. Somehow, Wacholder was able to get a hold of this concordance. A concordance is a list of every word that appears in the corpus; and so, for example, when Word A appears in a particular document, it may also appear in another document from a different cave. Of course, Document X was assigned to one scholar, and Document Y was assigned to another scholar; so the team assembled in Jerusalem actually created for their own internal use such a concordance so that they would know where this word may also appear elsewhere in the Dead Sea Scrolls corpus. Then Wacholder, who had this privately circulating concordance, he mentioned this to his graduate student Martin Abegg who was a computer whiz, and Abegg said, "I can write a program and we would be able to reconstruct the Dead Sea Scrolls that are in the hands of everyone else"; and that is exactly what they did.

The volume they produced was published by the Biblical Archaeology Society, headquartered in Washington, D.C., headed by Hershel Shanks. The Biblical Archaeology Society (BAS) is an organization led by Mr. Shanks that attempts to bring together scholars on the one hand and the educated laypeople on the other. Shanks took up the campaign of agitating for the release of the entire corpus of scrolls. Shanks argued that since almost 40 years had passed and the majority of scrolls still had not been published, it was time for the scholars assigned to publish the documents to relinquish their control over them, to simply publish them, and thereby allow scholars anywhere to have access to the documents. It was in this volume that the reconstructed 4QMMT text appeared via the Wacholder-Abegg system; and then Shanks also published the same material in his journal *Biblical Archaeology Review*. It was these publications that sparked the lawsuit from Elisha Qimron that we described when we studied the MMT text earlier in our course.

Then, two weeks after the appearance of the Wacholder-Abegg volume, William Moffet, the director of the Huntington Library in San Marino, Calif., announced that his institution possessed a full set of photos of the Dead Sea Scrolls, which had been donated to the collection by Elizabeth

Hay Bechtel, a well-known California philanthropist, some years earlier, and that his library, the Huntington, would allow any qualified scholar access to these photographs. As far as I am aware, the first person who went to the Huntington to look at the photographs and began to read scrolls for the first time using this system was Robert Eisenman, whom we mentioned earlier as a professor at Cal State University Long Beach, not too far away from San Marino. In short, through this series of events here in the United States in 1991—the Shanks publication of the Wacholder-Abegg volume, and then the Huntington Library announcing that it had photographs of all of the documents—the cartel had been broken.

Back in Israel, meanwhile, Professor Tov, the new DJD editor, began to expand the official publication committee by including younger scholars including Jewish ones from Israel, the United States, and elsewhere. In the process, he reassigned texts that had languished in the hands of older scholars for decades, and he gave them to the younger scholars, now eager to publish the scrolls and make them accessible to their colleagues around the world. At the same time, with the publication of the primary sources of these Dead Sea Scrolls, these younger scholars would quickly make their mark at a relatively early stage in their academic careers.

Almost immediately, DJD volumes began to appear at a very quick pace. By 2001, an additional 25 volumes had appeared, most of them devoted to the fragmentary texts from Cave Four. In 2002, Tov published DJD 39, an introduction to the entire series with indices marking the occasion of the final publication of all the Dead Sea Scrolls. I should add, though, the DJD series continues with a republication of some of the Cave One texts published much earlier, in the late 1940s and early 1950s, by Professor Sukenik and the various scholars at the American Schools of Oriental Research in Jerusalem. Thus, for example, a new edition of 1QH, the Thanksgiving Hymns, was released in 2009 as DJD 40, under the editorship of Hartmut Stegemann (we've referred to him earlier in our course), Eileen Schuller, and Carol Newsom. Incidentally, Professor Newsom, of Emory University, is the one who coined that delightful expression that you've heard me use several times: "sectually explicit." I did not mention her name back in Lecture One when I introduced the expression "sectually explicit literature," not to want to throw all sorts of names of academicians at you then; but she deserves credit, and

I'm happy to mention the name of Carol Newsom here in connection with that phrase.

One would think that one's religious affiliation would not matter in scholarship, especially as scholars study ancient texts seeking objective truth without theological or denominational bias. Unfortunately, however, such is not the case. We saw, for example, that de Vaux and his colleagues understood the Qumran community as an early celibate monastery; indeed, they used the word "monks" at times when referring to the individual members of the *Yahad*. In addition, by and large, scholars of Jewish law and Talmud tend to be Jews; though one must note that today professors of Talmud who are not Jewish may be found at outstanding universities such as Yale, Princeton, and UCLA. But such was not always the case; so when it came to studying the Dead Sea Scrolls in those early years (late 1940s and 1950s), Christian scholars paid most attention to the theological and doctrinal issues present in the text; and once more, this correlated with Josephus's descriptions of the sects. When Jewish scholars joined the mainstream of Qumran research in the 1980s and 1990s, they paid more attention to the Halakhic material in the scrolls.

We have seen, for example, how this history of scholarship affected our understanding of the Dead Sea Scrolls, especially once the Halakhic Letter (4QMMT) finally was published for all to read and see how the sect defined itself vis-à-vis the other sects at the time. Scholars continue to ask: How might Dead Sea Scrolls scholarship have been different had the Temple Scroll and the Halakhic Letter, both of which focus on legal issues, if they had been the first texts to appear, instead of, for example, the Community Rule and the War Scroll, important as they are with a focus on doctrinal issues. The above description of the course of scholarship in recent decades sets the stage for our next topic: Jewish practices, ritual practices, reflected in the Dead Sea Scrolls. Rabbinic law from the Mishna and the Talmud, as well as later medieval sources, prescribes a host of practices that continue to this day among traditionally observant Jews. Here one may mention the use of *tefillin*, the use of *mezuza*—again, I'll explain those terms in a moment—and the recitation of Grace after Meals.

First, one of the most amazing finds at Qumran is the oldest examples of *tefillin* in our possession. The New Testament refers to these objects, worn on the head and the arm, as "phylacteries," the Greek word for "amulets" or "protective device" (see Matthew 23:5), and even though Jews have never considered them as such, that term "phylacteries" has become part of the English language. Since the word *tefillin* derives from the Hebrew word *tefilla* ("prayer"), perhaps it is better to refer to these items in English as "prayer accoutrements." The discovery of about 20 extremely tiny *tefillin* scrolls—well, all of our *tefillin* scrolls by their very nature are going to be tiny—along with a few of the cases in which they were kept, all made out of leather, now represent our earliest evidence for this practice. The practice derives from a literal interpretation of Exodus 13:16 and Deuteronomy 6:8, 11:18. Let me read for you those passages. Exodus 13:16: "And it will be as a sign on your hand and as a symbol between your eyes"; and "between your eyes" is understood to mean "forehead." Then the two Deuteronomy passages, Deuteronomy 6:8, 11:18: "And you shall bind them as a sign on your hand and they shall be as a symbol between your eyes"; once more, "between your eyes" referring to your forehead.

We know that the Pharisees, and their rabbinic successors, interpreted these biblical passages in such fashion—that is, they took them literally; you are literally to bind these biblical passages, these little documents written on parchment, on your head and on your arm at the time of prayer—and now we know that the Qumran community (and perhaps all Essenes) did likewise. While we do not have explicit evidence for this, we assume that the Sadducees would have understood these passages metaphorically and therefore would not have worn *tefillin*. This is certainly the case with the Karaites, the medieval sect of Jews who rejected the Oral Law, for they understood the biblical passages that I have just read from Exodus and Deuteronomy figuratively.

The rabbinic tradition records different opinions as to the order of the four passages—two come from Exodus, two from Deuteronomy—to be written on separate tiny scrolls and then placed in the *tefillin* case. The Qumran *tefillin*, interestingly, present yet another order; plus we have still further variations including exactly which passages are to be written and installed in these tiny little cases. These extremely tiny finds were published by (yet again) Yigael Yadin in a monograph entitled *Tefillin from Qumran*, published in 1969, and they remain on display—with a magnifying glass so that the viewing public can see them—at the Shrine of the Book, the special pavilion at the Israel museum in Jerusalem dedicated to the finds from Qumran.

A related phenomenon in Jewish tradition is the use of *mezuza*; a tiny scroll placed in a case and then affixed to the doorposts of one's house in accordance with two passages from Deuteronomy, one is 6:9 and one is 11:20. This is understood literally by all Jews, since the word "write" actually appears in the biblical verse. Let me read that verse for you: "And you shall write them on the doorposts of your house and upon your gates." A later rabbinic tradition held that a single scroll including the two passages that refer to this custom is to be placed on the doorpost; but the rabbis also were aware that some sectarians included the Ten Commandments in their tiny little *mezuza* scrolls; the Ten Commandments found in Exodus 20, with a parallel text in Deuteronomy 5. Strikingly, the Qumran *mezuza* texts have the Ten Commandments included.

Another example of such a scroll is the Nash Papyrus, which we discussed earlier in our course, found in Egypt, dated to the 2nd century B.C.E., which places the Ten Commandments and the *Shema* prayer (Deuteronomy 6:4–9) on a single scroll. The Samaritans also take this commandment literally—again, since the word "write" is explicitly used—though their *mezuzot* take the form of plaques above the doorway, and theirs also contain the Decalogue, the Ten Commandments.

The third ritual practice that the Qumran texts refer to as a subject for this lecture is the blessing of food both before and after eating, with a priest performing the task. In the Community Rule, we have the following comment: "When the table has been prepared for eating, and the wine for drinking, the priest shall extend his hand first to bless the first of the bread and the wine"; so blessing the food, the bread, and the wine conducted by a priest. From a period several centuries later than the Dead Sea Scrolls, we possess the specific language of Grace after Meals as created by the rabbis. Professor Moshe Weinfeld of the Hebrew University identified a small gragment—4Q434 frg. 2—as a precursor to the rabbinic formulation, with a special focus on the expression "to eat of its fruit and of its goodness"; that's what our little Qumran fragment says. We know that same phrase from the rabbi's formulation centuries later.

Furthermore, a Deuteronomy manuscript found at Qumran—its official siglum is 4QDeut[n]—which includes Deuteronomy 8, includes a space between verses 8 and 9 of that chapter. That is to say, when it writes out Deuteronomy 8 versus 8 and 9, it includes a space between verses 8 and 9. This space is not included in our later medieval biblical manuscripts, but Weinfeld was able to determine what the purpose of that space was right here. The later rabbis decreed that only after eating bread is one required to recite the complete Grace after Meals. After eating other food items, one is required to recite only a much shorter prayer. Since Deuteronomy 8:8 refers to other items—grapes, figs, pomegranates, olives, and dates—and then mentions bread in the next verse, verse 9; and then in the following verse 10 it states, "and you shall eat and be satiated, and you shall bless the LORD your God for the good land that he has given to you," the rabbis deduced that the full Grace after Meals is required only after eating bread. Verse 8 other food items, verse 9 bread, verse 10 the commandment to bless God after eating; therefore the rabbis deduced only for the bread in verse 9, not for the other food items mentioned in verse 8, is one required to say the full Grace after Meals. By placing the space between verses 8 and 9 in this Deuteronomy text from Cave Four, the Qumran scribe is anticipating the rabbinic opinion from centuries later; again, that is to say that the rabbinic system was already in place in the 2nd and 1st centuries B.C.E., as Professor Weinfeld was able to determine from that tiny little space in between those two verses in a Qumran fragment of the book of Deuteronomy 8.

Before the discovery of the Dead Sea Scrolls, we knew about the practices discussed in this lecture from the Mishna, dated to the early 3rd century C.E. A scholarly debate arose as to whether practices mentioned in this important rabbinic text—this codification of Jewish law, the Mishna—but not specifically indicated in the Torah. The question was: Were these innovations of the rabbis of the 2nd and 3rd centuries C.E., or was it that the Mishna was simply codifying practices that had existed for centuries earlier? The existence of the Dead Sea Scrolls tilts the scales of this debate greatly in favor of the latter opinion, which now should serve as the default opinion for those of us who study Judaism in antiquity. Unless we can say with certainty that the rabbis of the Mishna innovated a particular custom or ritual, we may assume that the practices incorporated into this code of Jewish law, such as the use of *tefillin* and Grace after Meals, hark back centuries earlier.

Now we return to the subject of the first part of this lecture. As we saw with the passage of time, more and more Jewish scholars entered the fray of Dead Sea Scrolls research; and it was mainly these Jewish scholars who began to focus their work on the topics described in this lecture. The paradigm shifted so that the scrolls came to be seen as more connected to Judaism than to Christianity. It is for this reason that Lawrence Schiffman calls his book *Reclaiming the Dead Sea Scrolls*, which is to say, the subject of the Scrolls has been reclaimed to its rightful home, the larger field of Jewish Studies. There is no better way to present this turn of events than to read from a portion of Professor Schiffman's book; early on, it appears on page 18 of his book. He talks there about the earlier trend, what he calls the "Christianizing" of the Scrolls, and then the more current trend, which is to return these documents to the world of Jewish studies. Let me quote at length for you Professor Schiffman here:

> To show how important terminology can be, let me [the "me" here is Lawrence Schiffman] present a composite portrait of the sect as drawn from these Christianizing analyses. [Then he begins] The monks of Qumran were ascetics who practiced a baptismal rite and were led by a Teacher of Righteousness. They ate together in a refectory after taking ablutions, and they shared a Eucharist of bread and wine. After the teacher died, they were led by an episkopos [bishop]. They practiced community of goods and dedicated themselves to the healing of the sick and the clothing of the poor. They composed hymns in which they praised God, and they eagerly awaited a savior who combined priestly and Davidic aspects. The monks copied manuscripts in the scriptorium, leaving us the Dead Sea Scrolls.

Then Professor Schiffman goes on as follows: "Correspondingly, the same community [the Qumran sect] could be reconfigured in Jewish terms." Then he rewrites the paragraph using terminology more familiar to us from the field of Jewish Studies as follows:

The inhabitants of Qumran were observant Jews who practiced ritual purity and were led by their rabbi, a Teacher of Righteousness. They ate communal meals in their dining room after immersion in the mikvah (ritual bath). They recited Hamotzi [that's the blessing over bread] over the bread before the meal, and made a special barak (blessing) over wine. After the teacher died, they were led by another rabbi. They were always willing to lend their possessions to others, and dedicated themselves to the mitzvah [commandment] of healing the sick and giving charitable donations to clothe the poor. They composed prayers in which they praised God, and they eagerly awaited a Messiah who combined priestly and Davidic aspects. The scribes among the sect copied their most important texts for their library, leaving us the Dead Sea Scrolls.

Then Professor Schiffman goes on: "Both of these descriptions, made up by me, demonstrate how easy it is for language and terminology to influence our perception of the Scrolls." Personally, I have a bit of a problem with Schiffman's use of the word "rabbi" for the leader of the Qumran community, but I hope you get the main point presented in his two descriptions here.

In our next lecture, we will continue this thrust, as we turn in greater detail to the topic of prayer, another important Jewish ritual practice. Our discussion there will include a thorough examination of the one remaining text from Cave One that we have not scrutinized thus far: the Thanksgiving Hymns.

Prayers, Hymns, and the Synagogue
Lecture 20

> Only after an immersion into the Dead Sea Scrolls corpus as a whole is it possible to tease out some of the theological expressions of this document.

When the Temple stood in Jerusalem, it remained the locus of the worship of God via the daily animal sacrifices, with additional sacrifices on the Sabbath and festivals, as prescribed in the Torah. Since the Qumran sect saw the Temple as polluted and beyond repair, they sought other means for the worship of God, particularly through communal daily prayer. While other Jews may not have viewed the Temple in such a negative light, we also know that the synagogue was a developing institution even while the Temple still stood. Once the Temple was destroyed, the synagogue burgeoned even in the rabbinic tradition, as we know from archaeological discoveries dated mainly to the Byzantine period, especially in the Galilee region in northern Israel. Given all this, it is noteworthy that there is no synagogue found at Qumran. Most likely, the communal nature of the entire site obviated the need for one: Recall that "synagogue" means "the place of the people coming together." Presumably the Qumran sect gathered in the largest room at the site for synagogue activities. Also, the community as a whole, the *Yahad*, was a substitution for the Temple. The Damascus Document states, "Anyone who enters the house of prostration, let him not enter impure, but rather let him be washed" (CD MS B 11:21–22). This indicates that the Qumran community saw entering their house of worship (call it "synagogue" or whatever) in a state of ritual purity as akin to entering the Temple. The rabbis, however, did not see the synagogue in this light.

A number of Dead Sea Scroll texts refer to morning and evening prayers, no doubt in imitation of the morning and evening sacrifices performed in the Temple, along with prayers for Sabbath and festivals. A section near the end of the Community Rule presents the leader of the community as offering praise to God at these appointed times (1QS 10:1–6), ending with "with the offering of my lips I bless him, as a statute engraved forever." We have a series of texts that are clearly prayers and blessings, but unfortunately they are very fragmentary. A better preserved text is entitled Songs of the Sabbath Sacrifice, preserved in nine copies at Qumran (4Q400–407, 11Q17), with an additional fragment found at Masada, presenting the hymns recited by the angels in heaven for each of the first 13 sabbaths of the year. It is not clear whether the Qumran community recited these songs as part of their own Sabbath liturgy, but the presence of this text is significant nonetheless.

> **The Qumran community saw entering their house of worship in a state of ritual purity as akin to entering the Temple.**

Of all the Qumran texts that qualify as prayers, the one on which we should focus the most attention is a document known as the Thanksgiving Hymns, or Hodayot (1QH). This document was one of the original seven scrolls found in Cave 1, purchased and published by Eliezer Sukenik. At 18 columns, plus dozens of fragments that need to be incorporated at different places, the Thanksgiving Hymns is one of the longest of the scrolls. The text presents a series of individual hymns, about 25 in number, of varying lengths, which begin with the phrase *'odekha 'adonay* ("I give thanks to you, O Lord"). Since the single scroll was no longer intact when it reached Sukenik's hands, scholars disagree as to the ordering of the individual columns and thus the arrangement of the individual hymns.

Now that we have mastered so many of the other texts, we will be able to contextualize this document all the better. The hymns are praises of God, and in many ways they resemble the book of Psalms. Some appear to express the sentiments of the community as a whole, while others (especially hymns 1, 2, and 7–11) appear to refer to the experiences of a single individual. Some scholars have proposed that the Teacher of Righteousness is the author of the Hodayot text. Many of the sect's theological points are presented in poetic terms in this collection, though many of these ideas were part of common Judaism: the Glory of God, reward of the righteous, punishment of the wicked, predetermination, and the existence of angels. The reward of the righteous and the punishment of the wicked point once more to the dualism present in the Dead Sea Scrolls; and they also indicate a developing belief in an afterlife.

The Thanksgiving Hymns are centered totally on the community. There is no appeal to biblical texts (such as in the Prophets) that describe the conversion of the pagans to the worship of the one God. There is not a single reference to the Jerusalem Temple, which was the focus of all other Jewish groups at the time. In short, on the scale of particularism and universalism, the Dead Sea Scrolls community is geared totally toward the former. The Qumran community is concerned only with itself in this document. One reads again and again how the author feels inadequate in the presence of God, referring to himself more than once as "a creature of clay." But the author goes even further, describing his origins as follows: "Behold, [I have been taken] from dust [and] fashioned [from clay], from a fount of impurity and the nakedness of shame" (1QH 20:24–25). Schiffman has made the very interesting observation that the expressions "fount of impurity" and "nakedness of shame" refer to the female genitalia. While typically Jewish tradition has viewed sexuality in a positive manner, these phrases, he says, suggest that "sexuality is basically an impure and undesirable feature of human existence."

One is tempted to consider the possibility that the Thanksgiving Hymns were used liturgically by the Qumran community. We have no real evidence of liturgical use from the document itself. There is, however, an intriguing reference in Philo to the liturgy of Shavu'ot (a.k.a. Pentecost) among the Therapeutae (an Essene-like sect living in Egypt). Their leader would deliver a commentary on scripture, followed by his recitation of a hymn, at which point he invited other members of the community to recite hymns as well. One could imagine the leader of the Qumran community using these hymns in a similar fashion on special occasions.

Naturally, we cannot be sure how the Hodayot scroll may have been used by the Qumran community, but once more the contents of these poems afford us an opportunity to see their unique thinking and theology at work. ∎

Essential Reading

Vermes, *The Complete Dead Sea Scrolls in English*, 67–90, 243–300, 321–330.

VanderKam, *The Dead Sea Scrolls Today*, 60–64.

Schiffman, *Reclaiming the Dead Sea Scrolls*, 145–153, 289–301, 355–360.

Questions to Consider

1. How important was the development of the synagogue to the continued existence of Judaism in antiquity?

2. Does the order of the columns (and thus the individual poems) in the Thanksgiving Hymns document really matter? Is there a substantive difference? Or is this merely a matter of scholarly curiosity?

Prayers, Hymns, and the Synagogue
Lecture 20—Transcript

This lecture continues the subject of Jewish ritual as attested at Qumran, with special attention to prayer. We begin with a discussion of the synagogue, which developed as an alternative locus for the worship of God outside the context of the Temple in ancient Judaism. We will note a series of references to prayer within the Dead Sea Scrolls corpus, along with some actual prayer texts. We then turn to a presentation of the last of original seven documents to be examined in this course, a lengthy collection of poetry known as the Thanksgiving Hymns. These poems are praises of God, modeled very closely after the biblical book of Psalms. Some appear to express the sentiments of the community as a whole, while others appear to refer to the experiences of a single individual, perhaps the Teacher of Righteousness. Finally, we will consider the possibility that the Thanksgiving Hymns served the Qumran community in similar fashion to that described by Philo concerning the Therapeutae, an Essene-like sect in Egypt, according to whom the leader of the community recited hymns as part of the liturgy of Shavu'ot.

When the Temple stood in Jerusalem, it remained the locus of the worship of God via the animal sacrifices offered daily—with additional sacrifices for the Sabbath and the festivals—by the priest on the altar exactly as prescribed in the Torah. Since the sect saw the Temple as polluted and beyond repair— as we've mentioned several times in our course—they sought other means for the worship of God. First, they apparently saw their collective entity— their *Yahad*—as embodying the sacred; the community itself was an element of sanctity. Second, they instituted communal daily prayer as a means of worship. In the Bible, prayer was mainly a private affair, as illustrated best of all by the story of Hannah in 1 Samuel 1; at Qumran, you get public, communal group prayer. While other Jews may not have viewed the Temple in such a negative light, we also know that the synagogue was a developing institution even during the period when the Temple stood.

Clearly there were synagogues in the Diaspora, outside the land of Israel, where other Jewish communities lived. In 1902, an inscribed marble slab was found near Shedia, 26 kilometers from Alexandria, Egypt, mentioning the dedication of a synagogue during the reign of King Ptolemy III. The book 3

Maccabees 7, a non-canonical work, mentions the founding of a synagogue at Ptolemais, also in Egypt, during the reign of King Ptolemy IV. Philo mentions a synagogue in Alexandria during his day. It may be the same one that was destroyed by Roman emperor Trajan early on in the 2nd century C.E. as punishment for Jewish revolts during his reign. Later rabbinic tradition described this synagogue of Alexandria in great detail, indicating its size, grandeur, and beauty. The New Testament refers to Paul—later on now in the 1st century C.E.—preaching in synagogues in Damascus, and throughout Cyprus, Asia Minor, and Greece in cities such as Thessalonica and Corinth. There's a wealth of information concerning synagogues outside the land of Israel from all of these sources.

Archaeologists have excavated at least three synagogues in Israel itself, all dated prior to the destruction of the Temple in 70 C.E.: at Gamla in the far north, and at Herodion and Masada in the southern part of the land of Israel. In addition, the Gospels—1st century C.E.—refer to Jesus teaching in the synagogues of Nazareth and Capernaum; Matthew 13, Mark 6 refer to the Nazareth synagogue, Mark 1 refers to the Capernaum synagogue. Josephus, meanwhile, still a few decades later in the 1st century C.E., mentions synagogues in the following cities: Tiberias, Dor, and Caesarea. The synagogue appears to have been used mainly for the study of sacred texts; the Bible, that is. The rabbinic tradition would have to face the same issue once the Temple was destroyed, at which point the synagogue burgeoned, certainly in the land of Israel, as we know from archaeological discoveries dated mainly to the late Roman or Byzantine Period, especially in the Galilee region of northern Israel.

Given all this, it is noteworthy that there is no synagogue found at Qumran. Most likely, the communal nature of the entire site obviated the need for a specific communal building; recall that the word "synagogue" means "the place of the people coming together." Presumably the Qumran sect gathered in the largest room at the site, the dining hall, for synagogue activities such as prayer and the study of the sacred texts. Plus we repeat our earlier comment that the community as a whole, the *Yahad*, represented its substitution for the Temple. The sanctity of the Temple was transferred to the sanctity of the community. The Damascus Document states as follows: "Anyone who enters the house of prostration, let him not enter impure, but rather let him we washed" (Damascus Document 11). This indicates that the Qumran community saw entering their house of worship—call it "synagogue" or "house of prostration" or whatever—in a state of ritual purity; one had to be ritually pure to enter the prayer hall, exactly akin to entering the Temple in a state of purity.

The rabbis, by contrast, did not see the synagogue in this light. The structure of the synagogue was important, its activities were crucial to religious worship, and over the course of centuries the synagogue became the centerpiece of Jewish life; but never was it considered a sacred precinct on a par with the Temple, so that did not need to be ritually pure in order to enter the synagogue. If one came in contact with the dead, or if a woman had her menstrual period, none of these things prevented you from actually entering the synagogue. One did not have to undergo that ritual purity that was necessary for entering the Temple when it stood. The most that is expected, according to the custom of many Jews, is a symbolic hand washing before prayer as a token reminder of what once was, when the Temple stood and real ritual immersion was required upon entering and the sacred precinct and worshipping. The rabbis take one view of the synagogue that does not require this kind of ritual purification; the Qumran community, however, as we saw from this Damascus Document text, states that one must be ritually pure before entering what they call the house of prostration. Incidentally, this expression, "house of prostration," is the lexical equivalent of the Arabic word *masjid*, "place of prostration," from which our word "mosque" comes; *masjid*, English: mosque.

A number of Dead Sea Scrolls texts refer to morning and evening prayers, no doubt in imitation of the morning and evening sacrifices performed in the Temple, along with prayers as well for Sabbath and festivals. A section near the end of the Community Rule (1QS) presents the leader of the community as offering praise to God at these various appointed times, and then it ends with the passage, "with the offering of my lips I bless him, as a statute engraved forever." We have a series of unfortunately very fragmentary texts that clearly are prayers and blessings. For example, 4Q507, 4Q508, and 4Q509—three fragmentary texts from Cave Four—present prayers for festivals, with particular mention of Yom Kippur, the Day of Atonement, and Shavu'ot, the festival, in this case, of First Fruits; you'll recall from a previous lecture Shavu'ot marks the wheat harvest, the harvest and the offering and the bringing of the first fruits to the Temple, and also the revelation of Sinai. Here you have a specific Qumran text that refers to these special prayers on these holidays, Yom Kippur and Shavu'ot.

4Q408 praises God for creating light and darkness, paralleling to a great extent, in very similar language, the later rabbinic formulation recited before the declamation of the *Shema* (that's the central prayer of Judaism, derived from Deuteronomy 6). Let me read the most relevant portion of this Qumran text. It reads as follows: "You have created the morning (as) a sign for the appearance of the dominion of light, as a boundary for the day ... to bless your holy name, you created them, that the light is good ... You have created the evening (as) a sign for the appearance of the dominion of [darkness, as a boundary for the night] ... to bless [your holy name]"; again, that's from 4Q408.

A better preserved text in the Dead Sea Scrolls corpus is entitled *Songs of the Sabbath Sacrifice*. It is preserved in nine copies found at Qumran, eight of them in Cave 4 (their numbers are 4Q400–407) and a copy from Cave 11 as well (11Q17), and an additional fragment of this text, the *Songs of the Sabbath Sacrifice* was also found in the excavations at Masada. The composition presents the hymns recited by the angels in heaven for each of the first 13 Sabbaths of the year; that is, the first quarter of the solar year: 52 weeks, the first 13 Sabbaths each get their own song in this document as proclaimed by the angels in heaven. It suggests that there is a simultaneous recitation of prayers by humans on earth as the angels sing in heaven. The hymns are based mainly on the biblical material in the book of Ezekiel, chapters 1–10 especially, which provide for us rare glimpses of heaven; most of the biblical books focus on what's going on on Earth, the beginning of the book of Ezekiel gives us parts, gives us views, of heaven, and then the *Songs of the Sabbath Sacrifice* builds from that. This document, by the way, intersects with Jewish mystical material, especially as known from later centuries when we get more texts from the field of Jewish mysticism. The rabbis actually would later warn against the use of various Ezekiel passages in the synagogue or in private study as too esoteric and too mystical. It's not clear if the Qumran recited these songs as part of their own Sabbath liturgy, but the presence of this text is significant nonetheless.

As to the Masada fragment: Earlier in our course, we noted that the discovery of one copy of this text at Masada suggests that the Qumran sect sought refuge at the Zealot stronghold there on top of Masada once their own community center was besieged by the Romans. But another option is possible as well: Perhaps this text—the *Songs of the Sabbath Sacrifice*—was not a sectarian document at all. There is no mention of the *Yahad* in this composition; there is nothing specifically Qumranite about it; but rather it may have been just one of the documents belonging to common Judaism, or at least that other groups of Jews would have been using at this time as well. Early on in Dead Sea Scrolls research, most scholars held to the former opinion that the Qumran community left its site and fled to Masada, and at least one of these documents from Qumran is found there in the excavations at Masada as well. Now, however, the pendulum has shifted and scholars are more likely to accede to the latter opinion; which is to say that the text is simply one that was used by different groups of Jews during this period, last several centuries B.C.E., 1st century C.E. This issue intersects with the ongoing problem of how to identify "sectually explicit" literature.

But of all the Qumran texts that qualify as prayers, or served as prayers, the one upon which we should focus the most attention is a document known as the Thanksgiving Hymns. It's Hebrew title is *Hodayot* ; *Hodayot* is the Hebrew word for "thanksgiving" or "thanksgiving hymns," and therefore its official siglum used by Dead Sea Scrolls scholars is 1QH: "1Q," Cave One; and then the "H" for *Hodayot*, although conveniently it also serves as the abbreviation for "Hymns." This document was one of the original seven scrolls found in Cave One, purchased and published by Eliezer Sukenik; you'll recall the story from the beginning of our course.

We have mentioned this story and this text several times in our course, though only now, towards the end here in Lecture 20, will we examine this composition in detail. You may ask: Why only now do I present this text? Why wait until now to present one of the original seven scrolls from Cave One? Several reasons: First, the subject fits very nicely at this point since there is a connection between the ritual of prayer, which we've been discussing, and the recitation of hymns. Second, this document, 1QH, is less polemical than the other texts from amongst the Dead Sea Scrolls, including those from Cave One, mainly because our text is a collection of hymns, poetry that is, as opposed to the polemical discourse of the type encountered in prose texts such as 1QS, the Community Rule, and other crucial Dead Sea Scrolls documents. Only after an immersion into the Dead Sea Scrolls corpus as a whole, to my mind, is it possible to tease out some of the theological expressions of the Thanksgiving Hymns, this Hodayot Scroll; and now that we have studied so many of the other texts, we will be able to contextualize this document all the better.

At 18 columns, along with dozens of fragments that need to be incorporated at different places, the Thanksgiving Hymns document is one of the longest of the Dead Sea Scrolls. The text presents a series of individual hymns—about 25 in number, of varying lengths—which begin with the phrase (in Hebrew) "*odekha 'adonay* ," "I give thanks to you, O Lord"; that's the refrain that repeats introducing each of the individual hymns. Since the single scroll was no longer intact when it was found or when it reached Professor Sukenik's hands, scholars disagree as to the ordering of the individual columns and thus the arrangement of the individual hymns. Let me explain this to you. Typically a scroll is created in the following way: Individual sheets of parchment are taken, and you write several columns of a text on those sheets. Then you sew them together and you get a single large roll or scroll, the entire document found in a single scroll. But what happened in this particular case is that the seams that were used to hold the various sheets together had come apart, and at some point—either when it was in Kando's hands or when it was given over to Professor Sukenik—and the individual sheets, each housing several columns, were no longer connected to the other. Therefore the question arose how to put them back together again; in what order to put them in. Sukenik presented one order in his initial publication of the document; and then the French scholar Émile Puech, also associated with the École Biblique in Jerusalem, suggested a different arrangement in a very important article that he wrote published in the *Journal of Jewish Studies* in 1988. In the end, this issue is of only minor importance, but it indicates once again the difficult task facing scholars in their publishing, understanding, and translating these ancient and often difficult to read manuscripts.

The hymns—the individual hymns in this document—are praises of God, and in many ways they resemble the biblical book of Psalms. Some appear to express the sentiments of the community as a whole, while others—and I'll even give you some of their numbers, hymns 1, 2, and then hymns 7–11— appear to refer to the experiences of a single individual. Regarding the latter, we take note of the "I" voice that is used throughout this document. For example, the phrase that I quoted earlier: *'odekha 'adonay*; emphasis on the "I," "I give thanks to you, O Lord." Indeed, some scholars have proposed that "I" here is the Teacher of Righteousness who therefore serves as the author of the *Hodayot* text, the composer of these hymns.

Many of the sect's theological points are presented in poetic terms in this Thanksgiving Hymns collection, though to be sure many of these same ideas were part of common Judaism. Let me give you some examples and read some of the passages from these hymns. The Glory of God; this is stated, of course, throughout these hymns, but let me give you a flavor from one particular passage; it's in 1QH 6:23. It reads as follows: "I praise you, O Lord, for the greatness of your strength and for the magnitude of your wonders, forever and ever." Another issue that arises: the reward of the righteous. This comes up several times in this document; let me read a sample passage again from 1QH 4: "Endowing them [referring to the righteous] with all the glory of man and the magnitude of days"; "magnitude of days" referring to long life; that's the reward that the righteous will receive. By contrast, you have the punishment of the wicked, another topic that comes up several times in the Thanksgiving Hymns. 1QH 7 gives us a fine example of this: "And the wicked you created for the end-time of your wrath, and from the womb you dedicated them for the day of slaughter, for they have walked in a way not good, and they have rejected your covenant." I want to reread the beginning of that: "And the wicked you created for the end-time of your wrath, and from the womb you dedicated them for the day of slaughter"; do you see that there is predestination, predetermination built into this passage as well? God is responsible for the creation these wicked individuals who will, in turn, have to be punished according to the way this is stated here in this poem. You can begin to see how this poem, again, dovetails nicely with the theological stances of the Dead Sea Scrolls.

While we're on the topic of predetermination, let me give you another passage that spells it out very clearly; it's from 1QH 4:22: "And I understand that you have chosen [for the one] his way," after which the text goes on and implies that even if one were to wish to sin against God, this could not happen, since the path of—in this case, the righteous person—has been predetermined. I'll read it again: "And I understand that you have chosen [for the one] [the righteous one] his way." Yet another element that comes out from reading the Thanksgiving Hymns is the belief in angels. Let me read that passage for you; this one from 1QH 14:12–13: "For you have brought your truth and your glory to all the men of your council, in the lot together with the angels of your presence." The humans and the angels are together in a single community according to this passage from the Hodayot Scroll.

The reward of the righteous and the punishment of the wicked—passages I've just read—point once more to the dualism present in the Dead Sea Scrolls, and they also indicate a developing belief in an afterlife which therefore would put a distance between the Qumran sect and the Sadducees, notwithstanding some of the Halakhic points of agreement we referred to earlier in our course.

The Thanksgiving Hymns are centered totally on the community. There is no appeal to biblical texts, such as occurs in the Prophets, which describe the conversion of the pagans to the worship of the one God; the *Yahad* is not concerned about such individuals. There is not a single reference in this long document to the Jerusalem Temple, which was so much the focus for all other Jewish groups at the time. The Qumran sect, of course, as we've stated, removed itself from Temple worship. In short, on the scale of particularism and universalism, the Dead Sea Scrolls community is geared totally towards the former; towards particularism. That is to say, the one point on which all Jews could agree, the centrality of the Jerusalem Temple to religious life, not only for themselves, but even by extension for the people of the world at large; all of this finds no expression whatsoever in the *Hodayot Scroll*. The community—the Qumran *Yahad*—is concerned only with itself in this document, though once more we note that for the *Yahad*, the community was the substitution, the replacement, the surrogate for the Temple with all the requisite holiness and purity attached to the Temple.

One reads again and again how the author feels inadequate in the presence of God, referring to himself more than once as "a creature of clay," for

289

example in 1QH 20:27. But the author goes even further when describing his origins as follows; let me read the text: "Behold, [I have been taken] from dust [and] fashioned [from clay], from a fount of impurity and the nakedness of shame," that's also from 1QH 20:24–25). Lawrence Schiffman has made the very interesting observation that the expressions "fount of impurity" and "nakedness of shame" refer to the female genitalia. While typically Jewish tradition has viewed sexuality in a positive manner, these phrases suggest that, I'm quoting now from Schiffman, "sexuality is basically an impure and undesirable feature of human existence"; that's from his book *Reclaiming the Dead Sea Scrolls*. As an aside, we may note that this view forms another nexus with early Christianity, since many early Christians viewed sexuality as impure, deemed marital relations as a necessary but undesirable component of human existence, and instead considered celibacy and freedom from family ties as the ideal state.

One is tempted, especially in light of the material presented at the beginning of this lecture, to consider the possibility that the Thanksgiving Hymns were used liturgically by the Qumran community. Unfortunately, though, we have no real evidence forthcoming from the document itself. Regardless, the fact that the Thanksgiving Hymns are collected on a single long manuscript demonstrates that the Qumran sect held these poems in very high regard, for such practice was reserved only for their crucial texts: the War Scroll, the Community Rule, the Temple Scroll, these very long documents, along with, of course, the biblical manuscripts, most famously 1QIsa[a], the entire book of Isaiah.

There is, however, the intriguing reference in Philo to the practice of the Therapeutae, an Essene-like sect living in Egypt. According to Philo, the Therapeutae would recite hymns. Philo describes the liturgy of the holiday of Shavu'ot amongst this group, in which the leader of the Therapeutae would deliver a commentary on a portion of Scripture, followed by his recitation of a hymn; at which point the leader would invite other community members to recite hymns as well. One could imagine the leader of the Qumran community using these hymns in a similar fashion on special occasions. For example, at 1QH 6:17, the psalmist refers to his oath, one which brings him into the community. Let's read that passage: "And I know that with the magnitude of your goodness and with the oath, which I set upon myself, not to sin before you and not to do any evil before your eyes, and thus I was brought into the *Yahad*, (with) all the men of my council." Could this hymn have been used as part of the initiation rite, when individuals joined the community as full-fledged members? In like fashion, the Hodayot Scroll speaks of individuals joining the community, with such key phrases as "I cling to the congregation" and "I will hold fast to the truth of your covenant." Again, could this hymn have been used as part of the initiation rite, when individuals joined the community as full-fledged members? Naturally, we cannot be sure how the Thanksgiving Hymns scroll may have been used by the Qumran community, but once more the contents of these poems afford us an opportunity to see their unique thinking and their theology at work.

At several points in our course, we have mentioned the unique variety of ancient Hebrew employed by the Qumran scribes who've left us these documents. This topic will perforce bring us into an especially technical area of Dead Sea Scrolls research. Nevertheless, I will do my best in the next lecture, to present this material in an accessible way, to allow you to see how even at the level of language the Qumran sect made every effort to distance themselves from the Jewish world at large from which they had separated.

Qumran Hebrew as an Anti-Language
Lecture 21

Qumran Hebrew includes grammatical forms unlike those found in any other variety of ancient Hebrew. What is the origin of these forms?

The specific Hebrew dialect used to write the majority of the Dead Sea Scrolls is a different Hebrew register from all other Hebrew varieties known to us. Biblical Hebrew is divided into standard biblical Hebrew, used to compose the Torah, historical books, and prophetic books; and late biblical Hebrew, used from the time of the Exile onward (550–200 B.C.E.) to compose books such as Ezra, Nehemiah, Esther, Chronicles, and so forth. Hebrew works from the immediate postbiblical period include the book of Ben Sira (c. 180 B.C.E.), but since this work is written in poetry, with a heavy influence from the like-minded biblical book of Proverbs, we cannot use the prose continuum to the extent that we would like. Other works of the Apocrypha and Pseudepigrapha are in prose, but their Hebrew originals were lost in late antiquity, after which they were transmitted only in Greek and other translations.

We have recovered some later works in Hebrew such as Jubilees (c. 175 B.C.E.), but unfortunately they are very fragmentary and do not allow a full linguistic analysis. Some letters written

> **The Qumran community … devised their own variety of Hebrew, with its own vocabulary and grammar.**

by Simeon Bar-Kokhba and his contemporaries between 132 and 135 C.E. were also discovered in caves near the Dead Sea, though further south in the Ein Gedi region. These letters are written in a Hebrew with some similarities to Mishnaic Hebrew. The very large rabbinic corpus, especially the Mishna and the Tosefta (c. 200 C.E.), along with other elucidations of biblical material, are written in a dialect called Mishnaic Hebrew, which diverges considerably from the old biblical Hebrew standard. Most likely this dialect grew out of the everyday spoken Hebrew. The Qumran community refers to its opponents—most likely meaning the Pharisees—as using an inferior brand of Hebrew. But the Qumran community could not use simple biblical Hebrew either, for such was the inheritance of all Jews. They thus devised their own variety of Hebrew, with its own vocabulary and grammar.

Linguists refer to the phenomenon of an in-group language as "linguistic ideology" and use the expression "anti-language" to refer to the idiom developed by the in group. Convenient examples in English are the use of the word "queer" by the gay community to describe themselves, which otherwise could not be used by outsiders, and the very offensive word "nigger" used by African Americans among themselves but that certainly cannot be used by nonmembers of the group. In another example, all sorts of coded languages exist in the world of criminals, in the realm of prostitutes, and in drug culture. Most striking is the phenomenon noticed by those who study modern-day cults, which also tend to construct an in-group language. This is not to say that the Qumran community is akin to a modern-day cult, but the analogy may be helpful.

William Schniedewind adopted the linguistic ideology/anti-language approach and applied it to Qumran Hebrew. Examples of anti-language within Qumran Hebrew include the following. The use of the word

Backlash against 17th-century English Quakers affected speech patterns.

"*Yahad*," typically rendered "community," as the group's self-designation. Archaisms and pseudo-archaisms that give a patina of antiquity—and thus authority—to their literature. Most strikingly, the dialect is relatively devoid of loanwords, in stark contrast to late biblical Hebrew, which is filled with words borrowed from Aramaic, Persian, and even (in the case of the book of Daniel) Greek. Finally, there is the very strange Qumran Hebrew usage of adding -*a* to pronoun forms.

Earlier in our course, we noted that some of the biblical manuscripts, most famously 1QIsa[a], are linguistically updated, somewhat akin to seeing an updated Shakespeare play. Mainly this means that the Qumran scribes introduced late biblical Hebrew features into a text written in standard biblical Hebrew. But it also means that they introduced their own unique anti-language usages into the biblical text, such as the pronoun forms ending in *-a* mentioned above.

There is one feature of Qumran Hebrew that does occur elsewhere—namely, the unusual second-person masculine plural pronoun *'attema*, along with the corresponding possessive form *kimma*—that is, "your" (masculine plural). These forms are attested not only at Qumran but in Samaritan Hebrew. Could Samaratians too have engaged in an anti-language usage to distinguish themselves from general Judaism? As with so many questions that we raise in this course, there is no definitive answer. ∎

Essential Reading

Qimron, *The Hebrew of the Dead Sea Scrolls*.

Rendsburg, "Language at Qumran."

Schniedewind, "Qumran Hebrew as an Antilanguage."

Weitzman, "Why Did the Qumran Community Write in Hebrew?"

Questions to Consider

1. Do you think that the anti-language approach to Qumran Hebrew is valid? Are any other explanations possible?

2. Can you think of other instances of linguistic ideology within English or any other language you may know? Can you think of specific lexical or grammatical usages that may point in this direction?

Qumran Hebrew as an Anti-Language
Lecture 21—Transcript

This lecture concerns the dialect of Hebrew used in the Dead Sea Scrolls, what scholars call Qumran Hebrew; an important subject, as we shall see. Qumran Hebrew includes grammatical forms unlike those found in any other variety of ancient Hebrew; they are absent from earlier Biblical Hebrew, from the roughly contemporary sources such as the book of Ben Sira, and from the later Mishnaic Hebrew, the language of the Mishna and associated rabbinic texts. What is the origin of these forms? While much debate about Qumran Hebrew swirls in scholarly circles, we will follow the approach that understands this dialect as an anti-language. This term refers to the sociolinguistic phenomenon of a specific sect or group using "in" language in order to distinguish its dialect from that of the "out" group; that is, the majority population. We will provide ample illustrations of such Hebrew forms from our texts, using English analogies and translations along the way to illustrate the point. By so doing, we will realize the extent to which the Qumran sectarians attempted to distinguish themselves from the general Jewish population, which no doubt used a more standard Hebrew. That is to say, not only was their legal practice and belief system different, even their Hebrew dialect was different.

Before moving to a discussion of the unique brand of Hebrew used to compose the Dead Sea Scrolls documents, we present here once more some of the information conveyed earlier in our course. The vast majority of the Dead Sea Scrolls are in Hebrew. Of the 700 non-biblical scrolls, 560 (or 80 percent) of them are written in Hebrew, 120 (or 17 percent) are written in Aramaic, and a small number, 20 texts (or 3 percent of the corpus) are in Greek. Though we also need to note that all of the longest scrolls are in Hebrew—the only real exception is the Genesis Apocryphon, written in Aramaic as we discussed in an earlier lecture—so that the amount of material given the long Hebrew documents that we have is probably about 90 percent written in Hebrew.

The specific Hebrew dialect used to write the majority of the Dead Sea Scrolls is a different Hebrew register than all other Hebrew varieties known to us. Let me review for you here our other sources of ancient Hebrew. We begin with Biblical Hebrew, the language of the books of the Bible, divided into two strata: First, Standard Biblical Hebrew, used down to the time of the Exile (from about 1,000 B.C.E. until the 6th century B.C.E.), and Standard Biblical Hebrew is used to compose the Torah, the historical books such as Joshua, Judges, Samuel, and Kings, books of the prophets such as Amos, Hosea, and Isaiah, and more. The second stratum we call Late Biblical Hebrew, used from the time of the Exile in the 6th century B.C.E.—let's say 550 to give it a rough date—down to the end of the Biblical Period, and then slightly into the Postbiblical Period around 200 B.C.E., used to compose books such as Ezra, Nehemiah, Esther, Chronicles, and others.

Hebrew works from the immediate postbiblical period comprise our next category of documents for the history of the Hebrew language. The book of Ben Sira, for example, written 180 B.C.E.; but since this work is written in poetry, with a heavy influence from the like-minded biblical book of Proverbs, we cannot use this work, and we cannot put it into the prose continuum as we would like to do to give us a chronology of the history of the Hebrew language. Other works of the Apocrypha and books from this period were written in prose, but their Hebrew originals were lost in late antiquity, after which they were transmitted only in Greek and in other translations. We have recovered some of this material—we've referred, for example, to the copies of the book of Jubilees found among the Qumran texts—but unfortunately these documents are fragmentary and they do not allow a full linguistic analysis. Moving further chronologically towards the present: We then come to some letters written by Simeon Bar-Kokhba and his contemporaries in 132–135 C.E., also discovered in caves near the Dead Sea, though further south in the Ein Gedi region. These Bar-Kokhba letters are written in a Hebrew with some similarities to the language of the Mishna, which brings us to the next category of text for the history of the Hebrew language.

The very large rabbinic corpus—especially the Mishna and the related companion volume the Tosefta, both from approximately 200 C.E.—are written in a dialect called Mishnaic Hebrew (after the main rabbinic work, the Mishna), and this dialect diverges considerably from the old Biblical Hebrew standard. Most likely this dialect, Mishnaic Hebrew, grew out of the everyday spoken, colloquial Hebrew as opposed to the literary register used to compose the biblical books. Then there is the question of Aramaic once more, which as we saw was being used more and more widely on a daily basis. In the urban centers especially, which were more susceptible to Hellenization, Greek was making major inroads; and this trend continued with the arrival of the Romans, who administered the eastern half of their empire by using Greek as opposed to Latin. We will return to these Greek and Aramaic languages in just a few moments.

The Qumran community refers to its opponents as using what to their mind was an inferior brand of Hebrew. The following phrases appear in the Dead Sea Scrolls to refer to their opponents or their manner of Hebrew: *lashon 'aheret*, "another tongue"; *'arul safa*, "uncircumcised of lip"; *lo'eg safa*, "disparaging lip"; those three occur in the Thanksgiving Hymns document. Then a fourth phrase, *leshon giddufim*, "tongue of scorners"; that occurs in both the *Serekh ha-Yahad* 1QS, the Community Rule, and in the Damascus Document. To whom may these expressions refer? Most likely they refer to the Pharisees, whose later rabbinic successors wrote their works in Mishnaic Hebrew; and while the Mishna and related works are from three centuries later, the ideas related in these collections, and apparently, the mode of expression for these ideas, were present already in circa 100 B.C.E., the time of the Qumran community.

But the Qumran community could not use simple Biblical Hebrew either— either the Standard Biblical Hebrew of earlier times or the Late Biblical Hebrew of the later Biblical Period—for this variety of Hebrew was the inheritance of all Jews. The Qumran community, the *Yahad*, thus devised their own variety of Hebrew with its own vocabulary and its own grammar. Linguists refer to this phenomenon as "linguistic ideology," and they use the expression "anti-language" to refer to the idiom developed by the "in-group." One can find examples of this phenomenon in various places, in urban settings especially. Take, for example, Cockney English. Indeed all sorts of coded language exist in the world of criminals, in the realm of prostitutes, and in drug culture as scholars of sociolinguistics have noticed. Most striking is the phenomenon noticed by those who study modern-day cults; that is, they too tend to construct an in-group language. This point was emphasized in the research of Margaret Singer. This is not to say that the

Qumran community is akin to a modern-day cult, but the analogy that I'm presenting here for you may be helpful.

My friend and colleague William Schniedewind of UCLA adopted the term "linguistic ideology" or "anti-language"; he took this approach and applied it to Qumran Hebrew. I, for one, fully subscribe to his considerations here about this variety of Hebrew that we call Qumran Hebrew or the Hebrew of the Dead Sea Scrolls.

Let me give you some examples of anti-language within Qumran Hebrew: The use of the word "*Yahad*," typically rendered "community," as the group's self-designation. That appears to be a term that they use for themselves, and while it's true that we don't have contemporary documents to see what others—the Sadducees or the Pharisees—may have been using to refer to our *Yahad*, our sense is that this is their in-group term, their self-designation. Then, the Dead Sea Scrolls use a whole array of archaisms, to give a patina of antiquity, and thus authority, to their literature. First example: Biblical Hebrew has two forms for "his father." There is an archaic form, pronounced *'avihu*, used only 7 times in the Bible; and then the standard form, *'aviw*, used 217 times in the Bible. Amongst the Dead Sea Scrolls, however, the scribes clearly favor the first of these: They use *'avihu* 24 times, while the word *'aviw* is used only 3 times.

A second example: Biblical Hebrew has an archaic form, *lamo*, which means "to them"; it's used 57 times in the biblical corpus but only in poetry, which naturally uses a more archaic idiom. That's a linguistic universal: Poetry is typically written in a more archaic style. Therefore, it's not surprising to see this archaic form *lamo* ("to them" or "for them") used only in poetry in the Bible. In Qumran Hebrew, however, this form becomes rather standard; it's used 22 times, mainly in prose texts, and thus it appears in the Damascus Document, the Community Rule, the War Scroll, the Pesher Habakkuk, all texts that we have read during our course.

A third example: The form *'el* is a term for God in Biblical Hebrew, used mainly in poetry, again as an archaism. In Qumran Hebrew, it is used exceedingly commonly, almost beyond counting. For example, 11 times in the first column of the Community Rule; 7 times in the first column of the

War Scroll. Other Jews, by contrast, were using the longer form, *'elohim*, to refer to God. They did not use this shorter form *'el* that was being used by the Qumran scribes. The term "Yahweh," by the way—the proper name of God as it were—was less and less used in the postbiblical period; and therefore scholars, scribes, writers, authors, and composers used either *'elohim* typically, or in the case of the Qumran community, *'el*, an archaism being used for God.

A pseudo-archaism occurs in these documents when the adverbial suffix "-a"—this is known from Biblical Hebrew—is attached to a host of other adverbs, even when it does not belong there. Thus, for example, in Biblical Hebrew there's a word *šam*, it means "there," and then there's a word *šama*, with the ending "-a," and it means "whither," or "to there." But since the latter form (*šama*) has an air of superior language, the Qumran scribes would use this latter form *šama* even when the former *šam* was called for according to the strict grammatical rules. Compare, for example, the misuse of English "from whence," even though "whence" already by itself means "from where." Hopefully that's an English analogy that works for you. Do your ears cringe when you hear someone say "from whence?" Mine do; that is how it sounds to the Hebrew ear to hear the word *šama* used when *šam* would suffice.

By the way, I once was curious to learn when the expression "from whence" began in English, and upon checking the *Oxford English Dictionary* I learned that both Shakespeare and Dryden used this phrase. Oh well, what did they know about the English language?

Back to Qumran Hebrew: Most strikingly, the Hebrew of the Dead Sea Scrolls is relatively devoid of loanwords; words borrowed from other languages. This stands in stark contrast to Late Biblical Hebrew, which is filled with words borrowed from Aramaic, Persian, and even (in the case of the book of Daniel) Greek. This trend would continue in the postbiblical period, especially in the light of the ever-increasing use of Aramaic and Greek in the land of Israel as we indicated a few moments ago. Writing only a century or two after the period of Late Biblical Hebrew, with Aramaic and Greek to be heard throughout the land of Israel, it is actually quite staggering that the Qumran scribes studiously avoided loanwords, lexical items borrowed from these languages.

One might wonder how the Qumran scribes knew which words were native Hebrew ones and which words were loanwords from other languages. For example, again using English: If I were to ask you about words such as "cow" and "beef," or "sheep" and "mutton," you probably would not know which are the words inherited from Old English and further back from Germanic, and which are borrowings from French during the Middle Ages. But scholars who spend their lives with texts, as clearly was the case with the members of the Dead Sea Scrolls community, are able to keep track of such things. As parallels to this trend, one can look at a few examples: During the Middle Ages, William of Tyre (12th century writer) and Thomas of Aquinas (13th century writer) decried the incursion of vulgarisms into Latin; and thus they made the concerted and mostly successful effort to write in classical Latin, even though they are a millennium removed from the heyday of ancient Rome. Closer to our times, let's take the famous British author J. R. R. Tolkien. He was professor Anglo-Saxon and Old English at Oxford University, and he attempted to recreate that stage of the language— Anglo-Saxon and Old English—as much as possible in his own writings; which is to say, Tolkien limited the number of French loanwords that became part and parcel of English starting with the Middle English period after 1066 C.E., the year of the Norman conquest, after which dozens, hundreds, eventually thousands of loanwords from French enter the English language. Thus, most famously, Bilbo Baggins (Tolkien's character) lives at Bag End instead of cul-de-sac.

Finally, there is the very strange Qumran Hebrew usage of adding "-a" to pronoun forms as well. We saw a few moments ago how they took this adverbial "-a" and put it where it didn't belong; they took the same "-a" and they added it to pronoun forms. Thus, for example, while all other forms of ancient Hebrew, in fact down to modern Hebrew, use the word *hu'* for the pronoun "he," and *hi'* for the pronoun "she," in the Dead Sea Scrolls we encounter the forms—can you predict them already now that you get the trend here?—*hu'a* and *hi'a*. Similarly, while all other forms of Hebrew use *'attem* for the second-person masculine plural pronoun—that is, "you," masculine plural—in the Dead Sea Scrolls, we encounter the form *'attema*, again with the addition of the "-a" suffix (the feminine equivalent, by the way, is unattested in our Qumran corpus of texts). Note the additional "-a"—*hu'a*, *hi'a*, and *'attema*—similar to the suffix "-a" that we mentioned for the form *šama*. All of this, once more, sounds very strange to the Hebrew ear.

Let me give you an analogy regarding pronouns. Let me present for you what happened to the English second-person pronouns in the 17th century; how to say "you." Until the 17th century, the words "thou," "thee," and "thy," were used for the singular, and the words "you," "ye," and "your" were used not only for the plural, but also as a formal or honorific form, when speaking to superiors, in imitation of the French and German systems that have a formal "you," as to other European languages. The Quakers, however, in 17th century England, objected. According to their approach, they see everyone as equals, and therefore they refused to use the formal "you" forms, and thus used only the "thou" forms even when addressing superiors. The reaction of everyone else in England, for fear that they would be seen as Quakers or as Quaker-sympathizers; what did everyone else do? They started to use the "you" forms at all times, even for the singular; and thus the "thou" forms died out in our English language, with the "you" forms serving ever since the 17th century in all cases, singular, plural, informal, and formal.

Something like this is what transpired with the pronouns in Qumran Hebrew. With everyone else using the standard forms *hu'*, *hi'*, *'attem*, along with other similar forms, the Qumran sectarians developed their unique pronoun forms that would distinguish them very clearly; thus *hu'a*, *hi'a*, *'attema*, along with other similar forms. We see these throughout their documents.

Earlier in our course, we noted that some of the biblical manuscripts—most famously 1QIsa[a]; that's the entire complete book of Isaiah from Cave One, all 66 chapters of the biblical canonical prophetic book of Isaiah on a single scroll—are linguistically updated, somewhat akin to seeing an updated Shakespeare play. Mainly this means that the Qumran scribes introduced Late Biblical Hebrew features into a text that was otherwise written in Standard Biblical Hebrew. But it also means that they introduced their own unique Qumran Hebrew anti-language usages into the biblical text, such as the pronoun forms ending in "-a," which I've mentioned in this lecture. The use of anti-language by the Qumran group demonstrates to what extent the

Yahad saw itself as different from the other Jewish groups of the time. They accentuated these differences even to the extent of linguistic usage.

I should state that the view I am presenting to you here, introduced by William Schniedewind, is not yet accepted by most scholars. In fact, when my friend and colleague first proposed this explanation for Qumran Hebrew, I myself was skeptical. Like many scholars, I questioned whether any group could use language so consistently and with such effect. True, we know of the phenomenon of "in-group" language, but typically this is restricted to lexical choices—that is, vocabulary items—and not to an overarching grammar. In 2008, however, I was asked to participate in a conference marking the 60th anniversary of the Dead Sea Scrolls hosted by Lawrence Schiffman at New York University with the idea that I would speak on the language of the Dead Sea Scrolls. I happily accepted the invitation, and then spent months rereading the all the secondary literature concerning Qumran Hebrew. Most scholars simply detailed the different linguistic usages and then described them in comprehensive grammatical treatments. Scholars debated whether Qumran Hebrew represents a brand of literary Hebrew only, or whether the *Yahad* members actually spoke this way in their daily discourse, regardless of where these unusual forms originate. But in the main, there was no agreement as to how to explain the usages that I have outlined for you in this lecture.

After months of reading and rereading, poring over the opinions of scholars from around the world, I came to the conclusion that Schniedewind was correct; that the notion of linguistic ideology or anti-language best explains the peculiar nature of Qumran Hebrew. I was spurred by my having read books and articles on the general subject of linguistic anthropology where the notion of linguistic ideology was first developed; and indeed it was during this period of my research that I discovered the parallel of the pronoun usage among the Quakers. Now that I had a real parallel—in fact, one dealing with pronouns, the same issue we have in Qumran Hebrew—a real parallel from a real language usage closer to our own day (early Modern English), one readily accepted by linguists, I became convinced that Schniedewind was correct. Had I not been invited to deliver the lecture at New York University, had I not spent months working on this issue, I undoubtedly would have remained part of the larger group of scholars who remained skeptical of Schniedewind's analysis, even without being able to express a real alternative.

As I have said, this variety of Hebrew is unknown from anywhere else in ancient times. There is one feature, however, that I have mentioned, that does occur elsewhere: namely, the unusual second-person masculine plural pronoun *'attema* (that is, "you" masculine plural), along with the corresponding possessive form *kimma* (that is, "your" masculine plural). These forms are attested not only at Qumran, but in Samaritan Hebrew as well; that is, the dialect used by the Samaritans. You will recall that the Samaritans are an offshoot of Judaism who expressed their individuality in different ways, most prominently by rejecting Jerusalem and honoring Mount Gerizim, where they had their own Temple with their own altar with their own priests, offering the sacrifices to the God of Israel. Could the Samaritans also have engaged in an anti-language usage in order to distinguish themselves from general Judaism? Is that how the pronoun usage in both Qumran Hebrew and Samaritan Hebrew is to be explained? Were both of these groups, the *Yahad* members and the Samaritans, seeking to differentiate themselves through the use of language? Some mornings I wake up and think that the answer to this question is yes, these two groups share this goal, using language as a mark of distinction vis-à-vis other Jews of this time period. Other mornings, however, I wake up and think that the presence of similar grammatical forms in Qumran Hebrew and Samaritan Hebrew is merely a matter of convenience to be explained by random grammatical drift, as linguists would call it.

You may recall that at the outset of this course I mentioned my own interest in the history of the Hebrew language. As you can imagine, then, I find all of this material especially fascinating. I love to listen to the way people speak; I love to read and pay attention to the words that authors select; and I obviously love my ancient texts in which I can combine my interest in language and literature. Whenever I consider the material from Ancient Hebrew, especially the unusual linguistic patterns present in Qumran Hebrew, I try to imagine the sounds as they were spoken and as they were heard 2,000 years ago. I can just about hear them; I hear them in my ears. I hear regular Hebrew, whatever that term "regular Hebrew" means; Standard Biblical Hebrew; Late Biblical Hebrew; the Hebrew of Ben Sira from 180

B.C.E.; the Hebrew of the rabbis of the Mishna from 200 C.E.; and I hear the unusual Hebrew of the Qumran *Yahad* members.

Let's take a moment, then, to place ourselves at Qumran 2,000 years ago as we enter their world, imagining their texts being read aloud, standing in awe and wonder at our heroes of old living their live in a remote desert outpost, a life they have created for themselves via their own sacred and pure community, and with the individual members devoted to their sacred writings expressed in a unique variety of the Hebrew language.

The Dead Sea Scrolls continue to raise questions that do not always have clear definitive answers; and we have saved perhaps the best for last. For in our next lecture, we turn to what remains the greatest enigma in all of Qumran scholarship: the unique Copper Scroll, its official siglum 3Q15; unique because of the material on which this text is written, copper. Unique because of its contents, a treasure map describing hordes of gold and silver. and unique because we are not even sure, notwithstanding the fact that the document was found in Cave Three, whether or not it belongs to the Dead Sea Scrolls corpus. When we come back: the Copper Scroll.

The Enigma of the Copper Scroll
Lecture 22

The Copper Scroll is the most unusual text discovered in the Qumran caves.

In earlier lectures, we have mentioned the Copper Scroll (3Q15). As its name implies, this text, which was found in Cave 3 in 1952, consists of 12 columns incised on sheets of copper rolled together. The text actually was found as two separate rolls, each one badly corroded, so that they could not be unrolled. In 1956, the Jordanian authorities sent the two sections to the laboratory of Professor H. Wright Baker. Within the course of months, Baker cut the metal into strips so that the entire text was revealed, and he then returned the document to Jordan. On inspection by competent scholars, it was realized (as had already been suspected) that the two sections comprised a single scroll. The Copper Scroll is one of the few documents not housed in Jerusalem but rather in the Amman Archaeological Museum in Jordan, where it is contained in a specially constructed glass cabinet.

The text of the Copper Scroll lists, typically in coded language, 64 hiding places in Jerusalem and elsewhere in which are to be found huge amounts of gold, silver, vessels, scrolls, and more. The 64th and final hiding place informs us where another copy of this scroll is to be found. On occasion the text presents Greek letters, though always as abbreviations of a sort. What are these? Just one more riddle within our larger enigma.

The amounts of gold and silver listed are extraordinary.

The amounts of gold and silver listed are extraordinary. According to one reckoning, it lists 1,300 talents of gold, 65 bars of gold, 3,000 talents of silver, 608 pitchers of silver, and 619 assorted gold and silver vessels. To translate these amounts into their modern equivalents (using approximately 60 lb. per talent), one reaches an estimate of 26 tons of gold and 65 tons of silver. By way of comparison, we note that the famous gold coffin of King Tutankhamun weighs about 240 lbs. and his gold mask weighs about 24 lbs.—paltry sums in comparison!

The questions that scholars ask are whether the treasure is real, and if so, did it belong to the Qumran community or to another entity, such as the Jerusalem Temple. It is easy to conclude, given the huge amounts of gold and silver, that the treasure is imaginary. With the passage of time, however, more and more scholars have come to believe that the treasure is real. Among other arguments, scholars say that, if the treasure were fictional, no one would have taken the great time and effort to incise it on copper. The argument that the treasure belongs to the Qumran community is based on the Copper Scroll's discovery in the Qumran caves. But virtually none of the other 14 texts found in Cave 3 can be considered truly "sectually explicit."

The argument that treasures belong to the Jerusalem Temple is based on the treasure's size; after all, only as large and wealthy an institution as the Temple could have amassed this much gold and silver. Presumably, Temple officials hid these materials and then composed the enigmatic text, which they stashed in Qumran Cave 3. The treasures are items collected for a planned rebuilding of the Temple some time after its destruction in 70 C.E. Alternatively, the gold and silver may have been the hidden treasures of the Bar Kokhba rebels from the Second Revolt against Rome in 132–135 C.E.

The language of the Copper Scroll does not match the Hebrew dialect used in the other Dead Sea Scrolls. Instead, it approximates Mishnaic Hebrew. The same is true of the Bar Kokhba documents that we possess. However, the language of the Halakhic Letter also diverges from general Qumran Hebrew and has some features in common with Mishnaic Hebrew, though its Halakhic positions clearly belong to the Qumran sect. Unlike other Qumran documents, the Copper Scroll uses Greek terms rather liberally. Does the presence of so many Greek words in our text separate this document from the general Qumran corpus? Again, another question without a secure answer.

Several individuals have explored the Judean desert, starting with the caves at Qumran and fanning out in different directions, in an effort to locate the treasure listed in the Copper Scroll. The first such person was John

Allegro, a controversial figure in Dead Sea Scrolls scholarship. He was a member of the original international team, and in fact he was the only scholar to publish the texts assigned to him with alacrity. But then he did the unthinkable: Somehow, he obtained a copy of the text of the Copper Scroll and published an edition of the document two years in advance of Milik's official publication in 1960.

Allegro then spent several seasons exploring the Judean desert, hoping to find the treasures, though to no avail. Pesah Bar-Adon and Vendyl Jones also have explored the area, with some success at finding objects from the general time period, though clearly these relatively meager finds do not come close to the amounts of gold, silver, and objects listed in the Copper Scroll. How did anyone know where to begin to look? One distinctive cave is mentioned in the scroll, and thus these explorers have looked for a cave with two openings that might have a natural pillar or column as a marker. But just to show you how complex the whole problem might be, another hiding place mentions a Mount Gerizin (3Q15 12:4). Is this the Mount Gerizim of the Samaritans, about 65 kilometers north of Jerusalem, or another mountain with the same or similar name in the region of Jericho and Qumran?

Let us digress for a moment to discuss how interested and educated lay people can best read and study the Dead Sea Scroll texts on their own. Geza Vermes's *The Complete Dead Sea Scrolls in English* includes a 90-page introduction and an English translation of all the texts, with each document introduced in a lucid manner by the editor. For readers of Hebrew, I would recommend the two-volume set by Florentino Garcia Martinez and Eibert Tigchelaar, entitled *The Dead Sea Scrolls Study Edition*, with the Hebrew (or Aramaic) original and the English translation on facing pages as easy to use and clearly presented. The Discoveries of the Judean Desert series is the for the scholar only. Volumes are to be found mainly in major research libraries, and the entire set of 40 large folio volumes costs several thousand dollars. But I invite you to visit a library near you that has this set in its collection to get a flavor of how scholars go about the task of presenting these ancient texts to the academic community. The *Dead Sea Scrolls Electronic Library*, prepared by the Maxwell Institute for Religious Scholarship at Brigham Young University and edited by Emanuel Tov of the Hebrew University, is a computer program that includes every single nonbiblical scroll with the both the Hebrew (or Aramaic) originals and English translations and the photographs as well. Best of all, the program is fully searchable and includes a concordance of all the texts. To read more about the texts and their significance, I would recommend Lawrence Schiffman's *Reclaiming the Dead Sea Scrolls*, along with a shorter, more concise, and superb introduction by James VanderKam called *The Dead Sea Scrolls Today*.

The possible connection of the Copper Scroll to the Bar Kokhba rebellion, and the exploration in the caves by serious scholars (and adventure seekers) looking for these treasures leads us to a tangential discussion. Early in our course, I mentioned that scholars combed all the caves in the Qumran area, with 11 yielding scrolls and others yielding material remains. Scholars explored areas more removed from Qumran as well, and in fact met with success in two main places, both near Ein Gedi: Wadi Muraba'at, to the north of Ein Gedi, and Nahal Hever, to the south of Ein Gedi. The documents found in these caves relate to the Bar Kokhba rebellion. From both sites we have letters written by Simeon Bar Kokhba himself. These texts, as precious to us as the Dead Sea Scrolls, provide yet another window into Jewish religious life during the Roman period. Are there still more texts awaiting discovery? Many scholars believe so. ■

Essential Reading

Vermes, *The Complete Dead Sea Scrolls in English*, 583–589.

VanderKam, *The Dead Sea Scrolls Today*, 68–69.

Shanks, *The Dead Sea Scrolls after Forty Years*, 41–55.

Schiffman, *Reclaiming the Dead Sea Scrolls*, 397–399, 404–409.

Yadin, *The Message of the Scrolls*, 156–159.

Wolters, *The* Copper Scroll.

Supplementary Reading

Lefkovits, *The* Copper Scroll.

Questions to Consider

1. Of all the possible scholarly opinions concerning the Copper Scroll, which do you think is the most likely?

2. Do you think it is worth the effort to explore the general region, with the goal of decoding the clues in the treasure map, to find these objects?

The Enigma of the Copper Scroll
Lecture 22—Transcript

The Copper Scroll (3Q15) is the most unique text discovered in the Qumran caves. As its name implies, the Hebrew text is incised on copper sheets rolled together. Once more, we will narrate the tale of discovery and decipherment, in this case how this document was taken to a laboratory in Manchester, England where its corroded metal sheets were cut into strips to allow scholars to read the text. The Copper Scroll's contents provide for a veritable treasure map that will guide the reader, with obscure hints—as is usually the case in such texts—to locate vast amounts of gold, silver, and other precious commodities. Are the contents described here real? Did the Qumran community really own such wealth? Or does the text have nothing to do with the Qumran community? In this case, perhaps, the text records the whereabouts of the Jerusalem Temple treasury, distributed in various secret locations in the area, with the text itself deposited in Qumran Cave Three for safekeeping. In this lecture, we will show all of these and many other points of information and interpretations of this fascinating document.

Twice in our course we have alluded to and mentioned the Copper Scroll. As its name implies, this text was found in Cave Three, and it consists of 12 columns incised on sheets of copper rolled together. The text actually was found as two separate rolls, each one badly corroded so that they could not be unrolled or unfolded. After sitting with the text for several years, in 1956, the Jordanian authorities responsible for the preservation of this text and all the Dead Sea Scrolls coming out of the caves during those years sent the two sections of the Copper Scroll to the laboratory of Professor H. Wright Baker of the Manchester College of Science and Technology in England. Within the course of months, Baker cut the metal into strips—he actually devised a new machine in order to cut the Copper Scroll into the sheets—so that the entire text was now revealed, and then the document, now with single sheets that could be read by scholars, was returned to Jordan. Upon inspection by competent scholars, it was realized—as already had been suspected—that the two sections comprised a single scroll, a single document.

A few points related to the physical properties of the Copper Scroll. The metal itself is 99 percent pure copper, with only 1 percent additional elements present. The sheets are exceptionally thin, one millimeter. They were fastened together with rivets, and then the whole thing was rolled up to create the scroll in imitation of the way a parchment scroll is created. I hardly need to state that writing on metal sheets of any sort is extremely rare. One example, found by archaeologists in a burial site in Jerusalem: two silver amulets dated to the 7th century B.C.E., in which are inscribed a few lines from Numbers 6, the priestly blessing, "May God bless you and keep you," and so on. But those are tiny, tiny little silver amulets, only a couple of centimeters high; they are displayed, by the way, at the Israel Museum, and again with a magnifying glass to allow the museum visitor to see the objects better. Here, however, we're talking about an entire scroll, the Copper Scroll. As an aside, as I mentioned earlier, the Copper Scroll is one of the few documents not housed in Jerusalem, but rather in the Amman Archaeological Museum in the Jordanian capital, where it is contained and displayed in a specially constructed glass cabinet.

Now to the text: The text lists 64 different hiding places, in Jerusalem, the Judean Desert, and elsewhere, though typically by using coded language in which are to be found huge, enormous amounts of gold, silver, vessels, and more. Let me read for you a few sample passages. Let's start out where the text beings. The text simply opens up; there's no title, no description of what's going to happen, it simply begins as follows. This is the first hiding place; incidentally, the text does not give you hiding place number 1, number 2, and so on. This is something that the scholars have determined, that there were 64 individual hiding places listed in the text, and we give them numbers just to keep track of these different hiding places, though naturally we also refer to column such-and-such line such-and-such. The first hiding place, and this is how the text opens: "In the ruins, which are in the Valley of Achor, under the steps that go eastward forty cubits: a box of silver and its vessels, weighing seventeen talents." A talent, by the way, is approximately 60 pounds; 28 kilos, about 60 pounds. We'll come back and talk about the enormous weights in a few minutes. The Valley of Achor, which is mentioned here at the beginning of this text, is actually known from the Bible as a place near Jericho; and, by the way, Jericho itself is mentioned later on in the Copper Scroll in 5:13 (that's hiding place number 26, by the way). So all you need to do is go find the ruins that are in the Valley of Achor under the steps that go eastward 40 cubits and there you will find, according to this text, a box of silver and its vessels weighing 17 talents.

Let's read a few more passages from this amazing document. Hiding place number 7, from 2:3–4: In the cave of the old Washer's House, on the third platform [or the third ledge]: sixty-five gold bars." Where may that be found? The old Washer's House: Go right there to the cave of the old Washer's House. The text continues with hiding place number 8: "In the underground cavity that is in the courtyard of the House of Logs, in the midst of which is a recess: vessels and silver, seventy talents." On it goes; hiding place number 12: "In the pond that is east of Kohlit, at a northern angle, dig four cubits: twenty-two talents." And on and on the text goes in this fashion. The 64th and final hiding place—this is how the text ends—informs us that another copy of the scroll is to be found in the following location. Is that other copy also written in a copper scroll, or is it written on a parchment scroll? It doesn't say; but let me read for you the text: "In the underground cavity that is in the smooth rock north of Kohlit [that was the same place that was mentioned in the previous passage that I read; we do not know where Kohlit is located], whose opening is towards the north, with tombs at its mouth, there is a copy of this writing and its explanation and the oils [we're not quite sure what it means, but that's what is says right here] and the protocol of each item" (3Q15 12:10–11, the end of our text).

We will return to this discuss this word "protocol," which you just heard me read aloud from this passage. In the meantime, though, we are struck by the mention at the end of the Copper Scroll that a copy of this text exists elsewhere "in the underground cavity that is in the smooth rock north of Kohlit," wherever that may be.

On occasion, the text presents Greek letters—that is to say, the text is written in Hebrew, and every once in a while there are few Greek letters, two or three Greek letters interrupting the Hebrew text—though always as abbreviations of sort. 1:4, the first of them: *kappa-eta-nu*; 1:12: *chi-alpha-gamma*; 2:2: *eta-nu*; 2:4: *theta-eta*; 2:9: *delta-iota*; and so it goes. What are these Greek letters; are these fraternity and sorority houses? Seriously, we have no idea whatsoever; just one more riddle within our larger enigma of the Copper Scroll.

The amounts of gold and silver are extraordinary. According to one reckoning: 1,300 talents of gold, 65 bars of gold, 3,000 talents of silver, 608 vessels or pitchers of silver, and 619 gold and silver assorted vessels of different types. To translate these amounts into their modern equivalents, using approximately 60 pounds per talent, one reaches an estimate of 26 tons of gold and 65 tons of silver; 26 tons of gold, 65 tons of silver, if you add up all the wealth that is listed in the Copper Scroll. By way of comparison, let me tell you that the famous gold coffin of King Tutankhamen, the ancient Egyptian pharaoh, weighs about 240 pounds, and his gold mask weighs about 24 pounds; paltry sums in comparison to the amounts listed in the Copper Scroll. That is to say, one would need about 200 sets of gold coffins and gold masks of the type found in the tomb of King Tutankhamen (King Tut) in order to achieve the 26 tons of gold accounted for in the Copper Scroll, not to mention the silver as well.

The questions that scholars ask are: Is the treasure real? And if so, did it belong to the Qumran community, or to another entity, such as the Jerusalem Temple? It is easy to conclude, given the huge amounts of gold and silver listed here, that the treasure is imaginary. The contents of the Copper Scroll are the stuff of legend, adhered to by the Qumran community or by some other Jewish group of the time period. This approach was the route taken by the scholar first entrusted with the publication of this document, namely, Father J. T. Milik, you'll remember him as the "fastest man with a fragment," the article in *Time* magazine referred to him in such fashion. Milik's official edition of the text appeared in DJD series (Discoveries in the Judaean Desert: Volume 3, 1962), and Milik was followed in this opinion that the treasure is imaginary, legendary, by such scholars whom we've met earlier in our course, as Roland de Vaux and Frank Cross, for example.

With the passage of time, however, more and more scholars have come to believe that the treasure is real. Among other arguments, scholars ask: If the treasure list were the fictional creation of someone's imagination, why would the author have taken the great time and effort to incise this list of objects and their hiding places on copper. The following options have been proposed. First: The treasures belong to the Qumran community. How else can one explain how this document was found in a cave with other Qumran documents? In truth, however, virtually none of the other 14 texts found in Cave Three—there are only 15 documents altogether from Cave Three, the Copper Scroll is 3Q15 you'll recall—can be considered truly "sectually explicit," that is to say, part of the Qumran sect; in fact, they are all extremely fragmentary. One includes a small portion of Jubilees; we know that Jubilees was read at Qumran, but it was also read by other Jewish groups of late antiquity. Another text includes a tiny portion of the book of Isaiah; that's a biblical text read by all Jews. the rest of these documents from Cave Three have only a few words, or even a few letters. This view that it belongs to the Qumran community is associated with André Dupont-Sommer. He was one of the two originators of the Essene hypothesis in the early years of Qumran scholarship, and he believed that the treasure here is the treasure of the Qumran group.

A second option is that the treasures belong to the Jerusalem Temple. After all, only as large and wealthy an institution as the Temple in Jerusalem could have amassed this much gold and silver in its treasury. The argument goes: Presumably, Temple officials hid these materials in the various hiding places and then composed the enigmatic text, which they then stashed in Qumran Cave 3. Presumably in advance of the Romans' arrival, they emptied out the Temple treasury and placed it in Cave 3, so the argument goes. Indeed, as we noted in an earlier lecture when we surveyed the location of the caves at Qumran, Cave 3 is the northernmost cave of the 11 caves that have yielded documents. It is located about 2 kilometers north of the site of Khirbet-Qumran, the community center, and thus perhaps there is no connection between this document and the other texts found in Cave 3 and the scrolls found in the other caves and the site of Qumran where the *Yahad* members lived. An early proponent of this view, associating the treasure with the Jerusalem Temple, was John Allegro. You'll recall him as the author of *The Sacred Mushroom and the Cross*, and we'll have more to say about Professor Allegro regarding the Copper Scroll in just a few minutes. As you might imagine, Norman Golb of the University of Chicago also adheres to this view, especially since it dovetails with his larger hypothesis that the scrolls as a whole—all the documents from all 11 caves—represent the Jerusalem Temple library.

The treasures are items collected for a planned rebuilding of the Temple; that's another option. That sometime after 70 C.E., the Jews wanted to rebuild the Temple and they collected this amount of wealth to rebuild the Temple. That's a third option that scholars have proposed. Then a fourth option: The gold and silver represent the hidden treasures of the individual rebels in the Bar-Kokhba rebellion, the Second Jewish Revolt against Rome, 132–135 C.E., in which case we are now well beyond the period of Qumran altogether; we're in, again, this post-70, post-destruction of Jerusalem period. Any of these hypotheses has found adherents among different scholars in the academic community.

Also of note—and this point may be relevant to the discussion we're just had—is the fact that the language of the Copper Scroll does not match the Hebrew dialect used in the other Dead Sea Scrolls, which we discussed in the previous lecture. Instead, the dialect in this text, in the Copper Scroll, approximates the language of the rabbinic texts, called Mishnaic Hebrew. As an aside, the same is true of the Bar-Kokhba documents that we possess, found further south in the Judean Desert near Ein Gedi; they, too, approximately Mishnaic Hebrew. This fact should not lead us to conclude that either the third or the fourth options that I mentioned earlier are correct, that the treasures recorded in the Copper Scroll speak to a rebuilding of the Temple (under the rabbis perhaps?) or that they belonged to the Bar-Kokhba movement. In fact, we should add here, which was not noted earlier, that the language of the Halakhic Letter (4QMMT) also diverges from general Qumran Hebrew and has some features in common with Mishnaic Hebrew; and this is a text—the Halakhic Letter, 4QMMT—that clearly emerges from the sect, as it seeks to define its Halakhic positions vis-à-vis other Jewish groups of the time. The different language used in 4QMMT simply may be due to the genre of that text. That is to say, the missive uses a less formal language register in order to speak more openly and frankly to the addressee; less formal, that is, than the language register used to compose literary texts such as the Damascus Document, the War Scroll, the Community Rule, and the other major Qumran scrolls.

I also should note that unlike other Qumran documents, the Copper Scroll uses Greek terms rather liberally, such as the words for "peristyle," "stoa," and "exedra," all Greek architectural terms rendered from Greek into Hebrew in this text; and, in the final expression which we read earlier, the word "protocol," meaning something like a copy of the document or further details concerning the contents of the document. Does the presence of so many Greek words in our text separate this document from the general Qumran corpus? Again, another question without a secure answer.

I next want to note that several individuals have explored the Judean desert, starting with the caves at Qumran and fanning out in different directions, in an effort to locate the treasure listed in the Copper Scroll. The first such person was John Allegro, whom we mentioned a few moments ago, a controversial figure at all times in Dead Sea Scrolls scholarship. You'll recall he was a member of the original international team, and in fact he was the only scholar to publish the texts assigned to him with alacrity, but, as I mentioned, also went off and wrote *The Sacred Mushroom and the Cross*. In this particular case, Allegro he did the unthinkable: Somehow he obtained a copy of the text of the Copper Scroll and published an edition of the document two years in advance of Father Milik's official publication in the DJD series; Milik's book 1962, Allegro's book 1960. Then Allegro spent several seasons exploring the Judean desert from cave to cave, from ravine to ravine, hoping to find the treasures of the Copper Scroll, though to no avail.

In an earlier lecture when I was also referring to some of the archaeological excavations in the area, I mentioned two individuals: Pesah Bar-Adon, an Israeli archaeologist, and Vendyl Jones, an American. I mentioned that these two people have also explored the area, in their case with some success at finding objects from the general time period; though clearly these are relatively meager finds, and they do not come close to the amounts of gold, silver, and so on listed in the Copper Scroll.

How did anyone know where to begin to look in this empty landscape for any of these places? One distinctive cave is mentioned in the Copper Scroll; it's hiding place number 29, it's at the top of column six, so it's column 6:1–6 and it reads as follows: "In the cave of the pillar, the one with two openings, facing east, in the northern opening, dig three cubits: a jug is there, in it is one book, under it are 42 talents." Again, you see how the treasure map works: "In the cave of the pillar, the one with two openings, facing east, in the northern opening, dig three cubits," apparently you have to dig down into the ground three cubits, and there you'll find a jug, in the jug is a book, and under it are 42 talents. So for starters, these explorers—Bar-Adon and Jones, and before them Allegro—would look for a cave that matched this description; a cave with two openings that might have a natural pillar or a column as a marker of some sort. But just to show you how complex the whole problem might be, another hiding place listed in the text (12:4, towards the end of the document) mentions Mount Gerizin, with an "n" on the end, though this is a phonological issue in Hebrew at the time, where final "m" and final "n" often merge, so most likely this term Mount Gerizin equates with Mount Gerizim, with an "m" on the end. Is this the Mount Gerizim of the Samaritans, about which we have spoken during our course; about 65 kilometers north of Jerusalem, in which case it's removed from the Judean desert region? Or is there another mountain with the same or similar name in the region of Jericho and Qumran? In short, the Copper Scroll remains an enigma, probably the greatest riddle within the area of Qumran studies.

I want to take a moment at this juncture, as we near the end of our course, to discuss how best to access the Dead Sea Scrolls. That is, how can you, as an interested and educated layperson—a typical Teaching Company participant—read and study the texts on your own? Earlier in our course I mentioned the volume by Geza Vermes, *The Complete Dead Sea Scrolls in English*. This volume includes a 90-page introduction to the subject of the Dead Sea Scrolls, and then proceeds to include an English translation of all the texts, with each document introduced in a lucid manner by the editor, Professor Vermes. I commend that volume to you. If you know Hebrew, then I would recommend the two-volume set by Florentino Garcia Martinez and Eibert Tigchelaar entitled *The Dead Sea Scrolls Study Edition*, published in 1999, with the Hebrew original, or the Aramaic original as the case may be, and the English translation on facing pages. Very easy to use, clearly presented. I have referred to the DJD series in our course. These are for the scholar only; they are to be found mainly in major research libraries, and the entire set of 40 large folio volumes would cost you several thousand dollars. But I invite you to visit a library near you which may have this set in its collection to get a flavor of how scholars go about the task of presenting these ancient texts with the transcription, the translation, the commentary, and the photographs to the academic community.

Finally, I want to mention a project known as the Dead Sea Scrolls Electronic Library prepared by the Maxwell Institute for Religious Scholarship at Brigham Young University, edited by Emmanuel Tov of the Hebrew university with the copyright held by Brill Publishing House. DSSEL, as we call it—Dead Sea Scrolls Electronic Library—is a computer program that sells for about $350. I am fortunate to own the program and I use it on a very regular basis. Every single non-biblical scroll is included in the program, with both the Hebrew or the Aramaic original and the English translation, and photographs as well. While I am reading or studying a particular text, if I want to see the photograph I can simply click and there it is. Best of all, the program is fully searchable and includes a concordance of all the texts. If I want to know where a particular word or phrase occurs in the scrolls—let's say *bene or*, sons of light, or *Moreh Zedeq*, Teacher of Righteousness—I simply enter this info into the database search program and I gain every attestation. Ancient texts meet modern technology, a wonder to behold. To read more about the texts and their significance, I would mention once more Lawrence Schiffman *Reclaiming the Dead Sea Scrolls*, 1994; and here I add another volume, a shorter, more concise and superb introduction to our subject is James VanderKam of Notre Dame University, *The Dead Sea Scrolls Today*, also published in 1994.

Two topics raised in this lecture: a) the possible connection to the Bar Kokhba rebellion of this Copper Scroll; and b) the exploration of the caves by serious scholars, and some adventure seekers as well, looking for the treasures listed in the Copper Scroll leads me to a tangential discussion. Earlier in our course I mentioned that scholars combed all the caves in the Qumran area, with 11 of the caves yielding scrolls, and still other caves yielding material remains. What about areas more removed from Qumran? Scholars explored these caves as well, and, in fact, met with success in two main places near Ein Gedi: Wadi Muraba'at, slightly to the north of Ein Gedi, and Nahal Hever, slightly to the south of Ein Gedi. The documents found in these caves in these locations do not relate to our subject per se, they are not documents of the *Yahad*, but rather these are documents that belong to the Bar Kokhba rebellion. From both sites we have letters written by Simeon Bar Kokhba himself. Imagine how exciting these discoveries were for the scholars who found these texts, for unlike our Dead Sea Scrolls, which typically do not mention the names of real people, here we have not only a real person but actually a very important person, a key figure in ancient Jewish history, even if the Second Jewish Revolt led by Bar Kokhba met with disaster.

Let me quote a few of the letters for you, first a short text; it goes as follows. It begins: "Letter of Simeon bar Kosiba [bar Kosiba was his actual name; he was known as Bar Kokhba which means "Son of the Star" in Aramaic, but his Hebrew name was actually Simeon bar Kosiba] to Yehonathan, son of Be'ayan: Peace! My order is that whatever Elisha tells you, do for him and help him and those with him. Be well." In other words, it's a command; a missive from the commander to a subordinate. Then a longer one:

> Simeon to Yehudah bar Menashe in Qiryat 'Arabaya.
>
> I have sent two donkeys to you, and you must send with them two men to Yehonathan son of Be'ayan, and to Masabala, in order that they shall pack and send to the camp, towards you, palm branches and citrons. And you, from your place, send others who will bring you myrtles and willows. See that they are tithed and send them to the camp. The request is made because the army is big. Be well.

In this latter letter, we read of a directive to bring the four species—palms branches, myrtles, willows, and citrons—which are necessary for the observance of a ritual associated with the holiday of Sukkot. It is the middle of the war, the Second Jewish Revolt against the Romans, and yet the commander, Bar Kokhba, wishes to ensure that a religious ritual is performed correctly. This leads us beyond the subject of our course, but these texts, equally precious to us as the Dead Sea Scrolls, provide for us yet another window into Jewish religious life during the Roman period.

And then one more comment: Are there still more texts awaiting discovery? To be honest, many scholars believe that indeed other texts are to be found, though it may take an earthquake, even a small one, to reveal them. Recall that the area is part of the Syrian-African rift valley, and that an earthquake destroyed Qumran in 31 B.C.E., and that tremors are felt every once in a while to this day. Could an earthquake open up some more caves; that is to say, caves that once were open and accessible but which now are closed due to the vicissitudes of time? Stay tuned.

But you may not have to stay tuned for too long; for instance, in 2007 yet another startling discovery was made. We will examine this text, known as the Vision of Gabriel, or the Dead Sea Stone, in our next lecture, within the context of a thorough survey of the connections between the Qumran documents and early Christianity.

Connections to Christianity
Lecture 23

What was the relationship between the Qumran community and the early Christian movement?

Throughout our course, we have mentioned various connections between the Dead Sea Scrolls and the New Testament, or rather between the Qumran community and the early Christian community. In this lecture, we take a more systematic approach to this subject. First, however, we refer to (but do not adopt) the theories of some scholars that there is a direct linkage between the Dead Sea Scrolls and the New Testament. Robert Eisenman believes that many if not most of the scrolls date to the 1st century C.E. In addition to positing Zealot connections, he identifies James the Just, the brother of Jesus, as the Teacher of Righteousness referred to in Pesher Habakkuk and other documents. In his opinion, the scrolls have a very direct link to early Christianity. Barbara Theiring also believes that the scrolls originate in the 1st century with specific connections to early Christianity, though she goes even further by claiming that the Teacher of Righteousness is John the Baptist and that the Wicked Priest is Jesus. Jose O'Callaghan believed that 7Q5, written in Greek, is a copy of Mark 6:52–53, thus connecting at least one of the scrolls very directly to the New Testament. However, the only complete word in this tiny Greek fragment is the word *kai* ("and"), from which one cannot build an entire theory. A more recent theory is the interpretation of 4Q285, a fragmentary text, by Michael Wise and Robert Eisenman. These scholars read a particular passage to refer to a "pierced Messiah"; all other scholars, however, argue that their understanding of the grammar is totally wrong, that if anything the text refers to a "piercing Messiah."

Before proceeding, we take note of the scholarly view developed in the 19th century by the great French savant Ernst Renan, who in his book *Vie de Jésus* ("Life of Jesus") traced connections between the Essenes and early Christianity. This work appeared long before the discovery of the Dead Sea Scrolls, and indeed before the discovery of the Damascus Document in the Cairo genizah in 1896. We also mention, in passing, that the great Albert Schweitzer was highly critical of Renan's book. To Schweitzer's mind, the attempt to place the historical Jesus within the context of ancient Judaism was misguided. Schweitzer's critique of Renan won the day, and the "quest for the historical Jesus" movement came to a halt until it later in the 20th century.

Renan's approach received a new life with the discovery of the Dead Sea Scrolls. Eliezer Sukenik and André Dupont-Sommer saw Essene connections to the scrolls at a very early stage in scrolls research. Roland de Vaux and his colleagues understood the Qumran community as a precursor to early Christian (and even medieval Christian) groups. A transitive triangular relationship developed that began to see the Essenes, the Qumran community, and early Christians as an interrelated entity.

A transitive triangular relationship developed that began to see the Essenes, the Qumran community, and early Christians as an interrelated entity.

The majority view, including the position taken in this course, holds that the Qumran community was an Essene group. And since some of the Essenes were celibate (according to Philo, Josephus, and Pliny), and since celibacy entered Christianity at an early stage, there may be a connection here. On the other hand, we note that the New Testament does not promote celibacy per se. The concept of a celibate priesthood arose at a later time in the Roman Catholic Church. A copy of the Community Rule published in 1958 by two Jesuit scholars, Father P. Boccaccio and Father G. Berardi, uses the word "*regula*" to describe this important Qumran text—a clear attempt to see in the Community Rule as the first monastic rule for a (presumably) celibate community.

None of this, however, denies the fact that there are true links between the ideas expressed in the Dead Sea Scrolls, dated mainly to the 1st century B.C.E., and ideas expressed in the New Testament, dated to the 1st century C.E. The Qumran community saw biblical texts, especially the prophets, as speaking not in their historical setting centuries earlier but for the present. This method of interpretation is found throughout the New Testament as well. Both the Qumran sect and the early Christians used Habakkuk 2:4 as a key passage in their theology of a single individual (the Teacher and Jesus, respectively) through whom faith is to be directed, as opposed to individuals addressing their worship directly to God. The expression "sons of light" is a key term in the War Scroll, one of the sect's self-designations. The same term appears in the New Testament in John 12:38 and 1 Thessalonians 5:5.

The best represented of the biblical books among the Qumran manuscripts are Psalms, Deuteronomy, and Isaiah (with 34, 27, and 24 copies, respectively). These are also the most cited books in the New Testament. The Qumran sectarians viewed the Temple Scroll as a book of revealed scripture, which means that they saw revelation continuing in their day; the same holds in the New Testament, where revelation is seen as an ongoing process.

Communal life (including communal meals and communal property) is a distinctive feature of both Qumran society and the early Christian community. Baptism, or ritual immersion, plays a key role in the Community Rule and in the New Testament. Whereas all Jews practiced ritual immersion in antiquity for the removal of ritual impurity, these two sectarian sources present something new: immersion as initiation rite.

The Qumran community leader was known as the *mevaqqer* ("overseer"). This Hebrew term is the exact equivalent of the Greek term *episkopos*, from which our English word "bishop" is derived. As far as we can determine, no other Jewish group of late antiquity had such an official supervising its activities. While all Jewish groups held to some kind of eschatological view, only in the Dead Sea Scrolls (especially the War Scroll) and in the New Testament do we see an apocalyptic view expressed. One particularly notes the cataclysmic battle described both in the War Scroll and in Revelation.

Through what method might the two groups have such similar ideas? One theory, promoted especially by Otto Betz, holds that John the Baptist had contact with the Qumran community. Mark 1:4–6 and Matthew 3:1–6 present John the Baptist living in the desert region of Judah, baptizing people in the

Jordan River, and living on locusts and wild honey. The geography implies that this is the lower Jordan Valley, not far from Qumran. In the next verse in the Matthew passage (3:7), John castigates the Pharisees and Sadducees, which is the same attitude that pervades the Dead Sea Scrolls. While the vast majority of the scrolls come from a period a century earlier than John the Baptist, one recalls from Pliny that the Essene community was still resident in the area (if not Qumran specifically) well into the 1st century C.E.

Notwithstanding all these similarities, we need to mention three crucial differences between these sects. The Christian movement was much more focused on the Messiah figure than is the Dead Sea Scrolls sect. The Qumran community was intensely insular; the Jesus movement had a very active outreach program. Most importantly, time and again the Dead Sea Scrolls sect applied the strictest interpretation to Halakah; by contrast, the mainstream of the Christian movement relaxed Jewish law as much as possible.

While the Dead Sea Scrolls provide valuable information about the background of Christianity, it would be a mistake to view the Qumran community as the forerunner to the Jesus movement. Obviously Christianity sprang from Judaism, and indeed from a specific apocalyptic movement within Judaism. Perhaps we can word the situation this way: The scrolls provide a window into a Jewish sect much like the one that would emerge as the Jesus movement—parallel streams with much in common, though with important differences.

In 2007, a new inscription—not on parchment and not in a cave, but rather on a slab of stone—was made public. It is called the Vision of Gabriel, though the term Dead Sea Stone also has been used, and it dates to the 1st century B.C.E. While the details of its discovery are not known, apparently it was discovered around the year 2000, found its way to a Jordanian antiquities dealer, and was sold to a private collector. The collector was unaware of the significance of the object until a visitor to his collection read the inscribed words, at least as best as possible. The text is ink on stone, a rare medium, since usually one incises letters into the stone. The ink is very faded, so it is hard to read the entire inscription. The stone stands about one meter high, and the inscription comprises 87 lines in Hebrew. The best paleographer of

Hebrew in the world, Ada Yardeni, has authenticated the inscription. The text is known as the Vision of Gabriel because the angel Gabriel conveys an apocalyptic vision, or perhaps better a series of visions. The sense we get from the text is that an enemy nearly destroyed the "sons of the holy," but now their leader, the "prince of princes," will arise and overcome the adversary. Much of this, of course, sounds like phraseology known from the New Testament.

In short, wherever one turns, one finds connections between the scrolls (and now the Dead Sea Stone) and the books of the New Testament. The Qumran sect and the Jesus movement were parallel streams, each with its own apocalyptic vision, against the backdrop of the Roman Empire and the panoply of Judaisms under the umbrella of common Judaism. The one group had little or no continuity, while the other group spawned the largest religious movement in the history of the world. ∎

Essential Reading

Vermes, *The Complete Dead Sea Scrolls in English*, 187–189.

VanderKam, *The Dead Sea Scrolls Today*, 159–184.

VanderKam and Flint, *The Meaning of the Dead Sea Scrolls*, 321–377.

Shanks, *The Dead Sea Scrolls after Forty Years*, 18–38.

Schiffman, *Reclaiming the Dead Sea Scrolls*, 121–123, 344–347.

Brooke, *The Dead Sea Scrolls and the New Testament*.

Charlesworth, *Jesus and the Dead Sea Scrolls*.

Flusser, *Judaism and the Origins of Christianity*.

Knohl, "The Messiah Son of Joseph."

Rendsburg, "Linguistic and Stylistic Notes to the Hazon Gabriel Inscription."

Yardeni, "A New Dead Sea Scroll in Stone?"

Questions to Consider

1. Do you think we too quickly dismiss the views of Eisenman, Theiring, and O'Callaghan concerning direct connections between the Qumran sect and the Jesus movement?

2. If the Vision of Gabriel inscription was not recognized until 2007, what other discoveries may await scholarly detection in private collections?

Connections to Christianity
Lecture 23—Transcript

Throughout our course we have mentioned various connections between the Dead Sea Scrolls and the New Testament, or to word this differently, between the Qumran community and the early Christian community. In this lecture, we take a more systematic approach to this subject, clearly one of the major topics emanating from the study of the Dead Sea Scrolls.

First, we refer back to some earlier information that we presented: theories from some scholars that there is a direct linkage between the Dead Sea Scrolls and the New Testament. We distance ourselves from those interpretations, but we recall them here nonetheless. Robert Eisenman of California State University-Long Beach believes that many if not most of the scrolls date to the 1st century C.E. In addition to positing Zealot connections, he identifies James the Just, the brother of Jesus, as the Teacher of Righteousness referred to our texts. In his opinion, accordingly, the Dead Sea Scrolls have a very direct link to early Christianity.

Barbara Theiring, an independent scholar in Australia, also believes that the Dead Sea Scrolls originate in the 1st century with specific connections to early Christianity, though she goes even further by claiming that the Teacher of Righteousness is John the Baptist and that the Wicked Priest is Jesus.

Jose O'Callaghan, a Spanish Jesuit, believed that 7Q5, written in Greek, is a copy of Mark 6:52–53, thus connecting at least one of the scrolls very directly to the New Testament. In truth, however, as we saw, the only complete word in this tiny Greek fragment is the word *kai* "and," from which one cannot build an entire theory.

A more recent theory, not mentioned until now, is the interpretation of 4Q285, another fragmentary text, by Michael Wise and Robert Eisenman. These scholars read a particular passage to refer to a "pierced Messiah," with the assumption being that the text serves as a precursor to the idea developed by the Jesus movement. Let me read the text to you. It begins with a quotation from Isaiah 11:1, "there shall come forth a sprout from the trunk of Jesse," and then it continues—it's fragmentary; we are missing the beginnings of the lines, we only have the end of the lines—one line ends, "an offshoot of David, and they will be judged," and then there's a section of text missing. Then the next line, we have the latter part of it, "and he will kill him, the leader of the community, the offshoot (of David)," and then another part is missing, and then we read, "and with piercings, and the priest will command"; fragmentary.

All other scholars, however, have countered the Wise-Eisenman position, by arguing correctly that their understanding of the grammar is totally wrong; that if anything the text refers to a "piercing Messiah." The passage that they read—"and he will kill him, the leader of the community, the offshoot (of David)"—implies that the leader, "the offshoot (of David)," is the object ("he will kill him," that is to say, this individual), but most scholars, and I agree, would read the grammar to take that expression ("the leader of the community, the offshoot (of David") as the subject of the sentence, referring back to the "he." In this case it is a "piercing Messiah," not a "pierced Messiah." The reference is to a messianic figure that will militarily defeat his enemies.

Before proceeding further into this discussion—linkages between the Dead Sea Scrolls and early Christianity—we take note of the scholarly view developed in the 19th century by the great French savant Ernst Renan, who in his book *Vie de Jésus*, published in 1862 (an English translation appeared one year later, *Life of Jesus*) traced connections between the Essenes and early Christianity. Needless to say, this work appeared long before the discovery of the Dead Sea Scrolls, and indeed before the discovery of the Damascus Document in the Cairo genizah, found in 1896. Here we need to mention that the great Albert Schweitzer was highly critical of Renan's book in his own major work, *Geschichte der Leben-Jesu-Forschung* (1906; English translation: *The Quest of the Historical Jesus* [1910]). To Schweitzer's mind, the attempt to place the historical Jesus within the context of ancient Judaism was misguided. The phenomenon of Jesus was so unique, Schweitzer argued, that scholars should instead concentrate on the theology and eschatology forthcoming from Jesus's sayings and from the writings of his followers. This critique of Renan won the day, and the "quest for the historical Jesus" movement came to a halt, until it was revived later in the 20th century.

Renan's approach received a new life with the discovery of the Dead Sea Scrolls. Here we recall that Sukenik and Dupont-Sommer saw Essene connections to the scrolls at a very early stage in Dead Sea Scrolls. Then we recollect the view of de Vaux and his colleagues at the École Biblique and elsewhere to understand the Qumran community as a precursor to early Christian and even medieval Christian groups. As such, a transitive triangular relationship developed, which began to see the Essenes, the Qumran community, and early Christians as an interrelated entity.

Most prominently, de Vaux and his colleagues saw the Qumran community as a group of celibate monks, hard at work in their scriptorium copying biblical books and composing their own works. Clearly there is bias and exaggeration to this view, and it was in this context that we read the quotations by Schiffman. Let us look at the issue of celibacy in greater detail. The majority view, including the position taken in this course, holds that the Qumran community was an Essene group; and since many of the Essenes were celibate—according to all three sources: Philo, Josephus, Pliny—and since celibacy entered Christianity at an early stage, there may be a connection here. On the other hand, we note that the New Testament does not promote celibacy per se. For example, while the Corinthians may have stated, "It is a good thing for a man not to touch a woman" (1 Corinthians 7:1), in the subsequent verses Paul actually argues against this ascetic position. Similarly, in 1 Timothy 3:1–5, Paul argues that one desiring to accede to the position of episkopos (bishop) should be married with children, "for if a man does not know how to manage his own household, how can he take care of the church of God?" That's from verse 5. From these passages we infer that while there were ascetic and celibate Christians in the 1st century, the concept of a celibate priesthood clearly arose at a later time in the Roman Catholic church, since Greek Orthodox and other Eastern Orthodox priests may marry and have children.

As another indication of this approach, I present, as a case, my copy of the Community Rule or Manual of Discipline, which I used when I was a graduate student in the 1970s. The work was published in 1958 by two Jesuit scholars, Father P. Boccaccio and Father G. Berardi, under the title in Latin *Regula unionis seu manuale disciplinae*, the *Rule of the Community*, which is the Manual of Discipline. The key point here is the use of the word *Regula* to describe this important Qumran text, the Community Rule, because in a Catholic setting, the term is used to refer to specific texts such as *Regula Benedicti*, the book of precepts devised by Saint Benedict in the 6th century C.E., and followed ever since by members of the order of Benedictine monks that he founded. The oldest such community with a *Regula*, however—older than Benedict's—is the one established by the Coptic monk Pachomius in the early 4th century C.E. Before this time, monks typically were hermits, until Pachomius gathered them together in a single community with a communal lifestyle and rule to guide them. In other words, here we have very clear evidence of Catholic scholars in the 1950s working on the Dead Sea Scrolls and attempting to see in the Community Rule the first *Regula* for a presumably celibate community.

None of this, however, denies the fact that there are true links between the ideas expressed in the Dead Sea Scrolls, dated mainly to the 1st and 2nd centuries B.C.E., and ideas expressed in the New Testament, dated slightly later, the 1st century C.E. In fact, just to be perfectly clear, even Professor Schiffman would agree to this point, for the full title of his book is *Reclaiming the Dead Sea Scrolls: Their True Meaning for Judaism and Christianity*, with plenty of parallels between the Dead Sea Scrolls and the Jesus movement presented in his valuable book.

Let us, then, present the many correspondences between our scrolls and the New Testament, summarizing points noted at earlier junctures in our course. We begin with the Pesher method of interpretation. The Qumran community saw biblical texts, especially the prophets, as speaking not in their historical setting centuries earlier, but speaking rather to the present. This method of interpretation is found throughout the New Testament as well. For example, and most famously, Matthew 1:23 cites Isaiah 7:14 to refer to the birth of Jesus to his mother Mary. For 700 years, the Isaiah passage was transmitted by Jews with a meaning unrelated to the birth of Jesus, but the Christian community now saw this verse as speaking for the present. A key passage in Pesher Habakkuk is the following, Hab. 2:4 states, "But the righteous shall live by his faith," with the assumption being that the righteous person shall prosper by his own faith in God. But the Pesher author states that the faith is directed through the Teacher. Let's read that passage: "This concerns all those who observe the Law in the House of Judah, whom God will deliver from the House of Judgment, because of their suffering and because of their faith in the Teacher of Righteousness." As we saw earlier in our course, this passage is quoted three times in the New Testament—in Romans, Galatians, and Hebrews—as Paul sees this passage referring to a) Jesus, and b) the future life. Thus, both the Qumran sect and the early Christians used Hab. 2:4 as a key passage in their theology of a single individual—the Teacher, for the Qumran community; Jesus, for the Christian community—through whom faith is to be directed, as opposed to individuals addressing their worship directly to God; a second point of contact between the scrolls and the New Testament.

Our next item: The expression "sons of light" is a key term in the War Scroll as one of the sect's self-designations. The same term appears in the New Testament in John 12:38 and 1 Thessalonians 5:5. In the former passage, for example, let's read that one: Jesus says in John 12, "As long as you have the light, believe in the light, so that you may become children of light." There you have sons of light from our Dead Sea Scroll documents, and the same expression here in the New Testament.

The Damascus Document includes the following passage castigating the sect's opponents—Pharisees, in this context, apparently—who are "caught in two, fornication, by taking two wives during their lifetime"; you'll recall that we discussed this passage earlier. The syntax is difficult here; I've translated it as literally as possible, even though we know all the individual words and I've rendered this passage in hopefully a sensible way. The author defends his critique by invoking two prooftexts: Gen. 1:27 "male and female he created them," and Gen. 7:9, "two by two," with reference to those who entered the ark. Finally, the author cites Deut. 17:17, from the law of the king: "He shall not multiply wives to himself." All agree that the Damascus Document is prohibiting polygamy here; and such is implied in the New Testament as well, with the most illustrative passage being from 1 Timothy 3:2, where Paul writes that a "bishop must be blameless, the husband of one wife." At a later time, Saint Augustine, who bridges the 4th and 5th centuries C.E., wrote in his tractate *De bono coniugali (On the Good of Marriage)* as follows: "Now indeed in our time, and in keeping with Roman custom, it is no longer allowed to take another wife, so as to have more than one wife living." You see a continuity here all the way down through Saint Augustine that one husband one wife should be the norm, no polygamy.

But it is also possible that the Damascus Document goes further and prohibits divorce as well. In this context, we shall look at Mark 10:1–11, which is paralleled in Matthew 19:1–9, where Jesus contends with the Pharisees, he argues that divorce runs counter to the divine will, and he cites the same passage from Gen. 1:27 that the Damascus Document cites.

Next point of connection between our two groups of texts: The best represented of the biblical books among the Qumran manuscripts are Psalms, Deuteronomy, and Isaiah; 34, 27, and 24 copies, respectively. These are also the most cited books in the New Testament. Clearly the two groups were placing an emphasis on the same portions of scripture: Psalms, Isaiah, and Deuteronomy.

We reached the conclusion earlier in our course that the Qumran sectarians viewed the Temple Scroll as a book of revealed scripture, which means that they saw revelation continuing in their day, long after Moses had received the Torah and the later prophets had received the divine word. The same holds in the New Testament, where revelation is seen as an ongoing process. The most illustrative passage is 2 Peter 3:1: "I want you to recall the words spoken in the past by the holy prophets and the command given by our Lord and Savior through your apostles"; that's the present.

Another feature that links the Qumran *Yahad* and the Christian community: a communal lifestyle, including communal meals and communal property; a very distinctive feature of Qumran society, as indicated most of all in the Community Rule. The best New Testament parallel appears in Acts 2:42–45. The passage goes as follows: "And they devoted themselves to the apostles' teaching and fellowship, to the breaking of bread and the prayers. ... And all who believed were together and had all things in common; and they sold their possessions and goods and distributed them to all, as any had need." Then one recalls the story of Ananias and Sapphira, the couple in Acts 5:1–11, who were punished by death for retaining for themselves a portion of the proceeds from the sale of a piece of property. Communal lifestyle, another nexus between the Dead Sea Scrolls community and early Christianity.

Our next point: Baptism, or ritual immersion; this plays a key role in the Community Rule and in the New Testament. Whereas all Jews practiced ritual immersion in antiquity to remove ritual impurity based on the laws in Leviticus 12–15 and Numbers 19, it is only these two sectarian groups, the Qumran community and the early Christian community, which had a different take on the matter; they present something new. From 1QS 5:13–14, it reads as follows: "He shall not enter the water to touch the purity [that means the pure food] of the men of holiness; for they shall not be purified, unless they turn from their wickedness—for he is impure among all who transgress his word." According to this passage in the Community Rule, ritual immersion, this type of bathing, removes not only ritual impurity but also sin and transgression. Thus ritual bathing acts as a final act before one enters the *Yahad* to remove all types of impurity, ritual and moral, before you become a member of the group. Our parallels from the New Testament: In the New Testament we note the following. Mark 1:4: "And so John [reference to John the Baptist] came, baptizing in the desert region and preaching a baptism of repentance for the forgiveness of sins"; parallel to what we see at Qumran. Matthew 3:6: "Confessing their sins, they were baptized by him [John the Baptist] in the Jordan River"; same phenomenon. Another passage: In Romans 6:3, Paul refers to "all of us who were baptized into Christ Jesus." In short, in both communities, baptism or immersion is used for the removal of sin and for entrance into the congregation.

Another point: The negative view attached to sexuality, as we saw in the Thanksgiving Hymns; that passage: "Behold, [I have been taken] from dust [and] fashioned [from clay], from a fount of impurity and the nakedness of shame," the same essential view is expressed in early Christian writings as we saw in a previous lecture.

We have not yet mentioned another point of contact between the Qumran community and early Christianity. The oversight of the *Yahad* was done by an individual known as the *mevaqqer*, "the overseer." We have references to this individual in the Community Rule (1QS) and the Damascus Document. The Hebrew term *mevaqqer* (overseer) is the exact equivalent of the Greek term *episkopos*, which occurs five times in the New Testament as communal leaders; once in Acts 20:28, and then four times in the epistles. This Greek word *episkopos* is the root of our English word "bishop." As far as we can determine, no other Jewish group of late antiquity had such an official supervising its activities, only the Qumran group and the early Christians; *mevaqqer* and *episkopos*.

Finally, there is the obvious linkage of apocalyptic in the two groups. While all Jewish groups held to some kind of eschatological view, only in the Dead Sea Scrolls—in particular the War Scroll—and in the New Testament do we see an apocalyptic view expressed. More particularly, one notes the cataclysmic battle described both in the War Scroll and in the book of Revelation, the last book in the New Testament canon, in which the forces of good will destroy the forces of evil.

Through what method might the two groups have had such similar ideas? One theory, promoted especially by Otto Betz, holds that John the Baptist would have had contact with the Qumran community. Passages in Mark and Matthew reflect the fact that John the Baptist lives in the desert region of Judah, baptizing people in the Jordan River as an act that removes sin— we've just discussed this issue—all the while John the Baptist living on locusts and wild honey. The geography implies that this is taking place in the lower Jordan Valley, not far (perhaps 10 kilometers only) from Qumran. In the next verse in the Matthew passage (3:7), John castigates the Pharisees and Sadducees, which is the same attitude that pervades the Dead Sea Scrolls; and while the vast majority of the scrolls come from a period a century earlier than John the Baptist, one recalls that the Essene community still was resident in the area into the 1st century C.E. as we can determine from Pliny's report that he met a group of Essenes along the shore of the Dead Sea.

Notwithstanding all these similarities, however, we need to mention three crucial differences, one noted earlier explicitly, the other two not stated though perhaps implied earlier in our course. As we've indicated, the Christian movement—as its name implies—is much more focused on the Messiah figure than is the Dead Sea Scrolls sect. To repeat what we stated earlier in our course: The word "Christ" or "Messiah" appears more than 500 times in the New Testament; whereas in the much larger Dead Sea Scrolls corpus, the Hebrew word *mašiah*, "anointed" or "messiah," appears only 32 times. In the War Scroll, for example, the Hebrew term appears only once, in 1QM 11:7: "by the hand of your anointed ones [Messiahs, in the plural], they who discern the testimonies, you have told us the end-times of the battles of your hands, to fight against our enemies, to bring down the troops of Belial." That's the single reference, for example, in the War Scroll to a Messiah. Contrast the 500-plus instances of the attestation of this word in the New Testament books.

A second difference separating the *Yahad* group and the Christian movement is the attitude towards others. The Qumran community is intensely insular, seeing enemies all around. The Jesus movement, by contrast, had a very active what we today might call "outreach program," preaching to others, willing to meet people where they are, in order to bring them into the Christian fold; that's something we would have a hard time imagining the Qumran *Yahad* doing.

Third, and most important of all, though, is the following distinction between our two groups, it concerns their attitudes towards Jewish law. Time and again we have seen that the Dead Sea Scrolls sect applied the strictest interpretation to *halakha*. By contrast, although the Judaizing Christians headed by James sought to hold onto Jewish ritual practices, such as circumcision and the dietary laws, the mainstream of the Christian movement relaxed Jewish law as much as possible. For example: In Galatians 5:1–6, Paul argues that circumcision is not necessary. In Matthew 15:11, Jesus states, "It is not what goes into one's mouth that makes one unclean, but rather what comes out of one's mouth that makes one unclean." In Mark 2, Jesus permits the harvesting of grain on the Sabbath, even though all other Jewish considered agricultural work as one of the prime labors forbidden on the Sabbath.

In short, while the Dead Sea Scrolls provide valuable information about the background of Christianity, it would be a mistake to view the Qumran community as the forerunner to the Jesus movement per se, especially given their very different views of *halakha*. As we have seen in so many instances, the early Christians had much in common with the *Yahad*, but we need to recognize the salient differences along with the numerous points of contact. Obviously, Christianity sprang from Judaism, and indeed from a specific apocalyptic movement within Judaism. Perhaps we can word the situation this way: The Dead Sea Scrolls provide for us a window into a Jewish sect much like the one that would emerge as the Jesus movement, parallel streams with much in common, though with important differences.

The last point I want to make in this lecture concerns the discovery in 2007 of a new inscription, not on parchment, not in a cave, but rather on a slab of stone known as the Vision of Gabriel, though the term Dead Sea Stone also has been used, dated to the 1st century B.C.E. Where did this text come from? While the details of its discovery are not known, apparently it was discovered sometime around 2000, it found its way to a Jordanian antiquities dealer, and he in turn sold it to a private collector. At first, the collector was apparently unaware of the significance of the new find, until a visitor to his collection read the inscribed words, at least as best as possible. The text is ink on stone, a rare medium since usually one incises letters into the stone; and the ink is very faded, so it is hard to read the entire inscription. The stone stands about one meter high, and the inscription comprises 87 lines in Hebrew. You may wonder whether or not this inscription is a forgery, especially when I relate the story of how it was discovered and went from an antiquities dealer to a collection and so on. The best paleographer of Hebrew in the world, Ada Yardeni of Jerusalem, has authenticated the inscription, and most of us rely on her judgment. I, for one, certainly did so, especially in advance of my having published an article on the literary style of the Vision of Gabriel inscription as we call this text in the journal *Dead Sea Discoveries* in the volume for 2009.

The text is known as the Vision of Gabriel because the angel Gabriel conveys an apocalyptic vision, or perhaps better a series of visions. Let me read here for you a sampling of passages. "Thus says the Lord, God of Israel, now all the nations encamp on Jerusalem, and from it are exiled one two three, forty Prophets and the elders and the pious." (13–16) "In three days you shall know, for thus says the Lord [of Hosts], the God of Israel, the evil has been broken before righteousness." (19–21) "In a little while, I will shake the heavens and the earth." (24–25) "These are the seven chariots at the gate of Jerusalem and the gates of Judah." (26–27) "Seal up the blood of the slaughtered of Jerusalem, for thus says the Lord of Hosts, the God of Israel." (57–58) "Who am I? I am Gabriel," that's line 77. Most striking of all is what appears in line 80 of our text, "in three days, live, I, Gabriel [the angel Gabriel], command you, prince of princes." Let me repeat that: "in three days, live, I, Gabriel, command you, prince of princes." The sense we get from the text is that an enemy destroyed the "sons of the holy," but now their leader, called the "prince of princes," will arise and overcome the adversary. Much of this, of course, sounds like phraseology known from the New Testament.

In short, wherever one turns, one finds connections between our scrolls, including the Dead Sea Stone now, and the books of the New Testament. The Qumran sect and the Jesus movement were parallel streams, each with its own apocalyptic vision against the backdrop of the Roman Empire and the panoply of Judaisms under the umbrella of common Judaism. The one group had no continuity, or at least minimal continuity, while the other group spawned the largest religious movement in the history of the world.

We have one lecture remaining. We will look at some of the most intriguing of the fragments not yet discussed in our course, we will summarize the most salient conclusions forthcoming from the study of our texts, and we will present what I consider the most important lessons to be learned from scholarly inquiry into the Dead Sea Scrolls.

Scroll Fragments and a New View of Judaism
Lecture 24

> Like most professors, perhaps, I have a series of cartoons on my office door and walls. One shows a bunch of New York sophisticates enjoying a light repast; one of the women in the group says, "Who could have imagined that such a wonderful recipe for brownies would be hidden away in the Dead Sea Scrolls?"

In this course, we have examined maybe three dozen documents out of the 930 that emerged from Qumran caves 1–11, focusing on the longest scrolls. We have skipped many more, primarily because they are so fragmentary. Most of these fragments come from Cave 4, and some are merely scraps, though even with these some context can be teased out. Let us spend some time at least looking at three fragmentary texts. I have selected these three because each demonstrates an important point, as we continue, even here in our last lecture, to learn more about the Qumran community.

The first text is a blessing for King Jonathan, one of only a handful of instances where we get a reference to a real person in the scrolls. The obvious question is, who is King Jonathan? Esther and Hanan Eshel believe it refers to the Hasmonean monarch Alexander Janneus (r. 103–76 B.C.E.), whose name appears as "Jonathan" on some coins. The text may be a nonsectarian prayer in praise of the monarch. But we know from Josephus that Alexander Janneus was hostile to the Pharisees, and that alone may have been reason for the *Yahad* in particular to pray for the king's welfare. The second option is offered by Geza Vermes, who identifies him as Jonathan Maccabee (161–143 B.C.E.), an earlier Hasmonean monarch, who was seen as a liberator of Jerusalem, as the Maccabees continued to drive the Seleucids from the region. Again, if this is a sectarian text, perhaps the Qumran sect heralded Jonathan Maccabee for this achievement, even though things later turned bad. Even when we have a royal name attested in our documents, Qumran scholarship can be quite difficult. No text is simple!

The second text is known as the Florilegium, a technical word that is a synonym for anthology. It is like a *pesher* text, except that a *pesher* proceeds verse-by-verse through a biblical book, whereas the Florilegium garners verses from throughout the Bible. The common theme here appears to be the end of days (Hebrew *'aharit ha-yamim*), since we get references to the Temple that is to be built in the end of days, the end of the dominion of Belial, a figure known as the Shoot of David, and so forth. The one passage to highlight is proof that the *Yahad* served as the replacement or surrogate for the Temple. The humans who comprise the community are called in themselves a *miqdaš*, a holy place, a sanctuary, a temple.

The third text is 4Q159/4Q513–514, called Ordinances. Together these passages comprise a commentary on certain biblical laws. Exodus 30:11–16 contains a biblical commandment that each Israelite age 20 and up is to donate a half shekel of silver for the upkeep and maintenance of the Tabernacle. But is this a single one-time contribution or an annual levy? The main Jewish tradition calls for an annual contribution. But in Ordinances, we read, "He should give it only one time in all his days." A once-in-a-lifetime contribution allows one to fulfill the biblical command but allows the *Yahad* to withhold support for the Temple in Jerusalem on an ongoing, annual basis.

At several junctures in our course, we discussed what happened to the sects. In the main, the Sadducees and the Essenes disappeared from the landscape. In some way, eventually the Pharisaic/rabbinic system emerged as the dominant system. Some sectarian ideas, however, flowed into the rabbinic stream. The Mishna and the Talmudim often contain minority legal opinions, some of which are legal stances present in the Dead Sea Scrolls. It is clear that the Pharisees did not see their continuation as a defeat of the other sects. Quite the contrary, it appears that the Pharisees and their rabbinic successors saw room for the inclusion of their earlier competitors in the new post-Temple world.

At this point, I want to present what I consider the major takeaway points of our course. Before the discovery of the Dead Sea Scrolls, we would have understood the rabbis as very strict interpreters of Jewish law. One now realizes how much stricter the Qumran sect was in its interpretation of Jewish law. Approximately 1,000 years separated the Qumran copies of the Damascus Document and the two medieval copies of this text. The persistence of the Damascus Document into the Middle Ages opens up the possibility for some continuation of the Sadducee tradition throughout the golden age of the rabbinic literature. In light of our research, we can no longer speak of the rabbinic tradition as the normative one in Judaism. In fact, the scrolls lead us to conclude that there never was a normative position in Judaism during the period under discussion, and perhaps not for centuries afterward. This is a major paradigm shift in the study of ancient Judaism. Turning one last time to Christianity, we emphasize again that many of the ideas and beliefs of the Qumran community appear in the Jesus movement as well. The Christian religion would follow its own course, but its indebtedness to Judaism, specifically of the Qumran type, is realized more and more.

And now an admission: You may have gained the sense during our course that sometimes I hold that the rabbis emerged as the normative, mainstream construct within Judaism, while at other times I have emphasized that we cannot speak of a normative, mainstream anything for the period under consideration. Except for a few scholars on either side, most scholars today are hesitant to surrender the long-held belief of rabbinic normativity, even with evidence such as we have presented in this course. The main issue before us is that we have been trained to read history, philosophy, theology, and more only through the eyes of the rabbis. In the end, as so often happens in the study of antiquity, we simply do not have sufficient evidence to fully resolve this scholarly debate, and thus our questions remain.

> **The debates were not calm and collected, but rather replete with animosity and acrimony—"senseless hatred."**

Finally, we consider a rabbinic tradition concerning the destruction of the Second Temple in 70 C.E. Looking back on the event at some distance, the rabbis asked, why did this happen? And their response was *sinnat hinnam* ("senseless hatred"). Only after the discovery of the Dead Sea Scrolls did we come to realize this statement's truth and its import. When the Qumran sectarians call themselves the "sons of light" and include other Jews in the category of the "sons of darkness," we see the enmity between the different groups. When we realize that a Jerusalem priest (the so-called Wicked Priest) attacked the Qumran group's leader (the Teacher of Righteousness) on Yom Kippur, we again see the internecine hatred that existed. When we realize that the Halakhic Letter needs to demonstrate the priority of the sect's legal positions to the total exclusion of the other approaches, we see the sect's inability to embrace other approaches.

It may not be an exaggeration to see the Qumran community as a besieged group, one at odds with its more powerful Pharisee and Sadducee opponents, with a need to fight back with wrathful, even vengeful, words. The Essenes opposed the Pharisees mainly on religious-Halakhic grounds, and they opposed the Sadducees mainly on religious-political grounds. The debates were not calm and collected, but rather replete with animosity and acrimony—"senseless hatred." Even the New Testament books participate in this trend, with their very negative portrayal of the Pharisees especially.

The main lesson that we can extract from our study of the Dead Sea Scrolls and from this entire period of Jewish history is that Judaism at this time was ripe with vitriolic sectarianism. Let us stray far from this approach and follow a path of religious pluralism. Let us recognize our denominational differences but embrace them all as valid and appropriate ways to lead our lives, both our own lives and those of our neighbors. ∎

Essential Reading

Vermes, *The Complete Dead Sea Scrolls in English*, 331–332, 493–494, 497–499.

Schiffman, *Reclaiming the Dead Sea Scrolls*, 239–240.

Questions to Consider

1. How much of a fragmentary text do you think is necessary for a scholar to be able to gain a general sense of its contents? A few words? A few (broken) sentences? Half a column? Consider a parallel: a torn newspaper page, with only parts of lines and columns legible.

2. Are there any other takeaway points from our course that come to mind that we did not cover in this lecture?

Scroll Fragments and a New View of Judaism
Lecture 24—Transcript

Like most professors perhaps, I have a series of cartoons on my office door and inside my office walls. One of my favorites is a *New Yorker* magazine cartoon from October 14, 1991. A bunch of New York sophisticates are sitting around the living room enjoying a light repast, as one of the women in the group says, "*Who could have imagined* that such a wonderful recipe for *brownies* would be hidden away in the *Dead Sea Scrolls*?" Notice the date, by the way: October 1991, in the midst of the release of the scrolls to the public at large, based on the efforts of Ben Zion Wacholder and Martin Abegg, Hershel Shanks, and William Moffat of the Huntington Library, all of which I described earlier. We did not uncover any delicious brownie recipe in our study of the scrolls, but we have learned a lot and there is much more to learn.

In fact, have you been counting? Do you know how many scrolls we have examined? All the major scrolls—Damascus Document, Community Rule, War Scroll, Thanksgiving Hymns, Pesher Habakkuk, Genesis Apocryphon, Temple Scroll—and then the fragmentary but crucial 4QMMT, the Halakhic Letter. We've mentioned other texts from time to time, such as the *Messianic Rule*; the *Songs of the Sabbath Sacrifice*; 4Q177, which mentions the "sons of light"; 4Q477, which includes a list of names, including one person who was rebuked for disturbing the community; 4Q422, which paraphrases the narrative of the Ten Plagues; 4Q434, a text that includes the Grace after Meals; 4Q408, which praises God for creating light and darkness; 4Q285, the so-called "piercing Messiah" text (not the "pierced Messiah," we discussed that in the previous lecture); the Enoch material; the Jubilees material; plus a few others. That's maximally 25 texts, according to my count, out of 730 non-biblical manuscripts.

Then of the biblical texts, we've discussed 1QIsa^a and 1QIsa^b, two of the first seven documents from Cave 1; 4QExod^a, which reads 75 Israelites who went down to Egypt, instead of 70; 4QDeut^j and 4QDeut^q, both of which read "sons of God" instead of "children of Israel"; 4QSam^a, which has an additional portion of a narrative, something lacking in the Masoretic Text; 4QDeut^n, with a space between two verses, presumably telling us something about how Grace after Meals was recited; along with a few others mentioned only in passing. All told, maybe 10 or 12 biblical manuscripts, out of a total of 230 such documents. Or to total these two numbers, altogether, maybe we have looked at three dozen documents out of the 930 manuscripts that emerged from Qumran caves 1–11. Of course, I am being disingenuous here, since the amount of material that we read comes closer to 50 percent of the documentation from Qumran, since all of the major scrolls, some of them quite long—Temple Scroll, 67 columns for example—were treated in our course. But I hope you get the point.

Let me give you a sense here of the kinds of texts that we have not read in our course, primarily because they are so fragmentary. Just the titles alone, and these titles are assigned to these texts by the editors, will provide you with an idea of what awaits further study of the Qumran documents: the Vision of Samuel, Ages of the Creation, Wiles of the Wicked Woman, a scribal exercise, the Prayer of Nabonidus, Parable of the Tree, Zodiology and Brontology. You may ask, what are those? Zodiology, a text that talks about the signs of the Zodiac and how to interpret what you see in the heavens; and Brontology, a text that interprets what happens when you hear thunder, that's a Brontology text, how and what does the thunder say about the course of events still to understand. Other texts: a List of False Prophets, Accounting texts with accounts of cereal grains (one text in Hebrew, one text in Greek, rather mundane), the Rule for the Farmer, a Marriage Ritual text (that one, by the way, is written on papyrus), Physiognomic horoscope. What is that, you may ask? This is a horoscope text that tells the parents what the child might look like if the child is born, given the way the stars were aligned. It mentions the constellation Taurus in this text specifically, and then describes, "The nose will look like this, it will be a regular nose and not a long nose, and the hair will be in between these two colors, and so on and so forth." Then we have a text, Liturgical Curses, and another one called Allegory of the Vine, and on and on it goes. As you can imagine, most of these come from Cave four, all are fragmentary, some merely scraps, though even with these some context can be teased out.

But let's spend some time at least looking at three texts, also fragmentary again, all from Cave Four. I have selected these three documents purposefully, not just to give you a flavor of a few more Dead Sea Scrolls, but because each demonstrates an important point, as we continue, even here in our last lecture, to learn more about the Qumran community.

The first text to examine is one we that have mentioned in passing, 4Q448, a blessing for King Jonathan, one of but a handful of instances where we get a reference to a real person. The identity of this king is debated, but first let's read the relevant portions of the text. The text begins with "Hallelujah, a psalm, a song," and then continues with the usual praise of God, and then mentions King Jonathan twice as follows. First we read: "Rise, O Holy One, over King Jonathan and all the congregation of your people Israel, who are in the four winds of heaven, let there be peace on all of them and on your kingdom, blessed be your name." Then we read, in a fragmented section of this text 4Q448, "Remember them for a blessing / on your name that is called / the kingdom, to bless / on the day of war / King Jonathan."

The obvious question is: Who is King Jonathan? The first option, proffered by Esther Eshel and Hanan Eshel, a husband and wife team from Bar-Ilan University in Israel, is that King Jonathan refers to Alexander Janneus who reigned 103–76 B.C.E. For a while his Greek name was Alexander, his Hebrew name was Jonathan, as we know from coins that he minted with his Greek name on one side and his Hebrew name on the other. Why was there a prayer for this king among the Dead Sea Scrolls? If this text belongs to common Judaism, then it is simply a text in praise of the Hasmonean monarch. But if this is a sectarian text, we know from Josephus that Alexander Janneus was hostile to the Pharisees, and that alone may have been reason for the *Yahad* members to seek the king's welfare via this prayer to God.

The second option is offered by Geza Vermes, who identifies our Jonathan with Jonathan Maccabee several decades earlier, 161–143 B.C.E., an earlier Hasmonean monarch who was seen as the liberator of Jerusalem as the Maccabees continued to drive the Seleucids from the area. Why would there be a prayer to this king among the Dead Sea Scrolls? If the text belongs to common Judaism then the answer is clear; and if it is a sectarian text, then perhaps the Qumran sect heralded Jonathan Maccabee for this achievement, even though things clearly turned bad, in the eyes of the *Yahad*, since most scholars believe that Jonathan Maccabee is the Wicked Priest. All this to show you once more, even when we have a royal name attested in our documents (King Jonathan), how difficult Qumran scholarship is. No text is simple.

The second text that I would like to share with you in this lecture is 4Q174, a text known as the Florilegium, a technical word that is a synonym for anthology. In this text, a series of canonically disconnected verses are presented, from Samuel, Exodus, Amos, Psalms, Isaiah, Daniel, and so on, after which with each passage the author provides his explanation or interpretation of the verse. As such, the Florilegium is like a Pesher text, except that a Pesher text proceeds verse-by-verse through a biblical book as we saw when we studied the Pesher Habakkuk; whereas the Florilegium garners verses from throughout the Bible, though presumably there is a thematic linkage among the passages cited. The common theme in our text, 4Q174, appears to be the end of days, since we get references to the Temple that is to be built in the end of days, the end of the dominion of Belial—that's the Satan figure—a figure known as the Shoot of David, and yet other references to the end of days, the Hebrew expression *'aharit ha-yamim*.

The one passage to highlight, however, is a prooftext for what we have stated several times in our course, that the *Yahad* served as the replacement or surrogate for the Temple. The text reads as follows: "And he commanded to be built for him a Sanctuary [the Hebrew word *miqdaš*; we can translate it either as "sanctuary," "holy place," "sanctum," "Temple," or any of those things] of men [the Hebrew expression *miqdaš 'adam*] to offer incense in it to him, before him, works of Torah." The point is clear: The humans who comprise the community are in themselves a *miqdaš*—a holy place, a sanctuary, a temple, as it were—in lieu of the polluted and impure Temple that stands in Jerusalem, in which they offer the equivalent of incense on the altar, namely, works of Torah. What a stunning theological leap; a point I wanted to make clear in this, our last lecture.

The third text that I wish to share with you is 4Q159, and two other fragments, 4Q513 and 4Q514, which together comprise a commentary on certain biblical laws. As such, it is somewhat like the Florilegium again, though we reserve that title for the previous text, and we call this text simply Ordinances because it deals with a variety of biblical laws. I focus here on one of those laws. Exodus 30 contains a biblical commandment that each Israelite is to donate a half-shekel of silver for the upkeep and maintenance of the Tabernacle. The question arises in later Jewish deliberations: Is this a single one-time contribution, or is this an annual tax or levy? Obviously the Tabernacle was of old—today a Temple stands in its place—but the question remains: An annual tax or levy, or a single one-time contribution? The main Jewish tradition calls for an annual contribution. A couple of passages: Nehemiah 10, the people state, "We have placed upon ourselves obligations to give one-third shekel each year for the service of the house of our God"; we're actually not quite sure why now it's a third-shekel and not a half-shekel as per the book of Exodus, but it's clear from the words "each year for the service of the house of our God" that it's an annual contribution.

Matthew 17, in a story set in Capernaum, is our second text; while not stated explicitly in that passage, the implication is that the collectors of the Temple tax are making their regular annual rounds. Then the rabbis include in the Mishna a tractate called "Shekalim"—that's the plural of shekel—in which the contribution is deemed also to be an annual one. But in 4Q159 Ordinances—our Qumran text that we are reading now—the following is stated: "He should give it only one time in all his days," with the "it" referring to the half-shekel as commanded in Exodus 30. Clearly, once more the Qumran community has a different Halakhic standpoint, though in this case it would seem to be a more liberal opinion—if we can use that term—giving only once in one's lifetime, as opposed to contributing annually. But we can explain the difference as follows: A single once-in-a-lifetime contribution allows a member of the *Yahad* to fulfill the biblical commandment, at least according to one legal interpretation, but at the same this system allows the *Yahad* to withhold support for the Temple in Jerusalem on an ongoing, annual basis because of their views about the impurities and polluted nature of the Temple in Jerusalem. A brilliant case of legal thinking and accommodation. I repeat: Even from the so-called minor texts among the Dead Sea Scrolls, we learn new things over and over again. Laboring in the vineyard of Qumran continues to inform us, to teach us, and to open our eyes, time and again.

At several junctures in our course, we discussed what happened to the sects: How in the main the Sadducees and the Essenes disappeared from the landscape, though in some fashion they continued onward as well, as evidenced by the links between the Sadducees and the medieval Karaites on the one hand, and the Essenes and the readers of the Damascus Document in medieval Cairo on the other; and how notwithstanding these latter trajectories, and notwithstanding what we have stated about the lack of a normative, mainstream Judaism in the centuries not only before 70 C.E., but also following the destruction of the Temple, how, with all of those caveats and qualifications, in some way, eventually the Pharisaic/rabbinic system emerged as the dominant system.

What I have not presented until now, however, is the manner in which some of the sectarian ideas flowed into the rabbinic stream. You will recall that I mentioned that the Mishna and the Talmud*im* often contain minority legal opinions. Some of these minority opinions are legal stances present in the Dead Sea Scrolls. Two examples from among the issues that we discussed in our course: The first is the question of whether or not the sacrificing of a pregnant animal violates the law of Leviticus 22:28; not to sacrifice a mother and its young on the same day. As we saw, the rabbis followed a lenient position, stating that this occurrence did not violate the law of the Torah. The Qumran group felt it did violate the law of the Torah, but there is an exception to the rabbinic formulation in the Mishna. One particular sage, Rabbi Meir—this occurs in the Mishna tractate Hullin 4:5 which deals with this issue—believed that the practice of sacrificing a pregnant animal does contravene the passage in Leviticus; and yet his judgment is included in the codification of rabbinic law in the Mishna as a minority opinion. A ruling from Qumran finds its way into the Mishna through the voice of Rabbi Meir.

The second is the issue of whether or not fish require ritual slaughtering before eating. All Jews agreed that mammals and fowl require ritual slaughtering—you can look in Leviticus 11 and Deuteronomy 14 for the list of permitted creatures—the only issue was whether fish also require ritual slaughtering or not. According to the Damascus Document, we read the following in that text, from column 12: "They shall not eat fish, unless split while alive; for your soul is (in) their blood"; that is to say, you need to catch the fish while they're alive, and then split them and let whatever blood may exist in a fish to drain out exactly as occurs with mammals and birds. The rabbis do not accept this opinion; for them, fish do not require ritual slaughtering because fish were never sacrificed on the altar in the Temple. But this opinion is presented by an individual known as Jacob from Kefar Nevoraia, a town in northern Israel, in a text called *Genesis Rabba*—that is, a large Midrashic rabbinic collection that sits outside the Talmud of the land of Israel, from the 4th century C.E.—and while it is true that never in the rabbinic corpus is this individual Jacob accorded the title "rabbi," he clearly traveled in rabbinic circles, and this opinion, that fish require ritual slaughtering, makes it into a classical rabbinic text.

In light of these two illustrations, which could be multiplied, and in light of the general tenor forthcoming from the rabbinic corpus of texts, it is clear that the Pharisees did not see their continuation as a defeat of the other sects. Quite the contrary, given all that the Jewish community as a whole had endured—two revolts against Rome, destruction of the Temple, loss of Jerusalem—it appears that the Pharisees and their rabbinic successors saw room for the inclusion of their earlier competitors from the pre-70 destruction in the new post-Temple world that they are constructing anew. Differences of opinion are now acceptable, as the Mishna indicates, and no one will be ejected from the fraternity for holding a divergent judgment on a particular Halakhic issue or set of issues.

At this point, I want to present what I consider the major takeaway points of our course. Let us begin with the subject of *halakha* and state the following once more: Time and again we have sees that the legal opinion of the rabbis is the most lenient option available. Before the discovery of the Dead Sea Scrolls, we would have understood the rabbis as very strict interpreters of Jewish law. Some of this comes from the somewhat negative portrayal of their Pharisaic predecessors in the New Testament, though in general one can see from the Mishna and the later Talmudic material how many restrictions the rabbis held to; for example, in regard to Sabbath practice, recall that there are 39 individual actions prohibited on the Sabbath. But with the discovery of the Dead Sea Scrolls, especially when one reads the Halakhic texts such as the Damascus Document, the Halakhic Letter, and the Temple Scroll, one realizes how much stricter the Qumran sect was in its interpretation of Jewish law. To cite the most extreme instance, recall the prohibition against toileting on the Sabbath, as per Josephus's description of the Essenes.

Again, once more, approximately 1,000 years separates the Qumran copies of the Damascus Document found in Cave four, and the two medieval copies of this text, found in the Cairo genizah by Solomon Schechter. How did this text exist throughout this period, especially when we believe that the Pharisaic-rabbinic tradition eventually took hold as the normative one in the post-70 C.E. period? Or to word this differently: We have thousands upon thousands of pages of rabbinic literature, but not a hint that Jews continued to adhere to a different system of *halakha*; and yet they must have, for otherwise how can one explain the persistence of the Damascus Document into the Middle Ages? This also opens up the possibility for some continuation of the Sadducee tradition, in a *sub rosa* fashion, let's say, throughout the golden age of the rabbinic literature, only to emerge as Karaism in the 9th century. By the way, we have discussed the Karaites in their medieval manifestation, but I do not want to give the impression that they were a medieval sect only. Quite the contrary; the Karaites continue until today, though in smaller numbers, in Israel, in the former Soviet Union, and with one congregation in the United States, in San Francisco. Approximate population figures are 35,000 Karaites in Israel and 10,000 Karaites in the rest of the world.

Over the centuries, notwithstanding the official legal stance that forbade rabbanite Jews—that's the term we use for Jews who follow the rabbinic system—from marrying Karaites, in the main we know that rabbanite Jews and Karaites intermarried on a regular basis. Once more, by the way, this is information that we learn from the Cairo genizah medieval documents. In general, the rabbinic leaders of the rabbanite Jews have taken a liberal and understanding attitude towards the Karaites. The great medieval sage Maimonides, for example, wrote, with great sensitivity, that one could not blame the Karaites for the errors of their ways, that is, by rejecting the Oral Law and its concrete embodiment in the Talmud, because they merely were educated in this way by their parents.

Then a comment that we have stated several times: In light of our Dead Sea Scrolls research, we can no longer speak of the rabbinic tradition as the normative one in Judaism. Such was the view of scholars throughout Jewish history, well into the 20th century, and indeed this position still finds some adherents today. But the Scrolls lead us to conclude that there never was a normative position in Judaism during the period under discussion, and perhaps not for centuries afterward either. To be sure, we cannot say that the rabbis who produced the Mishna and the two Talmud*im* had the following of a large segment of the population. Quite possibly they were a closed circle, with only them and their colleagues and some adherents abiding by the rabbinic system. Eventually, of course, the rabbinic system did emerge as the norm, but our first real evidence for this may not be until the early Middle Ages, in places such as Spain of the 10th and 11th centuries. Back to our timeframe, though: The more we read our ancient texts, the more we realize how variegated Jewish life was during ancient times. The result of all this is a major paradigm shift in the study of ancient Judaism.

Turning one last time to Christianity, we emphasize again that many of the ideas and beliefs of the Qumran community appear in the Jesus movement as well. Most significantly, we note apocalypticism, which is prominent in the Dead Sea Scrolls, but which by and large vanished from the Jewish world, though this specific eschatological view persisted and indeed became an essential feature of Christianity. The Christian religion would follow its own course, separate from Judaism, but its indebtedness to Judaism, specifically of the Qumran type, is realized more and more upon our reading and studying the Dead Sea Scrolls. As one scholar once remarked, if we did not have the Dead Sea Scrolls, the New Testament would be our Dead Sea Scrolls.

And now a self-admission: You may have gained the sense during our course, even during this final lecture itself, that sometimes I hold that the rabbis emerged as the normative, mainstream construct within Judaism, while at other times—such as I have just done—I have emphasized that we cannot speak of a normative, mainstream anything for the period under consideration. If you have sensed this, then let me admit: Except for a few scholars on either side of the debate who hold firm to one opinion or the other, I believe that most scholars today are hesitant to surrender the long-held belief of rabbinic normativity, even when evidence such as we have presented in this course points in the other direction. The main issue before us is that we—we scholars and we laypeople—have been trained to read history, philosophy, theology, and more only through the eyes of the rabbis, both the ancient and the medieval, for their texts were the ones read and transmitted for more than 1,000 years. In the end, as so often happens in the study of antiquity, we simply do not have sufficient evidence to fully resolve this scholarly debate, and thus our questions remain. As one scholar has stated, all we have are islands of information in a sea of ignorance.

Finally, we consider a rabbinic tradition concerning the destruction of the Second Temple in 70 C.E. Looking back on the event at some distance, the rabbis asked: Why did this happen? Why was the Temple destroyed? Why was Jerusalem lost? Their response was *sinnat hinnam*, "senseless hatred." While we always possessed this view, embedded into the rabbinic literature, only after the discovery of the Dead Sea Scrolls did we come to realize its truth and its import. When the Qumran sectarians call themselves the "sons of light" and include other Jews in the category of the "sons of darkness," we see the enmity between the different groups. When we realize that a Jerusalem priest (the so-called Wicked Priest) attacked the Qumran group's leader (the Teacher of Righteousness) on Yom Kippur (the Day of Atonement), we again see the internecine hatred that existed. When we realize that the Halakhic Letter (4QMMT) needs to demonstrate the priority of the sect's legal positions, to the exclusion of the other approaches which are totally unacceptable, we see the sect's inability to embrace other views. Only my way is right, yours cannot be so. It may not be an exaggeration to see the Qumran community as a besieged group, one at odds with the more powerful Pharisee and Sadducee opponents, with the need to fight back with wrathful, even vengeful, words.

The Essenes opposed the Pharisees mainly on religious-Halakhic grounds—they were simply too liberal—and they opposed the Sadducees mainly on religious-political grounds, for the wrong line of priests was in control of both the Hasmonean kingdom and the Jerusalem Temple. As we have seen, the debates were not calm and collected, but rather replete with animosity and acrimony, exactly as is subsumed under this phrase *sinnat hinnam*, "senseless hatred." Even the New Testament books participate in this trend, with their very negative portrayal of the Pharisees especially.

Finally, just to relay a story narrated to us by Josephus; though first some Halakhic background. Another area of disagreement between the sects concerns how to perform a specific ritual on the holiday of Sukkot, whether the water used in a special water oblation ceremony should be poured on the altar (that's how the Pharisees held) or on the ground (that's how the

Sadducees held). When the Hasmonean priest-king Alexander Janneus performed the ceremony according to the Sadducee method, the crowd, convinced that the Pharisee system was the correct one, pelted the priest-king with their citrons, one of the four species used on the holiday of Sukkot. Incensed and in response, Josephus tells us that Alexander Janneus sent his army out and killed 6,000 Pharisees. This is the Alexander Janneus whom I referred to earlier in our lecture with a special hostility towards the Pharisees; and you can see here in this one instance how it played itself out.

All of this leads us to what is for me the main lesson that we can extract from our study of the Dead Sea Scrolls and from this entire period of Jewish history. Judaism at this time was ripe with sectarianism, with the different sects engaged in vitriol against each other, each believing that its way, and only its way, was the proper route to the worship of God. If I may be permitted a personal note upon which to close, let us stray far from this approach, and instead let us follow a different path, the one of religious pluralism. Let us recognize our denominational differences, but embrace them all as valid and appropriate ways to lead our lives, both our own lives and those of our neighbors.

Timeline

B.C.E.

c. 1200 .... Israel first appears in the historical record.

c. 1000–930 .... Period of Israel's United Monarchy under David and Solomon.

c. 965 .... Solomon constructs the First Temple.

c. 930–721 .... Kingdom of Israel, which ends in destruction by Assyria.

c. 930–586 .... Kingdom of Judah, which ends in destruction by Babylonia.

586–538 .... Babylonian Exile.

538 .... Cyrus the Great of Persia allows Jews to return to Judah and to rebuild Jerusalem and the Temple.

516 .... Second Temple completed.

331 .... Alexander the Great conquers the Persian Empire, including the land of Israel.

301–198 .... Ptolemy dynasty, based in Alexandria, Egypt, rules the land of Israel.

198–164 .... Seleucid dynasty, based in Antioch, Syria, rules the land of Israel.

175–164 .... Antiochus IV Epiphanes rules as Seleucid king, institutes anti-Jewish policies and persecutions.

164 .... Maccabean revolt results in independence for Judea and begins the Hasmonean dynasty.

c. 150 .... Founding of the *Yahad*, or Qumran sect.

134–104 .... Reign of Hasmonean king John Hyrcanus.

103–76 .... Reign of Hasmonean king Alexander Janneus.

63 .... Roman general Pompey captures Jerusalem.

37–4 .... King Herod the Great, a Hasmonean by marriage, rules Judea.

c. 6 .... Jesus is born in Bethlehem.

C.E.

6 .... Rule of the Hasmonean dynasty effectively ends; Judea is henceforth ruled directly by Roman prefects and procurators.

26–36 .... Pontius Pilate rules as Roman prefect of Judea.

c. 28 .... Jesus is baptized by John the Baptist and begins his ministry.

30 .... Jesus is crucified.

c. 47–64 .... Paul makes missionary journeys in the eastern Mediterranean.

65–70 .... Redaction of the Gospel of Mark.

66–73 .... First Jewish Revolt against Rome.

68 .... Qumran is destroyed by the Romans.

70 .... Second Temple is destroyed during the Roman assault on Jerusalem.

70–90 .... Redaction of the Gospels of Matthew and Luke.

73 .... Fall of Masada, the last holdout of the Zealots against the Roman legions.

90–100 .... Redaction of the Gospel of John.

132–135 .... Second Jewish Revolt against Rome, led by Simeon Bar Kokhba; Jews are barred from entering Jerusalem.

c. 150 .... The core of the Jewish canon (Torah, Prophets, Psalms) is fixed; other books' status remains pliable for some time.

c. 200	Redaction of the Mishna by R. Judah ha-Nasi.
313	Emperor Constantine issues the Edict of Milan, making Christianity a tolerated religion in the Roman Empire.
391	Emperor Theodosius makes Christianity the official religion of the Roman Empire.
c. 400	Redaction of the Talmud of the Land of Israel (a.k.a. Talmud Yerushalmi, or Jerusalem Talmud).
476	Fall of the Western Roman Empire; the Eastern Empire, or Byzantium, survives until 1453.
c. 500	Redaction of the Babylonian Talmud (a.k.a. Talmud Bavli).
890	Ben Ezra Synagogue is built in Cairo.
1000–1250	Zenith of the Jewish community of Cairo and heyday of the documents in the Cairo genizah, including the two copies of the Damascus Document.
1896	First Cairo genizah documents arrive in England for study by Solomon Schechter; among these are copies of the book of Ben Sira and the Damascus Document.

Spring 1947	First scrolls are discovered in Qumran Cave 1.
July 1947	Mar Samuel obtains four of the original Dead Sea Scrolls.
November 1947	United Nations approves the partition plan for Palestine; Eliezer Sukenik purchases three of the original Dead Sea Scrolls on behalf of the Hebrew University of Jerusalem.
February 1948	Mar Samuel entrusts publication of the scrolls in his possession to scholars associated with the American Schools of Oriental Research (ASOR).
May 1948	Modern state of Israel is proclaimed; seven Arab nations, including Jordan, attack Israel; six of the first seven scrolls are published by Sukenik and ASOR scholars.
1948–1956	Systematic exploration of the caves at Qumran, with 10 additional caves, numbers 2–11, yielding documents; Roland de Vaux excavates the nearby site of Khirbet Qumran.
1954	International team of scholars is established to publish the growing cache of Dead Sea Scrolls; Yigael Yadin purchases four of the original Dead Sea Scrolls from Mar Samuel via an ad placed in *The Wall Street Journal*.

1955	First volume of the Discoveries in the Judaean Desert series appears, including all Cave 1 fragments.
1956	Genesis Apocryphon, the most brittle and difficult to read of the original seven scrolls, is published.
1967	Six-Day War results in Israel gaining control of all of Jerusalem and the West Bank (including the site of Qumran); the Copper Scroll is placed on display at Amman, Jordan; Yadin obtains the Temple Scroll.
1977	Yadin publishes the Temple Scroll.
1984	Elisha Qimron and John Strugnell announce the existence of the Halakhic Letter.
1991	Ben Zion Wacholder and Martin Abegg reconstruct the unpublished scrolls by using a privately distributed concordance; the Huntington Library announces that it possesses a complete set of photographs of the Dead Sea Scrolls; due to slow publication of the scrolls, the Israeli Antiquities Authority removes Strugnell and appoints Emanuel Tov head of the publishing team.
1994	Qimron and Strugnell publish the Halakhic Letter.

2002 .... Official publication of the Dead Sea Scrolls in the Discoveries in the Judaean Desert series is complete.

2007 .... Discovery and publication of the Vision of Gabriel stone inscription.

Glossary

Aleppo Codex: Earliest extant codex of the Hebrew Bible; completed about 930 C.E. and now housed in Jerusalem.

American Schools of Oriental Research (ASOR): Academic research center in Jerusalem devoted to the study of the Bible, archaeology, and ancient history.

Amman Archaeological Museum: Main archaeological museum in Jordan that houses the Copper Scroll and some other texts.

anti-language: Language used by a specific group within a society to distinguish itself from the larger population.

apocalyptic: Subbranch of eschatology, with specific adherence to the notion that a cataclysmic battle will vault humanity into the eschaton.

Aramaic: Semitic language that spread in late antiquity and thus became the lingua franca of many Near East peoples, including the Jews.

Babylonian Exile: Period following the destruction of the First Temple in Jerusalem, 586–538 B.C.E.

Babylonian Talmud: Encyclopedic collection of rabbinic law and lore, completed around 500 C.E. in Babylonia.

Babylonians: Major power of Mesopotamia, responsible for the destruction of the First Temple and the conquest of Judah in 586 B.C.E.

B.C.E.: Before the Common Era.

Belial: Hebrew term referring to Satan.

Ben Ezra Synagogue: Medieval synagogue in Cairo, home of the Cairo genizah.

Ben Sira: Ancient Jewish poetic composition from about 180 B.C.E. that is canonized by Christians, though not by Jews.

Biblical Archaeology Society: Organization, located in Washington DC that seeks to bring archaeological discoveries and biblical research to an educated lay audience.

Boethusians: Offshoot of the Sadducees mentioned in the Talmud; unfortunately, little is known about this group.

Caesarea: Major harbor city on the Mediterranean coast of Israel.

Cairo genizah: Storeroom of the Ben Ezra Synagogue in which approximately 200,000 manuscripts of the medieval period were found.

canon: Set of books considered to be authoritative by a particular religious group.

Capernaum: Village on the shore of the Sea of Galilee in northern Israel.

carbon-14: Radioactive isotope of carbon whose half-life can be used to date any organic material.

C.E.: Common Era.

Chaldeans: Term used by some biblical writers to refer to the Babylonians.

Christ: Greek for "messiah," literally "anointed one"; applied to Jesus by Christians.

Christianity: Movement that developed in early Judaism and became its own religion, centered on the messiahhood of Jesus.

church fathers: Early Christian theologians, especially those who lived in the 2nd–5th centuries C.E.

compatabilism: Doctrine that holds that both free will and predestination are at work in human lives.

Dead Sea Scrolls: Cache of 930 documents found at Qumran.

Diaspora: Collective Jewish community living outside the land of Israel.

Discoveries in the Judaean Desert (DJD): Official publication series of the Dead Sea Scrolls published by Oxford University Press.

Dor: Harbor city on the Mediterranean coast of Israel.

Dositheans: Ancient Samaritan sect.

Ebionites: Jewish Christian sect that accepted Jesus as messiah but did not believe him to be divine.

École Biblique et Archéologique Française: Academic research center in Jerusalem established and administered by Dominican priests.

Edom: Country to the south of ancient Israel.

Ein Gedi: Oasis site 33 kilometers south of Qumran on the shore of the Dead Sea.

Enoch: Ancient Jewish composition, dated to the 3rd–2nd centuries B.C.E., that purports to describe the ancient hero Enoch's visit to heaven based on the reference in Genesis 5:24.

eschatology: Belief in the end of days, an end time, or the eschaton.

Essenes: Ancient Jewish sect; most scholars identify the Qumran sect with this group.

Ethiopian: Ancient Semitic language, also called Geez, now used only as a liturgical language by Ethiopic Christians.

Gamla: City in northeastern ancient Israel.

Genesis Rabba: Collection of legends related to the book of Genesis, dated circa 400 C.E.

Halakah: Hebrew term for Jewish law.

Hanukkah: Holiday established to celebrate the successful Maccabean revolt against the Seleucids in 164 B.C.E.

Hasmoneans: Dynasty founded by the Maccabees that lasted from 164 B.C.E. to 6 C.E.; they ruled first as high priests, then later as kings.

Hebrew: Ancient Semitic language in which the vast majority of the Dead Sea Scrolls are written.

Hellenism: General term for the spread of Greek culture, science, architecture, philosophy, and so forth into the Near East.

Herodion: Mausoleum of Herod, 12 kilometers south of Jerusalem.

Huntington Library: Educational and research institution located in San Marino, California, whose collections include a complete set of photographs of the Dead Sea Scrolls.

Idumea: Name of Edom in late antiquity; land to the south of Israel.

Israel, kingdom of: Kingdom established on the death of Solomon (c. 930 B.C.E.) comprising the nine northern tribes; it was destroyed in 721 B.C.E.

Israel Antiquities Authority: Official branch of the modern Israeli government responsible for all archaeological work in the country.

Israel Museum: Main archaeological museum in Jerusalem. It includes a special pavilion called the Shrine of the Book that houses and displays the major Dead Sea Scrolls.

Jericho: Nearest city in Israel to Qumran.

Jerusalem: Capital of Israel; site of the Temple.

Jordanian Department of Antiquities: Official branch of the modern Jordanian government responsible for all archaeological work in the country.

Jubilees: Jewish composition of the 2nd century B.C.E. that retells the stories of Genesis and Exodus via the framework of 50-year periods of history known as jubilees.

Judah, kingdom of: Kingdom established on the death of Solomon (c. 930 B.C.E.) comprising the three southern tribes; it was destroyed in 586 B.C.E.

Kabbalah: Jewish mysticism.

Karaism: Jewish movement that developed in the 8th century C.E. that denied the Oral Law and thus may descend from the Sadducees.

Karaites: Adherents to Karaism.

Khirbet Qumran: Literally "ruin of Qumran"; the archaeological site near the Qumran caves.

Kittim: Hebrew term used to refer to Crete in the Bible, though used as a coded term in the Dead Sea Scrolls for the Romans.

Leningrad Codex: Second oldest extant codex of the Hebrew Bible, dated 1009–1010 C.E. and now housed in St. Petersburg, Russia.

linguistic ideology: Anthropological notion that sees social, cultural, and/or political values reflected in language usage.

Maccabees: Family of Jews who led the successful revolt against the Seleucids in 164 B.C.E.

Masada: Remote fortress in the Judean Desert; last outpost of the Zealots in their revolt against the Romans in 73 C.E.

Masora: Hebrew term for the oral reading tradition transmitted by Jewish tradents from the biblical period into the early medieval period.

Masoretic Text: The authoritative text produced by the Masora tradents around 800 C.E.

messiah: Derived from Hebrew *mešiah*, "anointed one," eventually understood to be an individual who will vault humanity into the eschatological age.

mezuza: Small scrolls containing several biblical passages that are affixed to doorposts, in conformity with Deuteronomy 6:9 and 11:20.

Mishna: First codification of Jewish law, redacted by Rabbi Judah ha-Nasi around 200 C.E.

Modi'in: Town in ancient Israel that was home of the Maccabees.

Mount Gerizim: Mountain in central Israel; site of the Samaritan Temple in antiquity.

Nahal Hever: Wadi near Ein Gedi; documents written by Simeon Bar Kokhba and his colleagues were found in caves nearby.

Nash Papyrus: Small text containing the Ten Commandments (among other biblical texts) and dated to circa 100 B.C.E.; obtained in Egypt in 1898, it is now housed in the Cambridge University Library.

Nazareth: City in northern Israel; home of Jesus.

neo-Aristotelianism: Philosophical movement in the Middle Ages and earlier that adhered to the thought of Aristotle.

neo-Platonism: Philosophical movement in the Middle Ages and earlier that adhered to the thought of Plato.

neutron activation: Laboratory test used by archaeologists to determine the origin of the clay used in pots, vessels, and other objects.

New Testament: Collection of books canonized by Christianity detailing the lives of Jesus and his early followers.

Oral Law: Rabbinic concept of a legal tradition that originates at Sinai alongside the Written Law, or Torah.

ostracon: Inscribed piece of pottery.

Palestine Archaeology Museum (PAM): Museum in East Jerusalem where the Dead Sea Scrolls were taken for study and publication; later renamed the Rockefeller Museum.

pesher: Method of interpretation of biblical books, attested in approximately 20 Dead Sea Scrolls, in which the original historical context is disregarded and instead the ancient text is understood as speaking to the present. This type of exegesis is seen in the New Testament as well.

Pharisees: Ancient Jewish sect that later emerged as the rabbinic movement.

Ptolemies: Successor kingdom to Alexander the Great centered in Alexandria, Egypt.

Qumran: Site of the discovery of the Dead Sea Scrolls, situated on the northwestern shore of the Dead Sea.

rabbi: Hebrew for "my master"—that is, a master of the law.

Rockefeller Museum: *See* **Palestine Archaeology Museum**.

Roman Empire: The great ruling power of the Mediterranean basin, including the land of Israel, from 63 B.C.E.

Sabbath: Weekly day of rest in Judaism, occurring every Saturday.

Sadducees: Ancient Jewish sect that emphasized sacrificial worship of God, led by a priestly class.

Samaria: Capital of the northern kingdom of Israel and, by extension, the central hill country region of the land of Israel.

Samaritans: Offshoot of Judaism based in the area of Samaria; its adherents believed that Mount Gerizim was the place where God was to be worshipped, not Mount Zion in Jerusalem.

Satan: Hebrew for "adversary"; name of the embodiment of evil in early Judaism and Christianity.

Seleucids: Successor kingdom to Alexander the Great based in Antioch, present-day northern Syria/southern Turkey.

Septuagint: Translation of the Torah into Greek accomplished by the Jews of Alexandria around 250 B.C.E.

Shavu'ot: Literally "weeks"; Jewish holiday that occurs seven weeks (about 50 days) after Passover; thus it is also known as Pentecost.

Shrine of the Book: Special pavilion at the Israel Museum that houses and displays the major Dead Sea Scrolls.

Sicarri: Alternative term for Zealots.

synagogue: Literally "place of coming together"; locus of Jewish worship and study from the 1st century B.C.E. onward.

synoptic gospels: Term applied to the Gospels of Matthew, Mark, and Luke, which narrate essentially the same biography of Jesus, though with crucial differences.

Talmud: Literally "learning, study"; refers to the two great collections of rabbinic writings: the Talmud of the Land of Israel and the Babylonian Talmud.

Talmud of the Land of Israel: Encyclopedic collection of rabbinic law and lore completed around 400 C.E. in Tiberias in northern Israel.

Targum (pl. **Targumim**): Aramaic translation of a biblical book.

Teacher of Righteousness: Code name for the leader (perhaps founder) of the Qumran sect, or *Yahad*.

tefillin: Ritual objects consisting of leather straps and small boxes containing tiny scrolls with select biblical verses, used by Jews in the daily prayer service; usually rendered into English as "phylacteries."

Temple: Site of sacrificial worship of the God of Israel in Jerusalem until its destruction in 70 C.E.

Therapeutae: Ascetic group in Egypt.

Tiberias: City in northern Israel on the shore of the Sea of Galilee.

Torah: Literally "teaching"; refers to the first five books of the Bible (also called the Pentateuch, literally "five scrolls"), which form the first part of the biblical canon in both Judaism and Christianity. For Jews, these five books, which contain the most familiar stories of Genesis and Exodus along with the legal and cultic instructions in Exodus and Deuteronomy, remain at the core of religious life, liturgy, and tradition.

Tosefta: Companion volume to the Mishna—that is, a parallel collection of Halakah.

Wadi Muraba'at: Wadi near Ein Gedi; documents written by Simeon Bar Kokhba and his colleagues were found in nearby caves.

Wadi Qumran: Dry river bed (though it flows during the winter rainy season) that flows in the vicinity of Qumran.

Wicked Priest: Code name for the opponent of the *Yahad*, presumably referring to one of the Hasmonean leaders who assumed the position of high priest.

Yahad: Literally "community"; the self-designation of the Qumran sect.

Yahweh: Proper name of the God of Israel, traditionally rendered as "LORD" in English.

YHWH: English rendering of the four-letter name of the God of Israel.

Yom Kippur: Day of Atonement, occurring on month seven, day 10.

Zealots: Group of Jewish revolutionaries who led the First Jewish Revolt against Rome (66–73 C.E.).

Zoroastrianism: National religion of ancient Persia, characterized most of all by dualism and recognizing two gods: one embodying goodness and one embodying evil.

Biographical Notes

Premodern Individuals

Aaron (dates unknown): Brother of Moses.

Alexander Janneus (r. 103–76 B.C.E.): Hasmonean king.

Alexander the Great (r. 333–323 B.C.E.): King of Macedon, conqueror of the entire Near East and beyond.

Antiochus IV (r. 175–164 B.C.E.): Seleucid king.

Aristobulus I (r. 104–103 B.C.E.): Hasmonean king.

Augustine (354–430 C.E.): Church father.

Augustus Caesar (r. 27 B.C.E.–14 C.E.): Roman emperor.

Clement (c. 150–217 C.E.): Church father.

David (r. c. 1000–c. 965 B.C.E.): Second king of Israel.

Elazar ben Nahmani (dates unknown): Individual mentioned in a Qumran ostracon who apparently served as the overseer or bursar for the *Yahad*.

Eusebius (c. 260–340 C.E.): Church father.

Hananiah Nothos (dates unknown): Individual mentioned in a Qumran text as one who was punished for misconduct; since personal names are exceedingly rare in the Dead Sea Scrolls, he serves as the model average *Yahad* member in scholarly discourse.

Herod (r. 37–4 B.C.E.): Hasmonean king by marriage.

Herodotus (c. 484–c. 425 B.C.E.): Ancient Greek historian.

Jacob of Kefar Nevoraia (dates unknown): Individual named in the rabbinic text Genesis Rabba.

James (fl. 1st century C.E.): Brother of Jesus, leader of the Judaizing Christian movement.

Jason (fl. early 2nd century B.C.E.): Jewish priest who contested for the high priesthood.

Jerome (c. 347–420 C.E.): Church father who translated the Bible into Latin.

Jesus (fl. 1st century C.E.): Messianic figure whose followers launched the Christian movement.

John Hyrcanus (r. 134–104 B.C.E.): Hasmonean king.

John the Baptist (fl. 1st century C.E.): Early follower of Jesus.

Jonathan Maccabee (r. 161–143 B.C.E.): Hasmonean high priest.

Josephus (c. 37–c. 100 C.E.): Ancient Jewish historian whose voluminous writings provide essential information for the reconstruction of Jewish history in late antiquity.

Judah ha-Nasi (fl. late 2nd–early 3rd century C.E.): Leading rabbinic figure; compiler and redactor of the Mishna.

Livy (59 B.C.E.–17 C.E.): Ancient Roman historian.

Maimonides (1135–1204 C.E.): Great medieval Jewish philosopher, legal expert, and physician; lived in Spain and Egypt.

Malachi (fl. c. 450 B.C.E.): Last of the biblical prophets.

Menelaus (fl. early 2nd century B.C.E.): Jewish priest who contested for the high priesthood.

Moses (dates unknown): Prophet and leader of the Israelites in the books of Exodus through Deuteronomy.

Origen (185–254 C.E.): Church father.

Paul (fl. 1st century C.E.): Dominant figure in the earliest years of Christianity; leader of the non-Judaizing Christians.

Philo (c. 20 B.C.E.–c. 50 C.E.): Ancient Jewish philosopher in Alexandria.

Pilate (r. 26–36 C.E.): Roman governor of Judea.

Pliny the Elder (24–79 C.E.): Roman polymath (scientist, historian, naturalist, and admiral in the Roman navy); wrote *Natural History*.

Pompey (106–48 B.C.E.): Roman general; first Roman authority to control Judea, starting in 63 B.C.E.

Rabban Gamaliel (fl. 1st century C.E.): Major rabbinic figure mentioned in the New Testament; teacher of Paul.

Rabbi Meir (fl. 2nd century C.E.): Major rabbinic figure.

Saul (r. c. 1020–1000 B.C.E.): First king of Israel.

Simeon Bar Kokhba (fl. 2nd century C.E.): Leader of the Second Jewish Revolt against the Romans (132–135 C.E.).

Solomon (c. 965–930 B.C.E.): Third king of Israel and son of David.

Thomas Aquinas (1225–1274 C.E.): Medieval Christian theologian and philosopher.

Timotheus I (fl. c. 800 C.E.): Nestorian patriarch.

William of Tyre (c. 1130–1185): Medieval Christian prelate and historian.

Zadok (fl. c. 10th century B.C.E.): High priest in Jerusalem during the reigns of David and Solomon.

Modern Individuals

Abegg, Martin (b. 1950): Assisted Ben Zion Wacholder in the publication of *A Preliminary Edition of the Unpublished Dead Sea Scrolls* while still a graduate student at Hebrew Union College in Cincinnati; now a professor at Trinity Western University.

Albright, W. F. (1891–1971): Doyen of American biblical archaeologists; specialist in an array of ancient Near Eastern subjects; long-time professor at Johns Hopkins University.

Allegro, John (1923–1988): Professor at the University of Manchester and an early researcher into the Dead Sea Scrolls, he published all the texts assigned to him with alacrity.

Baker, H. Wright (fl. 20th century): Expert at the Manchester College of Science and Technology who cut the Copper Scroll into single sheets, thereby allowing scholars to read the text.

Bar-Adon, Pesach (1907–1985): Israeli archaeologist who explored caves in the general vicinity of Qumran off and on during 1971, 1972, and 1982, including a large cave near Cave 11 that yielded remains from the Hellenistic and Roman periods. *See also* **Jones, Vendyl**.

Betz, Otto (1917–2005): German Professor of New Testament studies who was a leading proponent of a John the Baptist–Dead Sea Scrolls connection.

Broshi, Magen (b. 1929): Israeli archaeologist and former curator of the Shrine of the Book (Israel Museum) who, together with Hanan Eshel, established a clear link between the Qumran caves and Khirbet Qumran, especially by discovering an ancient trodden path that connects the two.

Cansdale, Lena (b. 20th century): Independent scholar who believes that Qumran was an important commercial center on a north-south trade route through the Jordan Valley and the Dead Sea with no connection to the scrolls found in the nearby caves.

Cross, Frank Moore (b. 1921): Leading professor of the Bible at Harvard University; active in the publication of biblical manuscripts from among the Dead Sea Scrolls.

Donceel, Robert (b. 20th century): Belgian archaeologist who, with wife and colleague Pauline Donceele-Voute, posits that Qumran was a villa inhabited by wealthy individuals with no connection to the scrolls found in the nearby caves.

Donceel-Voute, Pauline (b. 20th century): *See* **Donceel, Robert**.

Driver, G. R. (1892–1975): Leading biblical scholar at Oxford University who believed that the Dead Sea Scrolls, especially the War Scroll, are evidence of composition by the Zealot group. *See also* **Rabin, Chaim**.

Dupont-Sommer, André (1900–1983): French scholar who first argued the *Yahad*-Essene connection in detail, especially in his monograph *Aperçus préliminaires sur les manuscrits de la Mer Morte*.

Eisenman, Robert (b. 1937): Professor at California State University at Long Beach who believes that many, if not most, of the scrolls date to the 1st century C.E. and that the Teacher of Righteousness is to be identified with James, brother of Jesus.

Eshel, Esther (b. 20th century): Professor of Ancient Jewish Literature at Bar-Ilan University; excellent representative of the younger generation of Dead Sea Scrolls researchers.

Eshel, Hanan (b. 1958): Israeli archaeologist and professor at Bar-Ilan University who, together with Magen Broshi, established a clear link between the Qumran caves and Khirbet Qumran, especially by discovering an ancient trodden path that connects the two.

Ginzberg, Louis (1873–1953): Leading Professor of Talmud at the Jewish Theological Seminary of America in New York who produced the basic interpretation of the Damascus Document, soon after its discovery in the Cairo genizah, under the title *Eine unbekannte jüdische Sekte* ("An Unknown Jewish Sect").

Golb, Norman (b. 1928): Professor at the University of Chicago who believes that the scrolls have no connection to Khirbet Qumran nor to the Essenes; rather, he opines that the scrolls represent the library of the Jerusalem Temple.

Hirschfeld, Yizhar (b. 20th century): Israeli archaeologist who claims that Khirbet Qumran constitutes the remains of a fortress; he places the Essene community referred to by Pliny the Elder in the cliffs above Ein Gedi. *See also* **Magen, Yitzhak** and **Peleg, Yuval**.

Humbert, Jean-Baptiste (b. 1940): French archaeologist and official heir to the materials excavated at Qumran by Roland de Vaux; he developed a hybrid view concerning Khirbet Qumran, suggesting that the site began as a villa rustica but that the Dead Sea Scrolls sect later came and occupied the site.

Jones, Vendyl (b. 1930): American explorer who assisted Pesach Bar-Adon and then continued to explore caves in the vicinity of Qumran in 1985–1986.

Kando (a.k.a. **Khalil Iskander Shahin**; fl. 20th century): Bethlehem antiquities dealer who served as intermediary between the Bedouin discoverers of the Dead Sea Scrolls and scholars in Jerusalem.

Magen, Yitzhak (b. 20th century): Israeli archaeologist who collaborates with Yizhar Hirschfeld.

Magness, Jodi (b. 20th century): Archaeologist and professor at the University of North Carolina at Chapel Hill who wrote the standard work *The Archaeology of Qumran and the Dead Sea Scrolls*.

Milik, J. T. (1922–2006): Polish-born priest who lived mainly in Paris; a major Dead Sea Scrolls scholar, he was heralded by *Time* magazine in 1956 as "the fastest man with a fragment."

O'Callaghan, Jose (1922–2001): Spanish Jesuit scholar who believed that 7Q5, a fragmentary text written in Greek, is a copy of Mark 6:52–53, thus connecting at least one of the scrolls very directly to the New Testament.

Peleg, Yuval (b. 20th century): Israeli archaeologist who collaborates with Yizhar Hirschfeld.

Petrach, Joseph (b. 20th century): Israeli archaeologist who explored dozens of caves in the Dead Sea region between 1984 and 1986 and then again in 1991. He found archaeological remains from the Second Temple period in 17 such caves.

Qimron, Elisha (b. 1943): Israeli scholar at Ben-Gurion University and expert in Qumran Hebrew who, with John Strugnell, is responsible for the publication of the Halakhic Letter. He sued Hershel Shanks in an Israeli court over the latter's publication of a reconstructed edition of this text.

Rabin, Chaim (1915–1996): Leading Professor of the Hebrew Language at the Hebrew University who believed that the Dead Sea Scrolls, especially the War Scroll, are artifacts of the Zealot group. *See also* **Driver, G. R.**

Renan, Ernst (1823–1892): Major French scholar who traced connections between the Essenes and early Christianity.

Roitman, Adolfo (b. 20th century): Curator of the Shrine of the Book at the Israel Museum; author and editor of *A Day at Qumran*.

Rossi, Azariah dei (1511–1578): Major figure of the Renaissance, a Jewish savant of 16th-century Italy, and the first to write a critical history of the Jews in ancient times using all available sources (including classical historians and church fathers, who had written in Greek and Latin).

Samuel, Mar (1907–1995): Head of the Syrian Orthodox Church in Jerusalem who at one point owned four of the first seven Dead Sea Scrolls to emerge from Cave 1.

Schechter, Solomon (1847–1915): Reader of Hebrew at Cambridge University, he identified the Hebrew original of Ben Sira among the documents of the Cairo genizah; published the Damascus Document, also found in the Cairo genizah; and was later president of the Jewish Theological Seminary of America.

Schiffman, Lawrence (b. 1948): Professor at New York University, leading expert on the Dead Sea Scrolls, proponent of Qumran-Sadducee connections, and author of *Reclaiming the Dead Sea Scrolls*.

Schniedewind, William (b. 1962): Professor of the Bible at the University of California, Los Angeles, who developed the notion that Qumran Hebrew served as an anti-language for the *Yahad*.

Schweitzer, Albert (1875–1965): Physician, humanist, and scholar who wrote about the uniqueness of Jesus and thus opposed the historical Jesus trend among scholars.

Shanks, Hershel (b. 1930): Founder and director of the Biblical Archaeology Society in Washington DC, he led the crusade for the release of the unpublished Dead Sea Scrolls during the 1980s and was sued by Elisha Qimron in an Israeli court over the publication of the Halakhic Letter.

Singer, Margaret (1921–2003): Clinical psychologist and professor at the University of California, Berkeley, who studied the use of in-group language among contemporary cults.

Stegemann, Hartmut (1933–2005): German scholar of New Testament studies who developed a unique way to correlate manuscript fragments with one another, mainly by looking at their physical properties.

Strugnell, John (1930–2007): Professor at Harvard University and the youngest member of the original international team of scholars entrusted with the publication of the Dead Sea Scrolls; brought Elisha Qimron on board to assist him in the publication of the Halakhic Letter.

Sukenik, Eliezer (1889–1953): Leading Israeli archaeologist of the Hebrew University who obtained and published three of the first seven Dead Sea Scrolls to surface; he is also the father of Yigael Yadin.

Sussman, Yaakov (b. 1931): Professor of Talmud at the Hebrew University who has proposed Essene-Boethusian connections.

Tabor, James (b. 1946): Professor at the University of North Carolina at Charlotte who explored Qumran with Joseph Zias and discovered a latrine about 500 meters northwest of the community center.

Theiring, Barbara (b. 1930): Independent scholar who believes that the Dead Sea Scrolls originated in the 1st century C.E. and have specific connections to early Christianity; she even claims that the Teacher of Righteousness is John the Baptist and that the Wicked Priest is Jesus.

Tolkien, J. R. R. (1892–1973): Professor of Anglo-Saxon and Old English at Oxford University and author of *The Lord of the Rings* and other major literary works; he is relevant to this course for his exemplary attention to language in the creation of a literary text.

Tov, Emanuel (b. 1941): Professor of Bible at the Hebrew University and expert in the Septuagint and the transmission of the biblical text through the ages, he was appointed head of the Dead Sea Scrolls publication committee in 1991 and oversaw the completion of the Discoveries in the Judaean Desert series.

Vaux, Roland de (1903–1971): French Dominican priest, director of the École Biblique et Archéologique Française in Jerusalem, and director of the excavations at Qumran in 1951–1956.

Vermes, Geza (b. 1924): Hungarian-born Professor of Ancient Judaism at Oxford University, leading Dead Sea Scrolls researcher, and editor and translator of *The Complete Dead Sea Scrolls in English*.

Wacholder, Ben Zion (b. 1921): Professor at Hebrew Union College in Cincinnati and expert on the Dead Sea Scrolls who, with Martin Abegg, published *A Preliminary Edition of the Unpublished Dead Sea Scrolls* (1991) based on a privately circulated concordance of the documents.

Weinfeld, Moshe (1925–2009): Professor of Bible at the Hebrew University, he identified 4Q434 fragment 2 as a precursor to the later rabbinic formulation of the grace after meals.

Wilson, Edmund (1895–1972): American literary critic who popularized the Dead Sea Scrolls via an essay in *The New Yorker* in 1955 and a book that appeared later that year, *The Scrolls of the Dead Sea*.

Wise, Michael (b. 20th century): Professor at the University of Chicago who believes that 4Q285 refers to a "pierced messiah" and thus serves as a precursor to the Jesus story.

Yadin, Yigael (1917–1984): Both a leading general in the Israeli army and a leading historian and archaeologist, he was a major figure in Dead Sea Scrolls scholarship. He published the Temple Scroll and was the son of Eliezer Sukenik.

Zeitlin, Solomon (1886–1976): Professor of Ancient Judaism at Dropsie College in Philadelphia who went against the scholarly consensus by proclaiming that the scrolls were of medieval origin.

Zias, Joseph: Israeli archaeologist who, together with James Tabor, explored Qumran and discovered a latrine about 500 meters northwest of the community center.

Bibliography

Abegg, Martin G., Jr. "The Calendar at Qumran." In *The Judaism of Qumran: A Systemic Reading of the Dead Sea Scrolls*, edited by Alan J. Avery-Peck, Jacob Neusner, and Bruce Chilton, 145–172. Leiden, Netherlands: Brill, 2001. A clear presentation of the complex issues of the calendar at Qumran and how it differed from the calendar that emerged as the standard one in Judaism.

Abegg, Martin G., Jr., Peter W. Flint, and Eugene C. Ulrich. *The Dead Sea Scrolls Bible: The Oldest Known Bible Translated for the First Time into English*. San Francisco: Harper, 1999. All of the biblical scrolls from Qumran represented in English translation.

Brooke, George J. *The Dead Sea Scrolls and the New Testament*. Minneapolis, MN: Fortress, 2005. A fine survey of all the relevant issues connecting the Qumran texts with early Christianity.

Charlesworth, James H., ed. *Jesus and the Dead Sea Scrolls*. New York: Doubleday, 1992. A collection of essays exploring connections between the *Yahad* and the Jesus movement.

Cohen, Shaye J. D. *Josephus in Galilee and Rome: His Vita and Development as a Historian*. Leiden, Netherlands: Brill, 1979. An investigation into Josephus as a historian, with a focus on his autobiography, *Vita*.

Collins, John J. *Apocalypticism in the Dead Sea Scrolls*. London: Routledge, 1997. An excellent survey of all the relevant Qumran apocalyptic texts, situated within the context of other Jewish apocalyptic trends.

Feldman, Louis. "Flavius Josephus Revisited: The Man, His Writings, and His Significance." *Aufstieg und Niedergang der Römischen Welt* 21 (1984): 763–862.

Flusser, David. *Judaism and the Origins of Christianity.* Jerusalem: Magnes, 1988. A basic survey of all the relevant issues, with special focus on the intersections between the *Yahad*, the Essenes, and early Christianity.

García Martínez, Florentino, and Eibert J. C. Tigchelaar. *The Dead Sea Scrolls Study Edition.* 2 vols. Grand Rapids, MI: Eerdmans, 1997. The complete Dead Sea Scrolls corpus, with Hebrew (or Aramaic) text and English translation on facing pages.

Golb, Norman. *Who Wrote the Dead Sea Scrolls? The Search for the Secret of Qumran.* New York: Scribner, 1995. The main challenge to the standard view that the scrolls were produced by the people at Qumran.

Horgan, Maurya P. *Pesharim: Qumran Interpretation of Biblical Books.* Washington, DC: Catholic Biblical Association, 1979. A convenient collection of the all the *pesher* texts in English translation and with extensive comments.

Jaffee, Martin S. *Early Judaism.* Upper Saddle River, NJ: Prentice Hall, 1997. A superb introduction to Judaism as a religious system and to the varieties of Judaism present in late antiquity that uses a social-scientific methodology, as opposed to the usual historical approach.

Knohl, Israel. "The Messiah Son of Joseph: 'Gabriel's Revelation' and the Birth of a New Messianic Model." *Biblical Archaeology Review* 34, no. 5 (September/October 2008): 58–62, 78. A rather speculative theory about the Vision of Gabriel, but this article presents the text in English translation for the first time. See also the Yardeni article.

Lefkovits, Judah K. *The Copper Scroll (3Q15): A Reevaluation; A New Reading, Translation, and Commentary.* Leiden, Netherlands: Brill, 2000. Massive, 600-page study of the enigmatic Copper Scroll.

Magness, Jodi. *The Archaeology of Qumran and the Dead Sea Scrolls.* Grand Rapids, MI: Eerdmans, 2002.

Neusner, Jacob. *Introduction to Rabbinic Literature*. New York: Doubleday, 1994. A survey of the basic rabbinic texts (Mishna, Talmud, etc.), plus a synthesis of the system as a whole.

Polliack, Meira, ed. *Karaite Judaism: A Guide to Its History and Literary Sources*. Leiden, Netherlands: Brill, 2003. A collection of scholarly essays about the Karaites, who arose during the early medieval period as a challenge to rabbinic hegemony.

Qimron, Elisha. *The Hebrew of the Dead Sea Scrolls*. Atlanta, GA: Scholars, 1986. The basic grammar of Qumran Hebrew.

Rendsburg, Gary A. "Language at Qumran (with a Trial Cut [1QS])." In *The Dead Sea Scrolls at 60: The Scholarly Contributions of NYU Faculty and Alumni*, edited by L. H. Schiffman. Leiden, Netherlands: Brill, in press. An article that builds on Schniedewind's understanding of Qumran Hebrew as an anti-language, with a focus on the Community Rule.

———. "Linguistic and Stylistic Notes to the Hazon Gabriel Inscription." *Dead Sea Discoveries* 16 (2009): 107–116. An article that addresses some language and stylistic issues in the Vision of Gabriel inscription.

———. "*lśwh* in 1QS 7.15." *Journal for the Study of the Pseudepigrapha* 5 (1989): 83–94. An article that treats in detail a difficult word in the Community Rule (1QS), column 7, line 15.

Roitman, Adolfo, ed. *A Day at Qumran: The Dead Sea Sect and Its Scrolls*. Jerusalem: Israel Museum, 1997. A collection of essays that nicely portrays daily life at Qumran.

Schiffman, Lawrence H. *From Text to Tradition: A History of Second Temple and Rabbinic Judaism*. Hoboken, NJ: KTAV, 1991. A basic introduction to Jewish history during the Hellenistic and Roman periods, with a focus on the emergent rabbinic tradition in the last section of the book.

———. *Reclaiming the Dead Sea Scrolls*. Philadelphia: Jewish Publication Society, 1994. An excellent introduction to the subject, with a special emphasis on contextualizing the Dead Sea Scrolls within the larger world of Jewish religious life, theological beliefs, and ritual practices.

Schniedewind, William M. "Qumran Hebrew as An Antilanguage." *Journal of Biblical Literature* 118 (1999): 235–252. The article that launched a new approach to Qumran Hebrew, understanding the unusual grammatical features and lexical usages to reflect a purposeful linguistic ideology.

Shanks, Hershel, ed. *The Dead Sea Scrolls after Forty Years*. Washington, DC: Biblical Archaeology Society, 1991. Four clear discussions presented at a public event at the Smithsonian Institution in 1990.

———. *Understanding the Dead Sea Scrolls: A Reader from the Biblical Archaeology Review*. New York: Random House, 1992. A collection of essays that appeared in the sister journals *Biblical Archaeology Review* and *Bible Review* during the years 1975–1992.

Talmon, Shemaryahu. *The Importance of the Qumran Calendar in Early Judaism*. North Richland Hills, TX: D. & F. Scott, 2002. Monograph devoted to the Qumran calendar and how it served as one of the key factors that forced the *Yahad* to separate itself from the general Jewish community.

Tov, Emanuel, ed. *The Dead Sea Scrolls Electronic Library*. Leiden, Netherlands: Brill, 2006.

———. *Textual Criticism of the Hebrew Bible*. Minneapolis, MN: Fortress, 1992. A scholarly treatment of the transmission of the biblical text in ancient times, covering all possible witnesses (Masoretic Text, Dead Sea Scrolls, Samaritan Torah, Septuagint, etc.).

VanderKam, James C. *The Dead Sea Scrolls Today*. Grand Rapids, MI: Eerdmans, 1994. The most accessible and straightforward introduction to the Dead Sea Scrolls available.

VanderKam, James, and Peter Flint. *The Meaning of the Dead Sea Scrolls: Their Significance for Understanding the Bible, Judaism, Jesus, and Christianity.* New York: HarperCollins, 2002. An excellent introduction to the subject, with many charts and tables that help present the material in fine and succinct fashion.

Vermes, Geza. *The Complete Dead Sea Scrolls in English.* New York: Penguin, 1997. The best English translation of all the scrolls, organized by genre (legal texts, hymns and poems, biblical interpretation, etc.), with a 90-page introduction on the Qumran community and its religious beliefs.

Weitzman, Steven. "Why Did the Qumran Community Write in Hebrew?" *Journal of the American Oriental Society* 119 (1999): 35–45. An article that relates to the issue of Qumran Hebrew as an anti-language, though it situates the predominant use of Hebrew at Qumran in the context of other options, such as Aramaic and Greek.

Wilson, Edmund. *The Scrolls from the Dead Sea.* 2nd ed. New York: Oxford University Press, 1969. Originally published in 1956 as an expansion of the author's *New Yorker* magazine article earlier that year, this monograph by a major American literary figure brought the subject of the Dead Sea Scrolls into the limelight.

Wolters, Al. *The Copper Scroll: Overview, Text and Translation.* Sheffield, UK: Sheffield Academic, 1996. Clear, concise introduction to the most enigmatic of the scrolls, with superb color photos, the Hebrew text, and English translations on facing pages.

Yadin, Yigael. *The Message of the Scrolls.* New York: Crossroad, 1992. Yadin's personal narrative concerning the scrolls written in 1957; this new edition, published after Yadin's death, includes an introduction written by James H. Charlesworth.

Yardeni, Ada. "A New Dead Sea Scroll in Stone?" *Biblical Archaeology Review* 34, no. 1 (January/February 2008): 60–61. First discussion of the Vision of Gabriel text in English (see also the Knohl article).

Credits

New Testament Scripture taken from the HOLY BIBLE, NEW INTERNATIONAL VERSION ®. Copyright © 1973, 1978, 1984 by International Bible Society. Used by permission of Zondervan. All rights reserved.

Reprinted from Reclaiming the Dead Sea Scrolls, © 1994 by Lawrence H. Schiffman, published by The Jewish Publication Society with the permission of the publisher.

Notes

Notes

Notes

Notes

Notes